Democratic Governance and Human Development

Democratic Governance and Human Development

Stocktaking and Future Strategies

Edited by

Yatindra Singh Sisodia

RAWAT PUBLICATIONS

Jaipur • New Delhi • Bangalore • Hyderabad • Guwahati

ISBN 978-81-316-0559-2

Published by
Prem Rawat for **Rawat Publications**
Satyam Apts, Sector 3, Jawahar Nagar, Jaipur 302 004 (India)
Phone: 0141 265 1748 / 7006 Fax: 0141 265 1748
E-mail: info@rawatbooks.com
Website: www.rawatbooks.com

New Delhi Office
4858/24, Ansari Road, Daryaganj, New Delhi 110 002
Phone: 011 2326 3290

Also at *Bangalore, Hyderabad* and *Guwahati*

Typeset by Rawat Computers, Jaipur
Printed at Chaman Enterprises, New Delhi

Dedicated to

My Reverend Guru and
Mentor (Late) Professor R.S. Gautam

for nurturing and developing
Social Science Community in
Madhya Pradesh

Contents

Part II
Democratic Governance and Initiatives for the Well-being

Part III
Scenario of Health Attainments and Educational Achievements and Areas of Concern

Part IV
Governance Issues at the Grassroots Level

Part V
Efforts for Livelihood, Social Security and their Future Needs

List of Tables and Figures

Tables

Figures

Preface

Governance is a political process involving exercise of different forms of power (social, political, economic, legal and administrative) within various institutional arenas. The real challenge in a democratic process is to ensure that the process of governance does not get subverted or appropriated or controlled by economic and political elites who control the institutions of government or powerful market forces. Human development can be defined as expanding the choices for all people in society. Defined in terms of the expansion of people's capabilities it has several aspects. Foremost among these are to lead a long and healthy life, to acquire knowledge and to enjoy a decent standard of living. These, in turn, raise such dimensions as access to basic social services, expansion of income-earning opportunities; and participation – both political and economic. Governance and human development – the two are indivisible. Human development cannot be sustained without good governance. Likewise, governance cannot be sound unless it sustains human development. It can thus be argued that from a human development perspective, good governance promotes, supports and sustains human, based on expanding human capabilities, choices, opportunities and freedoms (economic and social, as well as political), especially for the poorest and most marginalised persons of the society.

In India considerable attention has been paid to the development, and four priority themes have been identified by the Government of India to take this forward. These are: high economic growth, equitable growth and social justice, human development, and a crosscutting theme of reform and governance. Viewing the scenario in the context of the said priority themes it can be said that the issue of governance has emerged at the forefront of the agenda for sustainable human development. There is a general acceptance now that human deprivation and inequalities are not merely for economic reasons; rather they go hand-in-hand with social and political factors rooted in poor governance. However, looking from the perspective of human development large variations are seen within our country, or states within a region or even districts within a state, where development outcomes, in terms of social indicators, do not match with available resources and the inherent potential of the people. The variation may be established in the fields of education, health, poverty, and so on. They can also be seen across gender, castes, level of incomes and rural-urban divide.

All the aforementioned factors are posing grave challenges to the good governance of the country for the policy makers. In the matter of interface with the citizen, there is an enhanced accent on transparency and right to information. It is in this context that one has to analyse India's human development. Six decades of independent democratic India categorically put before us a scenario which needs stocktaking of the situation and to look into the multi-faceted aspects of human development to carve out strategies for future.

Keeping in view the significance of the issue, M.P. Institute of Social Science Research (MPISSR), Ujjain (Madhya Pradesh) organised a two-day National Seminar on Democratic Governance and Human Development: Stocktaking and Future Strategies to discuss threadbare the multi-faceted issues of democratic governance and human development in India. For articulation of views and presentation of papers in the seminar, the themes were as follows: Stocktaking of Democratic Governance and Human Development in the Proceeding Decades; Democratic Governance and Initiatives for the Well-Being (Poverty, Shelter, Sanitation, Drinking Water, etc.); Educational Achievements and Areas of Concern for Future; Scenario of Health Attainments and Issues of Immediate Priority; Efforts for Livelihood, Social Security and their Future Needs; Governance Issues for Achieving Human Development; Strategies and Road Map for the Human Development in India.

This volume is an attempt to identify, document and comprehend the broad trends on the democratic governance and human development. It is important to understand and analyse the process and direction of pace and pattern of the governance vis-à-vis human development, which would have a significant impact and critical lessons for charting out the future course of action for effective people-centric governance and development across the country.

I would like to acknowledge Indian Council of Social Science Research (ICSSR), Ministry of HRD, Government of India for providing financial support to organise this seminar. I would like to express my deep sense of gratitude to (Late) Professor R.S. Gautam for his valuable advice with appreciation and encouragement to work purposively. I am deeply indebted to Professor B.R. Purohit, Professor Emeritus, MPISSR, for his blessings and encouragement. I would like to express my gratefulness to Dr Neeta Tapan, Visiting Faculty, MPISSR, for taking pains to go through the papers of this volume. Her valuable input offered on individual papers helped me in identifying and rectifying inaccuracies in the papers.

I would like to express my sincere thanks to Professor Nalini Rewadikar, President, MPISSR and Professor Sandeep Joshi, Director, MPISSR, for inspiring me to edit this volume. I am thankful to my colleagues Professor D.C. Sah, Professor Y.G. Joshi, Shri L.P. Gautam, Dr Ashish Bhatt, Dr S.S. Chandel, Dr Manu Gautam and Dr Tapas Kumar Dalapati for their valuable suggestions and help extended during the editing of this volume.

My sincere thanks to all the contributors as without them this volume would not have been possible.

I would like to extend my personal thanks to my better half Mrs Surya for her constant encouragement and support in my academic endeavours.

Finally, I would like to express my thanks to Mr Pranit Rawat of the Rawat Publications, Jaipur for showing interest in this manuscript and bringing out the volume in time.

Dr Yatindra Singh Sisodia
Professor
MPISSR, Ujjain

Contributors

B.N. Prasad, Associate Professor, Giri Institute of Development Studies, Lucknow (UP). E-mail: prasad06bn@yahoo.co.in

D.C. Sah, Former Professor and Director, M.P. Institute of Social Science Research, Ujjain (MP). E-mail: dc_sah@yahoo.co.uk

G. Palanithurai, Professor, Rajiv Gandhi Chair for Panchayati Raj Studies, Gandhigram Rural Institute (Deemed University), Gandhigram (Tamil Nadu). E-mail: gpgri_hung1@rediffmail.com

Ganesh Kawadia, Professor and Head, School of Economics, Devi Ahilya University, Indore (MP). E-mail: ganesh.kawadia@gmail.com

Jharna Pathak, Assistant Professor, Gujarat Institute of Development Research, Ahmedabad (Gujarat). E-mail: fmjharna@yahoo.com

Kanhaiya Ahuja, Associate Professor, School of Economics, Devi Ahilya University, Indore (MP). E-mail: kanhaiya.ahuja@yahoo.com

Katar Singh, Chairman, India Natural Resource Economics and Management (INREM) Foundation, Anand (Gujarat). E-mail: singhkatar@gmail.com

N. Lalitha, Associate Professor, Gujarat Institute of Development Research, Ahmedabad (Gujarat). E-mail: lalithanarayanan@gmail.com

Neeraj K. Jain, Assistant Professor (Economics), G.S. Institute of Technology and Science, Indore (MP). E-mail: asaus343@yahoo.co.in

P. Padmanabha Rao, Associate Professor, Centre for Economic and Social Studies, Hyderabad (AP). E-mail: ppadmanabharao@cess.ac.in

Preeti Kathuria, Research Scholar, M.P. Institute of Social Science Research, Ujjain (MP). E-mail: preeti_kathuria20@yahoo.com

Radhika Dixit, Research Scholar, School of Economics, Devi Ahilya University, Indore (MP). E-mail: ganesh.kawadia@gmail.com

Rahul Banerjee, Development Practitioner, Indore (MP), (www.anar-kali.blogspot.com). E-mail: aarohini@rediffmail.com

Rajeev C. Bharathan, Department of Economics, Government College, Thrissur, University of Calicut (Kerala). E-mail: rajeevcb@gmail.com

S.K. Pant, Professor in Economics, G.B. Pant Social Science Institute, Allahabad (UP). E-mail: skpant@rediffmail.com

Sanjay Kumar, Fellow, Centre for the Study of Developing Societies, Delhi. E-mail: sanjay@csdsdelhi.org

Sanjay Lodha, Professor and Head, Department of Political Science, M.L. Sukhadia University, Udaipur (Rajasthan). E-mail: sanjay.kishti@gmail.com

Sanjay Singh, Assistant Professor (Sociology), Dr. Ram Manohar Lohia National Law University, Lucknow (UP). E-mail: sssocio@yahoo.com

Shailja Singh, Reader (Sociology), U.P. Viklang Uddhar Dr. Shakuntala Misra Vishwa Vidhyalaya, Lucknow (UP). E-mail: shailjasanjay@yahoo.com

Sujit Kumar Choudhary, Assistant Professor (Sociology), Hidayatullah National Law University, Raipur (Chhattisgarh). E-mail: sujitjnu@gmail.com

Tapas Kumar Dalapati, Assistant Professor (Sociology), M. P. Institute of Social Science Research, Ujjain (MP). E-mail: tapas273@gmail.com

Yatindra Singh Sisodia, Professor, M.P. Institute of Social Science Research, Ujjain ((MP). E-mail: yatindra15@yahoo.com

1

Introduction

YATINDRA SINGH SISODIA

Governance in democracy works when citizens and the most marginalised people have the capability to ask questions, seek accountability from the state and participate in the process of governance. Democracy becomes meaningful when people can shape the state and the state, in turn, enables social, political, economic and legal conditions wherein people can exercise their rights and achieve freedom from fear and want. It is not merely elections or universal adult franchise that defines the process of democracy. Quality of the democratic process depends on the capability and integrity of the organs of the state, institutions of governance and the extent of people's participation in governance. While constitutional framework and human rights guarantees can build the grammar of democracy, it is always people and the ethical quality of the political process that make democracy work. Democracy involves dignity, diversity, dissent and development. Unless the last person can celebrate his or her sense of dignity, exercise democratic dissent and involve themselves in the process of governance and development, democracy becomes an empty rhetoric. Democracy dies where discrimination begins and the politics of exclusion takes root. It is participatory, consensus oriented, accountable, transparent, responsive, effective and efficient, equitable and inclusive, and follows the rule of law (Chakarabarty and Bhattacharya: 2008).

Accountable and people-centred governance can provide an operational framework for making democracy work. Governance is a political process involving exercise of different forms of power (social, political, economic, legal and administrative) within various institutional arenas. The Human Development Report (HDR) described governance as 'the exercise of power or authority – political, economic, administrative or otherwise – to manage a country's resources and affairs. It comprises the mechanisms, processes and institutions, through which citizens and groups articulate their interest, exercise their legal rights, meet their obligations and mediate their differences'. The real challenge in a democratic process is to ensure that the process of governance does not get subverted or appropriated or controlled by economic and political elites who control the institutions of government or, powerful market forces and international financial institutions like the World Bank and International Monetary Fund (IMF).

Human development can be defined as expanding the choices for all people in society. It has several aspects when defined in terms of the expansion of people's capabilities. Foremost among these are to lead a long and healthy life, to acquire knowledge and to enjoy a decent standard of living. These, in turn, raise dimensions such as access to basic social services, expansion of income-earning opportunities; and participation – both political and economic. Governance and human development – the two are indivisible. Human development cannot be sustained without good governance. Likewise, governance cannot be sound unless it sustains human development. Promoting human development is not just a social, economic and technological challenge; it is also an institutional and political challenge (HDR, 2002).

It can thus be argued that from a human development perspective, good governance promotes, supports and sustains human well-being, based on expanding human capabilities, choices, opportunities and freedoms (economic and social, as well as political), especially for the poorest and most marginalised persons of the society. Good governance implies an administration that is sensitive and responsive to the needs of the people and is effective in coping with emerging challenges in society by framing and implementing appropriate laws and measures. It includes strict rules of accountability. It could be centred on community groups and individuals, and based on a notion of rights as inherently comprising duties. Rulers must be strictly bound by generally accepted norms and controlled by institutions to enforce those (Actionaid, 2004).

In India considerable attention has been paid to these developments, and four priority themes have been identified by the Government of India to take this forward. These are: high economic growth, equitable growth and social justice, human development, and a crosscutting theme of reform and governance. Viewing the scenario in the context of the above said priority themes it can be mentioned that the issue of governance has emerged at the forefront of the agenda for sustainable human development. Now there is a general acceptance that human deprivation and inequalities are not merely for economic reasons; rather they go hand-in-hand with social and political factors rooted in poor governance. However, looking from the perspective of human development large variations are seen within our country, or states within a region or even districts within a state, where development outcomes, in terms of social indicators, do not match with available resources and the inherent potential of the people. The variation may be established in the fields of education, health, poverty, and so on. They can also be seen across gender, castes, level of incomes and rural-urban divide.

It is in this context the critical review of governance with regard to human development is very appropriate and need a threadbare discussion. It necessitates confronting and addressing questions such as, why is it that governance standard declined in some regions or states over time? Why, for instance, some states have succeeded in turning around their institutional capacities to govern effectively while others have failed? Why has the gap between the developed and the developing regions/states not narrowed down at an adequate pace or in some cases even widened?

All the aforementioned factors are posing grave challenges before the policy makers in making the country a good governed one. In the matter of interface with the citizen, there is an enhanced accent on transparency and right to information. It is in this context that one has to analyse India's human development. In India, human development definitely and conceptually denotes progress-social, economic, political, educational, cultural, scientific, and technological. The unfortunate fact, however, is that despite considerable progress, there have emerged marked disparities in income and in the poor people's access to resources and economic opportunities. The social tensions that we are facing largely due to our single–minded pursuit to economic growth model of development putting the broader mandate of social transformation with social justice, equity, equality of opportunity and poor people's empowerment in development efforts in the background. Six decades of independent democratic India categorically put before us a scenario which needs stocktaking of the situation and to look into the multi-faceted aspects of human development to carve out strategies for future.

In This Volume

Keeping in view the significance of the issue, Madhya Pradesh Institute of Social Science Research, Ujjain (Madhya Pradesh) organised a two-day National Seminar on Democratic Governance and Human Development: Stocktaking and Future Strategies to discuss threadbare the multi-faceted issues of democratic governance and human development in India. For articulation of views and presentation of papers in the seminar, the themes were as follows: Stocktaking of Democratic Governance and Human Development in the Proceeding Decades; Democratic Governance and Initiatives for the Well-Being (Poverty, Shelter, Sanitation, Drinking Water, etc.); Educational Achievements and Areas of Concern for Future; Scenario of Health Attainments and Issues of Immediate Priority; Efforts for Livelihood, Social Security and their Future Needs; Governance Issues for Achieving Human Development; Strategies and Road Map for the Human Development in India.

To deal with the themes, as mentioned in preface, this volume is divided into five parts. The first part, *Stocktaking of Democratic Governance and Human Development in the Preceding Decades* has three chapters that review the governance and human development in India in preceding decades. This part provides adequate details of the background of human development and governance in the country as a whole. The second part, *Democratic Governance and Initiatives for the Well-Being* has four chapters. Two chapters are related to poverty and livelihood wherein the empirical papers are discussed at length while the other two chapters deal with the issue of institutional credit on agricultural productivity and profile of minority community. The third part, *Scenario of Health Attainments and Educational Achievements and Areas of Concern* has six chapters. Out of these, two chapters have analysed health and remaining four have discussed education in detail based on empirical evidences gathered from the field to understand relevance, potentials and demonstrations. The fourth part, *Governance Issues at the Grassroots Level* has three chapters. First chapter in this part provides a detail on human development. Second chapter elaborates the governance aspect at grassroots level in tribal areas. Third chapter deals with the democracy in Indian villages based on gender, caste and poverty. The fifth and last part, *Efforts for Livelihood, Social Security and their Future Needs* has three chapters. First chapter deals with the issue of poverty whereas remaining elaborates in detail the livelihood aspect.

Stocktaking of Democratic Governance and Human Development in the Preceding Decades

In this part, the first paper *A Strategy for All-Round Development of India's Human Resources* by Katar Singh makes a very pertinent and valid argument that human resources play an important role in determining the level and pace of development of a nation. At any level of economic development, proper development and utilisation of available human resources constitutes the bedrock of an economy. The quantity and quality of available human resources along with the intensity and efficiency of their use are equally important contributors to the process of development of a nation. Well developed human resources can be substituted to a large extent for natural resources in the process of development as is demonstrated by the examples of Japan, Denmark, Switzerland, Israel, and Hong Kong. These countries have compensated for their poor endowment of natural resources by highly developed human resources. As far numbers are concerned, India is relatively well-endowed with human resources but it has not been able to develop and utilise them fully and judiciously for the benefit of its people. He further argues that the low level of human resources development in India is evident in a number of indicators including level of literacy, life expectancy, per capita income, and Human Development Index. This explains to a large extent the relatively low level of economic and social development in India.

The strategy proposed in this paper for all-round development of India's human resources is pragmatic and multifaceted; pragmatic in the sense that it could be implemented in India under the prevailing socio-economic and political conditions including its governance system and multifaceted in the sense that it addresses all the dimensions of human resource development – physical, mental, spiritual, socio-cultural, and financial. Some of the elements of the proposed strategy are alleviation of poverty and inequality, food security, security of life and property, access to proper education, health care, and employment opportunities.

Sanjay Lodha in his paper on *Exploring the Nature of Democratic Governance* explains that in recent times, few concepts have enormously exercised the minds of the intelligentsia and the power managers of the world over. In this paper, Dr Lodha reflects upon the conceptual journey from human development to democratic governance and in the process tries to unfold the nature of democratic governance. It all started with the concept of human development as the basic indicator of the well-being of a population in any part of the world. The deficiency of the human development approach led policy makers and intellectuals to deliberate in terms of governance which later on got stretched to be good governance. But even these terms failed to capture the essence of changing needs and aspirations of the people. The end of the cold war and the democratic upsurge all over the world resulted in a mad rush among the academia and practitioners of democracy to quantify different countries on a democratic index. But even this approach had its limitations and democratic deficits became too glaring to be ignored. This dissatisfaction has led a section of social scientists and policy makers to emphasise on the concept of democratic governance as the yardstick to measure the success or failure of a state. As a concept, democratic governance envelopes the requirements of human development, good governance and democracy. It is thus inclusive in its nature. It solicits responsiveness from the state and the government. It provides for participation and empowerment of the people. However, what distinguishes democratic governance from all other concepts is the issue of 'access'. Access in this sense has three dimensions: access to material goods, access to decision making and access to normative resources. What gives access vitality is the combined presence of democratic processes (structures of governance) and democratic outcome (redistribution of public goods). Thus from the vantage point of democratic governance the issue of access entails four questions: Accessing what? Accessing by whom? Accessing how? And accessing how much?

Rajeev C. Bharathan's paper on *Governance and Human Development: Lessons from Kerala* elaborates that the governance is the exercise of political, economic and administrative authority in the management of a country/region. It comprises of complex mechanisms, institutions and processes through which common people articulate their interests and needs. Scholars have attempted to correlate quality of governance and the level of human development in a particular nation. Amartya Sen has been able to demonstrate a strong link between democracy and the reduction of hunger. In countries with a free press, and with political oppositions able to unseat unpopular regimes, governments cannot neglect the basic needs of the common people. He argues that the quality of governance is increasingly being recognised as a determinant of human development. It is generally maintained that human development is intrinsically related to education levels and health status of the people of the region. Thus, education and health has crucial roles to play in enhancing the dignity of human beings and freedom to choose their way of life. Education increases the ability of a society to absorb the technical skills needed to improve productivity; health of the citizens also enhances the quality of life. In this context, one can observe the relationship between the good governance and the high human development achieved by Kerala nationally. The region has exhibited a unique pattern of social sector achievements which are hailed internationally. The high human development achieved in the state was the cascading effects of several popular policies initiated by the democratic governments in modern Kerala. It should also be noted that many socio-economic and religious reforms were adopted by the erstwhile princely rulers of Kochi and Thiruvithamkore in response to public action since the late nineteenth century. The limited success of decentralised governance of the last decade also facilitated the process of human development in Kerala.

Democratic Governance and Initiatives for the Well-Being

D.C. Sah's paper is on *Livelihood, Food Insecurity and Well-being of Tribals: Evidence from Indian Central Tribal Belt.* The paper makes an argument on the interaction of livelihood, food insecurity and poverty in central tribal belt of India. Over 63 per cent time of the labours, among poor households, remain unutilised even after performing agricultural and labouring chores in and around village. As a result, even a small borrowing by them under shock triggers a process that traps them in chronic poverty. Food insecurity is significantly and positively associated with chronic poverty. As public distribution system supports about 7 per cent of cereal consumption of poor and chronic poor households, relevant question is why PDS is unable to influence their consumption behaviour. Dr Sah further elaborates that the credit and migration work as supplements as well as substitutes to each other in crisis. Absence of 'good' credit support is seen to be the major cause of migration, at least of distress type. However, in the case of the resource-poor, migration is clearly a more effective option because of the limited 'credit worthiness' of the migrant. In fact, migration in a dynamic context might help enhancing the credit worthiness, especially by improving the repayment schedule among these households. A 'good' credit support could reduce the burden of migration, whereas a 'bad' credit might increase it. Occurrence of a shock or lumpy borrowing for social events like death, son's marriage and at times sickness may further turn the equation against the poor borrowers. The social implications of the process varies across chronic poverty profile: poor households rely more on debt and social network to meet crises where non-poor households rely on economic process and do not believe much in social networking. The optimism of sustaining the economic well-being is significantly high among always non-poor compared to poor and chronic poor. The optimism of non-poor as well as pessimism among poor and chronic poor is a product of many forces that created environment for income generation for former or marginalisation for latter.

Kanhaiya Ahuja's paper is on *Impact of Institutional Credit on Agricultural Productivity*. It is based on a study conducted among 400 tribal farmers of Jhabua district of Madhya Pradesh, who are mainly dependent upon agriculture and allied activities, which is practiced on the poor soil of little depth with the help of primitive methods of cultivation and negligible irrigation facilities. Their problems over the years have multiplied due to economic backwardness, poverty and illiteracy. Agriculture has thus proved to be purely a subsistence economy. Therefore, the development of agriculture in the tribal economy is very essential for the overall development of tribals. The development of agriculture among tribals mainly depends on the supply of adequate, cheap and timely availability of credit. Over the years, due to the dependence of agriculture on vagaries of nature and various other inhibiting factors, the farming has become a difficult profession. Thus, the agricultural credit among tribals is considered as one of the most basic inputs for conducting agricultural development programmes. The study provides a brief and specific information about the prevailing agricultural and economic status of the tribals in the region. The study concludes that there is a positive and significant impact of loan disbursement among the farmers in terms of the increased usage of manure and chemical fertilisers and thereby affecting the cropping pattern and overall production in the district. It also shows that all the main crops have a significant difference in the mean productivity in the district. He concludes that the factors namely education status of tribal farmers, land holding of the farmers, number of employed persons in the family, quantum of institutional loan disbursed, household income of the farmers have been influencing the per acre, per farmer land productivity in the district.

B.N. Prasad's paper is on *Democratic Governance and Status of Minority: Reflections from the Field*. The paper makes an elaboration that minority constitutes one-fifth of the India population. They are yet to join mainstream of the Indian developmental trajectory. Majority of them are at the bottom of socio-economic stratification. Muslim constitutes the maximum minority population in the state of Uttar Pradesh as compared to the other religious minority groups like Sikh, Christian, Buddhist, Jain, and others. But majority of them are lagging far behind in terms of most of the human development indicators. Attempts have been made by the government, through policy initiatives and developmental measures, to ameliorate the conditions of Muslim community. Some of them have made perceptible progress, but perception remains that the gap between Muslim and rest of the religious communities has widened over the years. This 'development deficit' is a major stumbling block on the path of smooth functioning of democratic system. The purpose of this baseline survey was to identify the infrastructural gaps. Taking deficit as weight, the indicators representing specific sectors are ranked on eight point score scale, in which rank one indicates highest deficit and highest priority. Thus, an indicator is given highest rank, if the value of deficit between survey result and the estimate for India is higher. The other indicators are ranked in decreasing order according to their value of deficit. In case, the deficit is positive (survey result higher than the estimate of India) lower rank is assigned to the indicator. Findings of the survey indicate that top five major development deficit areas of the district are – electricity, pucca houses, work participation rate, female work participation rate, and literacy. Thus, these sectors, on priority basis, need urgent attention and policy intervention for its development.

Preeti Kathuria in her paper on *Poverty and Livelihood Diversification in Remote Tribal Areas of Madhya Pradesh: Study of Dhar District* attempts to analyse the livelihood structure of every individual which varies due to his/her socio-economic condition. In ancient period the structure of livelihood was governed by social and cultural milieu, which is now mostly economic. Economic factors determine that how the household should make ends meet. Madhya Pradesh is one of the third most economically poor regions in the country with 37.21 per cent of its population residing below poverty line. In remote rural areas poverty being 60 per cent, is a more serious problem than in other areas. To disclose this fact the study has focussed on the livelihood options opted by poor and non-poor in remote rural areas. How poverty influence livelihood pattern of individuals? What are the livelihood strategies adopted by households to cope up with shocks? The exploit of natural capital is high in rural areas especially in tribal villages. History provides evidences that the forests were initially the residence of almost all tribes, but they did not have any land rights. Due to state intervention, the tribals have been pushed out to an unsecured environment. Therefore, after independence these tribals are struggling for their survival. Though government's intervention in helping them fight poverty cannot be denied, a high proportion of tribals are still poor. Tribals are staying in these fringe forest areas in difficult conditions. Government has failed to reach in these forest areas, especially for maintaining law and development of the area. She argues that Dhar is also one of these types of district where a sizeable tribal population exists without adequate state support. Though, tribals expect a lot from the government for their welfare and livelihood, they get nothing in hand.

Scenario of Health Attainments and Educational Achievements and Areas of Concern

N. Lalitha in her paper on *Health Reforms in Tamil Nadu* makes an argument that as health security is limited to a small section of population working in the organised sector, the state governments have enormous responsibility to reach out to the people in providing health care. While public health expenditure in India accounts for 16 per cent of the total health expenditure, private expenditure constitutes the rest 84 per cent. It is well known that the inadequacy of services in the government health care in terms of health professionals and medicines force the consumers to depend on private health providers. In the private health expenditure, medicines account for a sizeable component. The National Sample Survey on Consumer Expenditure (55th Round) reports that, 77 and 70 per cent of the health expenses in rural and urban areas are on medicines. Realising the need to provide appropriate quality medicines to consumers, the government of Tamil Nadu has introduced an administrative reform measure since 1994 and has implemented through an autonomous agency called Tamil Nadu Medical Services Corporation (TNMSC). This autonomous supply agency functions like a utility service under private management and private sector employment conditions. However, since, its primary and priority client is government health services, it operates on a non-profit basis. This agency has streamlined the entire drug procurement and supply, ensuring the availability of quality medicines in all the government health care, thereby reducing the need for the consumers to buy the medicines from the retail market. She elaborates that the success and good will that this reform has created among the consumers being so huge, successive state governments with different political ideology have also consistently backed the functioning of TNMSC and Tamil Nadu has become a model for other state governments to replicate this health system of governance.

P. Padmanabha Rao's paper is on *Scenario of Education and Health Attainments in Krishna Basin Area in Andhra Pradesh.* The paper makes an attempt to discuss the education and health attainments in Andhra Pradesh. Andhra Pradesh is educationally backward with fourth lowest position in literacy among the major 16 states. Though the state showed higher performance in literacy than the national average in the nineties; its rank has not improved because of better performance of the educationally backward states than the developed ones. South Coastal Andhra occupies top position and North Telangana occupies bottom position in literacy. Illiteracy is more serious if all members in a household are illiterates than when at least one member in the family is literate. In Andhra Pradesh, more than 75 per cent of the rural households have no literate adult member. Regional variations in dropout rate exist at primary level, but they disappear at upper primary level. The Telangana region has higher dropout rate at primary level than the other three regions. Child labour influences dropout of boys only at upper primary stage. However, it is not clear whether child labour is the cause or consequence of dropout at upper primary stage. Low age at marriage and its consequence of child bearing at adolescent age are the major problems in Andhra Pradesh. Andhra Pradesh is one of the four states with high prevalence of HIV infection in the country. Despite this grave situation, awareness is low except in South Coastal Andhra and South Telangana regions. Further, the incidence of reproductive tract infection and sexually transmitted infection is higher in South Telangana. Regional variations exist in human development index and also in sectors like education and health. While inequality is narrowing down in literacy and primary education, it is not so in infant mortality. There has not been any substantial change in the ranking of districts in human development index. He argues that a shift in the approach in the provision of health facilities to the poor, social mobilisation and empowerment programmes along with higher public investment in underdeveloped areas would improve the overall human development.

Ganesh Kawadia and Radhika Dixit in their paper on *Opportunities and Challenges in Indian Higher Education* explain that today the world economy is experiencing an unprecedented change. New developments in science and technology, media revolution, internationalisation of education and the ever expanding competitive environment are revolutionising the education scene. A paradigm shift has been noticed in higher education now-a-days, from 'national education 'to 'global education', from 'one time education for a few' to 'life long education for all', from 'teacher centric educations' to 'learner centric education'. Knowledge is the driving force in the rapidly changing globalised economy and society. Quantity and quality of highly specialised human resources determine their competence in the global market. Emergence of knowledge as driving factor results in both challenges and opportunities. The benefits of globalisation accrue to the countries with highly skilled human capital and it is a curse for the countries without such specialised human capital. Developing countries are further challenged in a highly competitive world economy because their higher education systems are not adequately developed for the creation and use of knowledge. India is one of such developing nations. India has recently witnessed a big boom in the BPO/KPO sector, which absorbs and requires a large proportion of skilled and trained population of the country. This trend is certain to continue and India faces the challenge of generating an appropriate supply response to retain its existing advantage. They further argue that the real challenge therefore, is to expand capacities in higher education to keep ahead of the curve of rising domestic and global demand. Because of interdependence and integration of world economy in recent years, the Indian higher education system has a new role and a challenge to provide to the nation and the world at large, skilled human power at all levels, having breadth of knowledge and confidence to effectively confront the social and economic realities.

Sanjay Kumar in his paper *Disparities in Levels of Educational Attainment in India: A National Analysis* makes an attempt to comprehend that the issue of disparities in levels of educational attainment among various communities. Though the level of literacy has increased manifold in India over the last 60 years, this is not uniform across regions, states and among all the people. People of some states are more educated compared to other states. Similarly, the level of educational attainment is much higher in some regions compared to other region. There are also visible disparities in level of educational attainment amongst people belonging to different caste and communities. People belonging to the upper castes are more educated compared to the Dalits. There is a shared believe, this disparity in levels of educational attainment amongst people belonging to different castes is due to the economic disparities and less due to their castes identities. The paper which uses lot of survey data helps in establishing that though various factors contribute towards disparities in levels of educational attainment, but castes is still the most important factor. The paper uses two kinds of data, the data from the Census of India conducted every 10 years and the data collected through the National Election Study 2009 (NES, 2009) conducted by the Lokniti, Centre for the Study of Developing Societies (CSDS). There are disparities in levels of educational attainment among people belonging to similar economic class but from different castes. The rich upper castes are more educated compared to the rich dalits. There are also corresponding relationship between levels of educational attainment amongst poor upper castes and poor dalits. The dalits irrespective of their economic class are less educated compared to the upper castes. This also has some relationship with unequal opportunities available to the different communities. The inequality in opportunities may not be solely guided by castes based discriminations, but other factors also contribute towards it.

S.K. Pant's paper *Quality Education under Sarva Siksha Abhiyaan: A Performance Appraisal* explains that education of masses has always remained an area of priority for the planners, social activists, and like-minded people on account of its highly pervasive character, education has the capability to reach, influence and mould the human capabilities from a very low level to unprecedented heights, from being an unknown and unproductive class to becoming a highly competitive unity and from being a raw and uncultivated class to becoming a highly refined value added finished product. Based on the experiences of earlier programmes, the Central Government in 2001 launched a very ambitious programme called Sarva Siksha Abhiyan (SSA) throughout the country. It is unique programme that is to run on people-government partnership with missionary mode. The ensuing exercise attempts to study the impact of SSA on six contiguous districts of eastern part of Uttar Pradesh. The analysis shows that the performance of programme suffers largely on account of lack of people's participation, and poor implementation of the various social interventions that have been envisaged to provide check and balance.

Sujit Kumar Choudhary's paper is on *Medium of Instruction in Schooling among Tribes in India.* This paper argues that medium of instruction is considered to be one of the most important parameters which affect schooling at the primary and secondary levels of education. Here, in this paper, Dr Sujit discusses the various issues related to language in general and medium of instruction in schooling among the tribals in particular. In addition, it also focuses the status of medium of instruction in the tribal areas of various states in India and addresses some innovative and good work done by the Central or State governments, and also by the different civil society organisations.

In India, in fact, approximately 8 per cent people belong to the tribal communities. It is well known fact that most of the tribals in the country have their own dialect and they are always separated and neglected from other sections of society, especially when it comes to the issue of language in general and medium of instruction in schooling in particular. However, the Constitution of India allows the use of tribal dialect (mother tongue) as the medium of instruction in case the population of a tribe is more than one lakh. Even the Kothari Commissions, 1966, and onwards policy documents have suggested to provide education to the tribals in their own dialect. The governments of different states have been making attempts to implement the medium of instruction in schooling in their own tribal dialects. But several studies have highlighted the language as barrier is impeding the progress of formal schooling among the tribals.

Governance Issues at the Grassroots Level

G. Palanithurai's paper is on *Human Development Scenario in Rural Areas: An Analysis of Human Dignity Index.* He explains that in India, governance, administration and development are mystified and complicated and thereby major sections of population are excluded from the process of governance, administration and development. As a result, majority of the people are termed either beneficiaries or petitioners and they are never regarded as development participants. This process has enabled the capacitated, skilled and privileged to exploit the system, society and the nature and thereby the majority lead a luxurious and greedy life resulting in environmental degradation and ecological damage and leave around 60 per cent of people in poverty. The poor live in undignified sub human living conditions. So to the poor leading a dignified human life is always a dream in India. In human development, India has gone down but in economic growth it has fared well. Why this paradox despite the Government of India adopting inclusive policies and making increased outlays for social development sectors? Be it health or education or employment generation, the Government of India has introduced flagship programmes. The quantum of allocation for these sectors has also been increased. Despite all the schemes, programmes and resource allocation, human development indicators have not improved. While reviewing the development activities at the grassroots one can easily identify the root cause. Absence of participation of stakeholders in the process of development is the main reason. The macro issues of human development can be tackled in a disaggregated way. So the micro actions are the imperative need. He further argues that since local governance institutions are in operation, human development issues can be tackled locally at the grassroot level. Further the existing procedure of compiling data has to be changed in such a way that the functional units of local governance involved in the process of administration and development keeps data base at every level starting from Gram Panchayat. In the same way the evaluation of the government departments has to be changed so that outcome orientation is the centrality in the place of output evaluation. Active involvement of people through local bodies on the issues of human development will make human development issues the issues of the people and not the issues of the experts and thereby the committed action of the people will bring about needed transformation in the domain of human development.

Rahul Banerjee in his paper on *The Elusive Holy Grail of Tribal Self-Rule: An Analysis of the History behind PESA* attempts to explain that the biggest lacuna of all was Gandhi's conception of 'Gram Swaraj' or the promotion of grassroot democracy through the establishment of autonomous village republics was given a go by. Panchayati Raj was included in the directive principles of state policy which were non-justiciable, that is, unlike the fundamental rights these could not be enforced through the courts. Basic rights like free education, health and nutrition services and the means to a dignified livelihood too were included in this section. Thus provisions that could have created an aware, healthy and articulate population and provided them with an institutional structure for implementing their development according to their own genius and so curtail the power of the ruling classes were ignored totally by the governments both at the centre and the states after independence thus paving the way for the persistence of a form of internal colonialism and feudalism. Matters were compounded by the fact that fundamental rights too were not easily assured given the tremendous expenses involved in approaching the High Courts and the Supreme Court for redress. While the erstwhile princes, landlords and the capitalists often went to court to obstruct the path of justice for the poor, the latter could hardly afford to do so and so had to bear with the illegal actions of the ruling classes directly or through the organs of the state. This in effect meant that the checks and balances that form a basic part of a liberal democratic set up were disturbed in favour of the executive consisting of the council of ministers and the bureaucracy. The party system ensured that the council of ministers and its leader the prime minister would always be much more powerful than their fellow legislators. In the initial years after independence, the overwhelming majority of the Congress party and the charisma of its leader Nehru also meant that the opposition was not very vocal or effective in monitoring the actions of the government and parliament was reduced to being as ineffectual as a debating society. Moreover, preventive detention laws were enacted to silence the protests of people's organisations and their leaders outside parliament and thousands of such people were jailed. Finally the press too was not as combative and investigative as it is today and given the high level of illiteracy it did not have much of a reach. Thus the government and the bureaucracy rode roughshod over democratic niceties to push through a process of modernisation at the cost of the ordinary people by using colonial repressive laws and by flouting the progressive aspects of the constitution. He further explain that the bureaucracy, which continued in its colonial mindset, was a power unto itself as it not only framed all the laws but also interpreted and administered them to the detriment of an illiterate and unaware populace.

Sanjay Singh and Shailja Singh in their paper on *Democracy in an Indian Village: Interaction of Gender, Caste and Poverty* described that India became more democratic with reference to participation of men, women and other disadvantageous groups but it became less democratic in terms of democratic principles and ideologies after independence. The caste and faction ridden politics at local level in the village to the national level signifies the decline in democratic principles. The parochial attitude with reference to women and other disadvantageous groups leads to hardship in terms of economy and development. The distribution of political power, education and economic opportunity to the disadvantageous group mainly dalit and women community is the important indicator of development and decentralised governance. The change of grassroot democratic system from developmental to political unit shows a shift in the orientation and participation. The inclusion of dalit and women in the political process has initiated a new dimension to the grassroots democratic system. In the hierarchical traditional structure social distances were clearly defined and were more or less rigidly maintained. There was hardly any scope in this structure for people at the two ends of the hierarchy to sit together and discuss their private affairs on equal terms. As long as the traditional structure persists, the cognitive map or archetype of elite class is likely to continue. But the new leadership that controls the affairs of panchayat differs from the traditional elite of the village. This difference is not only in terms of caste, class but in terms of gender also. They argue that earlier the power structure was complete without including the factor of women in it. But changes in policy and promotion of women in politics led to the changing power structure. The present paper is based on the micro field study of one of the smallest unit of democratic governance, the village panchayat of Lucknow district. The emphasis in the present study is on economy, gender and caste. These variables are observed in the context of the politics and governance of village panchayat. The change in the panchayat under study led to the change in the socio-political configuration. This process of change leads to creation of not only new relations but also of new values, attitudes and aspirations. This process of change provides scope to the researcher to enter into new network of interpersonal relations where village, caste and other traditional bonds are observed in interaction with one another.

Efforts for Livelihood, Social Security and their Future Needs

Jharna Pathak's paper is on *Creating New Options for the Poor: A Case Study of Gujarat*. She argues that in view of the challenges facing farmers today, the structural transformation of agricultural extension systems around the world is unavoidable. However, the first major issue is who will pay for the extension service along with diffusion of inputs related knowledge – the government, farmers, or private nonprofit organisations. Agriculture is one of the most promising instruments for reducing poverty and securing local livelihoods. One of the critical conditions required for the agricultural sector is to ensure that good governance structures and related policies are put in place at all levels. Studies have shown that agriculture-based economies around the world are to be found mostly in developing countries and countries with economies in transition. It is in these countries, however, that scores for governance are at their lowest and often negative. Good governance has a number of dimensions: political stability; the rule of law; voice and accountability; effective government; regulatory quality and control of corruption are among others. In spite of the recommendations of the 1982 World Development Report that governments should focus on governance to improve agriculture, very little has been achieved in that regard to date. Project Sunshine, a programme implemented by the Tribal Development Department, Government of Gujarat is the step in the direction of reassessing potential contributions of private firms, non-governmental organisations and farmers. Dr. Jharna in this article defines the scope of involving private sector in an array of diffusing new technology, identifies critical and complementary roles for the government and non-governmental organisations, with a prime focus on institutional dimensions. This recognises weaknesses of partners of the programme and advocates the need for agricultural extension services and proper monitoring.

Tapas Kumar Dalapati's paper is on *Implementation of MNREGS and Its Impact on Livelihood Structure in Rural Madhya Pradesh.* The paper analyses the implementation process and impact of MNREGS upon the livelihood structure of the poor in Madhya Pradesh through empirical findings and raise some issues for better implementation of the programme. The paper makes an elaboration about the Constitution of India which emphasises about 'decent work' under Directives Principles of State policy. Article 41 of the Directives Principle of State Policy states that 'the state shall, within the limits of its economic capacity and development, make effective provision for securing right to work ...' Similarly, there is attention to improve the conditions of work and level of wages in Articles 42 and 43 of the Indian Constitution. Despite prevalence of these provisions our country has not been successful in promoting right to work among the poorer section of our society. Low level of productive employment generation in the aggregate, persistence of poverty and low educational levels are the most significant failures of Indian employment strategy till date. The ensuring of rural employment is further facing acute crisis due to neo liberal economic reforms from the past decade and a half. Against this background, the notification of National Rural Employment Guarantee Act (NREGA) on September 7, 2005 is a unique step towards realisation of economic right to work as envisioned in the Directive Principles of State Policy which strives to ensure socio-economic justice for the rural poor in rural areas in the contemporary situation. Madhya Pradesh (MP) has predominantly been an agrarian economy which shows co-existence of poverty and prosperity. The state socio-economic profile describes an economy of rural mass, poverty and growth led by agriculture. Despite five decades of planned economic development, Madhya Pradesh continues as a BIMARU state (it includes Bihar, Madhya Pradesh, Rajasthan and Uttar Pradesh which are relatively low in the human development). If we analyse the percentage share of agricultural workers in total rural work force, it is 82.5 per cent in 2004–05 (NSSO, 2006).Out of the total rural workers, farmers constitute 61.4 per cent and 38.6 per cent belongs to agricultural labourer category (NSSO, EUS Survey 2004–05). In the same survey it is found that out of the total agricultural labourers scheduled tribe, scheduled caste constitute 35.9 and 28.5 per cent respectively. If we look in to the data of Rural Labour Enquiry Report 1999–2000, an agricultural male and female labourer earned ₹ 30.1 and 24.44 for male and female respectively in Madhya Pradesh. Further, this amount is quite dismal for Scheduled tribes and Scheduled castes agricultural labourers households in the state. Against this background introduction of MNREGS is like a silver lining where sizeable section households depend upon agricultural labour for their livelihood.

Neeraj K. Jain's paper is on *Tribal livelihood and Poverty Issues: A study of South-Western Madhya Pradesh.* This paper deals with tribal livelihood and structure of economic poverty estimated on the basis of annual per capita expenditure (APCE). Consumption pattern, calorie intake and health and education have been investigated. Income generating and shock management strategies and their linkages with poverty have also been studied to understand livelihood struggle. Tribal society, among various socio-economic groups, has been found as most vulnerable in terms of its percentage in poor section with their high concentration in most economically deprived section, i.e., casual labour. Scheduled Castes and Scheduled Tribes among the working population are in the worst position, as they constitute larger share in casual labour than their share in total population. More disturbingly, their share is continuously increasing among unemployed and underemployed. The situation can be mirrored in poverty incidence of these population groups, which are found to be poorest among poor. The nature of poverty and its issues in tribal society are concerned with their special kind of livelihood struggles. This paper is an effort to investigate nature and issues of poverty across three blocks of Barwani district. The data, collected during the survey for author's doctoral work has been utilised in this paper. Two villages from each of three block – Barwani (administrative centre), Sendhwa (commercial centre), and Pati (remote block) – have been selected.

Looking Ahead

Human Development is a process which is sustainable in terms of resources over generations and across space. It recognises the legitimate claim of each individual in a society to be an active and productive participant in the development function. Augmentation in a country's resources and its material means is one of the essential steps towards achieving human development. Equally important is the process of transforming these means into valued outcomes and ensuring equal and effective participation and involvement of every section of society in this process. Governance is defined as the manner in which power is exercised in the management of a country's economic and social resources. Quality of governance is increasingly recognised as among the primary factors behind the most remarkable development of human history. This quality of governance is judged as good or bad on the basic criteria of achieving the goal of human development based on the principle of social and economic justice. Good governance is linked with government's capacity for knowledge, mediation, resource allocation, implementation and maintenance of key relationships. Among the various key factors determining good governance like reliability, predictability, participation, rule of law, etc., the factors of transparency and open information system are the most significant one. Transparency in government means making information open and available to the public and thereby it is essential for bringing accountability. Good governance, based on the democratic principle of social justice, gender equality and sustainable human development implies participative and transparent government.

Democratic governance and human development go hand in hand and therefore it is genuinely felt that people have to be in the forefront of the whole schema of governance. Institutions of governance have a pivotal role in solving many of these dilemmas and challenges by managing the policy initiatives in an effective manner (Social Watch India, 2009). The need is to strengthen the democratic institutions with the inherent principles of good governance with capacity building and sensitisation to meet the needs of human development in true sense.

References

Actionaid (2004). *Good Governance*, Bangalore: Book for Change, p. 14.

Chakrabarty, Bidyut and Mohit Bhattacharya (2008). *The Governance Discourse: A Reader*, New Delhi: Oxford Press, p. 7.

Human Development Report (2002). UNDP, New Delhi: Oxford Press, p. 51.

Social Watch India (2009). *Citizen Report on Governance and Development 2008–09*, Delhi: Daanish Books, p. 17.

Part I

Stocktaking of Democratic Governance and Human Development in the Preceding Decades

2

A Strategy for All-Round Development of India's Human Resources

KATAR SINGH

Human resources play an important role in determining the level and pace of development of a nation. At any level of economic development, proper development and utilisation of available human resources constitutes the bedrock of an economy. The quantity and quality of available human resources along with the intensity and efficiency of their use are equally important contributors to the process of development of a nation. Well developed human resources are a great asset for any nation and underdeveloped ones a great liability. Well developed human resources can be substituted to a large extent for natural resources in the process of development as is demonstrated by the examples of Japan, Denmark, Switzerland, Israel, and Hong Kong. These countries have compensated for their poor endowment of natural resources by highly developed human resources.

As far as numbers are concerned, India is relatively well-endowed with human resources but their quality is relatively poor in terms of knowledge and skills. Furthermore, it has not been able to develop and utilise them fully and judiciously for the benefit of its people. The low level of human resources development in India is evident from a number of indicators including level of literacy, life expectancy, infant mortality rate, per capita income, and Human Development Index. This explains to a large extent the relatively low level of economic and social development in India. In view of this, it is imperative for India to develop and implement a pragmatic and multifaceted strategy for all round development of its human resources.

In this paper, first a conceptual framework is presented connecting human resource development to overall development and then discussed the current status of human resource development in India. Finally, some of the basic elements of an appropriate strategy for all-round development of India's human resources are presented and briefly discussed. The paper is based partly on the author's own work done earlier (Singh, 2009: 68–69) and partly on a review of the literature available on the subject including the internet resources.

A Conceptual Framework

Human resources mean, the sum total of all physical and mental abilities, skills, and attributes of human beings which are partly inherited and partly acquired through education, training, health care, and pursuit of some spiritual methods like *yoga* or meditation. The Human Development Report 1990 (UNDP, 1990), defines human development as the process of increasing people's options. It emphasises that the most critical choices that people should have include the options to lead a long and healthy life, to be knowledgeable and to find access to the assets, employment and income needed for a decent standard of living.

The acquisition of human abilities and skills involves the investment of human effort and money and hence, in economics, this is also called human capital. There are many scholars who have emphasised the importance of human capital investment in the process of economic and social development. The simplest and most important of this type of model is a schooling model, which relates economic development to schooling. The classical and neoclassical economists did not explicitly include the quality of human resources in their theoretical frameworks; labour was taken to include both physical and mental effort (Alex, 1983: 3–12). It was Schultz (1964) who elaborated the concept of human capital and explicitly considered the investment in human capital as an important determinant of economic development. Subsequently, quite a few other scholars got interested in the economics of human capital, especially the economics of education, and a large number of studies were conducted on the subject. The model considers the totality of human potential, and emphasises the need to harness it for the good of people. It respects people's culture and religion, social values and structures. It is more applicable to countries like India than any other model. The human capital approach to development is based on the following two assumptions, which have been ignored in the classical theory of development:

- Human, physical and mental capabilities are partly inherited and partly acquired, and they vary from individual to individual, i.e., the classical assumption of homogeneous labour force does not hold; and

Human capital directly contributes to development through its positive effect on productivity and through reduction on resistance to diffusion of new technologies in the economy, especially in the rural sector.

Thus, this model shifts the emphasis from physical capital formation to human capital formation and from industrial development to rural development, as a basis for overall development. This model seems most appropriate for labour-surplus developing countries like India, where a lot of underdeveloped human resources having high potential for development exist. Besides, human resources are renewable and hence inexhaustible. Therefore, human capital can be substituted for exhaustible non-renewable physical capital in the process of development and thus relax the constraint on development imposed by inadequacy of physical capital to a large extent.

A few economists have also attempted a systematic theory of development which incorporates strategic sociological, cultural, and psychological factors. Outstanding among them are David McClelland and Everett Hagen (Higgins, 1966: Ch. 13). McClelland's 'Need-for-Achievement Motivation' (N-Ach) theory seeks to establish a relationship between N-Ach and economic development. His theory rests on two propositions: (a) that group differences in the average level of certain motives, such as N-Ach, predict differences in the rate of economic growth; and (b) that certain motive combinations predispose individuals to act like successful business entrepreneurs, who have played key roles in economic development. On the basis of his studies and analyses, he concludes that if we are to promote economic growth, it is necessary to first change the values and motives of individuals. This, in his opinion, can be done by: (a) persuasion or education; (b) introducing changes in the social system; and (c) early character training. Of these three, the third is by all odds the one most likely to succeed. For in this way, values can be in-built from the very beginning. Early character training can be imparted by a corp of specially qualified nursery and primary school teachers carefully selected for the purpose (Singh, 2009: 73–74).

Current Status of Human Resource Development in India: Some Indicators of HRD

There are many indicators which are and can be used to measure the level of human resources development. Having rediscovered the truth that people must be at the centre of all development, the United Nations Development Programme (UNDP) decided to bring out every year a report on human dimensions of development from 1990. The Human Development Report (HDR)-1990 was the first such report. The Report addresses the question of how economic growth does or does not promote human development. It discusses the meaning and measurement of human development, proposes a new composite index of human development, summarises the record of human development over the past three decades and sets forth strategies for human development in the 1990s (UNDP, 1990).

Development thus defined cannot be adequately measured by income alone. The Report therefore proposed a new measure of development, the Human Development Index (HDI), composed of three indicators: life expectancy, adult literacy and income expressed in logs. The subsequent Human Development Reports have made some refinements in the procedure of defining the component indicators and computing the HDI. The refinements include adjustment of income for differences in purchasing power and disparities in income distribution, combining adult literacy and mean years of schooling into an index of educational attainment, and computing disaggregated HDI for males and females and for different population groups. Now HDI has four components, namely, life expectancy at birth in years; adult literacy rate measured by per cent of literate people aged 15 years and above; combined gross enrolment ratio in primary, secondary and tertiary education; and gross domestic product per capita in terms of Purchasing Power Parity (PPP) in US dollars. In the Human Development Report 2009 (HDR 2009), estimates of HDI are presented for 182 countries for selected years over the period, 1980–2007. In addition, HDI is also supplemented by a human poverty index, and a gender related development index. In earlier reports, a human freedom index and indicators of human security were also presented for selected countries for which data were available.

HDI is by far the most widely accepted indicator of human development (and lack of development or poverty). In Table 2.1, we present the HDI values and trends in them for a few selected countries including India and China over the period, 1980–2007, as estimated in HDR 2009. As shown in the table, of the 182 countries, Norway had the highest HDI with a value of 0.971 in 2007 and Niger the lowest HDI with a value of 0.340. In 2007, India's HDI was 0.612 and its rank was 134th among 182 countries of the world. China had a higher HDI with the value of 0.772 in 2007 as compared to India's HDI (0.612). Two of India's neighbouring countries, Pakistan and Bangladesh had both lower HDIs than India but Sri Lanka had a higher HDI (0.759) in 2007. India's HDI increased from 0.427 in 1980 to 0.612 in 2007 whereas the corresponding figures for China are 0.533 and 0.772. Thus, India registered an increase of 43.33 per cent in its HDI over the period, 1980–2007 whereas China registered a marginally higher increase of 44.84 per cent over the same period of time. Bangladesh registered the highest increase of 65.55 per cent and the USA the lowest of 6.94. This is because the former had a lower base year value of HDI and the latter a much higher base year value. In India, Human Development Reports are now prepared by many state governments including Gujarat, Madhya Pradesh and Uttar Pradesh.

Table 2.1

Human Development Index and Trends in it for Selected Countries of the World, 1980–2007

Country	*1980*	*1985*	*1990*	*1995*	*2000*	*2005*	*2007*	*HDI rank (2007)*	*Increase in HDI from1980 to 2007 (%)*
Norway	0.900	0.912	0.924	0.948	0.961	0.968	0.971	1	7.88
Japan	0.887	0.902	0.918	0.931	0.943	0.956	0.960	10	8.23
USA	0.894	0.909	0.923	0.939	0.949	0.955	0.956	13	6.94
United Kingdom	0.861	0.870	0.891	0.929	0.932	0.947	0.947	21	9.99
Mexico	0.756	0.768	0.782	0.794	0.8 25	0.844	0.854	53	12.96
China	0.533	0.556	0.608	0.657	0.719	0.756	0.772	92	44.84
Sri Lanka	0.649	0.670	0.683	0.696	0.729	0.752	0.759	102	16.94
India	0.427	0.453	0.489	0.511	0.556	0.596	0.612	134	43.33
Pakistan	0.402	0.423	0.449	0.469	NA	0.555	0.572	142	42.29
Bangladesh	0.328	0.351	0.389	0.415	0.493	0.527	0.543	148	65.55
Niger	NA	NA	NA	NA	0.258	0.330	0.340	189	NA

Source: Human Development Report 2009, Statistical Annex, Table G (http://hdr.undp.org/en/media/HDR_2009_EN_Indicators.pdf)

Table 2.2

Components of Human Development Index for Selected Countries of the World, 2007

Country	*Human development index value*	*Life expectancy at birth (years)*	*Adult literacy rate (% aged 15)1999–2007*	*Combined gross enrolment ratio in education*	*GDP per capita (PPP US$)*
Norway	0.971	80.5	NA	98.6	53,433
Japan	0.960	82.7	NA	86.6	33,632
USA	0.956	79.1	NA	92.4	45,592
United Kingdom	0.947	79.3	NA	82.2	35,103
Mexico	0.854	76.0	92.8	82.2	14,104
China	0.772	72.9	93.3	68.7	5,383
Sri Lanka	0.759	74.0	90.8	68.7	4,243
India	0.612	63.4	66.0	61.0	2,753
Pakistan	0.572	66.2	54.2	39.3	2,496
Bangladesh	543	65.7	53.5	52.1	1,241
Niger	0.340	50.8	28.7	27.2	627

Source: Human Development Report 2009, Statistical Annex, Table H (http://hdr.undp.org/en/media/HDR_2009_EN_Indicators.pdf)

HDI is an aggregated measure of human development in a country and is comparable across countries. An examination of its components reveals why its value varied within a very wide range from 0.340 for Niger to 0.971 for Norway in 2007. Table 2.2 presents the values of components of HDI along with the value of HDI for selected countries for the year 2007. As shown in the table, the range of variation in the values of HDI is the highest for the component, GDP per capita (PPP US$). This means that GDP per capita (PPP US$) was the most important factor affecting the variations in the level of HDI in 2007. In terms of all the four components, China faired much better than India. The difference is most conspicuous in terms of GDP per capita and adult literacy rate.

Basic Elements of a Strategy for All-Round Human Resource Development

After having examined the current status of human resource development in India and a few other countries of the world, we now proceed to present some of the basic elements of a pragmatic and multi-faceted strategy of human resources development for India. According to Wikipedia, the free encyclopedia, a strategy is a long-term plan of action designed to achieve a particular goal, most often 'winning'. Strategy is differentiated from tactics or immediate actions with resources at hand by its nature of being extensively premeditated, and often practically rehearsed. The proposed strategy is designed taking into account the four components of HDI as elaborated in the preceding section of this paper.

Alleviating Poverty and Inequality through Higher Economic Growth

Poverty is the root cause of so many socio-economic problems such as illiteracy, unemployment, disease, hunger, and servitude. It degrades its victims physically, mentally, spiritually, morally, and socio-culturally. It is a big obstacle to human development. Any meaningful strategy of human development has to address the problems of a large number of people, who live in absolute poverty, i.e., who are unable to satisfy even the most basic needs. In India, the incidence of poverty is still very high despite almost 50 years of planned development. The Uniform Recall Period (URP)-consumption[1] distribution data of the 61st Round of the National Sample Survey Organisation (NSSO) yields a poverty ratio of 28.3 per cent in the rural areas, 25.7 per cent in the urban areas and 27.5 per cent for the country as a whole for the year 2004–05. The corresponding figures obtained from the Mixed Reference Period (MRP)-consumption[2] distribution data of the 61st Round are 21.8 per cent in the rural areas, 21.7 per cent in the urban areas and 21.8 per cent for the country as a whole. According to the HDR-2009, India's Human Poverty Index (HPI) in 2007 was 28 per cent and its rank among 182 countries was 88th as compared to China's HPI of 7.7 per cent and rank of 36. The percentage of India's population below poverty line (living on income of $1.25 per day) over the period 2000–07 was 41.6 as compared to 15.9 in China (HDR-2009, Statistical Annex, Table I). This shows how dismal India's performance has been in its effort to alleviate poverty vis-à-vis China.

Poverty reduces the people's capacity to use resources in a sustainable manner; it intensifies the pressure on the environment. A necessary but not a sufficient condition for elimination of absolute poverty is a relatively rapid rise in per capita incomes. Given the current population growth rate, this would require the overall national income growth of around 5 per cent per year in India.

Income distribution is an important element of sustainable human development. In India, there is a wide gap in the shares of incomes of the richest 10 per cent of its population and the poorest 10 per cent. According to HDR-2009, the share of the poorest 10 per cent of India's income in 2007 was 3.6 per cent and the share of the richest 10 per cent was 31.1. The Gini Index, which is a measure of income inequality, was 36.8 per cent. The corresponding figures for China were 2.4 per cent, 31.4 per cent and 41.5 per cent. This shows that in terms of income inequality India and China are almost comparable. A rapid economic growth combined with deteriorating income distribution may be worst than slower growth combined with redistribution in favour of the poor. If India focuses its efforts upon elimination of poverty and satisfying essential human needs, then domestic demands will increase for both agricultural products and manufactured goods and services. Hence, the very logic of sustainable human development implies an internal stimulus to economic growth.

Ensuring Food Security

Food, clothes and shelter are the basic needs of people everywhere. Meeting these basic needs is the primary function of all economic systems. The pace and pattern of economic development has to generate sustainable work opportunities at a level of productivity that would enable the poor to meet their basic needs of which food is most crucial. Therefore, ensuring food security is a prerequisite for sustainable livelihoods, which in turn, constitutes an integral element of sustainable human development. Food security at the national level may be defined as the secured access of all individuals and households in a country to adequate quantity of food for an active, healthy life on a long-term basis. Now, the concept of food security has been broadened and is used to connote livelihood security, i.e., secured physical and economic access to balanced diet, safe drinking water, environmental sanitation, primary education and basic health care (Swaminathan, 1996: 66). The three components of food security, namely, physical availability, economic access, and sustainability are essential for maintaining peace and social harmony both nationally and internationally. Therefore, it would be logically correct to say that food security is a *sine qua non* of peaceful sustainable development.

To attain food security, top priority must be given to promoting sustainable agricultural production systems. Increasing agricultural production at the cost of degraded soil and depleted and polluted water bodies is antithesis of sustainable agriculture. Growth in world cereal production so far has steadily outstripped world population growth. Land use in agriculture should be based on the scientific assessment of land capability. Furthermore, annual depletion of top soil, fish stock, or forest resource must not exceed the rate of natural regeneration. Future increase in productivity in India should be based on a better-controlled application of water and agro-chemicals, as well as on more extensive use of organic manures and non-chemical means of pest control. According to Purcell and Galati (1993), liberalisation of domestic and external trade in agricultural commodities may aggravate the food insecurity problem of the India's poor through higher cereal prices. To guard against the adverse effects of liberalisation, the public distribution system (PDS) will need to be better targeted and made more effective as a safety net for the poor.

In order to remove some of its drawbacks, the PDS was revamped in 1992 and the revamped system was launched in tribal, arid, hilly, drought-prone and other remotely located areas of the country. The objective of revamping the PDS was to increase its reach on the basis of area approach and to eliminate the leakages and malpractices that had crept in the system. In June 1997, a new policy of targeted PDS (TPDS) was introduced as an important constituent of the strategy of poverty alleviation. However, even now, the PDS suffers from several drawbacks including (i) proliferation of bogus ration cards; (ii) inadequate storage arrangements; (iii) ineffective functioning of Vigilance Committees; and (iv) failure to issue ration cards to all eligible households (Jena, 1998: 915). In 2007, the *Times of India* reported that wheat and rice worth ₹ 31,000 crore had been siphoned off the PDS in three years, 2004–07 (*Times of India* dated September 18, 2007). Such large scale leakages in the PDS have been known for decades now but no correctives have been taken to fix the problem.

Ensuring Security of Life and Property

In India, both man-made and natural disasters pose a serious threat to the lives and property of its people. Every day, in print and electronic media, we see reports of murders, rape, loot, and arson, abduction for extortion of money, communal violence and acts of terrorism committed by anti-national elements from both within and outside the country. Law and order situation in many parts of the country is at its worst. Thousands of innocent lives are lost every year in India mainly due to man-made mishaps and disasters. So much so that an average Indian always lives and works under the shadow of some unforeseen fear and threat to his/her life and property. This kind of situation is antithesis of human development and therefore requires measures for its amelioration.

Further, natural disasters have been a bane of India's economy since time immemorial. In ancient Indian literature, there are references to natural disasters such as prolonged droughts, flash floods, hail storms, land slides, cyclones and forest fires. About 60 per cent of the landmass in India is vulnerable to earthquakes; over 40 million hectares (ha) is prone to floods;[3] about 8 per cent of the total area is prone to cyclones; and about 68 per cent of the total area is susceptible to droughts. Eight thousand kilometre long coastline is prone to severe cyclonic formations. About 55 per cent of the total area lies in Seismic Zones III–V and is vulnerable to earthquakes. Sub-Himalayan regions and Western Ghats are vulnerable to land slides. (GoI, 2004 a: 32; Kanwar, 2001: 7). All this poses a serious threat to the lives and property of millions of people in India.

Economic development is unsustainable if it increases the vulnerability of people to natural and man-made crises. A drought may force farmers to sell their animals or other productive assets needed for sustaining production in future years. A pestilence may damage a crop wholly and leave the crop growers bankrupt. Similarly, a drop in the prices of farm produce may reduce farm incomes and thereby cause farmers to over-exploit natural resources. Although the central and state governments have introduced several measures to reduce the vulnerability of people in general and farmers in particular to floods and droughts, their effectiveness in redressing the problem is questionable. There is virtually no security of life and property against man-made disasters. To conclude, we could say that a development path that combines growth with reduced vulnerability to natural and man-made disasters is more sustainable than one that does not and hence there is a need for the government to initiate measures such as crop insurance, livestock insurance and life insurance so as to reduce the vulnerability of people to both natural and man-made disasters.

Reforming the Education System

Education is an important instrument of human development. It opens up doors of opportunities for human beings. *Sa vidya ya vimuktaye,* that is, education liberates individuals (from various types of servitudes and taboo). As stated earlier in this paper, there are many scholars who have advocated the human capital models of development. Education affects human development in several ways. First, it influences population growth. With rest all being equal, people with more education tend to have somewhat smaller families and to that extent population pressure on scarce resources is reduced. Second, education increases income, which is an important component of HDI. Third, it builds up technical knowledge and capabilities. Fourth, it can impart values and attitude which are conducive to development and help individuals cope with rapidly changing social, environmental and development realities. If development is to occur, an increase in income and wealth held either privately or publicly, must be one of the dominant goals in life. That is, people must have a desire to acquire, accumulate, or consume at increasing levels. If not, development is practically impossible. Research undertaken in developed and developing countries of the world reveals that for an increase in output, the quality of labour is more important than the quantity. A clear picture emerges if one looks at the experience of different countries. No country with an educated, technically trained labour force is poor, and no country with a predominantly illiterate, untrained labour force is rich. In general, the quality of the labour force is much more critical in economic development than is the availability of natural resources. Japan is a country which has almost no mineral or energy resources but has high economic productivity because of a highly literate, trained and efficient working population.

It has also been established that investment in education and training produces very high internal rates of return in economic output. Especially high are the returns to basic literacy. The rate of returns to investment in schooling is in the neighbourhood of 50 per cent per year in many rich countries, and in developing countries like India, the rate of return to primary schooling is even higher. Any poor country that wants to develop could do no better than use its scarce resources in schools, technical education, training, and management.

As two of the four components of HDI, viz., adult literacy rate and combined gross enrolment ratio in education, relate to education, so it is imperative for India to attach a very high priority to education if it wants to attain a high level of human development. As a matter of fact, strategies for development of the tertiary (service) sector, which is the fastest growing sector all over the world, requires skilled, experienced and innovative human resources for their success. And this is the path that India should choose to bring about overall development.

The quality of India's human resources, particularly the rural labour force, is poor in terms of skills, education, training, values, and attitudes. The literacy rate for the rural population in India in 2001 was as low as 59.40 per cent as compared to All-India average of 65.38 per cent. In terms of adult literacy rate and combined gross enrolment ratio in education, India was far behind China.

India's education system is dated and suffers from several drawbacks.[4] It produces young men and women who have no self confidence, are not self-reliant, and have no values and attitude congenial for their own development as well as national development. Another drawback of India's education system is that it involves a lot of wastage in terms of students who fail to pass an examination, particularly at the high school and higher secondary school levels.[5] In view of this, there is an urgent need for India to drastically reform its existing education system at all levels in general and primary and secondary levels in particular. Several Education Commissions and individual scholars and educationists have made recommendations from time to time to reform the education system but very little has been done to implement them. Some of the reforms required are as follows:

Value-based education: Today, we observe a high degree of degradation of moral and ethical values rampant in all walks of life in India, and the trend is increasing over time. This is partly due to the lack of value-based education and partly to the ostentatious consumption pattern of the elite section of our society. Education without values is merely a mechanical instrument which can be used for constructive as well destructive purposes, depending on the value-orientation of the person concerned. Further, life without values is like a rudderless boat, which keeps drifting in all directions in the absence of a particular destination. Socially desirable values can be in-built from the very childhood first in the families and later through character training by qualified and trained nursery and primary school teachers carefully selected for the purpose.

Exposure to world religions: In my opinion, ignorance about various world religions on the part of our people is responsible to a large extent for much of the communal violence and hatred in India. Therefore, courses in major world religions and cultures should be an integral part of course curricula in all secondary and higher secondary schools and colleges.

Education in yoga, meditation or other spiritual pursuits: This will help the students in their mental, spiritual and psychological development and inculcate in them a sense of worthiness and self-esteem. For this, there is a need for introducing practical courses in *yoga*, meditation and other arts of good living in secondary and higher secondary schools and colleges.

Higher emphasis on vocational education: In developed countries such as USA, UK, Canada, and France, education system at the high school and higher secondary school levels is designed in such a way that most of the students are equipped with the knowledge, skills and self-confidence necessary for taking up self-employment or wage-paid jobs in the trade and services sectors, in case they do not want or are not qualified to go for higher studies. Besides, there is virtually no wastage in terms of failed students.[6] In India, we need to reorient our education system in similar direction.

Allocation of higher budgetary resources to education: Current resource allocation priorities of India need to be changed to commit more public funds to education, particularly at the primary, secondary and higher secondary levels, to provide equal access to education to all sections of society. India could usefully redirect much of its current spending, over 2 per cent of its gross domestic product, toward education by reducing military expenditure, halt capital flight, combat corruption and privatisation of loss-making public enterprises.

It would be fair to say that both the Central and State governments have been conscious about the need to reform the education system and have initiated several programmes to revamp the existing system from time to time including the National Literacy Mission Programme (NLMP). There also have been several innovations in the education system at the primary, secondary and higher secondary levels such as the Delhi Public Schools, Navodaya Vidyalayas, and Navarachana schools and the schools run by several philanthropic organisations such a Rama Krishna Mission and Krishnamurthy Foundation. However, these are like a few drops in a big ocean. To sum up we could say that there is still a long way for India to go to revamp its education system to make it relevant, and equally accessible to all sections of society.

Improving the Delivery of Health Care Services

Life expectancy at birth is a component of HDI. It depends, among other things, on the availability of nutritious food, and health care facilities and services to the people at affordable cost. As shown in Table 2.2, life expectancy in India in 2007 was 63.4 years as compared to 72.9 in China and 82.7 in Japan. The probability of not surviving up to age 40 over the period, 2005–10 was 15.5 for India and 6.2 for China and underweight children aged below five over the period, 2000–06, was 46 per cent in India and as low as only 7 per cent in China (HDR-2009, Statistical Annex Table I). The infant mortality rate (aged under one) in 2005 was 56 per cent in India and 23 per cent in China (UNICEF, 2006, Basic Indicators Table 1). Further, the per capita public expenditure on health in India in 2006 was PPP US $21 as against PPP US $144 in China and 3,780 in Norway. In terms of total government expenditure, it was 3.4 per cent in India, 9.9 per cent in China and 17.9 per cent in Norway (HDR-2009, Statistical Annex, Table N). All this indicates the poor quality of public health care system in India and lack of access of most of the people to whatever facilities exist. However, it would be fair to admit that the quality of health care services available in India varies widely; there are world class hospitals in metropolitan cities like Mumbai, New Delhi, Chennai, and Ahmedabad and there are some hospitals, mostly in rural areas, without doctors and medicines. Rural areas and rural people are at a great disadvantage vis-à-vis their urban counterparts in terms of both the physical availability of health care services as well as financial access to whatever facilities and services are available.

Duly recognising the need for providing adequate public health care services to rural people, the Government of India had launched the National Rural Health Mission (NRHM) (2005–12) with the main objective of providing effective health care services to rural population throughout the country with special focus on 18 states, which have weak public health indicators and/or weak infrastructure. The Mission is an articulation of the commitment of the government to raise public spending on Health from 0.9 per cent of GDP to 2–3 per cent of GDP. However, the Mission suffers from several constraints including the shortage of doctors and lab technicians. For example, as in March 2008, 12.4 per cent of the Primary Health Centres (PHCs) were without a doctor, about 37.8 per cent were without a Lab technician and 16.3 per cent were without a pharmacist (GoI, 2008). In view of this, there is a need for the government to take effective measures to ensure that PHCs are adequately staffed and equipped so that the objectives of the Mission are achieved.

Increasing the Employment Opportunities

Poverty and unemployment are closely associated and there is a two-way relationship between them. This means that the people are poor mainly because they are unemployed and vice versa. Employment is a source of income and livelihood and also a reflection of the overall living condition of people. The Approach Paper to the Tenth Plan prescribed that in order to ameliorate poverty it is essential to create 'gainful high quality' employment to the existing as well as prospective additions to the labour force. Growth in employment is usually linked with growth in earnings of the households and hence has a direct bearing on the poverty levels. It is to be noted that the rural households which are around the poverty line are primarily engaged in occupations which since the initiation of the reforms have not experienced a significant increase in productivity. Hence, for this group, in the immediate future, amelioration of poverty has to come mainly through additional employment generation.

However, despite several steps taken by the Government of India to provide regular and productive employment in rural areas, the rural employment situation in the country is far from satisfactory. Most of the workers in the rural areas are engaged in low paid agricultural activities either as self-employed or casual labour. In many regions, in view of the low absorption capacity of subsistence agriculture and in the absence of any major organised sector industry, there is distress diversification of workforce to unorganised non-agricultural activities. Hence, it is widely acknowledged that creating adequate employment opportunities should constitute one of the important objectives of the development strategy of the country.

Labour force projections show that around 10 million persons will be added to the labour force during the period, 2005–15 and a major portion will be located in rural areas of the country. To achieve the goal of full employment by 2015, India will require an annual employment growth rate of 2.8 per cent to absorb the additions to the labour force and to clear the backlog of unemployed persons at the 7–8 per cent growth rate of the GDP (NIRD, 2005 RDR: 83–87).

Consequent upon the passing of the National Rural Employment Guarantee Act (NREGA)[7] on September 7, 2005, the National Rural Employment Guarantee Scheme (NREGS, now MNREGS) was launched on February 2, 2006 in 200 backward districts with a view to extend it to all the districts within five years. In view of the high potential that the scheme has to benefit the rural areas, especially the rural poor, it has been extended to cover all the 614 districts in the country. The scheme aims at enhancing the livelihood security of the people in rural areas by guaranteeing 100 days of wage employment in a financial year, to a rural household whose adult members volunteer to do unskilled manual work. For the first time in India, an employment generation programme recognises the right to work as a fundamental legal right. Besides providing 100 days of guaranteed employment in a financial year to every rural household, it also aims at developing rural infrastructure by undertaking generation of wage-paid employment schemes that addresses the causes underlying drought, deforestation and soil erosion.

According to the MNREGA website, as in March 2009, out of total of 99 million households who demanded employment, the number of households working under the scheme was 14 million and the cumulative number of households who got 100 days of employment was about 4 million. MNREGS suffers from several drawbacks such as poor quality of durable assets created under it, lack of transparency and accountability, lack of effort to improve the skills of rural youth and to enable them to earn more (Sharma, 2009: 4). What is needed is to ensure that full benefits of the MNREGS reach its intended target group and that it is not reduced to yet another subsidy programme with a huge financial burden on the public exchequer.

Mainstreaming the Gender in Development Strategy

Women play a more critical role than men in imparting the right kind of values, beliefs and attitude to their children. In Hindu mythology, they symbolise knowledge (Goddess Saraswati), wealth and prosperity (Goddess Lakshmi), and power and strength (Goddess Durga). Without their development and empowerment, no sustainable human development is possible. Despite the fact that development cannot be sustained unless it is a joint responsibility shared by women and men, there has been a glaring lack of gender perspective in development strategies in both developed and developing countries of the world including India. A gender perspective emphasises the relations between men and women and the relationships that both men and women have with their social and natural environment. It recognises that the success of projects to foster sustainable development largely depends on the extent to which both women and men participate in project design, planning, implementation and monitoring. There are many ways of institutionalising a gender-sensitive approach to sustainable development. The first and foremost requirement is the policy of equal development of both men and women in development projects.[8] Next, women should be assigned specific roles, responsibilities and rights in making various decisions rather than simply attending project meetings. Besides, the whole project team has to be sensitised to gender issues if gender awareness is to be encouraged. The whole team also has to be trained and made responsible for the implementation of the gender-sensitive approach. Finally, it is also important to clearly define the objectives to be achieved, measures to be employed to achieve each of the objectives and develop quality and process-oriented indicators in order to monitor the progress of the projects in achieving the intended objectives.

Concluding Remarks

Human resources play an important role in determining the level and pace of development of a nation. Both quantity and quality of human resources are equally important contributors to national development. Human resources are renewable and well developed human resources can be substituted to a large extent for non-renewable natural resources in the process of development. As far as numbers are concerned, India is relatively well-endowed with human resources but their quality is poor in terms of knowledge and skills.

The low level of human resource development in India is evident from a number of indicators including HDI; India's HDI in 2007 was 0.612 as compared to China's 0.772. This explains to a large extent the relatively low level of economic and social development in India vis-à-vis many other developing countries including China. In view of this, it is imperative for India to develop and implement a pragmatic and multifaceted strategy for all round development of its human resources.

The strategy proposed in this paper for all-round development of India's human resources is pragmatic and multifaceted. The main elements of the proposed strategy are: alleviation of poverty and inequality, ensuring food security and security of life and property, reforming the education system, improving the delivery of health care services, increasing the employment opportunities, and mainstreaming the gender in development strategy.

Notes

1. URP consumption refers to Uniform Recall Period consumption in which the consumer expenditure data for all the items are collected from a 30–day recall period.

2. MRP consumption refers to Mixed Recall Period consumption in which the consumer expenditure data for five non-food items, namely, clothing, footwear, durable goods, education, and institutional medical expenses are collected from a 365–day recall period and the consumption data for the remaining items are collected from a 30–day recall period.
3. India is one of the most flood-prone countries in the world and accounts for one fifth of the global death count due to floods. Over 30 million people are displaced annually due to the floods.
4. Of late, there have been many innovations in India in education, especially at the primary, secondary, and higher secondary levels, by a number of NGOs, who have set up good schools, mostly English medium, and have hired trained and motivated teachers. The quality of education imparted in those private schools is good in most of the cases but an average Indian household cannot afford the cost of education in such schools. Further, their impact on the quality of education at the national level is almost negligible; they are like an oasis in a large desert.
5. Every year hundreds of thousands of students fail in High School and Higher Secondary School examinations and become a burden to their parents and society at large.
6. To ensure that no students fail at the high and higher secondary levels, students in a particular standard are normally divided into three categories, viz., (i) those who are very good and do not need much of the teacher's help and guidance; (ii) those who are good but need some help and guidance; and (iii) those who are poor and need intensive guidance and special tutoring. It is the responsibility of the teacher concerned that the poor students receive all the guidance and help they need to pass the examination.
7. Recently, NREGA has been renamed as Mahatma Gandhi National Rural Employment Guarantee Act (MNREGA).
8. Recently, the Government of India has taken up several measures including reservation of seats for women in Panchayat Raj Institutions and other local bodies to empower women and provide them equal opportunity in employment and several other spheres of economic activities. To protect and promote the interests of women and to redress their grievances, a National Commission for Women has also been constituted.

References

Alex, Alexander V. (1983). *Human Capital Approach to Economic Development*. New Delhi: Metropolitan.

Government of India (2004). Agricultural Statistics at a Glance 2004, New Delhi: Department of Agriculture and Cooperation, Ministry of Agriculture, Government of India.

—— (2008). Bulletin on Rural Health Statistics in India 2008, Ministry of Health and Family Welfare, New Delhi: Government of India. http://www.mohfw.nic.in/Bulletin on RHS-March, 2008–PDF version

Higgins, Benjamin (1966). *Economic Development: Principles, Problems and Policies.* Allahabad: Central Book Depot.

Jena, A.C. (1998). 'PDS: An Overview of Policies and Programme Implementation' in R.C. Choudhury and S. Rajakutty (Eds). Fifty Years of Rural Development: Retrospect and Prospect, Vol. II. Hyderabad: National Institute of Rural Development.

Kanwar, Rakesh (2001). 'Disaster Management', *The Administrator,* XLIV, December.

NIRD (2005). India Rural Development Report 2005–06, Hyderabad: National Institute of Rural Development.

Schultz, Theodore (1964). *Transforming Traditional Agriculture.* Ludhiana: Lyall Book Depot.

Sharma, Jogender (2009). 'NREGA: Potential and Challenges', *Kurukshetra,* Vol. 58, No. 2, December Issue.

Singh, Katar (2009). *Rural Development: Principles, Policies and Management,* 3rd Edition, New Delhi: Sage Publications; California, London, Singapore: Thousand Oaks.

Swaminathan, M.S. (1996). 'Science and Technology for Sustainable Food Security', *Indian Journal of Agricultural Economics,* 51: 1, 2.

UNDP (1990). *Human Development Report 1990.* New York: Oxford University Press.

—— (1994). *Human Development Report 1994.* New York: Oxford University Press.

—— (1996). *Human Development Report 1996.* New York: Oxford University Press.

—— (1997). *Human Development Report 1997.* New York: Oxford University Press.

—— (2009). *Human Development Report 2009.* New York: Oxford University Press. (http://hdr.undp.org/en/media/HDR_2009_EN_Indicators.pdf)

UNICEF (2006). The State of the World's Children 2007, New York: The United Nations Children's Fund.

3

Exploring the Nature of Democratic Governance

SANJAY LODHA

A new genre of terms and concepts has occupied the interest and imagination of students, researchers and teachers in the discipline of political science in the last few decades. Many of these have been in the literature earlier too but have gained increasing currency recently. A core term like government has been stretched to governance, good governance, humane governance, and democratic governance. The concept of democracy has been added with a lot of prefixes and suffixes as well as adjectives. We now have a whole gamut of terms which seek to explain one or the other dimension of democracy. To name a few here – procedural democracy and substantive democracy, cyber democracy, ballot box/electoral democracy, radical democracy, democracy with/without accountability, accountability without democracy, democracy without people, people without democracy, democracy with/without associations, etc. (Tsai, 2007). Tagged along with these core terms have been a few satellite notions as well, such as responsiveness, accountability, transparency, participation, empowerment, trust, inclusion/exclusion, access, civil society and social capital, state capacity, and delivery. This proliferation of conceptual jugglery and terminological diversity has made the task of academic community more challenging as well as complicated.

This paper seeks to unravel some limited dimensions of this conceptual jungle and make some sense of the reason behind this terminological web. Part I briefly discusses the context of this unprecedented expansion in the lexicon and accounts for the factors responsible for this. Part II throws light on the concepts of governance, good governance and humane governance. Part III deliberates upon the features of democratic governance. The paper makes a few empirical observations towards the end.

The Context

It will be perhaps not out of place to ponder a little on the reason for this sudden spurt of lexicon in the stream of political science. In the post-war world, the cold war and the consequent multi-dimensional bipolarity of international politics had rendered the 'master science' sterile. Researchers and commentators on both sides of the iron curtain had fixed glasses to interpret and analyse events. Voices outside the two poles were either ignored or were too feeble to be taken care of. The orthodoxy and exclusive nature of the cold war system prevented the growth of alternative concepts and free thinking. The first rupture in this rigid milieu was noticed with the downfall of the Allende regime in Portugal in 1979. This was followed by introduction of state-directed reforms in China. Soon the tide became strong enough to encapsulate a large part of East Europe culminating not only in the downfall of the authoritarian regimes in most countries of East Europe but also the very disintegration of the communist bloc as well as dismemberment of the multi-cultural Soviet Union. It was not long before many other countries also switched over to democracy in other continents of the world. The new trend was referred to as the 'third wave of democracy' (Huntington, 1991). Thus, the dismantling of the iron curtain and the end of the cold war provided considerable scope for exploring new vistas and experiment with new concepts.

A notable feature of the post-cold war world was the growth of a vibrant civil society at the global level which raised a number of critical issues relating to poverty, empowerment, human rights, election watch, environment, trade, and development. The civil society has assumed the role of conscience keeper of 'the democratic upsurge' and played a critical role in both broadening and deepening the democratic agenda (Hertel, 2006). Its intervention has involved multifold pathways from awareness generation and capacity building to service delivery in partnership with the state or on its own. In its relationship with the state, the civil society has adopted collaborationist as well as confrontational positions depending upon the nature of the former. Where the states have been liberal, the civil society has successfully joined hands in consolidating and expanding the democratic space. Otherwise, it has confronted illiberal political regimes in mending their ways. What has facilitated its activities is the global reach which itself is an outcome of the revolution in the field of information and communication technology. The civil society thus has been a major enabling factor in pushing the democratic enterprise to hitherto untapped territories. Much of the satellite notions of the democratic juggernaut in the last few decades have been a contribution of the activities undertaken by the civil society agencies. What has furthered this exercise is the increasing engagement of academics with people's movements and community-based organisations as well as with policy making bodies of the state. This engagement has given greater resilience to the conceptual underpinnings of the subject.

The global march of democracy has made it the only game in the town. It has become more and more difficult for states to be otherwise. Even distinctly authoritarian states will masquerade as being democratic either to receive multilateral aid or to avoid the critical gaze of other members of the international community. This is clearly an authoritarian moment for the advocates of democracy. Concern has been raised about the illiberal nature of democracy or one can even label it as hegemony of democracy. One is reminded of Rousseau's dictum of 'being forced to be free'. The obsession with democracy in every walk of life has indeed led to a trivialisation of the concept itself. An overemphasis on the institutional and procedural basis of democracy has done considerable damage to the essence of the democratic spirit. There has been a great urge to assess and measure democracies on different scales adopting a multitude of variables. Checklists on the essentials of democracy have been prepared to quantify degree of democracy prevailing in a certain state. Most of these assessments have been done by western experts in collaboration with the elites of the subject states. Democratic assessments such as these have become the yardstick for rewards or punishments at the international level. Not many of these studies have taken into account the actual experience of the common men in negotiating with the state or engaging the state functionaries. This has led critics to decry western fixation with ballot box democracy. This process of growing democratisation and the concerns reflected thereby has led to the coinage of new terms to highlight the deficits and strengths of democracy.

The Content: Governance

Governance has been one of the buzz words that has simultaneously evoked critical response and also changed the vocabulary of political science. The concept has a rich history. It was way back in 400 BC that Kautilya in his *Arthashastra,* a treatise on governance, unfolded the key pillars of the art of governance, emphasising justice, ethics, and anti-autocratic tendencies. He identifies the duty of the king to protect the wealth of the state and its subjects and to enhance, maintain and safeguard this wealth as well as the interests of the kingdom's subjects. Despite its historicity, no strong consensus has emerged around a single definition of the concept. Since the 1980s it has come in vogue in development circles and assumed prominence in global public policy lexicon. The term connotes a complex set of structures and processes and is much broader than government.

The World Bank defined governance as 'the manner in which public officials and institutions acquire and exercise the authority to shape public policy and provide public goods and services' (World Bank, 1994). The Bank has identified three distinct aspects of governance: (i) the type of political regime; (ii) the process by which authority is exercised in the management of a country's social and economic resources for development; and (iii) the capacity of governments to design, formulate, and implement policies and discharge functions.

The Commission on Global Governance defines governance as 'the sum of many ways individuals and institutions, public and private, manage their common affairs. It is the continuing process through which conflicting or diverse interests may be accommodated and co-operative action may be taken. It includes formal institutions and regimes empowered to enforce compliance, as well as informal arrangements that people and institutions either have agreed to or perceive to be in their interest' (Commission on Global Governance, 1995).

UNDP, which has been in the forefront of development debates, has defined governance 'as the exercise of economic, political and administrative authority to manage a country's affairs at all levels. It comprises mechanisms, processes and institutions through which citizens and groups articulate their interests, exercise their legal rights, meet their obligations and mediate their differences' (UNDP, 1997).

For James Rosenau, governance 'encompasses the activities of governments, but it also includes the many other channels through which "commands" flow in the form of goals framed, directives issued, and policies pursued' (Rosenau, 1995).

Kaufmann, Kraay, and Zoido-Lobaton define governance as 'the traditions and institutions by which authority in a country is exercised. This includes the process by which governments are selected, monitored and replaced; the capacity of the government to effectively formulate and implement sound policies; and the respect of the citizens and the state for institutions that govern economic and social interactions among them' (Kaufmann et al., 1999).

A number of definitions can be quoted here to unravel similar or different aspects of governance. Most definitions do agree on the need of a capable state operating under the rule of law. There is also unanimity that governance is broader than government. However, different degrees of emphasis have been placed upon the role of democratic accountability of governments to their citizens. A few definitions also take into account traditional and informal authority structures which regulate relationships in a society. Some definitions also refer to civil society at various levels, from local to the global. It also subsumes within its fold the vast increase in the number and activities of non-state actors and also the implications of the revolution in the field of information and communication technology.

The term 'governance' came to occupy prominence due to dissatisfaction with the state-dominated models of social and economic development in many parts of the post-cold war world. Cold war and nationalist insecurities had blinded political actors and regimes to many new developments in the literature on development. Criticism was looked upon as interference in internal affairs. But end of the cold war led to increasing western pressure for economic liberalisation and political democratisation. There was now no need to turn a blind eye to the presence of excessively illegitimate political regimes. Nature and quality of local governance became issues of concern as the third wave of democracy set in. More and more countries adopted civilian rule, elections and multiparty democracy. Elections became the sine qua non for a democratic veneer. This was necessary for regime legitimacy and also to attract investors and aid agencies. The mushroom growth of civil society agencies further opened up the local and the global arena for pressure politics and contestation. The internal sovereignty of nation-states was thwarted by these bodies in collaboration with their global counterparts. Emergence of certain global challenges such as terrorism, global warming, terrorism, frequent natural disasters necessitated global action which further eroded national sovereignty.

Governance as a term has developed considerable elasticity given the fact that it has been adopted by people pursuing different ideological destinations (Kooiman, 1993). While it quickly captured the imagination of the elite in the south as well, it always had connotations of intervention. Alternatively, it surreptitiously legitimised the less than democratic ways of managing public affairs of societies. Many new democracies had a deplorable track record. It is true that the initial formulations of governance were informed more by concerns of investors and financial institutions. It was believed that once efficiency is attained and economic reform is ensured, democracy would become a more workable enterprise. Thus, the issue of democracy was sacrificed for the sake of administrative and managerial reforms.

Good Governance

The demise of the cold war brought to an end the need to organise the world in opposite camps on the basis of rival ideologies and political systems. The urge to amass the support of as many states as possible in a perceived game of numbers suddenly came to an end. For the lone global power, i.e., the USA, the end of the cold war may have implied 'a unipolar moment' or the 'end of history' but it also meant that now there was no pressing need to seek the support of states which had authoritarian political systems. Nor was there an urge to give aid and assistance to client states which had dubious track record in the handling of their internal affairs, including human rights issues. In the wake of the disintegration of the communist bloc, it was now felt that political systems in both post-colonial and post-communist states needed to be disciplined. Consequently, the developed North led by the United States and supported by the Bretton Woods international financial institutions now embarked upon the agenda of prescribing conditionalities for client states so that the latter could reform the management of their governmental affairs. These states were now goaded to restructure the nature and operation of their institutions to make these more efficient, effective, transparent, responsive, accountable and last but not the least democratic (OECD, 1995).

During the cold war days, the conditionalities were mostly external in nature in the shape of support for the warring powers in the international fora or by giving bases or resources. These externally directed conditionalities did not evince much interest in the internal administrative arrangements and policy making processes of the client states (World Bank, 1994). Nor was any effort made to dictate prioritisation of policy initiatives and the manner of implementing the same. However, in the post-cold war scenario, a new generation of political conditionalities persevered to engage in this enterprise. The new idea was to establish a grip on recipient developing countries' handling of political processes, and on the basic manner in which government and its constituent political processes—multi-partyism or other—would be restructured. For the international financial institutions it meant interfering in the internal affairs of nation-states overriding the norms laid down by the United Nations. In order to push the new regime of political and administrative reforms what was needed was a new set of criteria or standard. It was here that the notion of 'good governance' emerged. The term promised to embrace reforms of administrative-managerial as well as political nature. It had sufficient elasticity to give the agenda-setters enough discretion of action. What was pushed as universal or core values of the good governance agenda was dismantling of bloated state structures in the developing countries and multi-party democratisation.

Gradually, good governance sought to focus more on alleviating two undesirable features in many a political establishments: unrepresentative character of governments and inefficiency of non-market systems. If bad governance implied personalisation of power, violation of basic human rights, systemic corruption and non-responsive and unelected governments, the plate of good governance had to be more stuffed than just structural adjustments and bureaucratic reforms. Apart from economic liberalisation, it had to give space to elections, accountability and human rights. The list of other attributes which have assumed importance in more recent times is pretty formidable: universal protection of human rights; non-discriminatory laws; efficient, impartial and rapid delivery of justice; elected parliaments; transparent and accountable public agencies;

democratic decentralisation and meaningful participation by citizens in debating public policies and choices.

At the insistence of the UNDP, human development reports have regularly focused on the urgent needs of the more deprived sections of the population in different parts of the world. Poverty, increasing unemployment, glaring inequality, social exclusion and environmental damage have occupied the attention of the Human Development Reports of the UNDP for more than a decade. The Human Development Index (HDI) has brought to the fore these issues year after year. What this implies is that human well-being has to be conceived more broadly to include not only consumption of goods and services but also the accessibility of all sections of the population to the basic necessities of productive and socially meaningful life. Human development also pertains to expansion of people's choices with regard to education, knowledge, health, longevity. The question also deals with that of agency which will deliver these public goods. The free market logic that anything that the government can do, the markets can do better has come under a scanner. Public provisioning of these goods, especially for the impoverished and deprived social groups, has again come to the forefront. The Washington Consensus needed to be revisited. A proper balance between market and the state was needed. A strong state was looked upon as necessary to ensure equity, legitimacy and efficiency. An UNDP report stated, 'A legitimately strong government can be described as one that commands sufficient confidence in its legitimacy to allow for a strong civil society, and for a network of non-governmental institutions and regulations that ensure the development of a well-functioning economic system, the strengthening of democratic procedures, and a widespread participation by people in public life' (UNDP, 2002). Taking the lead from the UNDP, the World Bank, under the leadership of Joseph Stiglitz, sought to build state capacity.

Thus, as a result of rigorous intervention by the UNDP and a few other UN agencies, the implication of the good governance agenda became more humane and statist. The minimalist state has now given place to reforming and improving state institutions, including deepening and broadening the scope of democracy and also exploring more active and creative role for non-state actors. Good governance does not mean less but more appropriate government.

Humane Governance

The 1990s saw another powerful set of ideas that emerged from the advocates of human development. Mahbub ul Haq, the father of the human development approach, felt that the concept of good governance had failed to match the radicalism of the notion of human development (Mahbub ul Haq, 1999). Therefore, along with Richrad Falk, he launched the concept of 'humane governance' which included good political, civil and economic governance. Good political governance referred to structures, processes that support the creation of a participatory, responsive, and accountable polity; good civil governance implied a society in which people develop the ability to organise themselves and good economic governance posited competitive, non-discriminatory and equitable economy (Falk, 1995).

The idea of humane governance was to make governance more people-oriented. It focused on human rights and global security and endeavoured to redress 'inhumane governance' reflected in five persistent global problems: the failure to meet basic human needs; discrimination and denial of human rights to women, indigenous people and others; failure to protect the environment and to safeguard the interests of the future generations; lack of progress in abolishing war; and failure to achieve the spread of transnational democracy. Humane governance seeks to develop a more equitable world order in which the lives of the people are interlinked regardless of the boundaries of nation-states.

The end of the cold war unleashed a flurry of fresh ideas in the realm of welfare and development. Governance, good governance and humane governance have been extensions and improvements upon each other. These have elicited critical responses from scholars and development practitioners. Many governments the world over have introduced meaningful changes in their policy framework to give space to local, national, regional as well as global concerns. Good governance has moved ahead from mere efficiency and growth considerations to promote greater freedom, participation and sustainable human development. However, down the line the feeling has grown that there is a disconnect somewhere. The issue of fundamental importance is related to the interrelationship between democracy and governance. The two could not be separate compartments. There was a need to connect the two.

Democratic Governance

In the scholarly debate culminating in the UNDP edition of good governance, the early World Bank sidetracking of democracy was checked and partially corrected. Basic questions which led to this correction were governance for whom? Who will judge good or bad governance – elite experts wearing World Bank glasses or the common people? Whose development? In answering these questions the UNDP successfully shifted the focus away from the concerns of the donor countries and international financial institutions to the masses living in the developing world. But the UNDP effort is limited in terms of its appeal and the 'location' from which it views governance. It appears not to situate the idea in a normative framework as to why governments should reach the poor. It is this intellectual deficit which led to the concept of democratic governance. It is a firm belief now that democracy is not a mere appendage to governance for making the latter legitimate and politically acceptable. The two are not distinct concerns but are integral to the democratic mission. It may well be proposed that governance is democratic or else it is not governance meaning thereby that without democracy we cannot think in terms of good governance. What naturally follows from this is that democracy implies the ability of a society to self-regulate. It is only in a democracy that there can be an efficient and just management of conflicts. It is only in a democracy that a fair regulation and redistribution of resources is possible. It is only in a democracy that social peace and inclusion can be ensured. And it is only in a democracy that people can be promised access to power, goods, services, and dignity. As such, democracy means efficient governance and governance means vibrant democracy.

The concept of democratic governance turns the pyramid upside down. Democracy is usually taken to mean either a set of procedures to ensure fair and routine circulation of elites and/or an expression in the myth of efficacy on the part of the citizens. In the last instance, democracy must have the ability to translate itself in to concrete outcomes that generate support and legitimacy to the democratic enterprise. For the ordinary citizen, it is the end product which is of interest: what democracy delivers. People look at democracy as providing opportunities for uplifting life conditions. They want the government to deliver. If democracy with all its procedural niceties is unable to perform then it becomes only a legitimating strategy for one or the other set of incumbents. Not many people are interested in assuming powers of the government but they do understand the logic of power. The more radical formulations of people becoming the government or people 'participating' in government on a routine basis are, at least for now, not very popular.

Democratic governance involves engaging with a wide variety of laws, regulations, rules, and procedures. Three dimensions would merit attention: (i) How democratic has been the process of arriving at these laws, regulations, etc.? (ii) How much do these laws and regulations reflect popular sentiment and aspirations? (iii) Are the objectives with which these rules are framed get reflection in actual practice? No less important is the understanding that democratic governance is also about the capacity of a society and its citizens to these commonly accepted norms and principles. Self-regulation is as important as is state capacity. Democratic governance also needs to be understood in a social context. It believes in an inclusive society and privileges the deprived groups. Citizens have to be at the core of democratic governance. Usage of terms like clients, consumers, customers, stakeholders, recipients for the citizens has its allegiance to systems other than that of democratic governance (UNDP, 2002).

Responsiveness of the government is another key concern of democratic governance. Responsiveness of the government needs to be viewed not merely in terms of tangible outcomes as benefits from welfare programmes and schemes but also its capacity to secure dignity and respect to common citizens. The services and benefits that the state provides to its citizens could be divided into several categories: minimal responsibilities that every state has to fulfil – ensure law and order, dispute settlement, enforce contracts among citizens, protect basic liberties; collective services and benefits meant for citizens irrespective of one's social background, class or gender – such as transport, roads, electricity, education, health; collective services meant for citizens as members of some group based on ascriptive identity – dalits, tribals, minorities and OBCs; individual benefits based on some economic criterion-subsidies on cooking gas or petrol, on agricultural inputs, minimum support prices for crops, goods through the PDS, old age pension, credit at low interests, etc. Efficient and effective delivery of these services and benefits leads to the success of democratic governance.

Citizen's access to these services and benefits is the central theme which informs democratic governance. Access has three dimensions: normative dimension – acceptance of the right to access; institutional dimension – the establishment of appropriate institutions to ensure access; and empirical dimension – actual practice of access. Access has to be a routinely experienced fact. Based on these three dimensions, access is located in four issues: access to power – participation, political equality, responsiveness, transparency and accountability, decentralisation; access to material resources: employment, health, education, food, transport, house, etc.; access to cultural resources: dignity, identity, space, plurality, equality and justice; access to whom: poor, rural, women, minorities, children, elderly, differently abled, dalits, tribal, etc. It is on the issues of state delivery and citizens' access that democratic governance is premised. Performance of the state and its institutional network results in differential degrees of faith/trust legitimising different arms of the government. People's faith in democracy is correlated to the degree of success or failure of the government in delivering goods and services to the citizenry.

The UNDP in its strategic plan for 2008–11 has proposed to restructure its support to democratic governance into three broad areas: (i) fostering inclusive participation: empowering the poor, women, youth, indigenous people and other deprived groups through expanding the core channels of civic engagement – electoral channels, media, ICT, participation; these will strengthen the demand for democratic governance; (ii) strengthening responsive institutions: accountability, responsiveness, state capacity, representation, justice system; these will enhance the delivery of democratic governance; (iii) policies and principles: promotion of human rights, gender equality and anti-corruption; these will create an enabling environment for democratic governance (Sakiko and Ponzio,

2002). Democratic governance is thus integral to the Millennium Development Goals (MDGs) of the UNO. It would be only through appropriate blend of democratic institutions and democratic politics that the goals of democratic governance can be accomplished. There is no gainsaying the fact that the two are complementary to each other. Democratic governance involves a definite step forward from economic liberalisation and human development approach to political liberalisation and democratic development. That there is a greater global consensus on this speaks volumes about the promise of democratic governance.

Empirical Observations

The debate about concepts belonging to the governance family has been the concern of this paper so far. What may provide greater meaning to the debate is the findings of a nation-wide survey conducted by the Lokniti research programme of the CSDS as a part of its National Election Study. The post-poll survey was conducted in the immediate aftermath of the 2009 Lok Sabha elections.

People's faith in democracy was proved by the fact that nearly three-fourth of the respondents considered democracy better than any other system. Success of electoral democracy was confirmed by people's opinion that elections are conducted in a fair manner. An overwhelming majority felt that governance in the country cannot be done properly without political parties, legislatures and elections. People have greater trust in politically accountable governance than any kind of meritocracy or rule by the armed forces. They also do not subscribe to the view that a powerful leader can substitute for elected leadership. Non-performance by elected leadership should entitle voters to recall those elected and people are not averse to the idea of being empowered with the option of not to elect any candidate if no one is to their liking. But they do feel that their vote has an effect on the manner in which governance is carried out in the country.

People want greater devolution of power to local levels of governance. But they are less interested in engaging themselves with such institutions in a routine manner as is evidenced by their indifference towards attending meetings of Gram Sabha or Ward meetings. But their faith in public provision of services and goods is evidenced in their rejection of private sector as service provider in the fields of electricity, education, health, drinking water, and transportation. That the people expect the state functionaries to deliver on their own is also established by the fact that very few engage them frequently. The survey also reflected people's awareness about major welfare schemes of the government, viz., National Rural Employment Guarantee Act (NREGA), Mid-Day Meal Scheme (MDMS), Farmer's Loan Waiver Scheme, Indira Gandhi Pension Scheme, etc. But it also cuts a sorry picture because of a big gap between the degree of awareness and extent of delivery. At the same time, lack of performance by the state has not culminated in an explosive condition so far as people are overwhelmingly opposed to violence as a method of protest against non-delivery. They appear to be more comfortable with less strident modes of protest, such as *hartal*, *gherao* and demonstrations.

The empirical findings from NES 2009 give us a vivid picture of people's perceptions, opinions and attitudes about issues which are so intimately related to the whole debate about democratic governance. As awareness about access, delivery and responsiveness increases, people will be more assertive and demanding strengthening democracy and compelling those in power to be more efficient and responsive.

References

Commission on Global Governance (1995). *Our Global Neighborhood*, New York: Oxford University Press.

Falk, R.A. (1995). *On Humane Governance*, PSU: Pennsylvania.

Haq, M. (1999). *Human Development in South Asia*, Karachi: Oxford University Press.

Hertel, S. (2006). *Unexpected Power Conflict and Change among Transnational Activists*, London: Cornell University Press.

Huntington, S.P. (1991). *The Third Wave: Democratisation in the late 20th Century*, Oklahoma: University of Oklahoma Press.

Kauffman et al. (1999). *Governance Matters*, World Bank Policy Research Working Paper 2196, August.

Kooiman, J. ed. (1993). *Modern Governance: New Government-Society Interactions*, London: Sage.

OECD (1995). *Participatory Development and Good Governance*, Paris: OECD.

Sakiko, Fukuda-Parr and R. Ponzio (2002). *Governance: Past, Present and Future Setting the Governance Agenda for the Millennium Declaration*, Draft Paper for Fourth Global Forum, Morocco.

Rosenau, J. (1995). Governance in the 21st Century, *Global Governance*, 1, (1).

Tsai, L. (2007). *Accountability without Democracy*, New York: Cambridge University Press.

UNDP (1997). *Governance for Sustainable Human Development*, New York: UNDP.

—— (2002). *Human Development Report 2002: Deepening Democracy in a Divided World*, New York: OUP.

World Bank (1994). *Governance, the World Bank's Experience*, Washington DC: The World Bank.

4

Governance and Human Development

Lessons from Kerala

RAJEEV C. BHARATHAN

Of late, the critical role of governance in any development activity has been increasingly recognised the world over. Governance consists of the traditions and institutions by which authority in a nation is exercised. This includes the process of selection and monitoring government, the ability of the government to execute effective public policies and the respect of citizens and the state for the institutions which govern socio-economic interventions. It comprises of complex mechanisms, institutions and processes through which common people articulate their interests and needs. Experience from many countries demonstrates that while good governance promotes human development, poor governance reduces human well-being. It has been observed that sound governance is essential in achieving sustainable human development. The goal of governance initiatives should be to develop capacities that are needed to realise development that gives priority to the poor, advances women, sustains the environment, and creates needed opportunities for employment and other livelihoods (UNDP, 2005). Scholars have attempted to correlate quality of governance and the level of human development in a particular nation. Amartya Sen has been able to demonstrate a strong link between democracy and the reduction of hunger. In countries with a free press, and with political oppositions able to unseat unpopular regimes, governments cannot neglect the basic needs of the common people.

The paper is a modest attempt to explore the relation between governance and level of human development, based on the relative success of human development in the Indian state of Kerala. It is divided into three sections. The first section analyses the conceptual framework of governance and its role in human development of a region/country. The next section critically traces the human development experiences of Kerala from the middle of 19th century onwards. The penultimate section attempts to explore the major achievements and failures of Kerala experience by summarising the lessons learnt from the unique human development process of Kerala.

Conceptual Framework

The challenge facing all societies is to create a system of governance that promotes, supports and sustains human development. UNDP defined governance as the exercise of political, economic and administrative authority in the management of a country's affairs at all levels. It comprises mechanisms, processes, relationships and institutions through which citizens and groups articulate their interests, exercise their legal rights, meet their obligations and mediate their differences.[1] Governance embraces all the methods that societies use to distribute power and manage public resources and problems. Effective democratic norms of governance rely on public participation, accountability and transparency. Although governance encompasses every institution and organisation in society, from the family to the state, here our focus is on three important domains of governance that directly contribute to achieving sustainable human development. These are the State, civil society organisations and the private sector. In this canvas, the following major types of governance are identified: economic governance includes processes of decision-making that directly or indirectly affect a country's economic activities or its relationships with other economies; political governance refers to decision-making and policy implementation of a legitimate and authoritative state. The state should consist of separate legislative, executive and judicial branches, represent the interests of a pluralist polity, and allow citizens to freely elect their representatives; and administrative governance is a system of policy implementation carried out through an efficient, independent, accountable, and open public sector.

Governance exercises its influence, and in turn is influenced by institutions and organisations. The institutions and organisations of governance must be designed so as to contribute to sustainable human development by establishing the political, legal, judicial and social circumstances for poverty reduction, job creation, environmental protection and regeneration, and the advancement of women. Government institutions are also necessary for empowering the people they are intended to serve: providing equitable opportunities and ensuring social, economic and political inclusion. Empowerment can only take place within a conducive institutional environment comprising of properly functioning legislatures, legal and judicial systems and electoral processes. Legislative bodies, like parliaments, made up of freely and fairly elected members and representing various parties are crucial to popular participation and public accountability. Effective judicial system protects the rule of law and human rights, particularly those of disadvantaged groups.

Strengthening the enabling environment for sustainable human development depends not only on a state that governs well and on a private sector that provides jobs and income, but also on civil society organisations that facilitate socio-political interaction and that mobilise various groups in society to participate in public spaces. Civil society organisations provide important checks and balances on government power and on the private sector, but they can also strengthen the other two domains. They can help monitor the environment, resource depletion, pollution and social abuses; contribute to economic development by helping to distribute the benefits of economic growth more equitably within society; and offer opportunities for individuals to improve their standards of living.

Mahbub ul Haq's Human Development Centre views 'human governance as governance dedicated to securing human development'. It must enable the state, civil society and the private sector to help build capacities, which will meet the basic needs of all the people, particularly women, children and the poor.[2] The centre specifically put forth the need for the following three components for governance to be humane:

Good Political Governance

Free and fair elections in a multi-party setting; a constitution that is difficult to amend; and impartial judiciary.

Good Economic Governance

Maintains competitive markets; makes adequate budgetary allocation for social services; and equitable access to land and credit.

Good Civil Governance

A civil society combined with pro-poor media should raise its voice to get justice for the disadvantaged groups.

All developing countries must construct and legitimise a political system that promotes participation and can elicit at least a minimum public consensus on social and political goals; create the circumstances for constructive engagement with civil society; encourage political, business and civic leaders to articulate and pursue social and economic priorities; and guide the actions of public and civil society organisations towards social, cultural, environmental and economic objectives that are sustainable and beneficial to people and the environment.

The concept of social welfare has undergone structural changes as societies evolved over time. Thus, by the dawn of 20th century, it implied the right to education, to work, to rest and leisure, to provision in old age and to aid in sickness.[3] That is why many democratically elected governments included social welfare principles in their constitutions. India also made provisions for three articles under the Directive Principles of State Policy which directly promote human development in the country.[4] A state which honours the right to life has to ensure freedom from hunger, sickness, homelessness, and ignorance. Any further exposition of this matter may require us looking closely at the concept of human development and UNDP index of human development.

Concept of Human Development and Human Development Index

The human development approach, often forgotten in the immediate concern with accumulating commodities and financial wealth, is not new. Philosophers, economists and political leaders have for long emphasised human well-being as the purpose, the end of development. As Aristotle said, in ancient Greece, 'Wealth is evidently not the good we are seeking, for it is merely useful for the sake of something else.'[5] In seeking that *something else,* human development shares a common vision with human rights. The goal is human freedom. And in pursuing capabilities and realising human rights, this freedom is indeed crucial. People must be free to exercise their choices and to participate in decision-making that affects their lives. Human development and human rights are mutually reinforcing, helping to secure the well-being and dignity of all people, building self-respect and respect for others.

Many of its key principles, however, can be found in the writings of scholars and philosophers of the past, across the globe. Locke John maintained that the basic purpose of a state is to protect people's right by creating a system of laws and rights.[6] The age of the enlightenment in Europe especially the works of great thinkers like Voltaire, Rousseau and Immanuel Kant also had significant impact in evolving the concern for individual human worth. This new vision attempted to enhance human happiness by freeing individual from restraints so that he/she could act independently in accordance with his/her nature.[7] It was closely associated with the idea of perpetual human progress put forth by the rational philosophers of this era.

Much later, the works of Amartya Sen and Mahbub ul Haq provided the conceptual foundation for an alternative and broader human development approach defined as a process of enlarging people's choices and enhancing human capabilities and freedoms, enabling them to: live a long and healthy life, have access to knowledge and a decent standard of living, and participate in the life of their community and decisions affecting their lives. The capability approach developed by Sen provided the underpinnings for the evolvement of Human Development Index (HDI). This approach refers to the well-being of an individual in an effective way.

Freedom of an individual is important in capability approach, as a person requires the freedom to choose one's own life. Even if an opportunity is available under regulated system, it is not development in the real sense.

The human development paradigm has influenced socio-economic policies pursued by almost all countries of the world. Consequently, any serious debates on development naturally have to focus on human centred policies and actions. In short, this approach argues that the process of economic growth in any society has to be evaluated by considering its impact on the benefits and opportunities for the common man. The writings of Sen[8] and Haq[9] and Morris[10] surely influenced a shift in emphasis of development from income to non-income factors and finally UNDP launched its path breaking Human Development Report 1990. For preparing human development reports, UNDP is making use of a HDI consisting of three indices (life expectancy, adult literacy rate combined with gross enrolment rate and GDP per capita in PPP).[11] This is an indicator which makes use of selected quantifiable measures only. Here we are excluding many indicators like gender empowerment, civil society participation, political awareness, social capital endowments, and nutritional adequacy of the citizens.

The concept of human development is about creating an environment in which people can develop their full potential and lead creative lives satisfying their needs and interests. The central idea behind this approach is that people are the real wealth of nations. Therefore, any development strategy should focus on expanding the choices of people to lead the kind of lives that they cherish. Without these, many choices are simply not available, and many opportunities in life remain inaccessible. Human development has always been flexible and open-ended with respect to more specific definitions.

Kerala Experience

Kerala state attracted the attention of international scholars as it was the second region after French Guymon in the world where a Communist government through an electoral process came to power in 1957. This was a historic success for the century long popular struggles by the oppressed classes and castes in the state for social and economic justice (Parayil Govindan, 2000: viii). The dominance of Communist party in the state though has declined in the post-1990 period but has not been seriously challenged by other parties even now (2009). Apart from the political preferences, the region has exhibited a unique pattern of human development which was well documented in a seminal work by the Centre for Development Studies, Trivandrum.[12]

In the international discourse on development, Kerala is held up as one of the success stories, especially in comparison with other Indian states, and to some extent with the developing countries. It is generally maintained that human development is intrinsically related to education levels and health status of the people of the region. Thus, education and health have crucial roles to play in enhancing the dignity of human beings and freedom to choose their way of life. Education increases the ability of a society to absorb the technical skills needed to improve productivity. Like wise, health of the citizens also increases the quality and productivity of labour. All these facts logically call forth the need to look into the historical roots of the development of education and public health in Kerala.

Education is universally recognised as a crucial factor in enhancing socio-economic and cultural development of a region by aiding citizens of a nation to improve their knowledge, skills and thinking power to participate in productive activities. Scholars like Hicks, Schultz and Griliche have done substantial research studies to unearth strong correlations between education and socio-economic development.[13] Prior to the administration of Colonel Munro, princely states of Kochi and Thiruvithamkore had not taken any steps to introduce education for the people. The upper caste people (Nambutiris, Ambalavasis and Nairs) had made their own arrangements to educate their children. In the rural areas, every village had its own Ezhuthachan, hereditary teacher, who taught the students in his own house. They taught the children reading, writing, multiplication tables and recitation of Sanskrit rhymes. This teaching-learning process was very slow and consumed a lot of time. During the middle of 19th century, District Elementary Schools were opened in all talukas and subsequently were elevated to the status of high school. Towards the end of 19th century, a set of rules was framed to provide grants-in-aid to the private schools. As a consequence, a lot of private schools were opened in several parts of Travancore and Cochin. Government started to take active interest in female education towards the end of 19th century (Aiya, 1906; Menon, 1911).

Public health pays special attention to the social context of disease and misery and focuses on improving health through society-wide measures like vaccinations or the fluoridation of drinking water. The goal of public health is to improve lives through the prevention or treatment of disease. The focus of a public health intervention is to prevent rather than treat a disease through surveillance of medical cases and the promotion of healthy behaviours. In addition to these activities, in many cases treating a disease can be vital to preventing it in others, such as during an outbreak of an infectious disease. Vaccination programmes and sanitation measures are examples of public health measures. Many diseases are preventable through simple, non-medical methods. Public health plays a very important role in prevention efforts in both the developing world and in developed countries, either through local health systems or through international non-governmental organisations.

Kerala had plentiful supply of ayurveda physicians, who made medicines from herbs/plants from the forest and the planes of the region. They also prepared mixtures, powders, pills, medicated ghee and oils for special treatments. Thiruvithamkore and Kochi had introduced government ayurveda dispensaries from the middle of the 19th century. Unaware of the giant leaps made by modern medicine in the western world, the people continued to prefer ayurveda till the last decades of 19th century. Even in the 19th century, Travancore and Cochin states opened government ayurvedic hospitals and dispensaries. By the dawn of 20th century modern medical institutions were set up in Kerala. In the absence of municipal or local bodies in princely states of Kerala till the 1890s, no special arrangements could be made by them for keeping the towns/villages in hygienic conditions. The Royal Commission appointed to inquire into the health of troops in India had observed thus, 'Apart from the question of humanity, the introduction of an efficient system of hygiene in India is of essential importance to the interests of the empire.'[14] This report had been instrumental in creating sanitary Commissioners in princely states of Kerala and British Malabar.

Before going any further, it should be made clear that the human development of Kerala is only a recent phenomenon. In the old Kerala (upto the middle of 20th century) the cruelest system of high caste domination prevailed. A tiny proportion of population, mainly the *Nambutiris* (Brahmins) controlled land, the most important means of production at that time. They dictated the social customs and ways in which people in Kerala should live. Table 4.1 shows the share of high caste Hindus in the population of the three distinct political entities, Travancore, Cochin and Malabar. It can be observed that they constituted less than 20 per cent of the population. During the long centuries upto the early 20th century, the lower caste Hindus and Muslims were denied the basic human rights. They could neither get admission to schools nor obtain government jobs. These social outcasts lived in pathetic conditions with little hope for the future.[15] In such a situation, basic human freedom and rights were not

Table 4.1

Composition of Population, Kerala, 1941

Parameters	*Travancore*	*Cochin*	*Malabar*	*Kerala*
Population (Millions)	6.1	1.4	3.9	11.4
Lower Caste Hindus (%)	40	45	48	41
Higher Caste Hindus (%)	21	19	18	20
Muslims (%)	7	8	32	17
Christians (%)	32	28	2	22
Total	100	100	100	100

Source: Census of India, 1941, Vols. II, XIX, XXV.

ensured by the Princely States. It was the prolonged collective agitations by public that made the states to concede some of their demands. Naturally this historical context made the democratically elected governments in Kerala from 1957 to pursue their public policies to continue the social welfare model further. The passing of land reforms act and several other acts to ensure social security and basic human rights to the poor should be seen as an extension of the earlier people-centred policies.

Table 4.2

Human Development Index of States in India, 2001

States	*Index*	*Rank*
Kerala	0.638	1
Punjab	0.537	2
Tamil Nadu	0.531	3
Maharashtra	0.523	4
Haryana	0.509	5
Gujarat	0.479	6
Karnataka	0.478	7
West Bengal	0.472	8
Rajasthan	0.424	9
Andhra Pradesh	0.416	10
All India	0.472	

Source: Government of India, Planning Commission (2002).

Table 4.2 shows that Kerala has the highest HDI (0.638) compared to all the other states in India. It is also noteworthy that the state occupied the first position ever since the computation of National Human Development Reports from 1981 onwards. Another point that warrants our attention is that there is a huge difference (0.638–0.537) in the index values of Kerala and Punjab (second rank).

Table 4.3 shows that even during the pre-independence period, Kerala region (Travancore, Cochin and Malabar) exhibited high literacy rates compared to other regions of the country. It continued to have the first place in literacy during the post-independence period too.

Table 4.3

Literacy in Selected Regions/States of India (1891–2001)

Regions/States	*1891*	*1931*	*1971*	*2001*
Travancore	11.0	23.9		
Cochin	18.0	28.2		
Malabar	9.1	14.4		
Kerala			60.4	90.9
Tinnevelly	12.4	25.7		
Madras Presidency	6.3	13.0		
Tamil Nadu			39.5	73.5
Karnataka			36.8	66.6
West Bengal			38.8	68.6
Madhya Pradesh			27.3	63.7
India	5.8	9.5	34.5	64.8

Source: Census of India, various years.

Table 4.4 shows the various health indicators in the major states of India. Life expectancy in the state (74) is the highest in India. In respect of all the other indicators; Kerala has the least value indicating that it has a commendable health care and family planning systems in the country.

Table 4.4

Health Indicators in Indian States

States	*Life Expectancy 2002–06*	*Infant Mortality Rate 2007*	*Birth Rate 2007*	*Death Rate 2007*
Andhra Pradesh	64.4	54	18.7	7.4
Bihar	61.6	58	29.4	7.5
Karnataka	65.3	47	19.9	7.3
Kerala	74	13	14.7	6.8
Madhya Pradesh	67.2	58	28.5	8.7
Odisha	59.6	72	21.5	9.2
Punjab	69.4	43	17.6	7.0
Tamil Nadu	66.2	36	15.8	7.2
India	63.5	55	23.1	7.1

Source: GoI, Economic Survey 2008–09, A119.

Table 4.5 indicates that the Malayalees are politically more active than average Indians. In all the selected years, voter turnout rates in Kerala was phenomenally higher than all India pattern. It can be observed that voter turnout rates have steadily increased to 79.2 during 1957–77 and declined thereafter. At the national level, there was an increase during 1957–67 only. It remained less than 60 per cent during 1967–2009. This implies that after 1977, there is a relative fall in the interest of Malayalees in party politics than others.

Table 4.5

Voter Turnout in India and Kerala, General Elections

Election Year	*Kerala*	*India*
1957	66.1	45.4
1967	75.6	61.3
1977	79.2	59.5
1991	73.3	56.7
2004	71.4	58.1
2009	73.3	59.7

Source: http:/eci.nic.in/eci_ma.in/Statistical Reports/(accessed on December, 22, 2009).

Policy Initiatives in Kerala

In the preceding section, we have observed that Kerala has achieved high human development on the basis of literacy, health care and other quality of life indicators. However, one should be cautious to claim that these achievements were the direct consequences of the policies pursued by the Communist governments which were in power in the state on and off for 26 years during the period from 1957–2009. Instead, one has to concede that the high human development achievements of the state were the cascading effects of several popular policies initiated by the princely states of Kochi and Thiruvithamkore due to the socio-economic, religious movements and struggles of the late 19th and early 20th centuries. It is true that several progressive social and religious movements like Sree Narayana Dharma Paripalana (SNDP),[16] Sadhu Jana Paripalana (SJPS)[17] inculcated the idea of individual freedom and the need for education in the *Malayalee mind* strongly. The Muslim community also had their fair share due to the social reforms led by Vakkam Abdul Khader Moulavi and Sanaulka Makthi Tangal who strongly argued for the education of Muslims.[18] The socio-political movements initiated by Communist party of India during the early 1940s all over Kerala had attracted most of the working class population in the state because of the revolutionary ideas of human rights put forth by it.[19]

Kerala has accomplished impressive development achievements in many spheres including poverty reduction, health and education.[20] The period after the publication of 1975 CDS/UN study (this is a pioneering study carried out by Centre for Development Studies and sponsored by Committee on Development Planning of the United Nations in the mid-seventies) witnessed the publication of several studies which in fact glorified the Kerala development experience beyond rationality. Scholars extolling the virtues of Kerala experience failed to note that such a peripheral social development could not be sustained without government support for long. That is what has happened to Kerala when the state has to accept the neo-liberal economic agenda of the retreat of the state after the adoption of economic reform measures by the federal state in 1991.

Govindan Parayil maintains that what we observe in Kerala is not a model but just an alternative development experience (Parayil, 2000: 5). Some authors like Amartya Sen advise against the use of the term model to Kerala's development simply because the term carries too much normative baggage (ibid.: 12). The majority of others continue to look upon Kerala as a model, in a sense of a normatively circumscribed description of an entity that can be emulated and with features that can be replicated by others, taking into account their own specific contexts (ibid.). In effect, it does not matter if we call the Kerala pattern of development a model or an experience of development (quoted by Sen, ibid.). What matters is the overwhelming agreement that there are lessons to be learned from the development of Kerala. The importance of the Kerala model is that it demonstrated an alternative to the growth-based economic development model propagated by the International Monetary Fund (IMF) and the World Bank is possible. With all its failures, the example of Kerala shows that it is possible to make human lives better during their lifetime, without previous economic growth. This alone makes the Kerala development experiment a model that should be examined by other developing countries. However, Ram Mohan, (1991) observes that 'international agencies like the United Nations, comprador researchers in India and in the third world in general, have never lost a chance to glorify the Kerala case and uphold it as a model for the entire third world. The message has been that contradiction with imperialism is a big myth, expropriation by the bourgeoisie a figment of the imagination, revolutionary transformation of society unnecessary'.[21]

In this context, one would be interested to analyse the effects of decentralisation in the state on the well-being of people of Kerala. The fact is that the effects are mixed. Some success can be observed in certain areas like self employment generation through *Kudumbashree* and in providing basic services like water supply and housing. Local bodies were entrusted with a lot of responsibilities to improve the living conditions of the poor and excluded groups. The decentralised system of governance deliberately tried to address the gender issues by women component plans in local plans. Though the local governance has opened up the public space for the disadvantaged groups like SCs/STs and women, very little has actually been done to improve their capabilities. It is surprising to see that many of the Panchayats failed to utilise their allotted funds for the upliftment of weaker sections.[22]

It is true that the local communities have more knowledge about their dreams and aspirations. The direct participation of the local people in ensuring and enhancing the appropriate environment for human development is possible in participatory development projects. During the initial years of people's planning, a number of households actually participated in Gram Sabha meetings and voiced their concerns for a better future. Later due to disillusionment, many never bothered to attend such meetings.[23] One of the achievements of decentralisation has been that it has brought governments close to people in Kerala. It may be true in other states which have seriously attempted to help this common man to participate in the planning and implementation of local development.

Despite the high human development indicators, Kerala presents certain shortcomings, particularly in promoting environmentally sustainable development and in checking certain socio-economic issues like high suicide rates, food security and pre-school child undernutrition.[24] The decline in the quality of public and private sector services (education, health care, public distribution system, etc.) from the late 1980s has added to the vulnerability. There is also systematic exclusion of certain groups like women, tribals, dalits, fisher folks and backward communities. Further, the globalisation has increased the commodification of the education and health sectors of Kerala which may reduce the opportunities for the poor to get good jobs in the increasingly knowledge intensive manufacturing and service sectors. It is ironical to see that an average malayalee is not much interested in the public affairs. He is confined to the affairs of his family; if any one shows any social concern, it may be for some kind of gains. Gone are the days when politically motivated workers in Kerala and social activists voluntarily refused to get tied with families and jumped to the public spaces for the benefit of the society or the downtrodden. The post-reform Kerala seems to disprove the Seymour Lipset's proposition (1959) that the more economically developed a country/region, the more successful the democracy it would be.[25] As Kerala develops economically, people are getting more isolated from each other. It may be observed that economic development and human development in the state, to a certain extent are not correlated. Whenever the state develops economically, social concerns are fast declining leading to a hardening of human consciousness. The middle class which always spear headed social movements in Kerala and in every region that mobilised public action against social injustices are mere spectators now.[26] In such a situation, who is going to fight for the human rights and basic needs of the disadvantaged groups of the state/India remains the most critical question; which social scientists have to raise in this regard.

Concluding Observations

The paper is a modest attempt to link human development with unique governance of the state comprising of the public action taken by the various socio-religious movements since the late 19th century and a sympathetic State both before and after independence. One must also acknowledge the role of communists in awakening the class consciousness of the workers/poor and in empowering them to demand for their basic rights. The high HDI of Kerala should not make us to believe that the state has already achieved all the freedom associated with such a high human development. HDI does not show all features of human development. One could raise the following introspective questions to seek answers with regard to the status of human development in the state:

- Do the malayalees have the freedom to choose between alternative life styles?
- Can they have the freedom to access education and health care of their choices?
- Are they free to participate in socio-political movements of their own volitions?
- Do they get opportunities to earn adequate income for their basic needs?
- Does Keralite woman has the freedom to spend her money she earns the way she likes?

The present USA dominated world order implies that individuals have to enhance their capabilities to find a comfortable berth in the contemporary social life. Moreover, most people are motivated by private gains and not by selfless work to usher in the new world order where all vulnerable sections of society will be cared for by the state which itself is facing a loss of real power in the emerging order where the transnational powers are dictating terms to the political executives of big nations like India. In such circumstances, a regional power like Kerala finds it increasingly difficult to fight against the invisible imperial powers. The principal feature of the post-reform India has been the increasing concentration of governing powers with the union government relative to the state governments. This has restricted state governments from undertaking progressive social changes. The union government has been using these powers to force states to implement its neo-liberal agenda. An associated feature of the reduced autonomy of states in decision making has been the sharp deterioration in the finances of Indian states. Deficits and debts of states have risen significantly, primarily due to the inadequacy of the volume of statutory transfers of resources to the states relative to their growing financial commitments. Gross devolution and transfers from the centre to states, as a share of GDP, declined considerably. The fall in the financial health has seriously undermined the potentials of states to meet rising obligations in social services.[27]

Kerala experience shows that educating women enhances family planning measures resulting in reduced birth rate. It reveals how the freedom to protest and demand has pressurised both public and private sectors to adopt measures to increase the well-being of the common people. The state of Kerala has always been lauded for its developments in social infrastructure like hospitals, schools, etc., which in turn developed social sector. Though Kerala has been able to achieve human development to a certain extent, the economic sector is more or less stagnant. This calls for effective and timely government intervention so as to increase socio-economic infrastructure which will in turn promote investments in the state.

The current global socio-politico-economic structure largely favours economic models based on private capital accumulation, entrepreneurship, individual efforts and growing inequalities over Kerala's publicly funded socio-economic services and egalitarian concepts. Can the Kerala model of development that kept Kerala above all other Indian states from a human development perspective be sustained in such circumstances? The socialist welfare model of Kerala confronts innumerable challenges in the present highly globalised economic environment where all democratic governments are progressively retreating from the provision of basic services ushering in neo-liberal policies of free marketism. It is however true that the current knowledge capital based economic growth offers substantial opportunities for the people of Kerala if the state can modify its mindset by concentrating more on quality rather than quantity in imparting professional skills. The days are gone when the employers recruit graduates and post-graduates simply by considering their university examination performance. It is very difficult to get employment if one does not have adequate skills. Kerala has to restructure most of its courses to increase the employability of its students. This implies more investments in education particularly university education and primary health care. More efforts are needed to enhance the growth of agriculture and industry by supporting these sectors. Unless these urgent measures are taken to reverse the crisis, the Kerala's human development cannot be sustained for long.

Two decades back, Haq has posited that 'every governing institution, every policy action should be judged by one critical test: How does it meet the genuine aspirations of the people?'[28] Such a test, if done in Kerala will make the democratic state to rethink its development priorities and the civil society to spearhead popular struggles backed by a vigilant media for basic rights of the marginalised. Such a shift in policies can do wonders in enhancing human development and freedom in the model State.

Notes

1. See Government of India, Planning Commission, *National Human Development Report, 2001*, p. 115.
2. Mahbub ul Haq Human Development Centre, 2000, *Human Development in South Asia*, 1999, pp. 29–31.
3. The USSR constitution, 1936 granted all these rights to its citizens.
4. See Articles 38, 39 and 41 of Indian Constitution.
5. See Human development concept in *<http:/www.undp.org >*, accessed on December 10, 2009.
6. See John Locke (1690) *An Essay Concerning Human Understanding*, Peter H. Nidditch (ed.) Revised 1975, Oxford, Clarendon Press.
7. The Age of Enlightenment refers to the 18th century in European philosophy, and is often thought of as part of a larger period which includes the Age of Reason. This movement also provided a framework for the American and French Revolutions, the Latin American independence movement, and the Polish Constitution of May 3, 1791, and also led to the rise of capitalism and the birth of socialism.
8. 'Human development, as an approach, is concerned with advancing the richness of human life, rather than the richness of the economy in which human beings live, which is only a part of it.' Sen posited that only by enhancing entitlements and capabilities, we can reduce poverty and build a world where each individual can live with dignity. See for instance, Amartya Sen (1980), 'Inequality of what?' in Mcmurrin (ed.), *The Tanner Lectures on Human Value*, Vol. 1, Cambridge University Press.
9. 'The basic purpose of development is to enlarge people's choices. In principle, these choices can be infinite and can change over time. People often value achievements that do not show up at all, or not immediately, in income or growth figures: greater access to knowledge, better nutrition and health services, more secure livelihoods, security against crime and physical violence, satisfying leisure hours, political and

cultural freedoms and sense of participation in community activities. The objective of development is to create an enabling environment for people to enjoy long, healthy and creative lives.' Haq is credited with putting forth the theory of human development in his famous work (1976) which he expanded later (1996). See, for example Mahbub ul Haq (1976), *The Poverty Curtain: Choices for the Third World,* Columbia University Press, and Mahbub ul Haq (1995), *Reflections on Human Development,* Oxford University Press.

10. Morris proposed a non-income concept, which is a composite index of three indicators of development (infant mortality, literacy and life expectancy) which became popular as 'Physical Quality of Life Index' (PQLI). See D.M. Morris (1979), *Measuring the Condition of the World Poor: The Physical Quality of Life Index,* Elmsford, New York: Paragon Press.
11. See Technical Note 1 of *Human Development Report, 2005,* UNDP, New Delhi: Oxford University Press.
12. Centre for Development Studies/UN (1975). *Poverty, Unemployment and Development Policy: A Case Study of Selected Issues with Special Reference to Kerala,* Bombay: Orient Longman.
13. For more details on the relationship between education and economic development, see Todaro, P. Michael and Smith (2007), *Economic Development,* Delhi: Pearson Education, (8th edition).
14. Quoted by R. Radhika (1988) 'Imperial health in British India 1857–1900' in M. Roy and L. Milton (eds.), *Disease, Medicine and Empire,* London: Routledge, pp. 41.
15. See R. Jeffrey (1976) (2003), A. Aiyappan (1944), Gilbert Slater (1918), Edgar Thurston (1975).
16. Even before the formation of SNDP, Dr Palpu organised Ezhava memorials (1885, 1886) to highlight the sad plight of Ezhavas, a backward community and requested Diwan and Maharaja of Travancore to admit their children to government schools. Sree Narayana Guru exhorted the backward communities to get education and liberate from the oppressive caste system.
17. Sri Ayyankali (1863–1941) led this organisation which called for the right of Pulayas and other backward castes to travel in public roads and to defy the existing caste order. SJPS was instrumental in admitting the low caste children in government schools by 1910.
18. See Tharakan, 2008.
19. See M. Desai (2003) for a comparative study of the socio-cultural performance of the party in West Bengal and Kerala.
20. Government of Kerala, KSPB, (2006) *Human Development Report 2005,* Chapter 1.

21. See K.T. Ram Mohan (1991).
22. See Human Development Report, Kerala 2005, Chapter 9.
23. See E.M. Thomas (2004) and P. Krishnakumar (2009).
24. See IIPS, NFHS 3 Key-findings report, Kerala.
25. For a discussion of Lipset's arguments see Edmund Miller (1995).
26. See for instance Derne Steve (2008). *Globalisation on the ground*, New Delhi: Sage Publications, for a critique of the transformation of culture and class in India after globalisation.
27. See Rakesh Mohan (2007) for more details.
28. Mahbub ul Haq. *Human Development in South Asia*, Human Development Centre, p. 220.

References

Aiya, Nagam (1906). *Travancore State Manual*, Trivandrum: Government Press.

Aiyappan, A. (1944). Iravas and Culture Change, Bulletin of The Madras Government Museum, Madras: Government Press.

Derne, Steve (2008). *Globalisation on the ground*, New Delhi: Sage Publications.

Desai, M. (2003). *From movement to Party to Government: Why social policies in Kerala and West Bengal are so different*, in J.A. Gladstone (ed.) *States, Parties and Social Movements*, Cambridge University Press.

Edmund, Muller (1995). Economic determinants of Democracy, *American Sociological Review* 60(6): 966–82.

Jeffrey, Robin (1976). *The Decline of Nayar Dominance*, London: Sussex University Press.

——. (1987). *Governments and Culture: How women made Kerala Literate*, *Pacific Affairs*, Vol. LX, No. 3, 447–72.

——. (1992). *Politics, Women and Well-Being; How Kerala Became 'A Model'*, New Delhi: Oxford University Press (Revised edition 2003).

Jeromi, P.D. (2003). *What ails Kerala economy: A Sectoral Exploration*, Economic and Political weekly, No. 16, April 19–25.

——. (2005). Economic reforms in Kerala, *Economic and Political weekly*, July 23, pp. 3267–77.

George, K.K. (1998). Historical roots of Kerala Model and its present crisis, *Bulletin of the concerned Asian Scholars*, 30(4).

Govindan, Parayil (2000). *Kerala Economy*, New Delhi: Sage Publications.

Government of India. *Economic Survey 2008–09.*

Government of Kerala, KSPB (2009). *Kerala Economic Review, 2008.*

Government of Kerala (2006). *Human Development Report, 2005.*

Harris, John (2001). *Depoliticising Development: The World Bank and Social Capital,* New Delhi, Left World.

International Institute of Population Studies (2008). *NFHS 3 Key findings report, Kerala,* Mumbai.

Kabir, M. (2003). *Beyond Philanthropy: The Rockefeller Foundations Public Health Intervention in Thiruvithamkore*, Centre for Development Studies, Working Paper 350, Trivandrum.

Kannan, K.P. (2004). *Development as a Right to Freedom: An Interpretation of 'Kerala Model'*, Centre for Development Studies, Working Paper 361, Trivandrum.

Krishnakumar, P. and Mini Nair (2009). *Decentralised Planning and Marginalised Communities in Kerala,* Paper presented in the International conference on Development and Deprivation in the era of globalisation, December 14 and 15, Trivandrum: University of Kerala.

Lieten, G.K. (2002). The Human Development Puzzle in Kerala, *Journal of Contemporary Asia*, 32(1): 47–68.

Menon, C.A. (1911). *Cochin State Manual*, Cochin: Government Press.

Ram Mohan, K.T. (1991). Understanding Keralam: The Tragedy of Radical Scholarship, New York, *Monthly Review*, December.

Ratcliffe, John (1978). Social Justice and the Demographic transition: Lessons from India's Kerala State, *International Journal of Health Services*, Vol. VIII, No. 1, 423–44.

Sen, A.K. (1999). *Development as Freedom*, New York: Alfred A Knopf Inc.

Sundararaman, R. and S. Macpherson (2000). *Social Development in Kerala: Illusion or Reality*, London: Ashgate.

Tharakan, P.K.M. (1984). Socio-economic factors in educational development: The case of Nineteenth century Travancore, *Economic and Political weekly*, November 10 ...... (1998) Socio Religious reform movement, the process of Democratisation and Human Development: The Case of Kerala, South West India in L Rudebeck et al. (eds) *Democratisation in the Third world*, London: Macmillan.

—— (2008). *When the Kerala model of development is historicised: A Chronological perspective,* Kochi: Centre for Socio-economic and Environmental Studies, Working Paper 19.

Tharamangalam, Joseph (1998). The perils of Social Development without Economic growth: The Development debacle of Kerala, India, *Bulletin of the concerned Asian Scholars,* 30(1).

Tilak, J.B.G. (2001). *Higher education and Development in Kerala*, Kochi: Centre for Socio-economic and Environmental Studies, Working Paper No. 5.

Part II

Democratic Governance and Initiatives for the Well-being

5

Livelihood, Food Insecurity and Well-being of Tribals

Evidence from Indian Central Tribal Belt

D.C. SAH

It has been argued that chronic poverty[1] in central tribal belt of India is significantly associated with agricultural income whereas state intervention for income transfers to poor in the form of public distribution system (PDS) and benefits from panchayat and other government schemes could not help the poor significantly (Sah, Bhatt and Dalapati, 2008).[2] Households, in this central tribal belt of India have also experienced shocks in the form of droughts, population growth and land fragmentation, sickness, death, social ceremonies, etc. This adversely affects their agriculture and access to food, forcing them to either deplete their resources or supplement their income from borrowing, labouring and migration. In this paper, an attempt is made to understand the implications of food insecurity and coping mechanism under shock. The objectives of this paper are as follows: (i) examine the struggles for survival and dynamics of employment and income among a sample of 1,614 households from developed and underdeveloped groups of villages; (ii) understand the effects of scarcity on asset holdings over a period of time; (iii) interpret the coping mechanisms that households adopt in response to death, conflict and drought; and (iv) infer the continuity and changes the tribals face in their economy, polity and society over time.[3]

Livelihood and Income

Despite being near to the forest, natural resources do not provide substantive economic support to the tribals. Less than 2 per cent of gross income originates from natural resources (Table 5.1). Depletion of commons and forest resources over the years has made the forest cover thin and unsustaining for economic activities like gathering of minor forest produce and picking wood for sale in any significant way. Though agriculture is the major economic activity of the households that is contributing over 38 per cent to the gross income, agriculture in this undulating topography has serious limitations in the form of technology transfer. A large part of agricultural land falls under slopes that have thin soil cover and do not support intensive agriculture. Households located in relatively remote underdeveloped villages face this problem significantly more than the developed villages. The availability of irrigated land per household for cultivation in remote underdeveloped villages is nearly half of the average in relatively developed villages. This results in production of inferior cereal, and pulse in former, whereas in developed villages, jowar, bajra, cotton, soybean, and irrigated paddy and wheat dominate. On an average, the annual income from various sources of sample household is about ₹ 24,818. About 38 per cent of this income originates from own cultivation and another 34 per cent originates due to labouring in and around villages.

Table 5.1

Income, Sources and Expenditure among Tribals of Central Indian Belt

Income	*Chronic Poor*	*Non-Chronic Poor*	*Transitory Non-Poor*	*Always Non-Poor*	*All*
	₹ per Household				
Agriculture	8305 (36)	8629 (36)	8740 (37)	11389 (42)	9474 (38)
Labouring	7276 (31)	8747 (37)	9498 (40)	8169 (30)	8417 (34)
Service	1423 (6)	1688 (7)	773 (3)	4020 (15)	2301 (9)
Migration	5355 (23)	3561 (15)	3240 (14)	1893 (7)	3266 (13)
Other income	475 (2)	740 (3)	843 (3)	1229 (5)	867 (4)
Common Resources	323 (1)	455 (2)	468 (2)	632 (2)	493 (2)
Total income	23157 (100)	23820 (100)	23562 (100)	27333 (100)	24818 (100)
Expenditure	21029	19615	26529	26949	22881

Source: All the tables in the paper are culled from Sah et al. (2008).

Households also depend on non-agricultural activities for survival; this occupational diversity seems to be forced by failure of agriculture. Among the chronic poor, deteriorating access to land and income from agriculture forces the households to rely significantly upon migration and labouring, while among always non-poor about 42 per cent of the households' income accrues from own cultivation but their dependence on other sources of income, especially labouring, is not affected by their superior agriculture. Increasing expenditure of household forces even the well to do to supplement their income from other sources? This is evident in the case of transitory non-poor whose expenditure is even higher than their gross income and it can be presumed that the borrowing makes them sustain.

The pattern of income and its sources vary significantly across states (Table 5.2). Tribals in Odisha have relatively low income (₹ 14,596 per household) while Madhya Pradesh has relatively higher level of income (₹ 28,036 per household). Total expenditure is also higher than gross income in Odisha. Common property resources supplement the income significantly only in Chhattisgarh and Odisha, in other states dependence on forest is marginal. It is worth noting that migration as a major source of income is confined to Rajasthan, Madhya Pradesh and Gujarat, while in Chhattisgarh and Odisha migration as a source of income is insignificant. Labouring in and around the villages constitutes an important source of income in all the states, except where migration is high (Rajasthan and Madhya Pradesh).

Table 5.2

Income per household and its Sources across States (in ₹)

	Madhya Pradesh	*Chhattisgarh*	*Odisha*	*Jharkhand*	*Gujarat*	*Rajasthan*
Agriculture	12406 (43)	11747 (47)	5953 (41)	8343 (30)	7092 (29)	8003 (33)
Labouring	6079 (22)	9549 (38)	6475 (44)	10061 (37)	9799 (40)	5602 (23)
Migration	8098 (29)	170 (1)	347 (2)	2118 (8)	4029 (17)	9751 (41)
Service	1484 (5)	1465 (6)	851 (6)	5030 (18)	1577 (7)	219 (1)
Common resources	144 (1)	1385 (6)	648 (5)	156 (1)	- (0)	31[a]
Other	183 (1)	705 (3)	322 (2)	1446 (5)	1861 (8)	457 (2)
Total income	28036 (100)	25022 (100)	14596 (100)	27456 (100)	24358 (100)	24065 (100)
Total Expenditure	25037	23038	18113	23248	22914	23233

[a] less than 0.5

Note: Figures in brackets are percentage of total income.

Although the proportion of migration income significantly varies across chronic poverty profile, absolute migration income does not significantly vary across poverty profile. This means that on an average, income from migration is almost the same across chronic poverty profile, about 15 per cent. But the chronic poor household rely on migration significantly more; migration in their gross income contributes to an extent of 23 per cent. As total income of poor and chronic poor is significantly lower as compared to non-poor, the proportion of income originating from migration and labour around the villages turns out to be significantly higher for poor compared to non-poor. On the other hand, relative remoteness does significantly influence the income from labouring and migration, across groups of developed and underdeveloped villages (Table 5.3). Agriculture is though more paying in developed villages compared to relatively remote underdeveloped villages, its statistical significance is low. On the other hand, intensity of migration and income from labouring is about two times higher in underdeveloped villages compared to developed villages. The inability of local economy to sustain the livelihood forces a social process that engenders large borrowing for survival. The findings on borrowing when juxtaposed with poverty profile at a glance seem to be contradictory; a household would be 1.4 times more likely to be chronic poor rather than not, if located in underdeveloped village than in developed village. But borrowing both for agricultural and social purposes are not significantly different in the two groups of villages.

Table 5.3

Effect of Poverty and Remoteness on Income

Income	*Variations Across*	
	Poverty Profile[a]	*Remoteness*[b]
Agriculture	4.32 **	NS
Labour	3.74 ***	2.0 times more likely to be high in underdeveloped villages**
Migration	13.14 ***	1.9 times more likely to be high in underdeveloped villages**
Service	5.99 ***	NS
Forest resources	3.42 **	NS
Other income	2.31 **	1.6 times more likely to be high in underdeveloped villages *
Unpaid debts	94.2 *	NS
Farm loans	NS	NS
Chronic poverty		1.4 times more likely to be chronic poor in underdeveloped villages*

[a] F statistics across Chronic Poverty Profile.
[b] Odd ratio of income sources across developed and underdeveloped villages.
Significant at 1: ***, ** 5% and * 10%, NS: Not significantly different.

In this resource-poor economy under shocks, total income is much lower than the expenditure for households under transitory behaviour, either chronic poor or transitory non-poor. This negative income balance is prevalent in Odisha than the other states (Table 5.4). Borrowings sustain the households' economy in such crisis. Nonetheless, all borrowings need not be exploitative; borrowing when remains un-serviced from agricultural income – given highly unsustainable labouring avenues – creates social processes of borrowing that results in multidimensional poverty. With labour remaining unutilised annually between 70 and 63 per cent, unemployment remains as a serious problem with chronic and non-chronic poor (Table 5.5). Unemployment for resource poor households with marginal holdings and low irrigation, is a matter of serious concern. On the other hand, with less than 22 per cent surplus labour, unemployment is not a serious concern for households that are always non-poor and transitory non-poor. For the non-poor, ones own agriculture and labouring is enough for employment for their work force. But for over 50 per cent of the total workforce remaining unutilised in labour market, perpetual unemployment remains a serious concern in livelihood struggle of chronic poor and poor.

Table 5.4

Labour Absorption and Unemployment in Central Tribal Belt

	Chronic Poor	*Non-Chronic Poor*	*Transitory Non-Poor*	*Always Non-Poor*	*All*
Total family size	6.53	3.87	2.89	1.89	3.54
Workforces	3.76	3.63	2.96	2.81	3.37
Available labour days[a]	1090	1053	858	815	977
Area unirrigated	2.40	2.23	2.46	2.66	2.38
Area irrigated	0.31	0.48	0.86	0.72	0.56
Labour in agriculture[b]					
Irrigated	77	120	215	180	140
Unirrigated	360	334	369	402	357
Total	438	454	584	582	497
Available for labouring	653	599	274	233	480
Labour absorbed locally	187	221	214	200	210
Per cent surplus labour	70	63	22	14	56

[a] @ 290 days per annum.
[b] @ 250 days in irrigated and 150 days in unirrigated area.

Female participation in labour market is equal to male in this tribal area. Females are, however, burdened with cultivation as well as collection of fuel, fodder and animal care. As female work participation is over burdened, it may be assumed that surplus labour among female workers may be lower. But among the male, surplus labour could still be larger. For resource poor households, with income level a third of average and over 50 per cent labour remaining unutilised, even a small amount of borrowing during a shock could be an economic pressure on household that pushes it into chronic poverty. In this situation, a household faces access failure to food, remains unable to service its debt and in the process, loses its assets, especially animal herds and silver. This process of being trapped in perpetual poverty could be triggered among severely poor even without a shock. A marginal farmer is bound to be under a perpetual shock. For this category of households, even a small borrowing triggers a process of mortgage, income generation from labour and migration and repayment that pushes the household in chronic poverty significantly more than others.

Depletion of Asset

In around 1870 AD, tribals in the central belt of India were encouraged by British to stop shifting cultivations and settle down on forestland. Most of the land cultivated by tribal households, even today, consists of a significant part of depleted forestland. Such encroachment of forestland for self-cultivation is essential for subsistence in this land-starved economy. Although such encroachment results in deforestation and soil erosion, it is the only way out for them when employment opportunities are few and financial resources are lacking. The necessity to encroach on forestland needs to be appreciated within the social frame that values agriculture and the autonomy it provides to individuals. As income levels and opportunities are seriously constrained in this tribal economy, wealth and assets are relatively easy to measure. The task becomes further easy owing to the fact that savings as liquid money has remained confined to a minuscule. In fact, concept of saving and banking is alien to the tribal community. In this situation, land, animals and silver become major counts of wealth. In the last few years, another asset, well, has been added to this list.

Average possession of agricultural land is about 3.1 acre. Population pressure and thus fragmentation in holdings has resulted in depletion of about a third of land per household during the last five years. Despite agriculture being the major source of income, cultivation is practised without terracing the slopes. Consequently, less than 10 per cent of land is plane that is capable of retaining moisture. Market-oriented crops are cultivated on this patch. Irrigation has emerged as a prime mover of agriculture in this otherwise stagnant agricultural economy. But irrigation is a difficult and risky proposition in the central tribal belt; only about 26 per cent of gross cropped area is irrigated, bulk of which is in developed villages.

Livestocks are considered a major asset in this economy that has low agricultural productivity and experiences frequent and consecutive monsoon failures. The stock of livestock depletes frequently because of the shocks. Yardstick of wealth is number of cattle, goats and poultry a family possesses. Goats are important assets that can be converted into liquid money during times of shock. Depleted forest, wherever accessible, is the only source of fuel and house-building material. Over the last five years, a few households have acquired assets like wells for irrigation, electric pump and diesel engines. This made possible double cropping on these farms significantly more than others. As Table 5.4 shows, there is significant difference in possession of land across poverty profile; always non-poor possess relatively larger holdings than rest. Added irrigation with non-poor category of households has resulted significantly in higher gross cultivated area with these households in comparison to chronic poor and poor households. There has also been another addition to family possessions in the form of consumer items like radio, tape-recorder, television, cycle and motorcycle (Table 5.5). But these consumer items are possessed only by a miniscule of the population. Not surprisingly, though only 50 per cent of households in underdeveloped villages have domestic electricity while in developed villages, this proportion is over 70 per cent.

Table 5.5

Depletion of Assets (in last five years)

	Animal	*Silver*	*Land*	*Consumer Items*	*Tubewell*
Asset Today		*₹ per household*			*Total*
Chronic poor	7587	2908	109167	2889	7
Non-chronic poor	8720	2178	108992	2475	12
Transitory non-poor	7636	1943	103869	3685	7
Always non-poor	8560	2778	127584	3846	23
Total	8392	2456	114444	3098	49
F[a]	NS	*	*	**	*
Depletion of assets[b]					
Chronic poor	1326	1685	40607	–1877	–2
Non-chronic poor	1171	121	34326	–1133	–7
Transitory non-poor	2739	1497	58743	–2536	–4
Always non-poor	1450	179	47391	–1595	–11
F[a]	NS	***	*	*	*
All	1442	514	41915	–1534	–24

Note: Negative sign implies an increase in consumer items.
[a] F across chronic poverty profile.
[b] Loss in last 5 years; a negative sign imply an increase.

As indicated earlier, depleted forest resources do not allow households in this region to depend on forest during shocks. As a result, depletion of livestock constitutes easy source of much required liquidity. Consequently, a third of milch and draught-power animals, half of goat possessions and a fourth of poultry have depleted over time. On the other hand, new consumer gadgets have been added to households in the last five years. The addition of consumer goods as well as depletion in land, silver, animal and poultry have taken place across chronic poverty profile (Table 5.5). The always non-poor and transitory non-poor alone have neither experienced additions to the consumer goods nor the poor alone have faced depletion of their silver, land and animals. The process has taken place across all groups of poverty profile, though chronic poor have lost significantly more silver. Demographic pressure, in this region, has resulted in reduction of land resource to above two-thirds of what was a generation back. This has become a source of chronic poverty in this region. With resource base already depleted and with lack of employment opportunities around the villages, food security has been significantly threatened for newly formed households with marginal holdings, even in normal agricultural years.

Food Insecurity and PDS

As agricultural production significantly varies across chronic poverty profile (Table 5.6), it is observed that proportion of the agricultural output consumed also significantly varies across poverty profile. Although always non-poor households have higher agricultural production as compared to chronic poor, the poor consumes significantly higher proportion of their agricultural produce as compared to the non-poor. Moreover, despite consuming only a small proportion of agricultural produce, the home produced food of transitory non-poor and always non-poor lasts for

Table 5.6

Food Insecurity and Role of PDS in Central Tribal Belt

	Chronic Poor	*Non-Chronic Poor*	*Transitory Non-Poor*	*Always Non-Poor*	*All*
Cereal production (quintal)	8.85	11.31	10.11	14.49	11.84
Produce consumed (%)	81	81	75	67	75
Produce lasts (days)	230	259	244	273	260
(%) Respondents lasts less than 146 days	39	23	29	19	24
(%) Responding not enough	58	47	54	41	48
Steps when food is not enough	*Rab*[a] and *kanji*	Do	Do	—	—
Missed both meals (%) households	34		30		8
PDS card used last year	7	7	8	8	7
Sugar from PDS (%)	14.5	15.5	15.7	16.5	15.6
Cereals from PDS (%)	14.0	16.2	17.8	15.2	15.7

Note: [a] *Rab* is a liquid diet, barely giving required nutrition made out of maize and buttermilk.

significantly longer duration (273 days) in a year compared to chronic poor (230 days). Thus, food insecurity is significantly and positively associated with chronic poverty. Usually, when normal staple food is not available, the households in this tribal region consume *rab* a liquid diet made of maize and buttermilk (in Rajasthan, Gujarat and Madhya Pradesh), *mandia* and *kanji* (in Chhattisgarh) and a fermented liquid from rice, *handia* (in Jharkhand). This preparation has relatively low nutrition value but provides a filling meal. There are days for some households in distress, when even *rab* is not available. *Rab,* in situation of access failure to food provides coping mechanisms to fight hunger but going without *rab* and missing both the meals is not uncommon (Table 5.6). As public distribution system supports only 16 per cent of cereal consumption of poor and chronic poor households, relevant question is why PDS is unable to influence their consumption behaviour.

Eight out of ten households have ration cards meant either for below poverty line, *Annapurna* or above poverty line. But, on an average, only about 16 per cent of monthly cereal consumption is supported by PDS. In this tribal economy, where socio-economic environment is characterised by wide spread poverty, vulnerability owing to variation in own production and lack of purchasing power have not been protected by subsidised supply of cereals through PDS. This small proportion of cereal need is being met by PDS needs to be appreciated along with the fact that on an average the card is being used about seven out of maximum 12 times that a cardholder can use it per year. What unfolds from qualitative research is that most of the households used the PDS cards for getting kerosene rather than supplementing the cereal consumption. The availability of wheat and rice rather than maize from PDS was identified as a major constraint that affects adversely the lifting of the cereals. Even in critical periods of recurring droughts during the last four years, a miniscule dependence on PDS is an indication of inefficient functioning of the public distribution system. About three-fourth of those who use PDS complained that either information about the availability of supplies was not available to them or they had to make many trips to adjoining villages located about 5 km away, on foot, in order to get their supplies. Cardholders also have serious problems either in calculating their entitlements or cost of their purchase from the PDS.

Marginal farmers are the most vulnerable section of tribal society. They are farmers only for four months. They work as labourers around the villages for some time and work as either casual labour in informal sector or as agricultural labour in irrigated areas within or outside the state. For this vulnerable section, food insecurity is most vulnerable. The food consumption habits of tribals are different from non-poor groups in other part of the country because coarse cereals like maize and jowar constitute a major portion of tribal staple food. The evidences show that PDS is not only targeting both poor and non-poor but also the cereals of their choice are not available from PDS. Moreover, moving to a targeted PDS system from universal entitlement one in tribal areas has not helped in protecting the interests of most vulnerable section of society. The interventions have not influenced the problem of scarcity and rising prices during drought. Such interventions in the food economy were achieved with an operational cost that are three to seven times more than the procurement price of wheat and rice respectively (Tyagi, 1990). The state in its foodgrains marketing intervention through PDS, thus, is subsidising the consumers to a tune of ₹ 10,0000 million and this bill is expending rapidly without its benefits reaching the most needy. On the other hand, the operations are achieved some times with negative price differentials compared to open market (Acharya, 2001).

As there is no evidence to prove that operations of PDS have contributed significantly to managing food economy, there is a need for bringing a change in the system. Given the coverage and level of food security PDS has achieved in this vulnerable remote areas, asking the question whether to continue with PDS operation as it is, is not only justified but also relevant. For, in order to increase the purchasing power of poor there are a number of other measures that have been successfully adopted by other developing countries. Two of the most viable options are cash transfer to needy and food stamps. Kumar (1978) and Dreze (2003) have independently shown that cash transfer rather than food subsidy contributes to substitution of food by non-food items. Moreover, implementing cash transfer effectively in a large country like India is difficult. On the other hand, countries like Sri Lanka, Colombia and Trinidad have successfully attempted subsidisation of poor consumers through food stamps with a fraction of subsidy that is involved in PDS and FCI operations.

Notwithstanding the failure of state in protecting the consumption through subsidised food distribution, the implications of shock may significantly differ across poverty profile. The implications of shock in its turn engender the notion of well-being and its persistence. Some of these issues are explored in the next section.

Crises and Well-being

There are a number of socio-economic and political reasons that adversely affects life of a household in central tribal belt of India (Table 5.7). Although the events could take place in any household across poverty profile, their implications are disastrous for poor. Not only access failure to food is significantly more in underdeveloped villages than in developed, the incidence is significantly more among chronic poor households than others; missing a meal among poor households than non-poor is two times more likely for households located in underdeveloped villages than in developed. Borrowing for meeting household expenses is common phenomenon during rainy season when food stocks are low or exhausted and new harvest has yet to reach the hearth. Repayment of these loans as well as any other borrowing forces a household to migrate. Response to shock situations – death, drought and conflicts – was examined in terms of people's coping mechanism in tribal community (Table 5.8).

Table 5.7

Events that Adversely Affect the Life in Central Tribal Belt (Number of Households)

	Chronic Poor	*Non-Chronic Poor*	*Transitory Non-Poor*	*Always Non-Poor*	*All*
Socio-economic events					
Marriage	20	42	7	21	90
Drought	18	48	18	34	118
Sickness	18	24	16	12	70
Depletion of animals	0	4	1	5	10
Land mortgage	5	4	0	2	11
Death in family	6	13	5	8	32
Accidents	2	3	2	6	13
Political events					
Bad blood	14	16	18	15	16
Loosing election	0	1	1	2	4
Winning election	2	9	0	6	7

Looking out for a fresh loan stands out as a major coping strategy when households face death in the family. Such borrowings are a necessary condition, even among well-to-do to meet social obligation arising due to the unfortunate event; additional cash has to be arranged to meet expenditure on rituals and feasts. But if the main breadwinner from a marginal farm family dies, more severe is the effect on income, access to food and well-being. In conflict situation, households rely on social network and debt in settling the dispute. There is no significant difference in this process across poverty profile. This brings clearly the role that social network could play in tribal society. Social capital, manifests when economic stratification is low and poverty is intense. What emerged from this analysis is that households depend on social network irrespective of chronic poverty profile. Coping with drought reveals a peculiar pattern; chronic poor households rely more on labour and migration whereas always non-poor rely on labour, migration and borrowing. But coping mechanism notwithstanding, access failure to food has physiological impact on capabilities of the poor as well as psychological implications for people's perceptions about well-being; waiting for State to start doles is relevant in this context.

Table 5.8

Managing Major Crises by Tribal Household (Number of Households)

	Chronic Poor	*Non-Chronic Poor*	*Transitory Non-Poor*	*Always Non-Poor*	*All*
Drought					
Labouring	133	359	81	234	807
Debt from *bania*	31	133	22	82	268
Loan from friends	1	6	1	5	13
Depletion of assets	1	1	2	2	6
Jati Panchayat	5	10	4	7	26
Migration	57	121	40	130	348
Rely on saving	—	—	2	1	3
Wait for state dole	7	36	8	39	90
Others	4	13	—	14	31
	239	**679**	**160**	**514**	**1592***
Sickness					
Debt from *bania*	206	591	144	442	1383
Loan from friends	10	48	9	39	106
	216	**639**	**153**	**481**	**1489***
Conflict					
Jati Panchayat	87	296	64	222	669
Community	52	137	40	92	321
Debt from *bania*	71	157	37	112	377
	210	**590**	**141**	**426**	**1367***
Death					
Debt from *bania*	124	314	80	237	755
Rely on savings	52	175	26	105	358
Loan from friends	34	120	39	107	300
	210	**609**	**145**	**449**	**1413***

* The figures are total of responses for respective categories.

About 60 per cent of the households believe that the economic well-being they have experienced can be sustained in future as well (Table 5.9). This proportion is significantly large among those who have always remained non-poor, as over 70 per cent from this category believe so. On the other hand, among other poverty profile groups, including transitory non-poor, only about 54 to 62 per cent believe that economic well-being can be sustained. This feeling of well-being is a product of many forces. After independence, three important processes have brought considerable change in ideas and behavioural expectations of the tribals. Development interventions of state, political decentralisation and seasonal migration have influenced the social and economic outlook of them. In order to appreciate the struggles between continuity and change, each of these processes has to be located within the cultural constructs that tribal employ to interpret them. Development for tribals brings images of large projects, displacement and associated hardship.[4] Otherwise, large sections of the tribals have missed the fruits of post-independence development interventions and remained poor both in terms of coverage and quality. But except for elementary education and availability of subsidised grains from public distribution system, other amenities like access to electricity, all weather roads, health services, drinking water and sanitation, irrigation, agricultural extension, rural co-operatives, etc., are poor. In fact, their remoteness to administration and civil society institutions is overriding enough to allow these facilities to reach the area. What has, however, reached them is the fear of displacement due to development projects with administrative insensitivity that accompanies them. Presence of administration – in the form of police, forest and revenue officials – is synonymous with corruption, repression and exploitation.[5] The experiences of development in tribal consciousness imprint mistrust towards non-tribals, caution and apathy towards state interventions and bitter memories of loss of land and natural resources.

Table 5.9

Ways of Sustaining the Economic Well-being

	Chronic Poor	*Non-Chronic Poor*	*Transitory Non-Poor*	*Always Non-Poor*	*All*
Can well-being sustain					
Yes	151	375	100	349	975
No	74	261	55	137	527
Can't say	18	56	8	29	111
If yes, how					
Hard work	33	62	24	75	194
Employment opportunity	60	129	44	126	359
Investment in agriculture	27	81	15	73	196
State interventions	14	49	11	41	115
All	151	375	100	349	974

The change in the form of technologically driven agriculture, though restricted to a small subset of area, is not entirely an outcome of state intervention either. It happened because of seasonal migration. Seasonal migration for tribals is not only coping measure to meet scarcity and its social implications,[6] it is also experiencing development that has by-passed them.[7] What a migrating tribal learns during his stay as a labourer either on irrigated farms of fertile plains (in Odisha, Chhattisgarh and Jharkhand) or on the farms of irrigated HB cotton growers of *Khandesh* or on the fields of irrigated paddy and sugarcane growers in South Gujarat (in Gujarat, Rajasthan and Madhya Pradesh), is a main source of his knowledge about agriculture technology transfer. How to energise the well and distribute water; how to grow fertiliser-responsive cotton, soybean and wheat; utilisation of post-harvest technology of these market-oriented crops, etc., is learnt during seasonal migration. No matter how much the left-oriented civil society organisation discredits it, this process of acquisition of knowledge creates space for non-tribal institutions that induce conversion of subsistence way of agriculture to a market driven agriculture.[8] The process is, however, internalised without any state support. In irrigated areas, the *bania* provides agricultural credit without any security. The tribal also repay the loans promptly at least during good agricultural years. But in the process, they have started attaching a high degree of dependence on non-tribal institution they loathed the most, the market. This is an ideological contradiction that is the handiwork of modernity. This emerging consciousness about technological change – infused with conditions of larger tracks of poor quality of land – produced ethos in which *bania* finds that land as a source of exploitation is not as remunerative for their money-lending business as it used to be during pre-independence years.

The third important process that is impinging on the tribal consciousness is the process of decentralised governance. The essence and logic of decentralised governance is to bring decision-making nearer to the masses. In the last 10 years of its working in the region, decentralisation has brought considerable transformation (Sah et al., 2008). Traditional leadership and its social dominance have given way to elected leaders; many a role that traditional leadership used to play has become redundant when identity of traditional leader is subsumed into *Sarpanch (*village panchayat head*)*. But when traditional leader is unable to establish himself as elected leader, decentralisation has become a ground where traditional ideology would like to re-establish itself (Sah and Bhatt, 2006). This results in divisions and fractions in village polity. Nonetheless, social interests that used to be supreme are giving way to economic interests. Generation divide has sharpened with older people being sceptical to all economic changes, whereas the younger generation is receptive and adaptive to interventions and economic changes. Both sides with their experiences – marginalisation and exploitation versus modernity and economic affluence – have stood to their ideological stands. But the divide is apparent. Both the agents, the *Patel* with his social clout as well as the elected representative with his political clout and reach-up to high echelons of administration, are playing their respective roles. Changes are accepted slowly and with caution in tribal society.

Images of modernity and change are mirrored simultaneously with traditionalism and *status quo*. The process is a continuum of mistrust and trust at one level but on the other, it only reflects diversity and stratification in an apparently homogenous society.

Summing up

On an average, tribal households earn annually about ₹ 24,800. Not only the total income of chronic poor is lower than always non-poor, among chronic poor the proportion of the income originating from agriculture is about 70 per cent in comparison to those who remained always non-poor. Consequently, the chronic poor households rely significantly upon labouring, migration and gathering. Relative remoteness significantly influences households' dependence on labouring and migration. Agriculture is 1.4 times more paying in relatively developed villages whereas migration intensity and income from labouring is two times more in relatively underdeveloped villages. What has emerged strongly from the study is that borrowing may always contribute to chronic poverty; borrowing when remains unserviced, creates social processe that forces chronic poverty. Over 63 per cent labour time after performing their agriculture and labouring around village remains unutilised among households that are poor and chronic poor. As a result, even a small borrowing by the tribals under shock makes an economic pressure that traps them in chronic poverty. Demographic pressures and shocks have resulted in depletion of land, silver and animal wealth. There is, however, some addition to irrigation and consumer products like tape recorder, radio, cycle and motorcycle as well. But this depletion and addition has taken place across all groups in poverty profile; no group has lost or added assets significantly more than others. As addition in irrigation has taken place more among under-developed villages, though possession of land does not vary significantly across poverty profile, the gross cultivated area due to irrigation is significantly higher among always non-poor category more so in the developed villages. The agricultural produce of chronic poor is sufficient for consumption only for 230 days against 280 days for non-poor. As a result, missing a meal is two times more among poor located in relatively under-developed villages than those located in developed villages. The social implications of the process varies across chronic poverty profile: poor households rely more on debt and social network to meet crises where non-poor households rely on economic process and do not believe much in social networking. The optimism of sustaining the economic well-being is significantly high among always non-poor compared to poor and chronic poor. The optimism of non-poor as well as pessimism among poor and chronic poor is a product of many forces that created environment for income generation for non-poor or marginalisation for chronic poor and poor. This creates images of modernity and change that mirror simultaneously with traditionalism and *status quo* in this society. These processes are continuum of trust at one level; at the other level, they reflect stratification in an apparently homogenous society.

Notes

This paper is part of a larger study on Chronic Poverty in India, supported by CPRC Manchester University, UK and IIPA, New Delhi and Planning Commission, Government of India. Thanks are due to Ashish Bhatt, Tapas Dalapati, and B.R. Purohit for comments and suggestions. Usual disclaimers are applicable.

1. In this research, instead of calorie intake, we have tried to estimate incident of poverty based on annual expenditure. The total per capita annual expenditure may be used to identify economic poor among the sample households. The official norm for identifying households that are below-poverty-line works out at ₹ 426 per capita per month at 2005 prices. That means, any household that spends less than ₹ 426 per capita per month can be termed as poor. Among these households, having lower than ₹ 285 per capita per month expenditure could be identified as severely poor. The poverty categories can further be re-categorised by incorporating time dimension of poverty. One way to capture chronic dimension of poverty is comparing the consumption expenditure over time. The major problem in this method is non-availability of a panel of data that fixes chronic nature of poverty. Sah and Shah (2003) have used variations in cereal consumption from normal as an indicator of chronic poverty. But identification of chronic poor using variations in cereal consumption from normal may provide underestimation to chronic poverty. This is because experience shows that cereal consumption is relatively inelastic to shocks. Alternatively, Krishna (2003) has identified that in sequence of changes, if there is deterioration in food intake or increase in leasing-in land in sharecropping or fall in clothing over time or instalments of accumulated debts are irregular or children remained illiterate or leaking roof has remained un-patched, it is sign of culturally rooted poverty. Since in tribal area the variations in quality of clothing over time are difficult to capture and the house repair has only labour component using local material, these two may not be included as indicators of identification of socially constructed process of poverty. It is also argued that short-term land transactions in the form of leasing land-in is more a function of market failure that brings agencies together than a pure indication of sequence of change that points a deterioration in the quality of life of either landlord or tenant (Sah, 1999). On the other

hand, experiences show (Sah and Bhatt, 2004) that leasing-out land is a response of household in shock to optimising labour availability. As leasing-out land is a part of social process that culminate income poverty into multidimensional poverty, this indicator is better suited, along with other identified processes, for capturing chronic dimension of poverty. Thus, in this analysis we have proposed that if the household had lost silver in last 10 years or could not service its old debts or could not get even *rab* (cereal boiled in butter milk) or *mandi, kanji pej* – substitutes for major food – to eat and hence missed both the meals or had to seasonally migrate after leasing-out his land, the household is a transitory household either chronic poor if it is economically poor or transitory non-poor if the household is economically non-poor. Thus, poor and non-poor households could further be divided in to following mutually exclusive categories: (i) always non-poor, (ii) transitory non-poor, (iii) poor but non-chronic, and (iv) chronic poor.

2. Chronic poverty is not a product of economic forces alone; it manifests through complex process where many socio-economic and political factors interact and influence the process. Chronic poverty as a social processes rides over shocks or resourcelessness. Livelihood struggles under shocks like population pressure, crop failure, droughts, son's marriage, serious sickness, etc., prompt process of mortgage and asset losses, borrowing and inability to service debt, hunger and migration. Findings show that economic variables like assets, irrigation and agricultural growth reduce the incidence of chronic poverty but state's effort to reduce it through its programmes either food security intervention or PRIs interventions do not necessarily reach the most needy sections. Nevertheless, state sponsored programme for universal education has a positive influence in reducing chronic poverty; put other way, the best benefactor of education-for-all programme is non-poor. As state interventions have failed in influencing poverty as well as chronic poverty, the coping mechanism to fight these rests on individuals' own efforts like borrowing and migration. This coping mechanism engenders a social process that brings multidimensionality to economic poverty. But the most disturbing fact of chronic poverty is the interaction of these explanatory factors with remoteness. Relative remoteness plays a significant intervening role in accentuating the play of forces that sets-up chronic poverty (for details, see, Sah and Bhatt, 2008).
3. This research is a part of larger study on multi-dimensional poverty in remote rural areas. The Central Indian tribal belt spreads across Gujarat, Rajasthan, Madhya Pradesh, Maharashtra, Chhattisgarh, Jharkhand, and Odisha. If findings of our earlier study (Sah and Bhatt, 2008) has any suggestion on tribal poverty, it could be argued that with two thirds of

the population living in poverty in these remote areas, they not only represent very high incidence of income poverty but also faces a multiplicity of discriminations in terms of resource base, social inequality, geographical remoteness, infrastructure development and political representation. Together these factors place this tribal belt in a disadvantageous situation that is characterised as *Remote Tribal Area* with chronic poverty. Our study area is a subset of the central tribal belt. The choice of the area was also guided by the homogeneity in terms of cultural similarity and livelihood structure of the inhabitants. Thus, the attempt was to study multidimensional poverty dynamics in 10 tribal districts of six states; Gujarat (Bharuch and Panchmahals), Rajasthan (Banswara), Madhya Pradesh (Jhabua and Badwani), Chhattisgarh (Bastar and Raigarh), Jharkhand (Ranchi and West Singhbum) and Odisha (Koraput). The selected districts represent high concentration of tribal population in the respective state. The important step was to select two *Janpad* representing relatively high and low level of development in each of these districts. Thus, two tribal dominated *Janpad* from each of the 10 selected districts, one developed and other under-developed, were selected purposively. The selection of the villages was done on the basis of the following two criteria: high incidence of poverty represented by extent of dryness or lack of irrigation; and remoteness. Two villages, representing an average 'remoteness' in each of these 20 *Janpad* in the 10 districts, were purposively selected for the detailed study. The micro-study, thus, involves collection of primary and secondary data from the sample villages. This includes group discussions to get familiarised with villages and their people. This was followed by a survey of randomly selected sample of 50 households from each of the 40 villages. The quantitative database thus was randomly selected sample of 1614 households from the six states.

4. The Indian experience with R&R of large project affected PAPs lacks completeness and had been apathetic to local needs, resources. The R&R policy in forced and its implementation creates visible and invisible raptures in the social fabric in the short run and impoverishment in the long run (for details, see Sah, 1999).
5. Revenue official are remembered for their extortion in land sales which cost the seller about ₹ 4,000 per acre or for Land Transfer to a son that could be registered only after a bribe of ₹ 2,000 per entry. The police have duel images. First as an institution of settling disputes in such a way that each affected party has to bribe in order to resolve the dispute in his favour. Its second image is of a state apparatus that is used in intimidating involuntary relocation of PAPs. The forest officials connote a bureaucratic set-up that has denied tribal access to natural resources. But if one can bribe them, limited access may be granted.

6. Rehabilitation of involuntary migration begins with shifting of PAPs and ends with reconstructing their broken socio-economic fabric in new environment. It is prolonged and complex socio-economic and political process (for details, see Sah, 1998).
7. In drought prone areas, migration also works as asset formation device. Successive droughts render agriculture as unsustainable livelihood option and forces even large farmers to join the queue for doles. The marginal farmers and landless labourers accumulate assets due to their access to labouring options owing to migration.
8. This may also break the distrust syndrome with respect to non-tribals as noted above.

References

Acharya, S.S. (2001). 'Domestic Agricultural marketing policies, in eds., Acharya S.S. and D.P. Chaudhari, *Indian Agricultural Policy at the Cross Roads*, Jaipur: Rawat Publications.

Dreze, J. (2003). 'Food Security and the Right to Food' in eds., Dev M, Kannan KP and Ramchandran N, *Towards a Food Secure India*, New Delhi: Institute for Human Development.

Kumar, S.K. (1978). Impact of Subsidised Rice on Food Consumption and Nutrition in Kerala, Research Report 5, IFPRI, Washington DC.

Sah, D.C. (1998). 'Avoiding Impoverishment Risks', *Review of Development and Change*, 3 (1).

——. (1999). 'Pressure on Land, Employment and Migration', *Review of Development and Change*, Vol. 4 (2).

Sah, D.C. and Amita Shah, (2003). *Chronic Poverty in Remote Rural Areas of Southwestern Madhya Pradesh*, MPISSR, Ujjain, and GIDR, Ahmedabad (mimeo).

Sah, D.C. and Ashish Bhatt (2006). 'Shock, Livelihood and Debt-trap', *Madhya Pradesh Journal of Social Sciences*, Vol. 11 (2).

——. (2008). *Trapped in Poverty*, Jaipur: Rawat Publications.

Sah, D.C., Ashish Bhatt and Tapas Dalapati, (2008). *Chronic Poverty in Remote Rural Areas: Evidence from Central Tribal Belt of India*, MPISSR, Ujjain (mimeo).

Swaminathan, M. (2000). *Weakening Welfare: The PDS in India*, New Delhi: Leftword Publication.

Tyagi, D.S. (1990). *Managing India's Food Economy*, New Delhi: Sage Publication.

6

Impact of Institutional Credit on Agricultural Productivity

KANHAIYA AHUJA

In India, agriculture has been a predominant sector for production, employment and economic prosperity, where majority of the population depends on it for self-employment and food security. Introduction of technology in the recent years has transformed the nature of agriculture in India. The evolution of green revolution in the 1960s has led to the transformation in the agricultural sector. With the advent of modern agriculture, credit requirement of farmers has been for agricultural inputs, technology and allied activities. In the last few years, agricultural finance has become one of the most important economic and political issues. With the introduction of modern agricultural activities and improved method of agriculture, financial needs of the farmers have increased over the last few decades. Credit flow now assumes greater responsibility in reaching and fulfilling the needs of farmers and thus plays a role of an accelerator for agricultural development (Thorat and Sirohi, 2004; Belshaw, 1931; Galbraith, 1952; Myrdal, 1968; Schultz, 1964; Shandilya and Prasad, 2003). What is needed in agriculture now is a new mission mode akin to what was done in the 1970s with the green revolution (Rakesh Mohan, 2006).

There are many factors which derive the demand for credit for agriculture development. Widening gap between income-expenditure and capital, need for technological upgradations, and natural calamities (drought, flood, etc.) are some of the key factors which contribute to the demand for credit. There are studies which show that lack of adequate flow of institutional credit has deprived the farmers, especially small farmers from using improved variety of seeds, particularly high yielding variety (HYV), use of pesticides, insecticides, proper and adequate dose of fertilisers, adequate and timely availability of irrigation facilities and agricultural equipments. Nothing significant can be done unless adequate amount of investment is pumped in agriculture for enhancing agricultural production and productivity of farmers (Muthiah, 1972; Parthasarathy and Prasad, 1978; Schluter and Parikh, 1974; Balwinder Singh, 2000; Shahidur R. Khandker and Hans P. Binswanger, 1992).

The time has come when the old thoughts of agriculture being a 'labour-intensive venture' must be replaced with agriculture being a 'capital-intensive venture'. Thus, there is a need for a heavy dose of outlay in agriculture. Providing easy, adequate and timely institutional credit to the farmers can enable this. Need for agricultural credit becomes more essential for small or marginal farmers, especially the tribal farmers who often lack basic amenities of life and are exposed to various nefarious kinds of exploitations due to their poor and week status.

Disparities in access to institutional credit are too sharp. There are many studies which have focused on disparities in disbursement of institutional credit. Bhagwati and Shrinivasan (1993) observe substantial regional variation in institutional credit, especially between small and large farmers. Rath (1989) highlights the regional disparity in distribution of term loans among States in India. Singh (1990) focuses on the skewed distribution of bank credit between regions giving benefits to relatively prosperous areas and richer people within the region. According to Panda (1985), the farmers of irrigated regions are found borrowing larger amount of institutional credit on a lower rate of interest as compared to the farmers of non-irrigated areas. Various studies observe the existence of disparities in flow of institutional credit in India, which could be due to differences in resource endowments or lack of appropriate technology within regions.

The present study is conducted among 400 tribal farmers from Jhabua district of Madhya Pradesh, who are mainly dependent upon agriculture and allied activities, which are practised on the poor soil of little depth with the help of primitive methods of cultivation and negligible irrigation facilities. Their problems over the years have multiplied due to economic backwardness, poverty and illiteracy. Agriculture has thus proved to be purely a subsistence economy. Therefore, the development of agriculture in the tribal economy is very essential for the overall development of tribals.

The development of agriculture among tribals mainly depends on the supply of adequate, cheap and timely availability of credit. Over the years, due to the dependence of agriculture on vagaries of nature and various other inhibiting factors, farming has become a difficult profession. Thus, agricultural credit among tribals is considered as one of the most basic inputs for conducting agricultural development programmes. Mahalingam (1992) highlights various drawbacks that stand in the way of availing of credit by tribals. Operational weakness found in co-operative structure, long drawn cumbersome procedures, lack of integration between credit and marketing activities, lack of awareness among poor tribals, ill paid personnel in tribal co-operatives are few factors responsible for the failure of this structure.

Therefore, there is a need to examine the working of institutional term loan finance for agricultural purposes in general and development of tribal economy in particular. The present study is an attempt to assess various parameters of institutional finance in Jhabua district for the economic upliftment of tribal farmers. It focuses on the impact of institutional credit on cropping pattern and agricultural productivity. It also highlights various factors influencing per acre land productivity in the district.

Objectives

This paper focuses on the cropping pattern and agricultural productivity at the district and tehsil levels. The analysis is based on primary data collected through a sample survey of 400 farmers in Jhabua district. The basic objectives of the sample survey were to analyse the impact of institutional term loan finance on the production and income of tribal farmers in Jhabua district, the cropping pattern adopted by farmers in the district and to assess how far the institutional credit disbursed to them has influenced their crop and land productivity in the region.

Cropping Pattern Practised by the Tribal Farmers in the District

This section looks into the aspects of the cropping pattern practiced in the region. Cropping pattern denotes the rotation of crops and the intensity of cropping. The intensity of cropping is explained as the number of crops harvested within a given period on an area available for cultivation. Crop rotation is the sequence of crops planted within a season or in a given period. The rotation cycle largely depends on factors such as quality of soil, irrigation facilities, agro-climatic conditions, type of crops, variation in prices, etc. Cropping pattern, rotation and the cyclical factors have an influence on the level of agricultural production as well as the production potential of farmers.

Within the region, the household economies of the farming class are represented by the level of agricultural production and their production potential. However, the agricultural activities in the tribal economy continue to be of a low order and depend largely upon vagaries of the monsoon. With less than one third of the region's gross cropped area under irrigation, both agricultural production and productivity have shown considerable instability over the years. The data on the cropping pattern are presented in Table 6.1.

Table 6.1

Cropped Pattern in the District

Cropping Season	*Name of Tehsils*				*Total*
	Jobat	*Alirajpur*	*Petlawad*	*Thandla*	
Kharif	11	28	31	31	101 (25.25%)
Kharif and rabi	89	72	69	69	299 (74.75%)
Total	100	100	100	100	400 (100.00%)

Source: Field survey.

A survey of 100 farmers from each district shows that cropping is done in both seasons, namely; kharif and rabi. The region being predominantly rainfed, soybean, jowar, groundnut, cotton and maize are its main crops during kharif season. Crops like, wheat, gram and pulses are grown during rabi season which are cultivated using residual moisture and irrigation facilities.

Table 6.2

Cropping Pattern in the District: Before and After Credit

Crops	*Before Lending of Credit*				*After Lending the Credit*			
	Cultivated area before credit*	*No. of farmers*	*Mean cultivated area*	*% of cropped area*	*Cultivated area* after credit*	*No. of farmer*	*Mean cultivated area*	*% of cropped area*
Kharif								
Jowar	409	373	1.10	12.78	381.1	363	1.05	10.55
Maize	350.5	312	1.12	10.95	390.5	311	1.26	10.81
Cotton	403	274	1.47	12.59	445.95	289	1.54	12.35
Bajra	343.5	367	0.94	10.73	358.5	361	0.99	9.93
Kulthi	29	46	0.63	0.91	30.55	46	0.66	0.85
Groundnut	486	316	1.54	15.19	502.4	336	1.50	13.91
Pulses kharif	156.5	286	0.55	4.89	146.55	277	0.53	4.06
Chili	61.5	128	0.48	1.92	61.05	123	0.50	1.69
Soybean	418	299	1.40	13.06	454.09	317	1.43	12.57
Total	2657			83.03	2770.69			76.72
Rabi								
Wheat	273	161	1.70	8.53	580.3	299	1.94	16.07
Gram	142.5	114	1.25	4.45	64.5	58	1.11	1.79
Jowar rabi	44.5	31	1.44	1.39	21	12	1.75	0.58
Pulses rabi	8	14	0.57	0.25	14	29	0.48	0.39
Onion	53	121	0.44	1.66	100.7	242	0.42	2.79
Mixed crop	22	25	0.88	0.69	60.25	78	0.77	1.67
Total	543			16.97	840.75			23.28
Grand Total	3200			100.00	3611.44			100.00

* in acres.

Source: Field survey.

Table 6.2 presents the cropping pattern before and after the availability of credit. It may be observed that the gross cropped area 'before credit' of 400 tribal farmers was nearly 83.03 per cent in kharif season, which declined to 76.72 per cent 'after credit'.

The gross cultivated area in Rabi season during this phase has shown an increase from 16.97 per cent to 23.28 per cent after taking institutional loan. This is partly due to the fact that number of wheat cultivating farmers has increased from 161 to 299 during this phase. In terms of crops, wheat production shows a substantial increase in terms of cropped area and number of cultivating farmers. It may be considered that an increased irrigation facility on account of credit availability has facilitated such significant increase in its production. In overall comparison, the production in rabi season has shown a considerable increase as compared to kharif season.

An important aspect of agriculture at the district level is that the overall agricultural productivity is influenced by the yield of main crops. As supported by the figures of Table 6.2, the significant change in yield of main crops is on account of introduction of improved HYV seeds that are suitable for residual moisture conditions. The other reason is the state support for creating rural infrastructure and development of procurement markets, which inturn benefit agricultural production.

At this point the dependency of disbursement of institutional credit on agricultural productivity needs to be mentioned. The analysis of agricultural productivity is not limited to agricultural assets owned by the various categories of the farmers. Although it remains an influential factor, the use and quality of inputs, cropping pattern and its strategy emerge as the determining factors of productivity.

In order to assess the actual impact of institutional credit, we first address three major issues of: (i) agricultural inputs used by the farmers, (ii) level and status of agricultural equipments used, and (iii) productivity and cropping pattern followed in the district at tehsils levels. In all these cases, a comparative study is done to analyse 'before' and 'after' credit status of the above mentioned variables.

Level of Agricultural Inputs

Use of Manure, Chemical Fertilisers and Seeds

Agricultural production is a function comprising of some important inputs of manure, fertiliser and high yielding variety (HYV) seeds. Crop productivity is an increasing function of these variables and in usual course it follows that increase in use of these production inputs enhances productivity (Pani, 1966; Subbarao, 1980). However, use of agricultural inputs is constrained owing various limitations that the farmers face. In this section we look into the levels of agricultural inputs used in the region and present a comparative study on their before and after credit status. The data regarding use of inputs per farmer is measured as the total use of fertiliser and manure in two seasons. The units used for measurement are quintal and per acre use of inputs.

Level of inputs used is an indicator of farmer's overall productivity and potential. Inputs comprise of a variety of commonly used agriculture ingredients. For the purpose of our objective we have concentrated on the three major inputs, namely; (i) manure: traditional fertiliser, (ii) chemical fertiliser, and (iii) use of local seeds. The mode of measurement is the per acre use of inputs. Table 6.3 tabulates the before and after credit figures of levels of inputs in the district at tehsil level.

Table 6.3

Use of Agricultural Inputs Before and after Credit Disbursement

Name of Tehsils	*Quantity in quintals*					
	Manure		*Chemical Fertilisers*		*Local Seeds*	
	Before Credit	*After Credit*	*Before Credit*	*After Credit*	*Before Credit*	*After Credit*
Jobat	24.19	27.48	6.56	10.92	71.41	68.18
	(2.91)*		**(12.57)***		**(-0.38)**	
Alirajpur	22.79	27.54	5.95	7.95	71.55	69.1
	(4.27)*		**(4.84)***		**(-0.29)**	
Petlawad	27.06	30.04	5.4	7.92	83.83	82.01
	(3.08)*		**(6.94)***		**(-0.20)**	
Thandla	26.97	31.05	4.87	6.69	84.14	91.035
	(3.04)*		**(3.40)***		**(2.04)**	
Total	25.2525	29.0275	5.695	8.37	77.7325	77.5813
	(6.47)*		**(11.83)***		**(-0.03)**	

*Indicates significance at 5 per cent significance level.

Note: Figures in parentheses in each category are the *t* test values.

Source: Field survey.

As far as the input use before and after the credit lending is concerned, Table 6.3 presents the mean value of total consumption of inputs before and after credit. Figures in parenthesis in each category are the *t* test values computed to assess the significance of the change in value of use of inputs before and after credit availability. It reveals that the total consumption of manure as well as chemical fertiliser has increased after lending the credit in the district. However, the use of local seeds by farmers in a year shows a decline in the after credit category for three tehsils during this period. If we go through the mean of manure and chemical fertilisers used in different tehsils, it indicates a significant change over the time in each tehsils at 5 per cent level of significance.

Therefore, it may be concluded that there is a positive and significant impact of loan disbursement among the farmers in terms of the increased usage of manure and chemical fertilisers thereby affecting the cropping pattern and over all production in the district.

Use of Agricultural Equipments in Jhabua District

In the category of agricultural inputs, an important component is the use of equipments by farmers for cultivation. In this sub-section we briefly review the use and status of different agricultural equipments used by farmers for cultivation. The purpose of this exercise is to assess the quantity and overall productivity of farmers through use of these equipments. This assessment would further help the objectives of the study in taking productivity as a parameter to determine credit availability and disbursement. This section presents a brief account of the status of agricultural equipments used in the region.

Agricultural equipments constitute an integral part of production activities. In terms of productivity, it supports the rationale that farmers with proper and adequate equipments are able to produce better and larger quantities. In this region, commonly available equipments are the wooden plough, iron plough and spray pump. It may be observed that wooden ploughs and spray pumps are amongst the common equipments used in the region. Spray pump is essentially used by cotton growing farmers in the region. As these are vital production components, they constitute as important indicators for the explanation of variation in agricultural productivity in the region.

The comparison of figures of before and after credit availability with respect to equipments is assessed at the per farmer level. This assessment at tehsil level at periods before and after credit availability would provide a measure of the impact of such credit disbursement. A brief account of regional disparity at tehsil level is presented. To assess the impact of credit availability on the number and use of equipments, comparative statistics of usage before and after credit are presented in Table 6.4.

As far as the usage of agricultural equipments at periods of before and after the credit lending is concerned, it reveals that the total usage of iron plough and spray pumps has increased after lending the credit in the district. The difference in the mean of iron plough and spray pumps used in different tehsils indicates a significant change over the time in each tehsil at 5 per cent level of significance. Therefore, it may be concluded that there is a positive and significant impact of loan disbursement among the farmers in terms of the increased usage of iron plough and spray pumps thereby affecting the cropping pattern in the district. However, the change in usage of wooden ploughs by farmers before and after credit category is found to be statistically insignificant. It must be noted that figures in parenthesis in each category are the *t* test values computed to assess the significance of the change in value of use of equipments before and after credit availability.

Table 6.4

Average per Farmer Use of Agricultural Equipment after Credit Disbursement

Name of Tehsil	*Number of wooden plough used-BC*	*Number of wooden plough used-AC*	*Number of iron plough used-BC*	*Number of iron plough used-AC*	*Number of spray pump used-BC*	*Number of spray pump used-AC*
Jobat	1.78	1.69	0.67	1.55	1.55	2.02
	(–1.12)		**(8.22)***		**(5.18)***	
Alirajpur	1.65	1.7	0.34	0.64	1.53	1.65
	(0.65)		**(3.98)***		**(1.37)**	
Petlawad	1.87	2.04	0.27	0.77	1.54	1.88
	(2.20)		**(6.76)***		**(3.43)***	
Thandla	1.66	1.75	0.25	0.68	1.16	1.68
	(1.08)		(6.26)*		(5.65)*	
District	1.74	1.79	0.38	0.91	1.45	1.81
	(1.24)		**(11.58)***		**(7.65)***	

*Indicates significance at 5 per cent significance level.
BC is before credit and AC is after credit.

Note: Figure in parentheses in each category are the *t* test values.

Disparities in Crop Productivity among the Farmers

Farmers at the regional level undertake agricultural activity mostly for self-consumption and as sustenance for family members. As mentioned earlier, levels of farming activities are mostly determined by the social and economic status of respective farmers. Thus, disparities in productivity arise on account of agricultural assets, cropping pattern and affordability of inputs. The major crops of this region are wheat, jowar, bajra, maize, and groundnut. A comparison across the region shows that a sizeable number of farmers are producing wheat, maize, bajra, groundnut, soybean, jowar, and onion. At the district level out of 400 farmers more than 75 per cent of them are engaged in the production of main crops.

An important aspect of the assessment of impact of credit disbursement is the measurement of disparity in crop productivity across the region. Each region is assumed to possess different geographical and agricultural characteristics, which in turn are reflected in the productivity of the region. Table 6.5 presents the level of productivity of specific crops, before and after lending the credit and present status of productivity. It clearly shows that all the main crops excepting jowar, has a significant difference in the mean productivity of crops at district level. Apart from this, it is also observed, that there is a significant difference in mean productivity of maize, bajra and wheat respectively in Jobat, Thandla and Petlawad tehsil. Moreover, there is a significant difference in the mean productivity of Kharif pulses not only at district level but also at tehsil level too, except Jobat tehsil. Therefore, we can easily pronounce that each tehsil is specialised in enhancing the specific crop productivity after disbursement of credit to the farmer.

Table 6.5

Average Crop Productivity Before and After Lending Credit (Quintal/Acre)

Productivity	*Jobat*	*Alirajpur*	*Petlawad*	*Thandla*	*Total*
Jowar before credit	4.89	4.09	4.93	5.59	4.87
Jowar after credit5.53		4.71	5.44	5.67	5.33
(*t* values)	**2.326**	**3.083***	**1.6**	**0.285**	**3.31**
Maize before credit	6.89	3.46	5.09	5.38	5.26
Maize after credit7.63		4.08	5.58	5.87	5.85
(*t* values)	**3.668***	**1.777**	**1.314**	**1.487**	**3.154***
Cotton before credit	6.33	4.58	4.1	4.58	5.17
Cotton after credit	7.97	5.46	5.38	5.22	6.47
(*t* values)	**1.592**	**1.584**	**2.607***	**1.001**	**2.625***
Bajra before credit	6.63	6.97	7.29	7.22	7.04
Bajra after credit	7.19	7.83	8.28	7.82	7.8
(*t* values)	**2.368**	**7.643***	**5.239***	**2.13**	**7.161***
Groundnut before credit	9.66	6.72	6.86	6.88	7.11
Groundnut after credit	10.1	7.41	7.61	7.49	7.89
(*t* values)	**1.028**	**2.916***	**2.177**	**1.606**	**4.154***
Kharif pulses before credit	5.58	6.08	5.88	5.43	5.78
Kharif pulses after credit	6.33	7	6.65	6.32	6.62
(*t* values)	**1.662**	**3.171***	**3.421***	**3.346***	**5.781***
Soybean before credit	8.42	6.06	5.7	6.41	6.4
Soybean after credit	8.84	6.91	6.43	7.05	7.1
(*t* values)	**0.933**	**3.807***	**2.759***	**1.923**	**4.273***
Wheat before credit	9.63	8.81	9.44	9.82	9.41
Wheat after credit	9.75	9.6	10.81	11.35	10.34
(*t* values)	**0.283**	**1.967**	**3.804***	**2.963***	**4.296***
Gram before credit	6.5	5.29	5.8	5.29	5.8
Gram after credit	7.5	7.37	6.67	7.58	7.45
(*t* values)	**1.86**	**3.034***	**0.628**	**1.635**	**4.372***
Rabi pulses before credit	6	9	5.43	5.33	6
Rabi pulses after credit	5.6	8	6	4.57	5.86
(*t* values)	**0.802**	**0.291**	**0.795**	**0.414**	**0.184**

* Indicates significant at 5 per cent significance level

Source: Field survey.

Per Acre Productivity

Considering all the above aspects of productivity, an attempt is made to present a monetary analysis of the measurement of land productivity of farmers. This exercise would provide the economic status of farmers, which would in turn help in assessment of their credit requirements and also serve as a determining factor for credit disbursement by financial institutions.

In the rural tribal areas, the major economic activity is agriculture. Thus, in many ways agricultural productivity has its own importance in determining their overall economic and social welfare. However, measurement of per acre productivity has its own limitation and is not free from complications. In the present case, we consider the per acre per farmer productivity as a measure of economic and social welfare of the farmer. To assess the productivity in monetary terms, we have used the criteria of multiplying the per acre output with the prevailing minimum support price (MSP) in the year of study. To classify the farmers into different categories, a bracket of three levels of productivity measured in the unit of ₹/acre is presented. The results are tabulated in Table 6.6.

Table 6.6

Land Productivity per Acre per Farmer

Land Productivity (₹/Acre)	*No. of farmers*	*Percentage*	*Average Productivity (₹)*
Up to 7,200	141	35.3	7398.56
7,200 to 9,000	118	29.5	8777.244
More than 9,000	141	35.3	9329.88
Total	400	100.0	8437.5359

Source: Field survey.

After classification, the average productivity measured in terms of ₹/acre is ₹ 8,437 across the region. Around 35 per cent of farmers fall in lower productivity category of upto ₹ 7,200, and another 35 per cent in the higher category of more than ₹ 9,000. The middle bracket of productivity of ₹ 7,200–9,000 has a lower concentration of around 30 per cent of farmers in comparison to other categories. In other words, the farmers who represent the first category can produce maximum upto ₹ 7,200 of agricultural goods on their one acre area of cultivated land. Similarly, farmers belonging to second category produce agricultural goods worth ₹ 7,200–9,000. The table clearly illustrates a wide range of variation with respect to their land productivity among farmers in the district. The variation could be due to some economic factors, social factors or the regional divergence at tehsil level, which influence the level of land productivity among farmers in the district. It is thus very important to have an in-depth analysis of these factors which have been influencing the per acre land productivity in the district. The following factors are assessed to measure their influence on the per acre land productivity in the district:

(i) Size of land holding of the farmers
(ii) Regional diversity at tehsil level
(iii) Education status of the tribal farmers
(iv) No. of employed persons in the family
(v) Amount of institutional loan disbursed
(vi) Total household income of the farmers

In order to assess the association between per acre land productivity and above mentioned factors, the following hypotheses (H0) are tested by applying χ^2 test of independence. The results of the hypotheses are tabulated in the Table 6.7.

Hypothesis (H0)1 : The per acre per farmer land productivity is independent of size of land holding of the farmer.

Hypothesis (H0)2 : The per acre per farmer land productivity is independent of household income of the farmers.

Hypothesis (H0)3 : The per acre per farmer land productivity does not differ significantly among selected tehsils in the district.

Hypothesis (H0)4 : The per acre per farmer land productivity is independent of quantum of institutional loan disbursed.

Hypothesis (H0)5 : The education status of tribal farmers is not effective in influencing the per acre per farmer land productivity.

Hypothesis (H0)6 : The per acre per farmer land productivity is independent of number of employed persons in the family.

Table 6.7

Chi-Square Test for Independence

Hypothesis	*Chi-Square Value*	*df*	*Significance Level*
(H0)1	46.070	4	0.00*
(H0)2	54.302	6	0.00*
(H0)3	41.593	6	0.00*
(H0)4	15.191	8	0.056*
(H0)5	6.838	2	0.033*
(H0)6	31.457	6	0.00*

*Significant at 5 per cent level of significance.

Source: Field survey.

It is very significant to observe that all the above mentioned hypotheses are rejected at 5 per cent level of significance, which signifies that the per acre per farmer land productivity is not independent of these factors. The said factors namely education status of tribal farmers, land holding of the farmers, number of employed persons in the family, quantum of institutional loan disbursed, household income of the farmers have been influencing the per acre per farmer land productivity in the district. Also, the study depicts regional variation at tehsil level in per acre per farmer land productivity in the district.

Land Productivity and Land Holding of the Farmer

The result testing of hypothesis (H0)1 provides a very significant association between per acre per farmer land productivity and size of land holding among farmers in the district. It clearly illustrates the fact that size of land holding is one of the important factors in influencing per acre per farmer productivity in the district.

The development of agriculture to a larger extent depends upon availability of credit for irrigation and fertilisers. It is important to observe here that there are many farmers in the district with relatively low size of mean land holding, who are disbursed loans mainly for purchasing fertilisers. These farmers are generally deprived of availing credit for enhancing irrigation facilities on their farm lands. As the land is proving to be a deciding factor for the purpose of loan disbursal, it has deprived many farmers with small piece of land from meeting their irrigation needs.

Land Productivity and Household Income of the Farmer

The results of the χ^2 test (H0)2 clearly identify household income of the farmers as one of the influencing variables of the per acre per farmer land productivity in the district. It establishes a positive relationship between the household income and per acre land productivity of farmers. It is found that tribal farmers with low household income are not able to achieve better land productivity. It clearly derives the demand for institutional finance, especially among those farmers who are not able to generate adequate amount of income from agriculture.

Per Acre per Farmer Land Productivity among Tehsils

The results of the χ^2 test (H0)3 clearly depicts that there is regional variation in per acre per farmer land productivity at tehsil level. The result illustrates that per acre per farmer land productivity differs significantly at tehsil level in the district. The location of the farmer's farm is thus significantly associated with the level of productivity and the disparity could be due to some regional issues prevailing at tehsil level due to the geographical differences.

Land Productivity and Quantum of Institutional Credit

The χ^2 test (H0)4 illustrate the significant association between per acre per farmer land productivity and amount of institutional credit disbursed to the farmers. The results of the test establishes a strong association between the per acre land productivity and the amount of institutional credit disbursed. It has been found that tribal farmers with low amount of disbursement of institutional credit are found having low per acre land productivity in the district. This clearly depicts that quantum of institutional credit disbursed is one of the influencing factors of per acre per farmer land productivity in Jhabua district. It thus strongly supports the need for more amount of capital investment in tribal agriculture through institutional credit in Jhabua district.

Land Productivity and Education Status of the Farmers

Does illiteracy among farmers adversely affect their land productivity? The result of chi-square test (H0)5 provides an answer to this query and establishes a very significant and strong association between per acre per-farmer land productivity and education status of the farmers. It is important to mention that around 74 per cent tribal farmers are found to be illiterate. The result proves that per acre per farmer land productivity in the district is not independent of the educational status of the tribals. Literate farmers are found to have much higher land productivity as compared to illiterate farmers. The results definitely give a strong call of improving literacy standards among tribal farmers to improve their productivity.

Land Productivity and Employed Persons in the Family

Lastly, the land productivity is assessed with respect to number of employed persons in the family. Does the number of earning members in the tribal family affect their per acre land productivity? The result of chi-square test (H0)6 categorically establishes a very significant and strong association between per acre per farmer land productivity and number of earning members in tribal family. The findings establish a positive relationship between per acre land productivity and number of earning members in the family. It is found during the study that tribal farmers having more number of earning members are able to achieve better land productivity. It is suggested that capital investment through institutional credit can play an important role in reducing the dependency ratio and provide employment opportunities to more number of tribal people for the betterment of their agriculture and economic development in Jhabua district.

The analysis of the study thus provides us brief and specific information about the prevailing agricultural and economic status of the tribals in the region. In overall terms, the purpose of the survey on cropping pattern, agricultural equipments, and levels of inputs was to assess and measure the status of agricultural productivity in the region and also to analyse the impact of institutional term loan finance on tribal farmers on their farm activities and land productivity. The study concludes that there is a positive and significant impact of loan disbursement among the farmers in terms of the increased usage of manure and chemical fertilisers thereby affecting the cropping pattern and overall production in the district.

It also shows that all the main crops have a significant difference in the mean productivity in the district. Also each tehsil has been able to enhance the specific crop productivity after disbursement of credit to the farmer.

It is very significant to conclude that the factors namely education status of tribal farmers, land holding of the farmers, number of employed persons in the family, quantum of institutional loan disbursed, household income of the farmers have been influencing the per acre per farmer land productivity in the district.

References

Bhagwati, J. and T.N. Shrinivasan (1993). *India's Economic Reforms*, a report submitted to Ministry of Finance, Government of India, New Delhi.

Belshaw, H. (1931). *The Provision of Credit with Special Reference to Agriculture*, Cambridge: Auckland University Press, Texts No. 1.

Galbraith, J.K. (1952). 'The Role of Agricultural Credit in Agricultural Development' in proceedings of the *International Conference on Agricultural and Cooperative Credit*, Berkeley: University of California Press.

Khandker, Shahidur R. and Binswanger, Hans (1992). 'The Impact of Formal Finance on the Rural Economy of India', *Policy Research Working Paper Series from the World Bank*, No. 949.

Mahalingam, S. (1992). *Tribal Co-operative System: A Study of North-East India*, Jaipur: Rawat Publications.

Muthaih, C. (1972). 'The Green Revolution: Participation by Small and Large Farmers', in seminar on *Rural Development for Weaker Section*, Indian Society of Agricultural Economics, Bombay, October.

Myrdal, Gunnar (1968). *Asian Drama: An Enquiry into the Poverty of Nations*, Volume II, The 20th Century Fund Inc.

Panda, R.K. (1985). *Agricultural Indebtedness and Institutional Finance*, New Delhi: Ashish Publishing House.

Pani, P.K. (1966). 'Cultivator's Demand for Credit: Across-section Analysis', *International Economic Review*, 7 (2).

Parthasarathy, G. and D.S. Prasad (1978). *Response to the Impact of the New Rice Technology by Farm Size and Tenure: Andhra Pradesh in interpretative analysis of selected papers from changes in rice farming in selected areas of Asia*, Philippines: IRRI.

Rakesh, Mohan (2006). 'Agriculture Credit in India: Status, Issues and Future Agenda', *Economic and Political Weekly*, Vol XLI, NO. 11, March 18–24, 2006.

Rath, N. (1989). 'Agricultural Growth and Investment in India', *Journal Indian School of Political Economy*,1 (1).

Shandailya, Tapan Kumar, and Umesh Prasad, (2003). *Agricultural Credit and NABARD*, New Delhi: Deep & Deep Publications.

Schluter, M.G.G. and G.O. Parikh (1974). 'The Interaction of Cooperatives Credit and Uncertainty in Small Farmer Adoption of New Cereal Varieties', *Artha Vikas*, 10 (2), July.

Schultz, T.W. (1964). *Transforming Traditional Agriculture*, New Haven: Yale University Press.

Singh, Balwinder (2000). *Agricultural Credit: Sources, Problems and Emerging Issues*, New Delhi: Deep & Deep Publications.

Singh, Surjit (1990). 'Rural Credit: Issues for Nineties', *Economic and Political Weekly*, November 17, 2231–34.

Subbarao, K. (1980). 'Institutional Credit, Uncertainty and Adoption of HYV Technology: A comparison of East U.P with West U.P.', *Indian Journal of Agricultural Economics*, 35(1):69–90.

Thorat, Sukhadeo and Smita Sirohi (2004). *Rural Infrastructure*, Vol. 4, State of the Indian Farmer, New Delhi: Academic Foundation.

7

Democratic Governance and Status of Minority

Reflections from the Field

B.N. PRASAD

Social stratification has been a ubiquitous presence in human society. But larger the gap between layers of social system, the system is more prone to crises. G. Lenski in his magisterial survey of social development noted that unequal development of the society has been a major stumbling block in the way of successful representation of democracy. That is why, even today, democratic regime of India is burdened with severe contradictions. Hitherto marginalised social categories, instead of occupying mainstream are lagging far behind in terms of crucial developmental indicators. Indian Constitution is committed to the doctrine of socio-economic and political *justice* to every Indian citizen. It is the basic duty of Indian state to preserve and assure the *equality* of opportunity and dignity of every individual and promote 'participatory development'. Protection of these basic rights, especially to the downtrodden sections of the society assures political and social stability and peace of the country. Impartial functioning of the state in these matters is an acid test of its being a just state.

However, with the acceleration of economic development, pressures are likely to build up and intensify when there is unequal development and some groups lag behind in the developmental process. Ideally, the development process should remove or reduce socio-economic inequalities and enhance mutual respect among all groups in the country. If the developmental process is misdirected, this may be proved counter-productive.

In the post-independence period, Uttar Pradesh has achieved significant growth and development. It has been successful in reducing poverty and improving crucial human development indicators, such as level of literacy, income level and health. Indicators show that all social groups have not shared equally the benefits of the growth process. Minority community lags behind in terms of most of the human development indicators. Serious attempts have been made by the government, through policy initiatives and developmental measures, to ameliorate the conditions of the minority. The community has made some perceptible progress in socio-economic and political spheres, but perception remains that the gap between minority community and rest of the socio-religious communities has widened over the years. This 'development deficit' is a major stumbling block on the path of smooth functioning of democratic system. Situation becomes alarming and grim if one looks at this development deficit in terms of stratification and differential mobility within the minority community itself. However, under the impact of emerging new socio-economic and political forces, minority is confronting with two major and interrelated factors - problem of *security;* depends on social development and intensity of cordial relationship among the members of the socio-religious communities, and issues related to *equality,* i.e., distributive justice of developmental measures and deprivation of the benefits of opportunities. The above issues are intricately linked in complex ways and determine the course of social dynamics of Uttar Pradesh.

However, a survey conducted by the central government highlighted the fact that 90 districts of the country, having minority concentration, are backward. Out of these, 21 districts are identified in Uttar Pradesh alone. Out of 21 identified backward and minority concentrated districts of Uttar Pradesh, a survey has been conducted in 19 districts by Giri Institute of Development Studies, Lucknow. Bijnor district is one of them. Survey findings of this district are presented in the paper. The main aim of this baseline survey has been to identify the developmental deficit in these districts and identify areas for intervention. In order to identify the development deficit and identification of priority areas for policy intervention, the indicators have been identified as (i) religious-specific socio-economic indicators: literacy rate, female literacy rate, work participation rate, and female work participation rate; (ii) indicators of basic amenities: proportion of households with *pucca* walls, proportion of households with safe drinking water facilities, proportion of households with electricity, proportion of households with WC latrines; (iii) indicators of health: percentage of fully vaccinated children, percentage of institutional deliveries.

Objective of the Study

The main objective of the survey is to identify the gaps in infrastructure such as schools, health and drinking water; in housing and sanitary facilities; in other infrastructure like roads, banking and marketing facilities, etc.; and to point out income generating activities, e.g., artisan/handicrafts, in which villagers have a comparative advantage.

Methodology and Sample Design

Tehsils of the district were classified into three strata by arranging them in descending order of minority population in the 2001 census. Then 30 villages were selected from each district. A door-to-door survey was conducted to do the house listing in each village with a population up to 1,200. In larger sized villages, two hamlets were selected. The first was the one with highest minority population and the second was any other hamlet of the villages. From each village, 30 households were selected in proportion to the religious categories of people living in the village. Thus, a total of 900 households was identified and surveyed from the district.

Uttar Pradesh, India's diverse, most populous and key political state, is rich in natural resources but inhabited by poor people. Economy of the state is generally characterised as backward, with low level of income and productivity, preponderance of agrarian sector, low level of urbanisation and literacy, underdeveloped infrastructure and low level of investment (for details, see Singh, 2001). In terms of important development indicators, out of 17 major states of India, the state is just above two states from bottom. Within the general stagnating economy, the western region of the State is better placed in terms of socio-economic development, as compared to other regions (central, eastern and the southern region or Bundelkhand). Agriculture in this region has experienced significant impact of green revolution. Capitalist mode of production is relatively more pronounced and the economy is progressively market-oriented. Urbanisation and modernisation are more marked here, rate of literacy is also little higher. Western region has 26.30 per cent of urban population as against 19.80 per cent of the state as a whole (Singh, 2001). Further, Bijnor is one of the developed districts of western region. In aggregate indicators show that this district is better placed in terms of development indicators. *pucca* road in the district is 86.30 km per lakh population, which is much higher than the state figure of 67.90 km per lakh population. Credit-deposit ratio is also higher, i.e., 54 for the district and 37 for Uttar Pradesh consumption of electricity is key to economic development. In Bijnor per capita consumption of electricity is 185.60 kwh and for the whole state it is 183.30 kwh. There are positive signs of development in Bijnor district in terms of other economic infrastructure like post offices, telegraph offices, telephone connections, PCOs, banks, etc. (for details, see District Sankhyaki Patrika, Bijnor, 2005). But socio-economic indicators of rural areas of the district are quite discouraging. Except few rural infrastructural facilities like *pucca* road and electrified villages, other economic indicators, e.g., veterinary hospitals, animal husbandry centres, co-operative marketing societies, primary agricultural credit societies, regulated markets per lakh hectare of net area sown, etc., are far below the state figure.

Demographic Status, Condition of Housing and Basic Amenities

Out of 900 surveyed households in 30 sample villages, Hindus constitute 58.56 per cent; Muslims 38.33 per cent, Christians, Buddhists, Sikhs and others are only 3.11 per cent. Average family size of Muslims is higher (6.20) than Hindus (5.43). In terms of age composition, the proportion of Muslims population below 15 years is higher than that of Hindus, which is 45.14 and 38.55 per cent respectively. But, in the age group of 15–45 years, which is the most active age, Hindus constitute 46.21 per cent and Muslims 41.11 per cent. In 60 years and above age group, Muslims have lesser population (i.e., 5.33%) than that of Hindus (i.e., 6.54%) being. One of the possible reasons for shorter longevity of Muslims may be due to their poor living conditions (Tables 7.1 and 7.2).

Table 7.1

Distribution of Sample Households by Religion and Family Size

Religion	*Number of Households*	*Percentage*	*Average Size*
Hindu	527	58.56	5.43
Muslim	345	38.33	6.20
Christian	2	0.22	5050
Sikh	21	2.33	5.81
Buddhist	1	0.11	7.00
Others	4	0.44	3.25
Total	900	100.00	5.72

Table 7.2

Classification of Population by Age

Religion	*Age Groups (in Years)*					
	Below 15	*15–30*	*30–45*	*45–60*	*60 and above*	*Total*
Hindu	1103 (38.55)	765 (26.74)	557 (19.47)	249 (8.70)	187 (6.54)	2861 (100.00)
Muslim	965 (45.14)	527 (24.65)	352 (16.46)	180 (8.42)	114 (5.33)	2138 (100.00)
Christian	2 (18.18)	5 (45.46)	1 (9.09)	1 (9.09)	2 (18.18)	11 (100.00)
Sikh	36 (29.51)	33 (27.05)	27 (22.13)	16 (13.11)	10 (8.20)	122 (100.00)
Buddhist	3 (42.86)	2 (28.57)	2 (28.57)	0 (0.00)	0 (0.00)	7 (100.00)
Others	3 (23.08)	4 (30.77)	0 (0.00)	4 (30.77)	2 (15.38)	13 (100.00)
Total	2112 (41.00)	1336 (25.93)	939 (18.23)	450 (8.73)	315 (6.11)	5152 (100.00)

Figures in parentheses are percentages.

Status of housing and basic amenities is not very encouraging in the surveyed households. Although 95.89 per cent houses are owned by the dwellers and 31.89 per cent are pucca houses, Muslims own only 24.93 per cent, but 36 per cent are semi-*pucca* and 32 per cent are mud (*kuccha*) and thatched houses, in the case of Muslims, it is 36.52 per cent. Further, 36.33 per cent houses have one room (Muslims: 40.58%) and 42.44 per cent have two rooms (Muslims: 44.93%). Only 21.22 per cent have three and more than three rooms' facility (Table 7.3).

Table 7.3

Distribution of Households by the Type of Ownership of Houses

Type	*Hindu*	*Muslim*	*Christian*	*Sikh*	*Buddhist*	*Others*	*All*
Type of ownership							
Owned	501	334	2	21	1	4	863
	(95.07)	(96.81)	(100.00)	(100.00)	(100.00)	(100.00)	(95.89)
Indira Awash/ government provided	26	10	0	0	0	0	36
	(4.93)	(2.90)	(0.00)	(0.00)	(0.00)	(0.00)	(4.00)
Rented	0	1	0	0	0	0	1
	(0.00)	(0.29)	(0.00)	(0.00)	(0.00)	(0.00)	(0.11)
Total	527	345	2	21	1	4	900
	(100.00)	(100.00)	(100.00)	(100.00)	(100.00)	(100.00)	(100.00)
Sources of homestead							
Owned	501.00	335	2	20	1	4	863
	(95.07)	(97.10)	(100.00)	(95.24)	(100.00)	(100.00)	(95.89)
Provided by Government panchayat	20.00	7	0	0	0	0	27
	(3.80)	(2.03)	(0.00)	(0.00)	(0.00)	(0.00)	(3.00)
Landlord's land	5.00	2	0	1	0	0	8
	(0.95)	(0.58)	(0.00)	(4.76)	(0.00)	(0.00)	(0.89)
Others	1	1	0	0	0	0	2
	(0.19)	(0.29)	(0.00)	(0.00)	(0.00)	(0.00)	(0.22)
Total	527	345	2	21	1	4	900
	(100.00)	(100.00)	(1.00)	(100.00)	(100.00)	(100.00)	(100.00)
Type of house							
Thatched	84	64	0	0	0	3	151
	(15.94)	(18.55)	(0.00)	(0.00)	(0.00)	(75.00)	(16.78)

Cont'd...

...Cont'd

Kachcha khaprail	75	62	0	0	0	0	137
	(14.23)	(17.97)	(0.00)	(0.00)	(0.00)	(0.00)	(15.22)
Semi-pucca	183	133	0	6	1	1	324
	(34.72)	(38.55)	(0.00)	(28.57)	(100.00)	(25.00)	(36.00)
Pucca	184	86	2	15	0	0	287
	(34.91)	(24.93)	(100.00)	(71.43)	(0.00)	(0.00)	(31.89)
Others	1	0	0	0	0	0	1
	(0.19)	(0.00)	(0.00)	(0.00)	(0.00)	(0.00)	(0.11)
Total	527	345	2	21	1	4	900
	(100.00)	(100.00)	(100.00)	(100.00)	(100.00)	(100.00)	(100.00)
No. of rooms							
One	183.00	140.00	1.00	0.00	0.00	3.00	327
	(34.72)	(40.58)	(50.00)	(0.00)	(0.00)	(75.00)	(36.33)
Two	222.00	155.00	0.00	3.00	1.00	1.00	382
	(42.13)	(44.93)	(0.00)	(14.29)	(100.00)	(25.00)	(42.44)
Three	86.00	38.00	0.00	7.00	0.00	0.00	131
	(16.32)	(11.01)	(0.00)	(33.33)	(0.00)	(0.00)	(14.56)
Four	31.00	8.00	0.00	5.00	0.00	0.00	44
	(5.88)	(2.32)	(0.00)	(23.81)	(0.00)	(0.00)	(4.89)
Five	4.00	3.00	0.00	5.00	0.00	0.00	12
	(0.76)	(0.87)	(0.00)	(23.81)	(0.00)	(0.00)	(1.33)
Six and above	1.00	1.00	1.00	1.00	0.00	0.00	4
	(0.19)	(0.29)	(50.00)	(4.76)	(0.00)	(0.00)	(0.44)
Total	527.00	345.00	2.00	21.00	1.00	4.00	900
	(100.00)	(100.00)	(100.00)	(100.00)	(100.00)	(100.00)	(100.00)

Figures in parentheses are percentages.

In terms of area and basic amenities, it is found that maximum of 49.44 per cent residence occupies 501 to 1000 sq ft area, Muslims having 53.04 per cent, followed by less than 500 sq ft occupied by 38.44 per cent in all religious category, Muslims have 41.45 per cent. Only 28.56 per cent house holds have electricity connection and 71.44 per cent houses do not have this facility, for Muslims, it is 25.22 and 74.78 per cent respectively. Source of drinking water is largely dependent on personal initiatives as government support is insufficient. About 49.11 per cent households are using own hand pump/tube well and 40.44 per cent use public hand pump/tube well. Tap water facility is available to just 9.33 per cent. Majority of the households, i.e., 67.78 per cent, do not have toilet facility in their houses, in spite of total sanitation campaign. Almost 92.89 per cent houses are still dependent on wood as a source of cooking (Table 7.4).

Table 7.4

Availability of Basic Amenities

Type	*Hindu*	*Muslim*	*Christian*	*Sikh*	*Buddhist*	*Others*	*All*
Area of house (sq ft)							
Below 500	197	143	0	1	1	4	346
	(37.38)	(41.45)	(0.00)	(4.76)	(100.00)	(100.00)	(38.44)
501–1,000	254	183	2	6	0	0	445
	(48.20)	(53.04)	(100.00)	(28.57)	(0.00)	(0.00)	(49.44)
1001–5,000	72	16	0	11	0	0	99
	(13.66)	(4.64)	(0.00)	(52.38)	(0.00)	(0.00)	(11.00)
5,000 and above	4	3	0	3	0	0	10
	(0.76)	(0.87)	(0.00)	(14.29)	(0.00)	(0.00)	(1.11)
Total	527	345	2	21	1	4	900
	(100.00)	(100.00)	(100.00)	(100.00)	(100.00)	(100.00)	(100.00)
Electricity facility							
Yes	150	87	2	18	0	0	257
	(28.46)	(25.22)	(100.00)	(85.71)	(0.00)	(0.00)	(28.56)
No	377	258	0	3	1	4	643
	(71.54)	(74.78)	(0.00)	(14.29)	(100.00)	(100.00)	(71.44)
Total	527	345	2	21	1	4	900
	(100.00)	(100.00)	(100.00)	(100.00)	(100.00)	(100.00)	(100.00)
Sources of drinking water							
Own hand pump/tubewell	269	160	2	11	0	0	442
	(51.04)	(46.38)	(100.00)	(52.38)	(0.00)	(0.00)	(49.11)
Public hand pump/tubewell	215	149	0	0	0	0	364
	(40.80)	(43.19)	(0.00)	(0.00)	(0.00)	(0.00)	(40.44)
Tap in dwelling	35	34	0	10	1	4	84
	(6.64)	(9.86)	(0.00)	(47.62)	(100.00)	(100.00)	(9.33)
Public tap	1	2	0	0	0	0	3
	(0.19)	(0.58)	(0.00)	(0.00)	(0.00)	(0.00)	(0.33)
Others	6	0	0	0	0	0	6
	(1.14)	(0.00)	(0.00)	(0.00)	(0.00)	(0.00)	(0.67)
Toilet facility							
In house	109	164	1	15	1	0	290
	(20.68)	(47.54)	(50.00)	(71.43)	(100.00)	(0.00)	(32.22)
Outside house	418	181	1	6	0	4	610
	(79.32)	(532.46)	(50.00)	(28.57)	(0.00)	(100.00)	(67.78)
Total	527	345	2	21	1	4	900
	(100.00)	(100.00)	(100.00)	(100.00)	(100.00)	(100.00)	(100.00)

Cont'd...

...Cont'd

Type of fuel							
Wood	483	329	2	17	1	4	836
	(91.65)	(95.36)	(100.00)	(80.95)	(100.00)	(100.00)	(92.89)
Coal	5	2	0	0	0	0	7
	(0.95)	(0.58)	(0.00)	(0.00)	(0.00)	(0.00)	(0.78)
Kerosene oil	0	1	0	0	0	0	1
	(0.00)	(0.29)	(0.00)	(0.00)	(0.00)	(0.00)	(0.11)
Hay/leaves	19	4	0	0	0	0	23
	(3.61)	(1.16)	(0.00)	(0.00)	(0.00)	(0.00)	(2.56)
Cow dung cake	3	2	0	0	0	0	5
	(0.57)	(0.58)	(0.00)	(0.00)	(0.00)	(0.00)	(0.56)
Agricultural waste	1	2	0	0	0	0	3
	(0.19)	(0.58)	(0.00)	(0.00)	(0.00)	(0.00)	(0.33)
LPG	16	5	0	4	0	0	25
	(3.04)	(1.45)	(0.00)	(19.05)	(0.00)	(0.00)	(2.78)
Total	527	345	2	21	1	4	900
	(100.00)	(100.00)	(100.00)	(100.00)	(100.00)	(100.00)	(100.00)

Figures in parentheses are percentages.

Value of productive and other assets have less than ₹ 25,000 for 82.44 per cent households and only 5.78 per cent possesses these assets worth of ₹ 1,00,000 or above. Among Hindus and Muslims, proportion of Hindus is higher in all value slabs than that of Muslims except below ₹ 25,000 slabs, where Muslims constitute 90.43 per cent and Hindus 80.46 per cent (Table 7.5). The data shows pitiable condition of Muslim community in the region.

Table 7.5

Distribution of Household by Value of Productive and Other Assets

Value (₹ in thousands)	*Hindu*	*Muslim*	*Christian*	*Sikh*	*Buddhist*	*Others*	*All*
Below 25	424	312	1	1	1	3	742
	(80.46)	(90.43)	(50.00)	(4.76)	(100.00)	(75.00)	(82.44)
25–50	43	17	0	2	0	1	63
	(8.16)	(4.93)	(0.00)	(9.52)	(0.00)	(25.00)	(7.00)
50–75	21	7	0	1	0	0	29
	(3.98)	(2.03)	(0.00)	(4.76)	(0.00)	(0.00)	(3.22)
75–100	9	5	0	0	0	0	14
	(1.71)	(1.45)	(0.00)	(0.00)	(0.00)	(0.00)	(1.56)
100 and above	30	4	1	17	0	0	52
	(5.69)	(1.16)	(50.00)	(80.95)	(0.00)	(0.00)	(5.78)
Total	527	345	2	21	1	4	900
	(100.00)	(100.00)	(100.00)	(100.00)	(100.00)	(100.00)	(100.00)

Figures in parentheses are percentages.

Educational Status

Rate of illiteracy among the surveyed households is 31.71 per cent, which is higher in Muslim community, i.e., 33.52 per cent. Muslims' representation in education up to primary level is higher (32.34%) as compared to all religious communities (29.40%). But this trend changes very rapidly in the higher academic stratification. At upper primary and matriculation level Muslim's share is 15.32 and 4.73 per cent, lower than the total, which is 17.92 and 7.97 per cent respectively. Among Hindus, it is 19.42 and 9.97 per cent. Muslims' share decreases sharply at higher secondary, graduation and post-graduation levels compared to all other religious communities taken together, which are 1.69, 0.73 and 0.17, and 3.54, 1.57 and 0.50 per cent respectively. In Hindu community, it is 4.36, 1.94 and 0.69 per cent (Table 7.6). Thus, overall educational status of Muslim community is quite discouraging in the region.

Table 7.6

Classification of Population by Level of Education

Level	*Hindu*	*Muslim*	*Christian*	*Sikh*	*Buddhist*	*Others*	*All*
In relative term							
Illiterate	768	595	1	20	1	4	1389
	(31.01)	(33.52)	(12.50)	(18.69)	(16.67)	(33.33)	(31.71)
Below Primary or	98	197	0	2	0	0	297
Informal Education	(3.96)	(11.10)	(0.00)	(1.87)	(0.00)	(0.00)	(6.78)
Primary	692	574	0	21	0	1	1288
	(27.94)	(32.34)	(0.00)	(19.63)	(0.00)	(8.33)	(29.40)
Upper Primary	481	272	1	25	2	5	785
	(19.42)	(15.32)	(12.50)	(23.36)	(33.33)	(41.67)	(17.92)
Matriculation/High	247	84	2	15	1	1	349
School/Secondary	(9.97)	(4.73)	(25.00)	(14.02)	(16.67)	(8.33)	(7.97)
Higher Secondary/ Pre-	108	30	1	13	2	1	155
University/Intermediate	(4.36)	(1.69)	(12.50)	(12.15)	(33.33)	(8.33)	(3.54)
Graduate (General)	48	13	1	7	0	0	69
	(1.94)	(0.73)	(12.50)	(6.54)	(0.00)	(0.00)	(1.57)
Post-graduate (General)	17	3	0	2	0	0	22
	(0.69)	(0.17)	(0.00)	(1.87)	(0.00)	(0.00)	(0.50)
Total Literates (%)	(68.99)	(66.48)	(87.50)	(81.31)	(83.33)	(66.67)	(68.23)

Figures in parentheses are percentages.

Enrolment Status, Reasons for Dropout and Parents' Aspiration

About 72.66 per cent of the children are enrolled in government schools and only 24.56 per cent are enrolled in private schools. In the case of Muslims, it is 73.91 and 20.47 per cent respectively. Generally, government schools are poorly maintained and quality of education is very low. Dropout cases are alarming in these schools. It becomes even more serious as we move from primary to higher levels. Students' enrolment up to class 5 is almost 14 per cent. This decreases to 9.41 per cent at class 8 and then very sharp decline has been observed at class 9 and 10 standards, which is 3.37 and 1.10 per cent respectively. In the case of Muslims this trend is more discouraging. Enrolment of Muslim children is 14.42 per cent at class 5, but it declines to 2.56 and 0.48 per cent at class 9 and 10. In most of the cases small children are sent to the schools mainly to receive scholarship and mid-day meal. Grown up children are forced to earn money, which although meagre, but is an important additional source of family income. In the case of girl students, situation is even worst. It has been observed during field work that maximum girls of the surveyed villages have left school education after upper-primary level mainly due to unavailability of secondary and higher secondary schools in the village or nearby villages. Average distance of secondary/higher secondary school per lakh of population is almost 6 km (Table 7.7). Due to distance and social reasons most of the girls are forced to stay back in their home after upper-primary and do the traditional domestic chores. However, dropout cases are a matter of serious concern for school administration and government, both at district and state level. The most important reason for dropout is parents viewing their children as an additional source of income (18.87%), followed by distance of school (7.55%), work at home

Table 7.7

Educational Institution and Distance

Type	*Place*				*Distance (average)*	*Type of road*			
	Within Village	*Within Block*	*Within Panchayat*	*Within District*	*(km)*	*Pucca*	*Semi-Pucca*	*Kutcha*	*Kutcha-Pucca Mix*
Primary School	24	3	3	0	0.27	6	9	5	10
Middle School	9	14	6	1	1.80	14	4	3	9
High/Higher Secondary (Boys)	2	23	0	5	5.77	22	5	0	3
High/Higher Secondary (Girls)	2	23	0	5	5.60	22	5	0	3
Religious School	13	6	0	1	0.83	4	7	2	7
Non-formal Education Centre	5	4	1	4	2.77	8	2	1	3
Others	0	0	0	1	0.33	1	0	0	0

Table 7.8

Educational Status of Children, Dropout and Parents Aspiration

	Hindu	*Muslim*	*Christian*	*Sikh*	*Buddhist*	*Others*	*All*
Characteristics of Enrolled Children							
Enrolled in Class I	107 (13.46)	101 (16.19)	0 (0.00)	4 (12.90)	1 (25.00)	0 (0.00)	213 (14.63)
Enrolled in Class II	107 (13.46)	97 (15.54)	0 (0.00)	6 (19.35)	0 (0.00)	0 (0.00)	210 (14.42)
Enrolled in Class III	105 (13.21)	81 (12.98)	0 (0.00)	2 (6.45)	0 (0.00)	0 (0.00)	188 (12.91)
Enrolled in Class IV	83 (10.44)	62 (9.94)	0 (0.00)	2 (6.45)	0 (0.00)	1 (50.00)	148 (10.16)
Enrolled in Class V	111 (13.96)	90 (14.42)	0 (0.00)	1 (3.23)	0 (0.00)	0 (0.00)	202 (13.87)
Enrolled in Class VI	86 (10.82)	65 (10.42)	0 (0.00)	5 (16.13)	1 (25.00)	0 (0.00)	157 (10.78)
Enrolled in Class VII	74 (9.31)	52 (8.33)	0 (0.00)	3 (9.68)	1 (25.00)	0 (0.00)	130 (8.93)
Enrolled in Class VIII	81 (10.19)	51 (8.17)	1 (100.00)	3 (9.68)	0 (0.00)	1 (50.00)	137 (9.41)
Enrolled in Class IX	29 (3.65)	16 (2.56)	0 (0.00)	4 (12.90)	0 (0.00)	0 (0.00)	49 (3.37)
Enrolled in Class X	11 (1.38)	3 (0.48)	0 (0.00)	1 (3.23)	1 (25.00)	0 (0.00)	16 (1.10)
Total	795 (100.00)	624 (100.00)	1 (100.00)	31 (100.00)	4 (100.00)	2 (100.00)	1456 (100.00)
Types of School							
Government	585 (73.40)	473 (73.91	0 (0.00)	7 (22.58)	4 (100.00)	2 (100.00)	1071 (72.66)
Private	207 (25.97)	131 (20.47)	0 (0.00)	24 (77.42)	0 (0.00)	0 (0.00)	362 (24.56)
Reasons for Dropout							
Work at home	2 (9.09)	1 (3.33)	0 (0.00)	0 (0.00)	0 (0.00)	0 (0.00)	3 (5.66)
Need to earn	4 (18.18)	6 (20.00)	0 (0.00)	0 (0.00)	0 (0.00)	0 (0.00)	10 (18.87)
Far distance of school	0 (0.00)	4 (13.33)	0 (0.00)	0 (0.00)	0 (0.00)	0 (0.00)	4 (7.55)
Marriage	0 (0.00)	1 (3.33)	0 (0.00)	0 (0.00)	0 (0.00)	0 (0.00)	1 (1.89)
Others	0 (0.00)	1 (3.33)	0 (0.00)	0 (0.00)	0 (0.00)	0 (0.00)	1 (1.89)
Aspiration of Parents for Education							
Boys Total	327 (62.05)	221 (64.06)	0 (0.00)	13 (61.90)	1 (100.00)	0 (0.00)	562 (62.44)
Girls Total	274 (43.77)	185 (70.61)	0 (0.00)	12 (200.00)	1 (100.00)	1 (100.00)	473 (52.56)

Figures in parentheses are percentages.

(5.66%) and marriage (1.89%), etc. Last three reasons are mostly related to the girl child. Maximum dropout cases have been reported in Muslim community, which is 43.33 per cent, in Hindu it is 36.36 per cent. However, parents have strong desire to educate their children. 62.44 per cent parents are in favour of educated male children, in which Hindu and Muslim percentage is 62.05 and 64.06 respectively. In the case of female child, percentage is relatively low, which may be due to patriarchal and patrilineal family norms, especially in north India. Only 52.56 per cent parents are interested to educate their girl child, but 70.61 per cent Muslims are aspiring their female child to be educated and only 43.77 per cent Hindus are interested in this direction (Table 7.8).

Status of Health

As shown in Table 7.9, fever (25.90%) is the most common disease in the region with maximum of 29.21 per cent for Muslims, followed by stomach-related problems (24.17%). Dreaded diseases like cancer and tuberculosis are relatively lesser evident, i.e., 3.59 per cent, than jaundice and typhoid (4.65%). Poor supply of safe drinking water and lack of sanitation are largely responsible for jaundice in the area. Average days of taking treatment are 48. This is the highest in Christians, followed by Sikhs, Hindus and for Muslims, it is of 41 days. Due to poor economic condition Muslims are unable to continue the treatment, which is quite often very expensive.

Table 7.9

Type of Diseases

Type	*Hindu*	*Muslim*	*Christian*	*Sikh*	*All*
Fever	107	85	0	3	195
	(23.88)	(29.21)	(0.00)	(25.00)	(25.90)
Jaundice/Typhoid	24	10	0	1	35
	(5.36)	(3.44)	(0.00)	(8.33)	(4.65)
ENT	9	7	0	0	16
	(2.01)	(2.41)	(0.00)	(0.00)	(2.12)
Accident	31	15	1	1	48
	(6.92)	(5.15)	(50.00)	(8.33)	(6.37)
Stomach-related	110	71	0	1	182
	(24.55)	(24.40)	(0.00)	(8.33)	(24.17)
Cancer/TB	16	11	0	0	27
	(3.57)	(3.78)	(0.00)	(0.00)	(3.59)
Any other	151	92	1	6	250
	(33.71)	(31.62)	(50.00)	(50.00)	(33.20)
Total	448	291	2	12	753
	(100.00)	(100.00)	(100.00)	(100.00)	(100.00)
Average days of treatment	52	41	137	66	48

Figures in parentheses are percentages.

Condition of Treatment

Majority of the surveyed households (67.33%) consult private health centres for treatment (Table 7.10). Only 15.80 per cent prefer government hospitals as they are in poor conditions and lack facilities. People also consult *jhola-chhap* doctors (13.15%). They are mostly quacks and easily available within the village or nearby villages. Traditional home treatment is followed by 2.26 per cent. Break-ups of data by social category show that 20.27 per cent Muslims go to government hospitals, which is higher than the average. Almost all Christians go to private health centres, followed by Sikhs, Hindus and Muslims who form the smallest group in this category. Further, 15.81 per cent Muslims consult *jhola-chhap* doctors, which is again higher than the average. It has been reported by the respondents that patients with serious diseases were not admitted in government hospitals. The average expenditure per patient is ₹ 2,662. Average expenditure is higher in Hindus (₹ 2,945) than Muslims (₹ 2,121).

Table 7.10

Place of Treatment of Diseases

Place	*Hindu*	*Muslim*	*Christian*	*Sikh*	*All*
Government Hospital	58	59	0	2	119
	(12.95)	(20.27)	(0.00)	(16.67)	(15.80)
Private Hospital	321	174	2	10	507
	(71.65)	(59.79)	(100.00)	(83.33)	(67.33)
Government and Private	3	3	0	0	6
	(0.67)	(1.03)	(0.00)	(0.00)	(0.80)
Traditional	1	0	0	0	1
	(0.22)	(0.00)	(0.00)	(0.00)	(0.13)
Homeopathic	0	3	0	0	3
	(0.00)	(1.03)	(0.00)	(0.00)	(0.40)
Local Government Health Worker	1	0	0	0	1
	(0.22)	(0.00)	(0.00)	(0.00)	(0.13)
Voluntary Health Worker	0	0	0	0	0
	(0.00)	(0.00)	(0.00)	(0.00)	(0.00)
Home Treatment	11	6	0	0	17
	(2.46)	(2.06)	(0.00)	(0.00)	(2.26)
Jhola-Chhap Doctor	53	46	0	0	99
	(11.83)	(15.81)	(0.00)	(0.00)	(13.15)
Others	0	0	0	0	0
	(0.00)	(0.00)	(0.00)	(0.00)	(0.00)
Average Expenditure (₹)	2945.49	2121.18	7500	4308.33	2662.18

Figures in parentheses are percentages.

Condition of Mother Care

Majority of the households prefer delivery at home, which account for 90.70 per cent. People who can afford, go to private hospitals (6.84%) where government hospitals are least preferred (2.47%). It is generally believed that facilities and attention available for the expecting mothers are very poor in the government health centres. Maximum deliveries (83.97%) have been conducted by untrained *Dais*. Deliveries under the

Table 7.11

Assistance to Mothers at the Time of Last Delivery

Detail	*Hindu*	*Muslim*	*Christian*	*Sikh*	*Buddhist*	*Others*	*All*
Place of Birth of Last Child							
Government Hospital	12 (2.30)	10 (2.92)	0 (0.00)	0 (0.00)	0 (0.00)	0 (0.00)	22 (2.47)
Private Hospital	30 (5.75)	22 (6.43)	1 (50.00)	7 (33.33)	0 (0.00)	1 (25.00)	61 (6.84)
Home	480 (91.95)	310 (90.64)	1 (50.00)	14 (66.67)	1 (100.00)	3 (75.00)	809 (90.70)
Total	522 (100.00)	342 (100.00	2 (100.00)	21 (100.00)	1 (100.00	4 (100.00)	892 (100.00)
Help at the Time of Last Delivery							
Doctor	45 (8.62)	32 (9.36)	1 (50.00)	6 (28.57)	0 (0.00)	0 (0.00)	84 (9.42)
Trained Midwife	21 (4.02)	12 (3.51)	0 (0.00)	1 (4.76)	0 (0.00)	1 (25.00)	35 (3.92)
Untrained Dai	444 (85.06)	286 (83.63)	1 (50.00)	14 (66.67)	1 (100.00)	3 (75.00)	749 (83.97)
Others	12 (2.30)	12 (3.51)	0 (0.00)	0 (0.00)	0 (0.00)	0 (0.00)	24 (2.69)
Total	522 (100.00)	342 (100.00)	2 (100.00)	21 (100.00)	1 (100.00)	4 (100.00)	892 (100.00)
Pre- and Post-delivery Assistance							
Yes	128 (24.29)	133 (38.55)	2 (100.00)	12 (57.14)	0 (0.00)	1 (25.00)	276 (30.67)
No	394 (74.76)	209 (60.58)	0 (0.00)	9 (42.86)	1 (100.00)	3 (75.00)	616 (68.44)
No Response	5 (0.95)	3 (0.87)	0 (0.00)	0 (0.00)	0 (0.00)	0 (0.00)	8 (0.89)
Total	527 (100.00)	345 (100.00)	2 (100.00)	21 (100.00)	1 (100.00)	4 (100.00)	900 (100.00)

Figures in parentheses are percentages.

supervision of doctors and trained midwives (ANMs and ASHA workers) are just 9.42 and 3.92 per cent respectively. Pre and post-delivery assistance is given only to 30.67 per cent mothers, while 68.44 per cent mothers have been deprived of this facility. In case of Hindus and Muslims, only 24.29 per cent Hindus and 38.55 per cent Muslims reported receiving pre and post-delivery assistance (Table 7.11).

Economic Status

Out of total surveyed households 62.67 per cent are landless and 14.44 per cent own below one acre of agricultural land. But 71.54 per cent Hindus and 88.69 per cent Muslims are either landless or own below one acre of land. About 15.33 per cent households own between 1–2.5 acres, 4.44 per cent between 2.5–5 acres and only 1.22 per cent have agricultural land above 10 acres. In terms of land ownership, condition of Hindus and Muslims is equally miserable, but Muslims are more vulnerable (Table 7.12).

Table 7.12

Distribution of Households by Size of Agricultural Land

Land Size (in acres)	*Hindu*	*Muslim*	*Christian*	*Sikh*	*Buddhist*	*Others*	*All*
Landless	282 (53.51)	271 (78.55)	1 (50.00)	6 (28.57)	0 (0.00)	4 (100.00)	564 (62.67)
Below 1	95 (18.03)	35 (10.14)	0 (0.00)	0 (0.00)	0 (0.00)	0 (0.00)	130 (14.44)
1.00–2.50	104 (19.73)	31 (8.99)	0 (0.00)	2 (9.52)	1 (100.00)	0 (0.00)	138 (15.33)
2.50–5	31 (5.88)	6 (1.74)	0 (0.00)	3 (14.29)	0 (0.00)	0 (0.00)	40 (4.44)
5.00–7.50	11 (2.09)	1 (0.29)	0 (0.00)	2 (9.52)	0 (0.00)	0 (0.00)	14 (1.56)
7.50–10	3 (0.57)	0 (0.00)	0 (0.00)	0 (0.00)	0 (0.00)	0 (0.00)	3 (0.33)
10.00 and above	1 (0.19)	1 (0.29)	1 (50.00)	8 (38.10)	0 (0.00)	0 (0.00)	11 (1.22)
Total	527 (100.00)	345 (100.00)	2 (100.00)	21 (100.00)	1 (100.00)	4 (100.00)	900 (100.00)

Figures in parentheses are percentages.

Employment Condition

Almost 49 per cent population of the surveyed households is either studying or unable to work due to old age or is too young to work. 23.89 per cent is engaged in domestic works, followed by casual non-agricultural labourers (10.85%) and casual agricultural labourers (10.48%). Little more than 1 per cent is either self-employed or belong to regular salaried private and government employee class. Percentage of Muslims' working population is higher in casual non-agricultural labourers (13.24%) than that of Hindus (9.61%), which is just opposite in the case of casual agricultural labourers, i.e., 12.76 per cent Hindus and only 7.11 per cent Muslims are engaged as casual agriculture labour. It has been observed during fieldwork that most of the casual Muslim labourers are engaged in construction work, mostly in the village or nearby villages (Table 7.13).

Table 7.13

Working Status of Population

Activity	*Hindu*	*Muslim*	*Christian*	*Sikh*	*Buddhist*	*Others*	*All*
Self-employed	41 (1.43)	28 (1.31)	2 (18.18)	12 (9.84)	1 (14.29)	0 (0.00)	84 (1.63)
Regular salaried (government)	24 (0.84)	6 (0.28)	1 (9.09)	2 (1.64)	0 (0.00)	1 (7.69)	34 (0.66)
Regular salaried (private including domestic servants)	28 (0.98)	22 (1.03)	1 (9.09)	1 (0.82)	0 (0.00)	1 (7.69)	53 (1.03)
Casual labourer non-agriculture	275 (9.61)	283 (13.24)	0 (0.00)	1 (0.82)	0 (0.00)	0 (0.00)	559 (10.85)
Casual agriculture labour	365 (12.76)	152 (7.11)	0 (0.00)	20 (16.39)	0 (0.00)	3 (23.08)	540 (10.48)
Unemployed	18 (0.63)	14 (0.65)	0 (0.00)	0 (0.00)	0 (0.00)	1 (7.69)	33 (0.64)
Only domestic work	679 (23.73)	515 (24.09)	3 (27.27)	31 (25.41)	1 (14.29)	2 (15.38)	1231 (23.89)
Domestic work but also engaged in gainful economic activities	20 (0.70)	15 (0.70)	0 (0.00)	0 (0.00)	0 (0.00)	1 (7.69)	36 (0.70)
Student	945 (33.03)	664 (31.06)	0 (0.00)	40 (32.79)	5 (71.43)	3 (23.08)	1657 (32.16)
Retired/pensioners	4 (0.14)	1 (0.05)	0 (0.00)	0 (0.00)	0 (0.00)	0 (0.00)	5 (0.10)
Too old/too young (unable to work)	434 (15.17)	413 (19.32)	4 (36.36)	15 (12.30)	0 (0.00)	1 (7.69)	867 (16.83)
Others (specify)	28 (0.98)	25 (1.17)	0 (0.00)	0 (0.00)	0 (0.00)	0 (0.00)	53 (1.03)
Total	2861 (100.00)	2138 (100.00)	11 (100.00)	122 (100.00)	7 (100.00)	13 (100.00)	5152 (100.00)

Figures in parentheses are percentages.

Status of Main Occupation

Table 7.14 shows that majority of the working population (65.44%) is employed as manual labour, followed by 24.32 per cent as cultivators. Only 3.83 per cent working population is engaged in sales/business activities, 1.95 per cent working as clerk/supervisor/accountants and 1.02 per cent working population is engaged in managerial and administrative profession. Break-up of data by social category reveals that majority of Muslims are engaged as manual labourers (80.62%), which is much higher

Table 7.14

Distribution of Working Population by their Main Occupation

Occupation	*Hindu*	*Muslim*	*Christian*	*Sikh*	*Buddhist*	*Others*	*All*
Professional, Managerial and Administrative Work	10 (1.33)	2 (0.41)	0 (0.00)	1 (2.86)	0 (0.00)	0 (0.00)	13 (1.02)
Male	8 (80.00)	2 (100.00)	0 (0.00)	1 (100.00)	0 (0.00)	0 (0.00)	11 (84.62)
Female	2 (20.00)	0 (0.00)	0 (0.00)	0 (0.00)	0 (0.00)	0 (0.00)	2 (15.38)
Clerk/Supervisor / Accounts	18 (2.40)	4 (0.82)	0 (0.00)	1 (2.86)	0 (0.00)	2 (40.00)	25 (1.95)
Male	15 (83.33)	4 (100.00)	0 (0.00)	0 (0.00)	0 (0.00)	1 (50.00)	20 (80.00)
Female	3 (16.67)	0 (0.00)	0 (0.00)	1 (100.00)	0 (0.00)	1 (50.00)	5 (20.00)
Sales/Business Work	17 (2.27)	25 (5.15)	0 (0.00)	6 (17.14)	1 (100.00)	0 (0.00)	49 (3.83)
Male	17 (100.00)	25 (100.00)	0 (0.00)	6 (100.00)	1 (100.00)	0 (0.00)	49 (100.00)
Female	0 (0.00)	0 (0.00)	0 (0.00)	0 (0.00)	0 (0.00)	0 (0.00)	0 (0.00)
Cultivator	233 (31.07)	53 (10.93)	3 (100.00)	22 (62.86)	0 (0.00)	0 (0.00)	311 (24.32)
Male	230 (98.71)	53 (100.00)	3 (100.00)	22 (100.00)	0 (0.00)	0 (0.00)	308 (99.04)
Female	3 (1.29)	0 (0.00)	0 (0.00)	0 (0.00)	0 (0.00)	0 (0.00)	3 (0.97)
Manual Labour	438 (58.40)	391 (80.62)	0 (0.00)	5 (14.29)	0 (0.00)	3 (60.00)	837 (65.44)
Male	428 (97.72)	373 (95.40)	0 (0.00)	5 (100)	0 (0.00)	2 (66.67)	808 (96.54)
Female	10 (2.28)	18 (4.60)	0 (0.00)	0 (0.00)	0 (0.00)	1 (33.33)	29 (3.46)

Figures in parentheses are percentages.

than Hindus (58.40%). Only 10.93 per cent Muslims earn their livelihood as cultivators, which is 31.07 per cent in the case of Hindus. The picture that emerges out of the table clearly shows the pitiable economic condition of Muslim community in the region. In order to minimise the pathetic condition, additional employment opportunities are urgently needed for the labouring poor of the area. In fact, majority of the poor of the region are anxious for additional employment opportunities and they are willing to participate in skill development programmes for self-employment. They are also willing to bear, partly, the cost of such training programmes.

Status of Seeking Additional Employment

In terms of additional employment, 25.87 per cent households are interested to start their own business, followed by 23.33 per cent who wish to take up dairy activity, 15.67 per cent want to work in industry, 10.35 per

Table 7.15

Households Seeking Additional Employment with Preference

Detail	*Hindu*	*Muslim*	*Christian*	*Sikh*	*Others*	*All*
Dairy	369 (25.10)	198 (20.63)	0 (0.00)	8 (20.00)	4 (33.33)	579 (23.33)
Poultry	92 (6.26)	164 (17.08)	0 (0.00)	0 (0.00)	1 (8.33)	257 (10.35)
Piggery	40 (2.72)	5 (0.52)	0 (0.00)	0 (0.00)	0 (0.00)	45 (1.81)
Sheep/Goat	79 (5.37)	85 (8.85)	0 (0.00)	0 (0.00)	2 (16.67)	166 (6.69)
Fisheries	49 (3.33)	22 (2.29)	0 (0.00)	0 (0.00)	0 (0.00)	71 (2.86)
Agricultural Labour	62 (4.22)	48 (5.00)	0 (0.00)	0 (0.00)	0 (0.00)	110 (4.43)
Non-agricultural Labour	48 (3.27)	29 (3.02)	0 (0.00)	0 (0.00)	0 (0.00)	77 (3.10)
Industry	246 (16.73)	129 (13.44)	0 (0.00)	13 (32.50)	1 (8.33)	389 (15.67)
Business	389 (26.46)	236 (24.58)	0 (0.00)	13 (32.50)	4 (33.33)	642 (25.87)
Service	85 (5.78)	39 (4.06)	0 (0.00)	6 (15.00)	0 (0.00)	130 (5.24)
Other	11 (0.75)	5 (0.52)	0 (0.00)	0 (0.00)	0 (0.00)	16 (0.64)
Total	492 (100.00)	320 (100.00)	0 (0.00)	14 (100.00)	4 (100.00)	830 (100.00)

Figures in parentheses are percentages.

cent want to start poultry farms, 6.69 per cent willing to rear sheep and goats, 5.24 per cent wish to work in service sector and 2.86 per cent house holds are willing to start fisheries. Table 7.15 reveals that 49.37 per cent Muslims and 42.78 per cent Hindus prefer additional employment in the primary sector. But 42.08 per cent Muslims and 48.97 per cent Hindus seek additional employment in the secondary and tertiary sectors. This shows that agrarian sector is no more a preferred region for economic improvement for the poor communities of rural India.

Preference for Training Programmes

Table 7.16 reveals interest of the surveyed population in training programmes. Out of 900 households, 91 per cent has shown interest to undergo some kind of training programmes for self-employment and for better job opportunities, within the district or outside their district. Only 2.11 per cent has shown disinterest in such programmes and 6.89 per cent households did not give any response. In terms of social category, 92.22 per cent Hindus and 89.86 per cent Muslims are interested in skill development training programmes for themselves and for their family members. Most sought after areas are stitching, ITI, computer training, carpet making and handicraft. Most of the respondents want short duration training programmes of around 3-6 months, so that they can quickly improve their economic status. Further, more than two third respondents are willing to share expenses of such training programmes, of course partially.

Table 7.16

Interest in Training Programmes

Religion	*Yes*	*No*	*No Response*	*Total*
Hindu	486	12	29	527
	(92.22)	(2.28)	(5.50)	(100.00)
Muslim	310	6	29	345
	(89.86)	(1.74)	(8.41)	(100.00)
Christian	2	0	0	2
	(100.00)	(0)	(0)	(100.00)
Sikh	17	1	3	21
	(80.95)	(4.76)	(14.29)	(100.00)
Buddhist	1	0	0	1
	(100.00)	(0)	(0)	(100.00)
Others	3	0	1	4
	(75.00)	(0.00)	(25.00)	(100.00)
Total	819	19	62	900
	(91.00)	(2.11)	(6.89)	(100.00)

Figures in parentheses are percentages.

Areas of Concern

The purpose of this baseline survey has been to identify the infrastructural gaps. Taking deficit as weight, the indicators representing specific sectors are ranked on 10-point score scale, in which rank 1 will indicate highest deficit and highest priority. Thus, an indicator is given highest rank, if the value of deficit between survey result and the estimate for India is higher. The other indicators are ranked in decreasing order according to their value of deficit. The developmental deficit of Bijnor district has been presented in Table 7.17:

Table 7.17

Development Deficit of Bijnor District

Indicators	*Survey Result of District (2008)*	*Estimate for India (2005)*	*Gap between India and District*	*Priority Ranking*
	1	*2*	*3 = 1–2*	
Socio-economic Indicators				
Literacy Rate	67.29	67.30	-0.01	8
Female Literacy Rate	56.82	57.10	-0.28	7
Work Participation Rate	24.65	38.00	-13.35	5
Female Work Participation Rate	1.76	21.50	-19.74	4
Basic Amenities Indicators				
Percentage of Households with Pucca Houses	31.89	59.40	-27.51	3
Percentage of Households with Safe Drinking Water	99.22	87.90	11.32	9
Percentage of Households with Electricity	28.56	67.90	-39.34	1
Percentage of Households with WC Latrines	32.22	39.20	-6.98	6
Health Indicators				
Percentage of Fully Vaccinated Children	71.11	43.50	27.61	10
Percentage of Institutional Deliveries	9.30	38.70	-29.40	2

Notes: Survey data of the district (col. 1) pertains to rural areas only, but data (col.2) pertains to total.
Data in col. 2 of Basic Amenities Indicators pertains to year 2005–06 from NFHS-3 and rest data in col. 2 pertains to the year 2004–05 from NSSO.

Major Development Deficit in Bijnor

Electricity, institutional deliveries, pucca houses, female work participation rate, work participation rate are areas which need urgent attention and policy interventions. Rural household connections and availability of power supply is the first priority area. Although, all sample villages have electricity, number of connections and availability of power supply is discouraging in the district. Out of total households only 29 per cent households have electric connection and on an average less than 7.36 hours of power supply is available per day . Among Muslim and SC households, electric connections are almost negligible. Due to lack of facilities, percentage of institutions for delivery is much lower in the survey result (9.30%) as compared to national estimate, which is 38.70 per cent. The deficit is –29.40 per cent. Therefore, more PHCs and sub-centres should be constructed within the cluster of villages to improve the health condition of the rural people, along with ambulance facilities. The condition of houses is unsatisfactory and it receives third priority place. Besides having a large number of *kuccha* houses, the living space for an average family is insufficient. The survey indicates that expenditure on house repairing and its maintenance is the major cause of indebtedness of rural poor. This increases distress to the lower section of the society. Female work participation rate has been extremely low as compared to the national level. Serious effort is needed to increase work participation rate in general and female work participation in particular. The condition of infrastructure in surveyed villages is very discouraging. Roads, toilets, drinking water, sanitation, etc., are in bad shape. Even the existing infrastructure facilities are very poorly maintained. Government schools are poorly maintained and drop out cases are alarming. It becomes even more serious from primary to the higher levels. The main reason of dropout is parents' attitude – they view their children as additional source of income. Maximum drop out cases have been found in Muslim community, i.e., 43.33 per cent, than in Hindu community, which constitutes 36.36 per cent. Acute poverty is one of the major reasons. Maximum girls in the surveyed villages have left the schools after upper primary due to unavailability of higher secondary schools in the village or nearby villages. Higher secondary schools are far away from villages (average 6 km). Due to social reasons, girls are forced to stay back in their houses and learn the traditional domestic chores. Health facilities are very inadequate in the rural areas. No primary health centres (PHCs) or sub-centres are located within the village or nearby villages. People go to block headquarters for treatment. The number of beds in allopathic hospitals for per lakh population is 22.1, which is very less as compared to the State (38.0). The situation is more alarming for pregnant women, children and aged people.

Frequency of visit of medical officer, lady health visitor and malaria inspector is less in almost all villages in the district. The problem of medicine is acute. Further, veterinary hospitals are practically non-existent in the surveyed villages, except two villages. There is unfavourable employment– unemployment ratio. Most of the poor are landless labourers without even a piece of land. 62.67 per cent surveyed household are landless in the district. In case of Hindus and Muslims, 78.55 per cent Muslim households are landless as compared to 53.51 per cent Hindus. Muslim community has minimum average land holding of 0.32 acres as compared to the rest of the religious communities. Irrigation by canal (5.10%) and government wells (1.11%) is almost negligible in the district. Most of the irrigation has been done by private tube wells, which is 67.26 per cent. Other sources like wells, ponds, etc., constitute 27.58 per cent. The survey shows that the living condition of rural people is very bad. They have very little assets. Muslims having lesser agricultural implements, transport facilities and financial assets as compare to Hindus. Further, main and secondary occupation of working family members is higher in manual work as compared to other occupational patterns. Number of Below Poverty Line (BPL) cardholders in surveyed villages is very less. It has been found that BPL cards have not been issued to the needy persons but those, whose living condition is better have BPL cards. It has been reported by most of the villagers that pradhan and village secretary demand commissions (about ₹ 200–1,000) and unethical favour, especially from poor women, for issuing BPL card. Corruption is one of the most important causes for under development of the area. It is recorded during the survey that pradhan and village secretary did not maintain the records properly. They procrastinated the matter, when the survey team demanded the information. Further, most of the rural people are not aware about the government developmental schemes. Even the pradhan and secretary are reluctant to circulate the information to the rural people. Thus, survey team sincerely feels that massive awareness campaign is urgently needed for the success of government sponsored development plans. There is no village level record of population and occupational activities, especially of minorities and weaker sections, at any level of district administration. This is a serious impediment for welfare measures for the poor section of the society. For minority and other deprived sections of the society, there are no credit facilities, supply of raw materials and marketing of finished goods. So, credit facilities, supply of raw materials and marketing of finished goods should be ensured by the government. This will encourage handicraft and household industries, which are very important for minorities and weaker sections of the society. Survey result indicates that 91.33 per cent rural people aspire for additional employment opportunities, in which Muslim percentage is higher

(91.62%). Development of rural and cottage industry may be very helpful to reduce the poverty in the area. This will not only provide employment opportunities in the rural areas, but also arrest the migration process. Vocational training centres should be more decentralised. There is an urgent need to minimise dropout cases of children in general and girl children in particular. This area needs urgent attention because education is the dominant means of social mobility.

References

Census of India (2001). Series-1, Registrar General and Census Commissioner, New Delhi.

District Sankhyaki Patrika, District Economics and Statistics Department, Bijnor, 2005.

NABARD, *Potential Linked Credit Plan (2008–09)*, Bijnor District, Regional Office, Lucknow, 2007.

Punjab National Bank, *Annual Credit Plan (2007–08)*, Bijnor District, Office of the Senior Regional Manager, Bijnor.

Singh, A.K. (2001). *U.P. Development Report 2000*, Lucknow: New Royal Book Company.

Statistical Abstract, *U.P., 2003, Economics and Statistics Division*, State Planning Institute, Lucknow.

8

Poverty and Livelihood Diversification in Remote Tribal Areas of Madhya Pradesh

Study of Dhar District

PREETI KATHURIA

In India, poverty has made its roots in every region. Despite government efforts, one-fourth of the Indian people are deprived of economic necessities. About 25 per cent of poor are chronically poor (Mehta and Shah, 2003). Poor in India do not just suffer from economic deprivation but social, political and environmental deprivation superimpose on economic poverty. Madhya Pradesh is one of the third most economically poor regions in the country with over 37 per cent of its population residing below poverty line. Amongst the Indian states, Madhya Pradesh mirrors forest, tribals and poverty (Sah, 2003b). In the year 2004–05, Madhya Pradesh projected 37.09 per cent of rural poverty, which was more than the national average of 28.03 per cent (GoI, 2007). In remote rural areas, poverty is a more serious problem than in other areas which is as high as 60 per cent (Sah, Bhatt and Dalapati, 2008). Despite the fact that these poverty measurements are based on economic dimensions, the state is incapable to eradicate income poverty in remote rural areas.[1] Around 60 per cent of the total population of Madhya Pradesh resides in rural areas. Poor in remote tribal areas depend on natural capital. History provides evidence that the forests were initially the residence of almost all tribes, but they did not have any land rights. Due to state intervention, the tribals have been pushed out to an unsecured environment (Sah and Bhatt, 2004). Therefore, after independence, these tribals are struggling for their survival. Despite government's intervention in helping them fight poverty, a high proportion of tribals are still poor. But, the fact also indicates that government has failed to reach these remote tribal areas for the maintenance of law and development of these areas (Sah, 2004). Owing to this, many of the tribals have adopted self made livelihood options like wage labour, migration and also illegal means such as theft.

Given this backdrop, this paper analyses the pattern of livelihood opted by households trapped in poverty in remote tribal areas of Madhya Pradesh by focusing on the following specific research questions: this paper has focused on the livelihood options opted by poor and non-poor in remote rural areas. How poverty and shocks[2] influence livelihood pattern of individuals? What are the livelihood strategies adopted by households to cope up with shocks?

The objectives of the study are: to examine the livelihood options adopted by chronic poor households; to know the impact of poverty on livelihood options of households; and to find out the sources of income for various poverty profile households.

Dhar is one of the districts where a sizeable tribal population resides. Moreover, 53 per cent of tribal population of the district is residing in remote areas. The movement in and out of poverty is very significant due to frequent natural disasters like draughts in remote and dry areas.[3] The study involved both primary and secondary data for analyses. The primary data were collected from 240 households from remote and non-remote tehsils. The identification of remoteness was done on the basis of lack of access to market, fair price shop, formal credit institutions, and transport facilities within the range of 5 km. Secondly, percentage of tribal population to total population was also one of the important determinants of remoteness of tribal area. The paper is divided in four main sections. The first section distributes the households of remote as well as non-remote villages into various poverty groups on the basis of measurement scale developed for the purpose. The second section deals with the different livelihood opportunities adopted by various poverty profile households and the role of local bodies in it. Section three elaborates the percentage share of income from various sources. Fourth and last section furnishes the concluding of the paper.

Poverty Incidence: Remote versus Non-Remote Villages

This section tries to examine the incidence of chronic poverty in remote and non-remote villages. It was hypothesised that people living in remote rural villages are more prone to be chronic poor than people residing in non-remote villages. Hence, for this purpose, remote and non-remote villages were selected for the study. The data reveals the fact that poverty incidence varies significantly across villages on the basis of backwardness.

The survey indicates that remote villages have a higher incidence of poverty as compared to the non-remote villages. About 84 per cent of chronic poverty is found in the three socio-economically backward villages. In the same way the proportion of 'always non-poor', i.e., nearly 83 per cent lies in the other three developed villages. Though these two variables are significantly positively correlated but, the value of correlation is not very high. It is because of the fact that there are still many other factors which can influence chronicity. Thus, remoteness is one of the major factors responsible for poverty, especially chronic poverty (Table 8.1).

Table 8.1

Incidence of Chronic Poverty across Various Villages

Village Profile	*Poverty Profile (in %)**			
	Always Non-Poor	*Transitory Non-Poor*	*Non-Chronic Poor*	*Chronic Poor*
Non-remote Village	83	29	39	16
Remote Village	17	71	61	84

*The value of correlation is positive and significant at 5 per cent level.

High incidence of chronic poverty in these areas is due to access failure of five forms of capital, viz., natural capital in the form of lack of fertile land, lack of irrigation sources due to frequent droughts, lack of access to physical capital due to lack of basic infrastructural facilities, presence of interlocked market, depletion of physical assets, human capital failure due to lack of education, training skill and high rate of disguised unemployment. Social capital which can be of some help to these people is also denied due to lack of participation and memberships in various institutions and organisations. Lastly households' access to financial capital is denied due to lack of savings and indebtedness. Two observations are important in this context: firstly, poverty is correlated with all the socio-economic dimensions of life and secondly, there cannot be a single remedy for poverty eradication.

Struggle for Livelihood, Governance and Poverty

Livelihood struggle is a part of human capital because it reflects the health and educational status of the households. As seen that among 'always non-poor' the livelihood options are favourable towards agriculture. While in 'chronic poor' category it is diversified due to lack of education and poor health and nutrition condition of these group households. Outstanding to this, vast significant differences exist in livelihood struggle of remote and non-remote, 'always non-poor' to 'chronic poor' households. Agricultural activities in remote villages are generally carried out with labour-intensive techniques and as a result the productivity is low. That is why, households here, though have a high access to land, have to depend on various sources of livelihood. Secondly, the access to resources like irrigation facilities, credit availability, fertilisers, etc., is possible only for large farmers. Due to these constraints in remote villages, the productivity in agriculture is low, which in turn results in low per capita real income for the people employed in these villages.

Table 8.2

Livelihood Options Adopted by Households across Villages and Poverty Profile

Village Profile	*Occupational Profile*	*Poverty Profile*				
		Always Non-Poor	*Transitory Non-Poor*	*Non-Chronic Poor*	*Chronic Poor*	*Total*
Non-Remote Village	Farming	19		15	—	16
	Labour	19	50	30	—	21
	Land and Labour	40.5	50	30	50	39
	Labour and Migration	2.5	—	15	30	7.5
	All Land, Labour and Migration	5	—	7.4	20	7
	Land and Other Work	14	—	3.7		10
Remote Village	Land and Labour	—	—	5	2	2.5
	Labour and Migration	—	—	2.3	4	2.5
	All Land, Labour and Migration	87.5	100	91	94	92.5
	Land and Other Work	12.5	—	2.3	—	2.5

It is noticeable from Table 8.2 that a large fraction of people in these areas does not perform a single specialised work. People often do more than one work and keep on moving in and out of village for unskilled jobs. In remote rural areas, a large number of people are engaged in multiple economic activities to earn their livelihood. They cannot depend merely on land for livelihood. The per capita productivity from land in remote villages is so meagre that it cannot sustain the whole family throughout the year. Due to the implementation of Mahatma Gandhi National Rural Employment Guarantee Act (MGNREGA) by the government in all the villages, the labourers in remote villages also got work in the village itself. Otherwise there is no labour work available in the village premises. About 92.5 per cent of labour force in remote villages depends on agricultural land, labour in the village and labour outside the village.

Level and pattern of income play an important role in assigning households a position in socio-economic realm. Realising this income effect on households, it is necessary to explore the empirical results based on primary data. Therefore, in this section, an attempt is made to discern levels and pattern of income among various categories of households. More specifically, the aim is to examine the distribution of income among different household groups. The analysis deals with the level of per household income across different categories of households. It contains an account of the relative shares of different components of income in the total income of poverty profile groups. The extent of inequality in the distribution of per household income prevailing among different poverty group people across villages has been worked out.

Table 8.3

Income Pattern across Poverty Profile Households

(per household values in ₹)

Income from Different Sources	*Poverty Profile of Household*				
	Always Non-Poor	*Transitory Non-Poor*	*Non-Chronic Poor*	*Chronic Poor*	*Total*
Income from Labour	15294.11	8850	6047.14	4252.46	9414.75
Agricultural Income	46496.74	8392.86	14725.71	6597.05	24866.29
Income from Forest	842.11	3157.14	2971.71	4037.70	2410.50
Income from Livestock	2310.53	0.00	110.00	0.00	946.67
Income from Migration	6404.74	20357.14	15721.43	18786.89	13083.12
Income from Other Economic Work *	4530.53	0.00	671.43	0.00	1989.17
Total Income	75878.74	40757.14	40247.43	33674.10	52710.50

*Income from other economic work includes income from self-employment opportunities like small tea or grocery shops. It also includes income from small cottage industries and skilled service.

Table 8.3 clearly shows that for all rural households, income from own agriculture is the most important component, followed by income from migration, labour and forest. The average values of income from these heads are found to be ₹ 24,866.29, ₹ 13,083.12, ₹ 9,414.75, ₹ 2,410.50 respectively. Another significant feature emerged is that as we move away from always non-poor category to chronic poor the level of income from all sources diminishes. It demonstrates the minimum level of living of chronically poor households. 'Transitory non-poor' and 'chronic poor' households do not have any access to income from livestock and other economic work, whereas, chronically poor people are the group which gain highest proportion of their income from migration. Income from livestock makes ₹ 946. 67 and income from labour stands at ₹ 9419.75. This leads to conclude that agricultural produce is the most important component of the existing levels of income in the rural areas.

The trend of the change in the levels of income across remote and non-remote villages also reveals that in remote villages the option for livelihood struggle is completely different from non-remote villages.

Table 8.4

Level and Pattern of Income from Various Sources across Villages

(mean values ₹)

Source of Income	*Village Profile*		
	Non-Remote Village	*Remote Village*	*Total Income*
Income from Labour	18754.50 (26.84)*	75.00 (.21)	9414.75 (17.86)
Agricultural Income	43687.42 (62.52)	6045.17 (17.00)	24866.29 (47.17)
Income from Forest	0.00	4821 (13.55)	2410.50 (4.57)
Income from Livestock	1376.67 (1.97)	516.67 (1.45)	946.67 (1.79)
Income from Migration	2278.75 (3.26)	23887.50 (67.18)	13083.12 (24.82)
Income from Other Economic Work	3770.00 (5.39)	208.33 (.58)	1989.17 (3.77)
Total Income	69867.3**	35553.6	52710.5

* Figures in brackets denotes percentages.

** Variations are highly significant.

Table 8.4 exposes the different levels of income from various sources across villages. There is a significant variation between the total income from all sources in remote and non-remote villages. Thereafter, the table makes clear that people or households in remote villages migrate to different places in search of work. Hence, the major source of income, i.e., 67 per cent in remote villages is earned through migration. It is second major source of income for rural people in the region. This livelihood diversification is due to lack of employment opportunities in village itself. Income earned through forest products is common only in remote villages. These villages are resident places of mainly of tribals and tribals since their beginning are found to be dependent more on forest as one of their source for livelihood. On the other side in non-remote villages, income from agriculture (62.52%) is the main source of livelihood. Definitely, there is no income from forest to households from non-remote villages, whereas this proportion of income from forest in remote villages is on an average ₹ 4,821. The PESA Act, 1996, has authorised tribal community to use forest produce for self-consumption as well as for marketing. Panchayats are made responsible to directly involve in the marketing of these produce. But these reforms have not been found fruitful as it has failed to reduce migration (67% of the total income in remote villages is earned through migration); secondly, the control over these resources is not in the hands of local community and panchayats take least interest in the marketing process of the produce brought by the villagers. This has weakened the Act in the region and lost people's reliance on it. The second chief source of livelihood in non-remote villages is income earned through labour within the village. The availability of labour within the village domain is less (₹ 75) as far as remote villages are concerned.

Pattern of Income

Selected shares of components of the total income are given in Table 8.5. The table reveals that always non-poor households received about 61 per cent of their total income by farming. This is because agriculture is the main occupation of rural people and especially for those who are land owners. The second major proportion of total income of this poverty category is 20 per cent from labour, followed by 6 per cent from migration. Income from forest indicates that some percentage of always non-poor households residing in remote villages also get meagre part of their income from selling forest products especially firewood. Livestock contributes three per cent to the total income which is comparatively less than other sources, but is significant only for this group of households.

Table 8.5

Income Pattern of Various Poverty Profile Households

(percentage of total income)

Source of Income	*Poverty Profile of Household*				
	Always Non-Poor	*Transitory Non-Poor*	*Non-Chronic Poor*	*Chronic Poor*	*Total*
Income from Labour	20.15	21.71	15.02	12.62	17.86
Agricultural Income	61.27	20.59	36.58	19.59	47.17
Income from Forest	1.10	7.74	7.38	11.99	4.57
Income from Livestock	3.04	0.0	0.27	0.0	1.79
Income from Migration	8.44	49.94	39.06	55.79	24.82
Income from Other Economic Work	5.97	0.0	1.66	0.0	3.77
Total Income	100	100	100	100	100

The highest proportion of total income of 'transitory non-poor' is about 50 per cent, i.e., half of their income from migration. It has been observed through above analysis that nearly 71 per cent of 'transitory non-poor' households also belong to remote villages. Hence, the major part of income from migration is obvious in their case also. Income from migration is followed by income from labour, i.e., 21.71 per cent. Income from agricultural constitutes about 21 per cent, indicating another important constituent of total income for 'transitory non-poor' households. The proportion of forest income to total income is 7.74 per cent which again interprets that a large number of these households reside in remote villages.

As far as poor but not chronic households are concerned, they receive their major part of the income again from migration (39%). At the same time the share from agriculture income is little less, i.e., nearly 36 per cent. The proportion of livestock income is meagre (0.27%). On the other hand income from labour is 7 per cent for households of this category.

The dependency of 'chronically poor' households is largely on income earned through migration to distant places. More than 55 per cent of total income is received by migration. Agriculture does not support substantially in the case of 'chronically poor' households living in geographically remote and dry areas. In spite of having large quantity of land, they cannot depend entirely on it, because of unavailability of irrigation sources. Second, major source of income for 'chronically poor' households is income from agriculture (20%), followed by income from labour. 'Chronically poor' people are those who are most benefited by forest in terms of their livelihood. Other income sources are relatively small for these households.

Taking all the categories together, the pattern appears to be somewhat uniform. About 47 per cent share of total income is from agriculture income, followed by income from migration and labour with a proportion of 25 and 18 per cent respectively. Migration contributes to one-fourth of total income, because this place is surrounded by many industrial units where people can get employment easily. Whereas, in remote villages people prefer to go to neighbouring states; like Gujarat for good employment opportunities. Forests as mentioned above contribute as a major source of income for households residing in geographically remote areas. Income from livestock is less (2%), because there are very few households in the sample area who could afford to set up dairy or can gain from selling up of livestock. Though there were few households found in non-remote villages who were mainly engaged in buying and selling of oxen and buffaloes in weekly market. Hence the proportion of income from livestock is not significant.

Per Capita Income

In the foregoing discussion, we analysed the total income levels and income pattern of different poverty profile groups. Since the family size across the different groups varies, it becomes relevant to look into the per capita income levels across the different poverty group households. The information regarding per capita income[4] earned by different category households in rural area is provided in Table 8.6.

The table clearly shows that the average per capita income in the sample households is ₹ 12,925.39. Further, ₹ 18,904.99 is average per capita income for 'always non-poor' households, followed by the category of 'transitory non-poor' with ₹ 11,886.98. 'Chronically poor' households are in the group getting minimum level of per capita income. The correlation and variation between poverty profile and per capita income is highly significant. As the level of income reduces people or households get deeper into poverty trap. Per capita income also considerably varies between remote and non-remote rural households. People residing in remote rural areas have less per capita income as compared to non-remote villagers. This again validates our previous conclusion that income level explains 25 per cent variations in poverty.

Table 8.6

Per Capita Income of Various Households

*Poverty Profile**	*Per Capita Income (₹ per annum)*
Always Non-Poor	18904.99
Transitory Non-Poor	11886.98
Non-Chronic Poor	9244.14
Chronic Poor	8075.60
Total	12925.39
Village Profile*	
Non-Remote Village	17622.72
Remote Village	8228.05
Total	12925.39

*The variations are significant at 5 per cent level of significance.

Table 8.7

Proportion of Forest Income to Total Income across Different Poverty Profile Groups

Percentage of Forest Income to Total Income	*Poverty Profile*				
	Always Non-Poor	*Transitory Non-Poor*	*Non-Chronic Poor*	*Chronic Poor*	*Total*
0	81038.9 * (79) **	48975.0 (4)	48355.1 (29)	42981.8 (11)	68886.8 (123)
Up to 15	51707.1 (14)	37470.0 (10)	43740.9 (22)	36663.1 (19)	42423 (65)
> 15	41250 (2)	—	23827.3 (19)	28539.3 (31)	27306.5 (52)
Total	75878.7 (95)	40757.1 (14)	40247.4 (70)	33674.1 (61)	52710.5 (240)

* Average total income

** Number of households

Notes: (i) The value of *F* is significant at .001 levels between Total Family Income and Poverty Profile 21.61 (.000). (ii) *F* is significant at .001 level between Total Family Income and Percentage of Forest Income to Total Income 26.38 (.000).

Table 8.7 reveals that as the level of total income increases the proportion of forest income decreases. In other words, when the average total income is the highest, i.e., ₹ 68,886, the forest income is zero. And, when the forest income is above 15 per cent of the total income, total income is minimum. 'Always non-poor' household category has an average total income of ₹ 81,038 which is the highest of all. But, at the same time, during this phase, their income from forest is zero. The same situation can be observed with 'transitory non-poor', 'non-chronic poor' and 'chronic poor' households, whose income levels also exhibit an opposite relation with forest income. The highly significant value of *F* also supports the theory that there is a high degree of cause and effect relationship between total income and poverty profile and total income and forest income.

Concluding Remarks

The livelihood struggle of tribals in Madhya Pradesh reveals huge diversification pattern because the dependency of all category households is not on any single source, except few households of 'always non-poor' category who depend only on their own land. All others have to collectively depend on two or more possible sources of occupation for income. Due to the failure of PESA Act, 1996 migration has come out with an important source of livelihood in distress situation for all households and for all time for 'chronically poor' households. Migration as a source of livelihood is significantly influencing poverty incidence also. The nature of work is unskilled at destination place. At the time of migration 75 per cent households work in agriculture sector. The major part of the income goes into the hands of local moneylender of big farmers from whom they take loans during odd season. This extra income earned by hard labour goes into the pockets of rich moneylenders who exploit them. The educational, health and occupational status are the examples of this phenomenon. The ST community adopts migration more frequently. Among general category, migration is not adopted as a source of alternative livelihood option in any situation. The income structure is highly diversified in 'non-chronic poor' and 'chronic poor' households. To earn income they have to depend on several sources, i.e., migration, forest, labour and land, whereas among 'always non-poor', more than 60 per cent of income is earned from agriculture.

Endnote

To identify poor households with chronic nature, three indicators, including economic poverty, were taken in study area. They were: (i) missing of meals due to poverty, (ii) pursuing BPL card, and (iii) suffering from shocks (natural or human). All these three indicators were given one point each. Therefore, we had maximum three points. On this basis, households were divided into four categories: (i) always non-poor (poor 0 and point <=2); (ii) transitory non-poor (poor 0 and point >2); (iii) poor but non-chronic (poor 1 and point <=2); and (iv) chronic poor (poor 1 and point >2).

Notes

1. Over 77 per cent people are dependent on agricultural and allied activities for livelihood, 15 per cent work in service sector and only 8 per cent in industries. Madhya Pradesh also has the highest Infant Mortality Rate (IMR) and death rate in the country. These indicators are much worse for the SC and ST population in comparison to other sections.
2. Shocks are uncertain and sudden happening which grab the household completely. It can make the condition of household pathetic and can force them to do those types of work which they would not do in normal situations.
3. In last 10 years, Dhar has faced draughts four times, which has disturbed the economic conditions of its tribal population violently.
4. Per capita includes the income of all male and female above the age of 14 years, from all sources.

References

Mehta, Asha Kapur and Amita Shah (2003). *Chronic Poverty in India: Incidence, causes and policies,* World Development, Vol. 31, No. 3, Great Britain.

Sah, D.C. and Amita Shah (2003a). *Chronic Poverty in Remote Rural Area's of Southwestern Madhya Pradesh* (mimeo), Ahmedabad: GIDR and Ujjain: MPISSR.

Sah, D.C. (2003b). 'Continuity and Change: Tribal Society in Southwestern Madhya Pradesh', *Madhya Pradesh Journal of Social Sciences,* Vol. 8, No.1, 2003, pp. 12–36.

Sah, D.C. and Ashish Bhatt (2004). *An In-depth Study of Chronic Poverty: Evidence from South Western M.P.,* Ujjain: MPISSR.

Sah, D.C., Ashish Bhatt and Tapas Dalapati (2008). *Chronic Poverty in Remote Tribal Areas: Evidence from Central Tribal Belt of India,* Ujjain: M.P. Institute of Social Science Research (mimeo).

Part III

Scenario of Health Attainments and Educational Achievements and Areas of Concern

9

Health Reforms in Tamil Nadu

N. LALITHA

Social spending, i.e., allocation of resources to education, health, water supply, and sanitation, depends on the social priorities and development status of the state and therefore differs from state to state. Least developed states like Uttar Pradesh and Bihar spent 7.5 and 11.8 per cent on health while the public expenditure in Karnataka and Tamil Nadu was more than 22 per cent. Hence, there is also a stark difference in the availability of health professionals between the developed and the least developed states (Table 9.1). Because of continued allocation of funds to the health sector, a huge government health care infrastructure, ranging from hospitals for specialised treatments and research to preventive health care facilities in rural areas, has developed. State governments cover more than 75 per cent of the health service costs and are responsible for providing quality primary health care. The concept of primary health care consists of eight elements: (i) education of the people regarding prevailing health problems and method of preventing and controlling them; (ii) production of food supply and nutrition; (iii) adequate supply of safe drinking water and basic sanitation; (iv) maternal and child health care; (v) family welfare; (vi) immunisation against major communicable diseases; (vii) appropriate treatment for common diseases and injuries; and (viii) provision of essential drugs.

India's public health investment is the lowest in the world with 0.9 per cent of its gross domestic product spent on health. Private health expenditure accounts for more than 80 per cent of the total expenditure. However, as Dreze and Sen (1995) observe,

> India has poor health achievements despite spending a comparatively large part of its GNP on health (if one adds up public and private

spending). Much of the mismatch between the resources and achievements is due to the poor functioning of the public health care system especially in rural areas. In some states, this system is little more than a collection of deserted primary health centres, filthy dispensaries, unmotivated doctors and chaotic hospitals. (p. 101)

Table 9.1

Human Resources for Health (Allopathy) (selected states)

State	*Population*	*No. of registered doctors*	*No. of Nurses*	*No. of ANMs**	*Total Human Resources*	*Human Resources per 1000 Population Norm 3.25/1000*
States Above Norm of 2.25/1000 Population						
Andhra Pradesh	78,892,000	48,402	84,306	94,395	2,27,103	2.88
Delhi and Punjab	40,583,000	62,107	40,568	16,281	1,18,956	2.93
Gujarat	51,057,000	36,521	85,406	35,780	1,57,707	3.09
Karnataka	54,692,000	65,789	48,458	46,817	1,61,064	2.94
Kerala	33,365,000	32,412	71,589	27,612	1,31,613	3.94
Odisha	37,091,000	14,712	45,830	30,077	90,619	2.44
Tamil Nadu	63,755,000	71,157	155,647	52,341	279,145	4.38
States Below Norm of 2.25/1000 Population						
Assam	27,520,000	15,723	9,659	12,187	37,569	1.37
Bihar and Jharkhand	107,632,000	35,110	8,883	7,501	51,494	0.48
Madhya Pradesh and Chhattisgarh	86,681,000	29,003	92,158	25,344	1,46,505	1.69
Haryana	21,000,000	1,285	15,821	13,112	30,218	1.44
Maharashtra	94,839,000	90,855	79,004	24,910	194,769	2.05
Rajasthan	57,463,000	22,506	31,063	21,932	75,501	1.31
West Bengal	83,079,000	52,274	44,035	55,855	152,164	1.83
Total	837,379,000	577,856	504,628	4,64,144	1,854,427	2.21

*Auxilliary Nurse Midwife

Sources: Medical Council of India 2004: Indian Nursing Council 1998, 2002. National Commission on Macroeconomics and Health, p. 58.

It has been observed that in spite of the huge private expenditure on health and many people living below poverty line, utilisation of public health facilities is low in India. Some of the factors attributed to this lower utilisation rate are: lack of doctors, medicines and facilities in the hospitals and the poor maintenance and poor physical condition of hospitals make people to turn to private sector. 'The results of the NSS 1986–87 and 1995–96 showed a considerable decline in the utilisation of public health services by the poor especially the rural poor' (Report of the National Commission on Macroeconomics and Health, 2005, p. 71).

An evaluative study of Community Health Centres (CHCs) in eight states show that medicines were in short supply more in the case of four states of Bihar, Madhya Pradesh, Odisha and Uttar Pradesh where majority of the sample beneficiary patients have not been able to get the medicines from the CHCs. The situation was better in Haryana, Maharashtra, Rajasthan, and Tamil Nadu comparatively.

With all its limitations, there is a strong reason for government to continue to provide health services. This is because, the poor cannot always afford health care that promotes productivity and well-being. Publicly financed investment in health can lead to the alleviation of poverty and its consequences. Private markets would either not produce them at all or produce too little. Government intervention can improve the functioning of these markets in health care and health insurance thus raising welfare (Misra et al., 2003).

Srinivasan's (2004) study is about a total of nine Primary Health Centres (PHCs) in Gulbarga and Belgaum districts in Karnataka. He found that while the manpower and the physical infrastructure are adequate in these PHCs, supply of medicines was not adequate, though quality of medicine was good. The PHCs in Karnataka were found to have inadequate supply of essential drugs and surplus of non-essential medicines having little relevance presenting a mismatch.

Realising this, Tamil Nadu has targeted one of the fundamental problems in health care sector of non-availability of medicines in the government health care by addressing the issues in health governance. Medicines formulate an important cost in any illness episode. The National Sample Survey on Consumer Expenditure (55th Round) reports that, 77 and 70 per cent of the health expenses in rural and urban areas are on medicines. Out of pocket medical cost alone may push 2.2 per cent of the population below the poverty line in one year (World Bank, 2001). Medicines constitute a significant portion of expenditure.

This paper provides evidence from the functioning of the Tamil Nadu Medical Services Corporation (TNMSC) that by introducing administrative reform measures, better health delivery systems could be established. This organisation has been set up primarily to streamline the drug procurement and supply to the government health facilities and thereby is directly responsible for access to medicines in Tamil Nadu government health care. This paper is organised as follows. The second section following this introduction discusses the modus operandi of TNMSC. The third section discusses the prices of the drugs procured by TNMSC. Drug procurement from TNMSC by the primary health centres (PHCs) and dispensation pattern scenario at the PHC level have been described in the fourth section. The concluding section presents the possibility of replicability of TNMSC model.

Modus Operandi of TNMSC

TNMSC, set up by the Tamil Nadu government, is one autonomous service agency that is responsible for procuring medicines for the government health utilities in Tamil Nadu. TNMSC was set up in 1995 in response to the total chaos that prevailed in the drug procurement and distribution procedure meant for government health care. This is an administrative reform measure, which had been planned and implemented entirely by the government to correct the then existing government system of purchase of medicines that was plagued by several loopholes. This has been carried out without any external help or private sector co-operation.

TNMSC is responsible for all the aspects that are associated with the drug purchase. These range from identifying the list of essential drugs that are to be bought, identifying the suppliers who can supply the required quantity at appropriate quality and prices, ensuring that it reaches the warehouses meant for drug storage, and monitoring their appropriate storage from where different health services draw the drugs.

TNMSC does not have a financial budget of its own. The various health directorates of the state in charge of providing health services at various levels transfer 90 per cent of their drug budget to TNMSC. The remaining 10 per cent is retained with the directorates to purchase any drug outside the list if considered essential. Directorate of Public Health, Directorate of Rural Medical Services and Directorate of Medical Education account for larger share of the total budget. These three directorates are responsible for the functioning of primary health centres, district and taluka hospitals and teaching and research medical institutions respectively.

A drug committee consisting of professors of medicine, pharmacology, and therapeutics, a representative from World Health Organisation (WHO), health secretary and the managing director of TNMSC identify the list of essential drugs that are to be selected. After the selection of drugs is made, the next stage is the selection of suppliers for which, TNMSC has laid strict and elaborate procedures to ensure uninterrupted and quality supply since making medicines available at the government health institutions is the primary purpose behind setting up of this organisation.

While selecting the drugs, the committee also decided that it would do away with the earlier form of dispensing the drugs in loose, which reduces the quality of the medicine and its impact on the disease. Hence, the committee decided that while the tablets and capsules will be supplied in aluminium foils and blister packs, syrups will be supplied in 40 ml or 60 ml packs and the ointments in small five or 10 gram tubes. This was planned to avoid wastages and also to prevent the reduction in the shelf life of the drug in store.

In order to avoid pilferages, it has been stipulated that all the tablets and capsules carry the logo TG meaning Tamil Nadu government. All tablets, IV fluids and the ampules carry the message that the said drug is meant for the supplies of Tamil Nadu government and not meant for sale.

TNMSC invites tender by advertising in various dailies, pharmaceutical newspapers and in its own website. Tender document consists of cover A and cover B. The salient features of cover A are: (i) the manufacturer should have license for the product quoted and should be manufacturing the same in his own premises (loan licensees are not allowed to bid); (ii) the said company should have a minimum turnover of ₹ 35 lakhs and the manufacturer should have market standing for the drug issued for a minimum period of three years; (iii) the company should have the 'Good Manufacturing Practice' certificate issued by the state government authorities and should not have suffered any legal conviction cases. If the tender committee is satisfied with details provided in cover A, then a technical team visits the unit (without prior notice to the unit) to assert the facts stated in the tender and to assert the company's production capacity. On the basis of recommendation from the team, the samples of drugs are obtained from the unit and sent for quality checks. On the positive recommendation from the quality control department, those manufacturers who satisfy the entire criterion mentioned in cover A are invited for the opening of cover B. These manufacturers are asked to bring sufficient number of photocopies of their quoted prices and a floppy containing the prices of the products tendered by them. While photocopies are distributed to all those who are present in the tender process, the prices are simultaneously displayed on a huge screen. This method apparently helps in keeping the system transparent since every bidder gets to know the price bid by the other. Obviously the one who has quoted the lowest price (called as L1) gets the tender. But if there is more than one manufacturer whose prices are close to the L1 rates, they are asked to match the price of L1. And, the entire purchase order is distributed accordingly. Price fixed during the tender process holds good for the whole year and cannot be changed. In the whole process, there is neither price preference nor special preference for small-scale industries (SSIs). More interestingly, suppliers in the current year do not automatically become eligible to supply in the next year. They will have to go through the same procedures but for the inspection of units, which again helps in maintaining transparency.

The other interesting feature is that, once the order is placed with the selected supplier, the selected supplier should start supplying within 30 days of the contract and complete within/on 60th day. A late delivery fee of 1.5 per cent of the entire purchase order is levied if the supplies are delayed even by a day. Because of this huge levy, suppliers stick to the delivery schedule. The supplier will have to send the supplies directly to the designated warehouses. On receipt of the drugs, the drug warehouse issues a material received certificate to the TNMSC office. A certain quantity of drugs from each batch is sent for quality control (QC) to the designated laboratories located in different parts of country again selected through the tender process. This is done in spite of the fact that suppliers send their goods with QC certificate, a testimony that the products were checked before they were sent. Quality control takes about two weeks to test tablets and capsules and three weeks to test the injections. Surgical and sutures are selected based on the recommendation of experts. Drug distribution takes place only after the receipt of report from the QC. If negative reports are received on a particular product, then that product is sent for QC to another laboratory. If it fails again, then the entire batch is sent back to the supplier, who will have to supply fresh stocks. If this happens twice, then the supplier is blacklisted. From May 2003, warehouses have been advised not to send samples of the same batch for testing, if samples of a particular batch have already been sent for QC. Similarly, if the QC passes a drug of a particular batch, then other warehouses can also start distributing. TNMSC makes payment to the supplier only after the report from quality control is received. An automated cheque clearance system of payment to the suppliers further helps in maintaining the transparency of the system. These details show that detailed procedures have been set to purchase only quality drugs.

Impact of TNMSC's Intervention on Prices

The above mentioned procedures should also help the government in keeping the medicinal budget within the prescribed limits which depends on the prices of the drugs purchased. In order to understand the price impact of TNMSC's intervention, the following methodology has been adopted. In the first step, percentage changes in the prices of individual drugs were calculated in different points of time according to the availability of L1 prices 2002–03 to 2006–07. In the second step, these were grouped according to the major drug category as presented in the TNMSC's list of essential drugs. In the third and final step, the percentage change of the individual drugs were added to arrive at the cumulative percentage change of that category which was further divided by the number of drugs in that particular drug category. Table 9.2 provides this information.

Table 9.2

Percentage Change in the Prices of Drugs Procured by TNMSC (2002–03 to 2006–07)

	Drug Category	*% Change*	*% group*
1.	Anaesthetics	–23.74	3
2.	Analgesics, Antipyretics and Anti-inflammatory Drugs	–7.98	1
3.	Anti-Allergics and Drugs Used in Anaphylaxis	–11.44	2
4.	Anti-dotes and Other Substances Used in Poisoning	–14.76	2
5.	Anti-epileptic Drugs	–18.46	2
6.	Anti-infective Drugs	–51.40	6
6.3	Anti-bacterials	–23.40	3
7.	Anti-neoplastic and Immunosuppressant Drugs	–33.47	4
8.	Anti-Parkinsonism Drugs	–22.98	3
9.	Drugs Affecting the Blood	20.05	3
10.	Cardio-vascular Drugs	–22.18	3
11.	Dermatological Drugs	–7.72	1
12.	Reagents and Diagnostic Agents	–29.15	3
13.	Disinfectants and Antiseptics	18.07	2
14.	Diuretics	–16.45	2
15.	Gastro-intestinal Drugs	–7.18	1
16.	Hormones, Other Endocrine Drugs	–29.91	3
17.	Immunologicals	–16.95	2
18.	Muscle Relaxants and Cholinestrase Inhibitors	–4.12	1
19.	Opthalmological Preparations	–35.27	4
20.	Oxytocics	–20.24	2
21.	Psychothropic Drugs	–10.05	2
22.	Drugs Acting on the Respiratory Tract	4.14	1
23.	Solutions, Correcting Water, Electrolyte and Acid Base Disturbances	–21.65	2
24.	Vitamins and Minerals	–1.29	1
25.	Miscellaneous Drugs	–29.49	3

Source: Lalitha (2006), Access to Medicines in Tamil Nadu (a report submitted to the Indian Council of Social Science Research, New Delhi).

As evident from the table, while the TNMSCs intervention has resulted in overall reduction in the prices of several drugs over the period 2002–03 to 2007, there were three drug categories which had witnessed positive price increase. These are drugs affecting the blood (20.05%), disinfectants and antiseptics by 18.07 per cent and the relatively least increase was in drugs acting on the respiratory tract system where the price increase was to the extent of 4.14 per cent. Basically, the price reduction has been in the range of 1 per cent to more than 50 per cent. In the first group, where the reduction in the price has been within the range of 1–10 per cent, we have analgesics, anti-pyretics and anti-inflammatory drugs, dermatological drugs, gastro-intestinal drugs, muscle relaxants, drugs acting on the respiratory tract. In the second and third group where the price reduction has been in the range of 10–20 and 20–30 per cent respectively, we have eight drug groups each. These are: anti-allergic and drugs used in anaphylaxis, antidotes, anti-epileptic drugs, disinfectants and antiseptics, diuretics, immunologicals, oxytocics, psychothropic drugs, solutions, correcting water, electrolyte and acid base disturbances.

In the third 20–30 category, we have anaesthetics, anti-bacterials, anti-parkinsonism drugs affecting the blood, cardiovascular drugs, reagents and diagnostic agents, hormones, other endocrine drugs and miscellaneous drugs (comprising of items like water for injection, sodium bicarbonate, ECG Gel, ultra sonagram gel, etc.). In the fourth category, where the price reduction has taken place in the range of 30–40 per cent, we have anti-neo plastic and immune suppressant drugs and opthalmological preparations.

Anti-infective drugs fall in the category where the highest price reduction has been observed between 2002–03 and 2006–07. Anti-infective comprises of anthelminthics, anti-filarials, anti-bacterials, anti-fungal, anti-malarial and anti-viral drugs. Thus, we find that TNMSCs has been consistently procuring some of the very important and commonly used life saving drugs at a lower price.

The Scenario at Primary Health Centres

Here discussion is on the drug procurement and distribution procedures followed by the eight PHCs in Pollachi taluka of Coimbatore and Thiruppathur taluka of Sivaganga districts. At the PHCs we used a structured questionnaire to collect relevant information on the availability of medicines from the doctors and pharmacists. We also conducted an exit survey among patients to get their views on the availability of medicines and doctors, quality of medicines, services, etc. In all, 80 patients were interviewed in different PHCs.

Table 9.3

Budget Allocation to Directorate of Public Health (DPH) for Drugs and Other Special Schemes

(₹ in crores)

Year	*DPH*	*DPH Special Schemes*
1995–96	10.02	0.06
1996–97	10.02	3.37
1997–98	10.02	4.26
1998–99	10.82	6.03
1999–2000	10.82	7.34
2000–01	9.82	11.8
2001–02	9.82	8.21
2002–03	10.31	10.72

Source: DPH, Chennai.

Budgets for PHCs

The total medical and surgical budget allocated to the PHCs and the budget allocated under special schemes and other allotments are provided in Table 9.3. Budget allotment to the PHCs usually follows the State Budget. This budget allotment is made on the outpatient strength of the PHC and the morbidity pattern observed in that PHC (Table 9.4). It is observed from the table that till 2002–03, PHCs with the outpatient strength that ranged from 30–90 were in the same budget band of ₹ 30,000. These PHCs reported that if they do not get additional allotment or drugs from special schemes, there will be shortages of these drugs.

Table 9.4

Outpatient Slab Determination for Drug Budget for DPH

Outpatient strength	*Amount allotted to each PHCs (in ₹)*
Less than 50	30,000
50–75	42,000
75–100	63,000
100–150	1,00,000
150–200	1,20,000
200–250	1,40,000
More than 250	2,00,000

Source: DPH, Chennai.

Table 9.5

Drug Budget for the PHCs

(amount in ₹)

PHC/ Year	*Average outpatient strength*	*2000–01*	*2001–02*	*2002–03*	*2003–04*	*average cost of medicine*
PHC 1	80/100	90000	90000	63000	63000	2.5
PHC 2	100	90000	75000	63000	63000	2
PHC 3	60/70	30000	30000	30000	30000	2.5–3.5
PHC 4	70/90	30000	30000	30000	42000	2.50–3
PHC 5	30/40	30000	30000	30000	30000	2.5
PHC 6	100/140	65000	65000	65000	100000	>5
PHC 7	50/60	30000	30000	30000	30000	>2
PHC 8	80/85	30000	30000	30000	42000	>2

Source: Field survey.

The amount allotted to each PHC and the withdrawals against it are reported in Table 9.5. We observed that after 2002–03, most of the PHCs have either overshot the budget allotted to them or just exhausted their quota. Both pharmacists at the warehouse and the PHCs reported that the unutilised part is not carried over to the next year; it is often reflected in the form of reduced allocation. PHCs pointed out that reduction in the following year's budget would definitely follow if they have not utilised their entire quota in the current year, however, increased demand for allocation is provided only after the outpatient flow for at least two consecutive years.

Drug Procurement for the PHCs

The PHCs can draw 54 drugs out of the TNMSC's essential drugs list without the approval of the Deputy Director, Health Services (DDHS). These drugs are distinguished with a star in the TNMSC drug list of 2000–01. Once the allotment is decided by the Directorate of Public Health (DPH) and communicated to the TNMSC, the latter sends two copies of the passbooks (with the budget noted on the front page) to the warehouses where one is retained and the other is given to the PHC. The warehouse marks the dates on which the PHCs collected their stocks in both passbooks. Usually, the main PHCs and the additional PHCs collect the medicines once in three months on the same date. This arrangement has been made since additional PHCs do not have a vehicle of their own and have to depend on the main PHC vehicle to lift their stock.

Table 9.6

Pass Book Utilisation Statement of PHCs

(amount in ₹)

PHC	*2001–02*		*2002–03*	
	Total allotment	*Availed by PHC*	*Total allotment*	*Availed by PHC*
PHC1	64200	64198	63000	62997
PHC 2	80250	74999	63000	63000
PHC 3	32100	30000	30000	29999
PHC4	32100	29998	30000	30000
PHC 5	32100	29999	30000	30000
PHC6	79200	79184	70320	70141
PHC 7	47100	46091	37320	37137
PHC 8	47100	47079	38540	38536

Source: Drug warehouses at Coimbatore and Sivaganga.

The price of each drug is added to arrive at the total expenditure and this is subtracted from the opening balance/budget of the PHC and the balance is indicated in both the passbooks. So, after each withdrawal, the institution knows its remaining balance. Normally, by the end of the year most of the PHCs had drawn their entire allotment (Table 9.6).

Drug Distribution at the PHCs

Almost all the pharmacists observed that paracetamol tablets and syrups, cough syrups, anti-allergic, antibiotic, and vitamin tablets are the fast moving medicines at the PHCs. Though the pharmacist and the ANM explained the dosage as well as the method of taking drugs, we observed that the different tablets create some confusion in older patients who repeatedly checked the dosages with the pharmacist or the ANM. But we also saw some of the illiterate patients clearly distinguish paracetamol from vitamins and demanded vitamins, even if the doctor had not prescribed the same. Distinguishing the medicines has become possible now for the illiterate patients because of the different colours that are used in the aluminium foil packs, unlike the old system where the medicines were distributed in loose packings and patients could not distinguish between two white tablets.

For cold and fever, the pharmacists dispensed medicines for two days and for hypertension or diabetes medicines were given for a week or till the patient's next visit. The dispensing pattern of tablets, syrups, and ointments in the different PHCs is given in Table 9.7.

Table 9.7

Dispensing Pattern of Medicine in PHCs

PHC	*Tablets*		*Syrup*		*Ointment*	
	Original	*Loose*	*Original*	*Loose*	*Original*	*Loose*
PHC 1	√		√*	√$		√
PHC 2	√		√			√
PHC 3	√			√		√
PHC 4	√		√@			√
PHC 5	√		√			√
PHC 6	√		√		√#	√
PHC 7	√		√			√
PHC 8	√		√			√

*only for three years and above, $ for patients below three years, @ dispensed in loose if it is in short supply, # dispensed in loose if treatment is of shorter duration.

Source: Field survey.

It has been observed that good quality medicines were being dispensed at the PHCs. The tablets and capsules were dispensed in their original blister packs. All the medicines carried the logo TG (meaning Tamil Nadu government) written either in Tamil or in English. We observed that medicines dispensed were fresh and not nearing the end of their shelf life. In all the PHCs, in the pharmacists' and the medical officers' rooms we saw a chart with names of different medicines and their shelf life status. The chart is displayed to remind and guide both the pharmacist and the medical officer to choose the medicine in a way which would prevent their wastage. In some PHCs, doctors and pharmacists who had been serving the PHCs for a long time observed that before the TNMSC came into existence, PHCs used to be dumped with medicines that all looked alike and many of them used to arrive closer to the end of their shelf life.

Although they were not involved in the selection of drugs meant for the PHCs, the doctors observed that the list of medicines meant for PHCs covered all the needs of the PHC. A couple of young doctors thought that a few higher order new antibiotics which would work more quickly could be added to the list, while the older doctors observed that the list consists of safe, essential drugs. Pharmacists of PHCs where the budget allotment was reduced in the last few years or has not been increased for a couple of years however believed that if they did not get the additional allotment from the Directorate of Public Health Services, they would definitely have a shortage of drugs. They also said that this additional allotment takes place around March or April. By then, if they have shortages, they do resort to drug transfer from nearby PHCs.

Patients' Views

It was found that patients literate and illiterate, rich and poor availed PHCs' services. In Anaimalai block, most of the patients had reported that they worked as labourers in the farms and agricultural fields. In Thiruppathur block some of the patients worked as casual labourers, drivers, or engaged in petty trade. Importantly, it was observed that patients, especially women, tended to pay attention to their illness and did not dismiss them. It was also observed that school children, both boys and girls, came with a friend (who served as an escort) on the advise of their teachers for ailments such as minor skin problems or fever to the PHCs.

Interestingly, it was noted that many of the patients with whom we spoke were regular users of the PHC and were able to distinguish the quality of the medicines provided by the PHCs 'then and now'. They said that they do not buy medicines from the pharmacies any more because they get similar products, including syrups, from the PHC. Earlier, they used to be appalled by the medicines that all looked alike and were reduced to powder in their hands. They sometimes threw away the medicine right inside the PHC premises. However, now they get good medicines and relief from their ailments in one or two days. They recommended the PHC to their neighbours.

The patients stated that the doctors no longer ask them to buy medicines from non-government pharmacies. They were always referred to the nearest General Hospital when needed. Almost all the patients noted that the doctors were available in the PHCs when they visited the PHC and attended to them. They also added that not even once did they have to return without seeing the doctor or getting medicines. It was found that they were vocal in voicing their opinion. It was learnt from most of the PHCs that if they are dissatisfied, patients did not hesitate to complain to the District Collector or the DDHS or the Joint Director or whosoever visited their area. Some people, who had visited the PHC in this study for the first time because of sudden illness, pointed out that even in their hometown they go to the PHC and get 'good medicines'. It was checked with the patients whether they came back to the PHC in case they were not cured within two days, and they affirmed that they did come back to continue the medicine for a couple of more days. Pregnant women and patients suffering from hypertension said that they get medicines for a week or 10 days and do not discontinue their tablets, because, they feel good after taking the medicine.

Table 9.8

Drug and Health Expenditure of States in 2001–02

(₹ in lakhs)

States	*Drugs*	*Material supplies*	*Total*	*Health expenditure (rev)*	*Drug exp% of health exp*
Punjab	N.A.	916.32	916.32 (16)	61826.45 (12)	1.48 (16)
Assam	0	1530.1	1530.1 (15)	32690.82 (14)	4.68 (12)
Odisha	1768.98	361.3	2130.28 (14)	42135.78 (13)	5.06 (11)
Bihar	1996.9	206.29	2203.19 (13)	71348.49 (10)	3.09 (15)
Chhattisgarh	1822.47	680.22	2502.69 (12)	22587.1 (16)	11.08 (5)
Gujarat	1253.76	1440.06	2693.82 (11)	71547.95 (9)	3.77 (14)
Haryana	N.A.	3096.12	3096.12 (10)	31470.98 (15)	9.84 (6)
West Bengal	5005.25	793.23	5798.48 (9)	131948.35 (3)	4.39 (13)
Uttar Pradesh	5938.25	1166.04	7104.29 (8)	135578.81 (2)	5.24 (10)
Karnataka	6927.17	856.82	7783.99 (7)	98633.19 (6)	7.89 (9)
Madhya Pradesh	3965.86	3956.04	7921.9 (6)	66689.3 (11)	11.88 (3)
Rajasthan	3952.8	5092.25	9045.05 (5)	97311.61 (7)	9.29 (8)
Kerala	N.A.	12420.68	12420.68 (4)	72931.59 (8)	17.03 (1)
Andhra Pradesh	7923.09	4781.45	12704.54 (3)	131424.08 (4)	9.67 (7)
Tamil Nadu	16428.68	1668.57	18097.25 (2)	118432.85 (5)	15.28 (2)
Maharashtra	10	20295.91	20305.91 (1)	178379.51 (1)	11.38 (4)
Central Govt *		72649.23	72649.23	597700	12.15
All India*	56993.21	131910.63	188903.84	1962636.86	9.63

*Includes only 16 states total reported in the table, which account for around 85 per cent. Figures in parentheses indicate the ranks.

Source: National Commission on Macroeconomics and Health, Financing and Delivery of Health Care Services in India, p. 189.

It would have been ideal to compare the Tamil Nadu's expenditure on drugs with that of a state which has not adopted a rational drug list, but the required data are not available. So, in the absence of such data, we have compared the health expenditure and the average medical expenditure per treated ailment for various states for the year 2001–02 (Table 9.8). Here, the medical expenditure includes expenditure on items such as medicines and other supplies. These data show that Tamil Nadu which ranks fifth in terms of health expenditure when compared with other major states, ranks second in terms of the drug expenditure which may be attributed to the reforms introduced in the drug delivery system of Tamil Nadu.

Replicability of TNMSC Model

The reform measures introduced by Tamil Nadu through the TNMSC are localised. If such advantages have to spread widely, other state governments should adopt similar systems. An important contributor to the success of this model is the adoption of the rational drug list. The list identifies important drugs that have to be bought so that a sizeable percentage of wastage of expenditure is controlled at this point. Shiva and Rane (2004) list that there are medical, economical, social and administrative advantages of adopting an essential drug list. The medical advantages are that; besides ensuring efficacy and safety of drugs, such a list reduces the risks of drugs and doctor induced (latrogenisis) problems. It also improves the possibility of better monitoring. The economic advantages are that it reduces wastage of scarce resources on non-essential drugs and reduces the need for aggressive marketing of non-essential formulations. It is most economical for patients as it reduces the costs. The social advantages of essential drugs are: it represents the real health needs of the people; it makes it compulsory to draw up 'priorities' to meet the urgent needs of the people. The administrative advantages are that since the list is of a fixed number of drugs, it is easy to maintain the quality and also easy to streamline production, distribution and storage. Phadke (1994) observes that the use of irrational drug use is less in public sector because of the use of essential drug lists and the doctors serving in the public sector have to prescribe only from this list. Though there could be irrational prescriptions in the public sector, yet he states that the use of irrational drug combinations and use of hazardous drugs is less in public clinics as evident in the Table 9.9.

Further, in the case of Tamil Nadu the freedom given to the institutions to purchase is limited to 10 per cent; centralised purchase covers 90 per cent of the budget, which again restricts pilferage. In other states where a state formulary exists, shortages are often the case since the percentage of procurement with the institution is high, varying from 50 to 90 per cent, allowing wastages, pilferage, and favouritism leading to corruption. Critics may argue that such a centralised purchase could also lead to pilferage. However, as long as the procedures and guidelines remain transparent, the system would be effective. It should also be noted that after the TNMSC started its operations, technology available in public hospitals have also started improving. While it would be extremely difficult to extend the rational drug approach to the private sector, any government with the political will and commitment can implement this model in its public utilities and also in the government funded/aided voluntary organisations.

Table 9.9

Comparison of Prescriptions in Private and Public Clinics

% of prescriptions containing one or more	*Public clinic %*	*Private clinic %*	*Average*
Irrational Drug combination	9.6	30.9	20.3
Hazardous drug	7.4	14.6	11.1
Unnecessary drug	46.3	56.7	51.0
Unncessary injection	24.6	25.5	25.7
Number of prescription studies	1814	1688	3502

Source: Phadke (1994).

Overall the system can be made operational in other states as well provided there is strong political and bureaucratic commitment to make the system work is present. It requires meticulous planning by both technocrats and bureaucrats. This planning team must have an impact on politicians because they will have to translate these planning into policies and further into effective implementation. While this model is definitely replicable, scaling up of the operations to extend this system to NGOs can be thought of. Taking it to the private sector will be a herculean effort since there will be tremendous opposition from the pharmaceutical industry. Given the fact that there are several NGOs playing significant role in the health sector, TNMSC's efforts can be extended to them also. In conclusion, a system like TNMSC would lead to further positive health outcomes when it functions in association with health care institutions, which are well provided with skilled human resources and adequate physical infrastructure. To actually transform the availability of medicines in the government health care system into positive health outcomes depends on further reforms. These reforms would ensure that India attains the millennium development goals of combating the infectious diseases, reducing child mortality and improving maternal health.

References

Dreze, Jean and Amartya Sen (1995). *India Economic Development and Social Opportunity*, Delhi: Oxford University Press.

Government of India (2005). Report of the National Commission on Macro Economics and Health, Ministry of Health and Family Welfare, New Delhi.

Lalitha, N. (2006). 'Access to Medicines in Government Healthcare: A Case Study of Tamil Nadu', submitted to the Indian Council of Social Science Research, New Delhi, November.

Misra, Rajiv, Rachel Chatterjee and Sujatha Rao (2003). *India Health Report*, New Delhi: Oxford University Press.

National Health Accounts India 2001–02, National Health Accounts Cell, Ministry of Health and Family Welfare, Government of India.

Phadke, Anant (1994). 'The Private Medical Sector in India, Foundation For Research', *Community Health*, April, Table 4, p. 25.

Shiva, Mira and Wishvas Rane (2004). 'Banned and Bannable Drugs: Unbiased Drug Information-Essential Drugs and Rational Drug Policy', New Delhi: Voluntary Health Association of India.

World Bank (2001). *India-Raising the Sights: Better Health Systems for India's Poor*, Washington D.C.

10

Scenario of Education and Health Attainments in Krishna Basin Area in Andhra Pradesh

P. PADMANABHA RAO

Man is dependent on socio-economic and infrastructure resources and one has to provide facilities for harnessing the resources to achieve development in multiple sectors. It is understood that man depends not only on economic resources but is also dependent on government help in various walks of life. It is argued that development initially leads to widening of the inter regional inequality in an economy. The gap between the developed and under developed regions tends to narrow down only in the later stages of development. Conversely, as long as the economy remains stagnant or manages to grow at very slow pace, the regional inequality is found to be at its lowest ebb.

The concept of poverty is multidimensional. It covers not only levels of income and consumption, but also of health and education. UNDP's annual Human Development Reports (HDRs) have popularised several indices relating to human development, gender development, capability, poverty and human poverty. Basically, all these indices emphasise more on non-income factors such as health, education, nutrition, and basic services.

Andhra Pradesh has done well in reducing income poverty ratio. It was only 15.8 per cent as compared to all-India poverty ratios of 26 per cent in 1999–2000. Andhra Pradesh's rank in terms of the Human Development Index (HDI) is 10. The literacy rate in Andhra Pradesh increased from 34 per cent in 1981 to 61 per cent in 2001. Andhra Pradesh ranked 22nd in terms of overall literacy and 29th in literacy for Scheduled Castes (SCs) and Scheduled Tribes (STs). Andhra Pradesh's literacy rate of 61 per cent is lower than only that of Bihar and Odisha. Even the literacy rates of Rajasthan and Madhya Pradesh are higher than that of Andhra Pradesh.

Social, economic and infrastructural resources are considered as sources to generate development particularly spatial development or sectoral development. These three resources should be utilised to a maximum possible extent to derive profits in the form of development over a period of time. Time and objective are the two important effects to achieve the targeted growth and development. Among the factors, population growth is a predetermining factor for the achievement of social and economic development. Agriculture, industry, education and infrastructural factors will contribute to development at the state/nation level.

Improvement in literacy is important for empowering women. Rural female literacy increased from 14 per cent in 1981 to 35 per cent in 1991. In other words, around 65 per cent of rural women were illiterate. The literacy rates for SCs and STs show that only 16 per cent of the SC women and 7 per cent of tribal women in rural areas were literate in 1991. The infant mortality rate (IMR) is an important health indicator. The level of IMR is lower where as compared to the all-India average. However, the IMR has not declined much in rural areas in the 1990s. During the 1980s, the IMR declined from 93 to 73 per thousand in rural Andhra Pradesh. However, in the 1990s it declined from 73 to 70 only. Child labour is another major human development problem. The region has the highest incidence of child labour whereas Kerala has the lowest incidence in the country. In the age group 10–14, around 34 per cent of the children are working and the malnutrition among children is around 50 per cent in the region, this is much higher than those for Tamil Nadu and Kerala.

According to the sixth All-India Education Survey, 1997, around 34 per cent of the primary schools in Andhra Pradesh had only one teacher and another 43 per cent of schools had only two teachers. Some estimates show that Andhra Pradesh has to spend 3.32 per cent of the State Domestic Product (SDP) every year for five years for universal schooling of children in the age group 6–11. In other words, Andhra Pradesh has to make additional resource requirements of 2.4 per cent of the SDP for basic education.

The above record shows that it has a long way to go to improve its human development. It examines the status of education and health, indicators relating to health status of women and an analysis of human development indices across the districts and regions.

This paper focuses on education and health attainments in Krishna basin area in Andhra Pradesh and trends in inter-regional disparities in Andhra Pradesh, particularly in Krishna basin.

Objectives of the Study

The overall objective of the study was to examine the levels of development in the Krishna basin and its dependent/service area (command area). The study had the following specific objectives: to examine the literacy levels and education attainment in the basin area; to examine the problems of health and health facilities in the study area; and to examine the levels of human development and human poverty.

Methodology

Data Collection

The methodology used in this study was mainly employed by the UNDP in its HDRs. It would be good to use multiple indicators for example, the use of female literacy in the backward districts, or the use of gender differentials in literacy to see if these are reducing over time.

This is prepared by using the data from the 1991 and 2001 census, data from Bureau of Economics and Statistics, Government of Andhra Pradesh, for the years 1993–94 and 2003–04, Central Statistical Organisation (CSO), National Sample Survey (NSS), National Council of Applied Economic Research (NCAER), National Family Health Survey (NFHS), etc. The State Government has in recent times, constituted a number of Taskforces and Commissions to suggest new policy directions in various sectors. We want to utilise these reports of the Committee for Regional Imbalance and the reports of the Task forces on education and health, the sector report on Education, the state's Fiscal Plan, etc. Existing secondary data sources and research reports and outputs will also be used wherever relevant. The study is based mainly on secondary data taking mandal as the unit of study.

The study was carried out in the river basin and command area/service area in the districts of Krishna, Guntur, Prakasam, Chittoor, Anantpur, Kurnool, Kadapa, Mahabubnagar, Nalgonda, Rangareddy, Medak, and Khammam districts. The state's performance in the Krishna basin area in human and regional development was measured in those priority areas that affect most the living conditions of the poor and the vulnerable: education and literacy, nutrition and health care, and livelihoods.

Study Area: Krishna Basin

The Krishna basin lies between Latitude 13° 7′ 0′′ N and 19° 20′ 0′′ N and Longitudes 73° 22′ 0′′ E and 81° 10′ 0′′ E. It is roughly triangular in shape with its base along the Western Ghats and apex at Vijayawada. The basin extends over an area of 99,980 sq miles (2,58,948 sq kms), which is nearly 8 per cent of the total geographical area of the country. It is bounded on the north by the range separating it from the Godavari basin, on the south east by the Eastern Ghats and on the west by the Western Ghats. The basin lies in the states of Karnataka, Andhra Pradesh and Maharashtra.

The Krishna river basin covers part of three states, viz., Maharashtra, Karnataka and Andhra Pradesh. The Krishna river basin is the fifth largest river system in India in terms of annual discharge and drainage area. The river originates in the Western Ghats at an elevation of about 1,337 metres just north of Mahabaleswar, 64 km from the Arabian Sea as the upper Krishna river in the Western Ghats of Maharashtra and Karnataka, and flows about 1,400 kms and drains the Deccan Plateau, and outfalls into the Bay of Bengal. The principal tributaries joining Krishna are the Ghataprabha, the Malaprabha, the Bhima, the Thungabhadra, and the Musi. The lower Krishna basin contains the sub-basins of the lower Krishna, Musi, Palleru, and Muneru rivers as well as the Krishna delta and a poorly delineated area in the east of the delta – the Kolleru Wetland.

Most of the lower basin (98.5%) belongs to Andhra Pradesh, with the remaining area lying in two districts of Karnataka. The lower Krishna Basin has an area of 80,742 sq kms and is the most densely populated part of the Krishna Basin (447 persons per sq km). In 2006, the lower basin accommodated 36.1 million inhabitants, that is, 48 per cent of the total basin population on an area representing just 30 per cent of the whole basin. The population is mainly rural (65%) and half the urban population is concentrated in Hyderabad (7.9 million inhabitants). The main stem of the Krishna river has two major tributaries, the Bhima river from the north and the Tungabhadra river from the south (Figure 10.1).

Figure 10.1

Krishna Basin, Andhra Pradesh

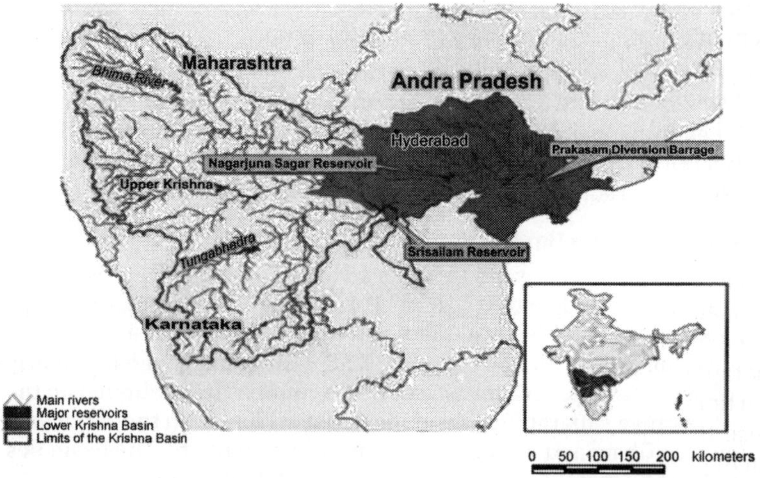

The interior of the basin is a plateau, divided into series of the villages sloping generally towards the east belt of country adjoining the western ghats in the upper Krishna, the upper Bhima, the Ghataprabha, the Malaprabha and the Tungabhadra sub-basins consist of undulating plains and broad flat valleys, interspersed by isolated and quartz rocky outcrops of hills. On the eastern side, lie the lower Krishna, the Musi, the Paleru and the Munneru sub basins comprising the coastal plains, the Eastern Ghats and series of valleys, partly covered by hills and dense forests.

The Telangana region covers the districts of Khammam (27 mandals), Mahabubnagar (64 mandals), Medak (9 mandals), Nalgonda (60 mandals), Rangareddy (36 mandals) and Warangal (33 mandals) (Figure 10.2). It is noted that 55 mandals (15.5%) of the Rayalaseema Region, 71 mandals (20%) of the Coastal Andhra Region and 229 mandals (64.5%) of the Telangana region are the regional components which helps to generate growth and development of the regions by the river water forming and termed as Krishna Basin or Basin area.

Socio-economic Conditions of the People

Overwhelmingly (81% of the sample), the population in the region belongs to the weaker sections of society, i.e., the Scheduled Castes (14%) and Backward Castes (67%). As in other regions of the country, the SCS are concentrated among the small and marginal farmers (66%) and landless labourers (20%). Backward castes are found in all classes but are the most predominant among those involved in non-agricultural occupations (84%). Among the other castes Reddys are predominant. People of other castes are more concentrated in the upper classes. They account for 42 per cent of the big farmers but only 5 per cent of the agricultural labourers. Of the total number of households, 17 per cent were those of big farmers, 16 per cent of middle farmers, 36 per cent of small and marginal farmers, and 17 per cent of agricultural labourers.

The soils of the river bank are very fertile and mostly black or red in colour. Farmers have been cultivating them for generations, if not centuries, growing a multiple variety of crops ranging from food crops like rice, jowar and other millets to cash crops like tobacco, chilli, groundnut, vegetables, onions, mustard, and wheat. The river bed was also cultivated in the dry season, especially by the weaker sections, harvesting a rich crop of water melons.

In addition to agriculture, small and marginal farmers are also involved in several subsidiary occupations such as sheep and goat rearing, toddy tapping, weaving, fishing and plying dinghies across the river. The proportion of agricultural labourers is comparatively low in these villages, because the poorer sections of the population are engaged in the cultivation of poromboke and waste lands.

Agriculture and Population

The basin is home to approximately 74.2 million people. The population density is high with 287 per sq kms with concentration of the population in the irrigated areas and metropolitan urban centres (e.g., Hyderabad has seven million people). About 68 per cent of the population live in rural areas and are dependent on agriculture for their livelihood. Basin closure has also resulted in interstate conflict, as three states share the shrinking water resources.

People living in the enroute command area are mostly dependent on agriculture and extending irrigation facilities to an extent of 1.68 lakh ha. will not only increase agricultural production but also create all-round prosperity.

Out of the total workforce, 48 per cent are agricultural labourers, 25 per cent are cultivators, 3 per cent are workers of household industry, 5 per cent are marginal workers and 19 per cent are other workers. Similarly, the people living in the districts situated further south, which will be benefited by the diverted water, are mainly dependent upon agriculture.

More than 70 per cent of the population in the command area is dependent on agriculture. The literacy rate is less than 50 per cent. More than 75 per cent of the agricultural land holdings are small. The growth of population was the strength and wealth of a nation as it was an underlying factor for technological development; however it was also a contributing factor to poverty and an impediment to development. After Independence, debates related to population growth and its consequences were encouraged among both academicians and planners, leading to policy measures to curtail the growth of population. Even though the growth of population in south India was much lower than that of the overall country, nevertheless within south India, Andhra Pradesh witnessed relatively higher growth rate for a long period.

Density of Population

The density of population is 275 per sq kms. Proportion of urban population to the total population is 27.08 per cent which is almost equal to the national average. The average rural population density of the state was about 175 persons per sq kms. Highest population densities are reported from the agriculturally well-developed coastal plains. This has 9 per cent of the area but houses 18 per cent of the rural and 21 per cent of the urban population. With excellent aquifers in this region, water shortage is not a major issue but these areas have problems of saline aquifers which necessitates long distance conveyance of water to some of the coastal communities. This region is one of the most irrigated regions of the state.

Figure 10.2

Population density map of the Lower Krishna Basin

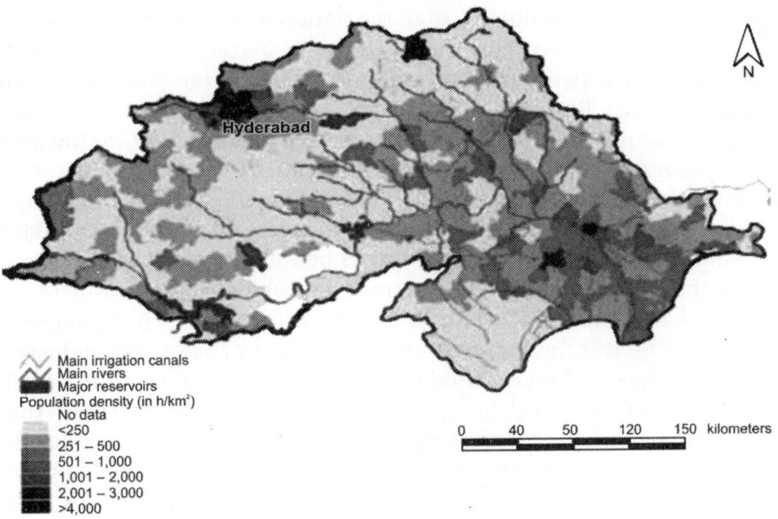

The lowest population densities are reported from forest tracts and hilly regions located mostly in the north eastern part of the state. The tribal settlements are generally dispersed and often found in hamlets. Since most of these regions are less accessible due to terrain conditions, transportation of rigs is a major problem. Groundwater availability is restricted to very few aquifers due to terrain conditions in these regions. A large proportion of the numerous streams in these regions have water during most part of the year and they are one of the common sources of domestic water. Water from these streams is often polluted due to utilisation by settlements en route and free use by animals, especially during the lean seasons. Perennial springs are another important source of water, especially in laterite-capped hill regions. Spring sources are tapped directly and usage at the spring itself often pollutes the sources.

Social Sector Development

Regional variations exist in Human Development Index (HDI) and also in sectors like education and health. While inequality is narrowing down in literacy and primary education, it is not so in the case of infant mortality (Dev, 2007). There has not been any substantial change in the ranking of districts in HDI during 1980s. A shift in the approach in the provision of health facilities to the poor, social mobilisation and empowerment programmes along with higher public investment in underdeveloped areas would improve the overall human development.

Andhra Pradesh is educationally backward with fourth lowest position in literacy among the 16 major states. Though the state showed higher performance in literacy than the national average in the 1990s, its rank has not improved since then because of better performance of the educationally backward states rather than the developed ones. South Coastal Andhra Pradesh occupies top position and North Telangana occupies bottom position in literacy. Among the districts in the state, Mahabubnagar occupies bottom position with 44 mandals falling in the category of very low literacy and the remaining 20 mandals falling in the category of low literacy mandals. Emphasis on female literacy should focus on weaker sections like Scheduled Tribes because gender gap is very high among them. Illiteracy is more serious a problem if all members in a household are illiterates than in household where at least one member in the family is literate. In Andhra Pradesh, more than 75 per cent of the rural households have no literate adult member. Regional variations in dropout rate exist at primary level, but they disappear at upper primary level. The Telangana region have higher dropout rate at primary level than the other three regions. Child labour results in dropout of boys at upper primary stage. However, it is not clear whether child labour is the cause or consequence of dropout at upper primary stage.

Low age at marriage and the consequent adolescent child bearing are the major problems in Andhra Pradesh. Such incidences are the lowest in South Telangana. The Reproductive Child Health programme (RCH) is more successful in South Coastal Andhra Pradesh. In the remaining regions less than one-half of the pregnant women could avail the services. The proportion of hospital deliveries was highest in South Coastal Andhra Pradesh and South Telangana regions. Development of private medical facilities in the former and proximity of the latter to Hyderabad seem to be responsible for this better performance. Andhra Pradesh is one of the four states with high prevalence of HIV infection in the country. Despite this grave situation, awareness is low except in South Coastal Andhra Pradesh and South Telangana regions. Further, the incidence of reproductive tract infection and sexually transmitted infection is higher in South Telangana (more than 20%).

Literacy

One of the most important characteristics of population is literacy, which is a prerequisite for the overall development of the country, both socially and economically. The literacy rate for Andhra Pradesh works out to 61.11 per cent in 2001 as against 44.09 per cent in 1991. The corresponding all India figures are 65.38 for 2001 and 52.21 in 1991. Among the males the literacy rate is around 70.85 as against 51.17 among females. When looking at the literacy rates in the urban areas the literacy rate among urban males is 83.21 as against 69.34 among urban females. What needs to be observed is that the literacy rate of Andhra Pradesh is lower than the all India literacy rate and the difference in the literacy rate in the rural and the urban between the male and female is very wide.

Levels and Trends in Literacy Rates

The literacy rate is generally considered to be one of the important indicators of development and the educational level of the population is an important determinant of the quality of life. Universal school education with special emphasis on the education of women is crucial for improving educational levels and also health practices in the community.

Table 10.1

Literacy in Andhra Pradesh and All-India

Year	*Andhra Pradesh*			*All-India*		
	Person	*Male*	*Female*	*Person*	*Male*	*Female*
1961	21	30	12	28	40	15
1971	25	33	16	34	46	22
1981	30	39	20	44	56	30
1991	44	55	33	52	64	39
2001	61	71	51	65	76	54

Source: Census of India.

The literacy rate (among population of age seven years and above) in Andhra Pradesh has always been lower than the all-India average. While the literacy rate in Andhra Pradesh was about three-fourths of the all-India rate in 1961, the state has made substantial progress in subsequent years, especially in the last two decades. However, the 2001 Census does not show a happy picture. Andhra Pradesh is among the three least literate states in the country (Table 10.1). While the overall literacy rate has gone up from 44 per cent in 1991 to 61 per cent in 2001, the male literacy rate has increased from 55 to 71 per cent. What is encouraging is that the female literacy rate has gone up by about 50 per cent, i.e., from 33 per cent in 1991 to 51 per cent in 2001. The ratio of male literacy to female literacy has come down after 1981, revealing the narrowing of gender inequality in literacy in the State.

The increase in literacy in Andhra Pradesh lagged substantially behind all-India during 1961 to 1981. During this period, the increase in male literacy in Andhra Pradesh was about 30 per cent as compared to about 40 per cent in India and the increase in female literacy was about 66.6 per cent in Andhra Pradesh as compared to about 100 per cent in India. However, if at the pattern over the longer period from 1961 to 2001, the picture is quite different and male and female literacy rates increased by about 80 per cent and 150 per cent respectively in Andhra Pradesh as compared to about 36 per cent and 80 per cent in India.

Gender equality in literacy (measured in terms of the ratio of female literacy rate to male literacy rate) increases as the female literacy rate goes up. It may be noted that gender equality in literacy increased with increase in female literacy rate across all the regions. The district-wise figures on gender equality in literacy shows that it was quite impressive (greater than 75) in West Godavari, Krishna, Nellore, and Guntur districts. However, it was lowest in Mahabubnagar (56.4) and was around 60 in Kurnool, Medak, Anantpur districts. These were the districts where the FLR was less than 30 in a large number of mandals. In fact there are 124 Mandals with FLR below 30 in the state and these Mandals should be given special attention to improve the overall level of literacy in the State. Further, it may be noted that Mahabubnagar district alone accounts for about 5per cent of the SC population and about 5.5 per cent of the ST population in the state. We also note that the percentage of children in the age group 0–6 years decreases with increase in the female literacy rate across all regions.

Across districts, the adult literacy rate was less than 50 in a majority of the districts (12 out of 23). Thus, the majority of the adults in these 12 districts are non-literate. The illiteracy rate was as high as 62.6 in Mahabubnagar, around 56 in Medak and slightly more than 50 in Nalgonda, Khammam, Warangal, Anantpur, and Kurnool. It is pathetic to note that more than 50 per cent of the adult females were illiterate in almost all the districts except in Hyderabad, West Godavari and Krishna. As expected, the literacy rate was lowest among the adult female population in rural areas. A little more than one-third of the adult female population in rural areas was literate whereas in the urban areas the literacy level of adult females was slightly less than two-thirds. The gender disparity index in literacy was also higher in rural areas than in urban areas.

The district-wise distribution of adult literacy rates broadly indicates the following: Mahabubnagar, Medak, may be classified as low literacy districts with literacy rates between 37.4 and 44.1. Kurnool, Anantpur, Warangal, Khammam, and Nalgonda may be classified as low medium literacy districts with literacy rates between 46.2 and 49.3. Prakasam, Kadapa, Guntur, Nellore, Chittoor, and Rangareddy may be classified as high medium literacy districts with literacy rates between 50.4 and 61.3. Krishna, West Godavari and Hyderabad may be classified as high literacy districts with literacy rates between 63.9 and 77.0 per cent (Table 10.2).

The percentage of households without any literate adult member or without any literate adult female member was much higher among the ST and SC as compared to the OBC or other categories both in rural and urban Andhra Pradesh in 2004–05. Between the two scheduled categories, the percentage of such households was much higher among the ST.

Table 10.2

District-wise Literacy Levels in the Krishna Basin

Districts	*Males*			*Females*			*Persons*		
	1981	*1991*	*2001*	*1981*	*1991*	*2001*	*1981*	*1991*	*2001*
Krishna	48.6	60.6	74.4	34.6	45.5	63.2	41.7	53.2	68.8
Guntur	45.3	56.5	71.2	26.6	35.9	53.7	36.1	46.4	62.5
Prakasam	40.5	53.1	69.4	18.0	27.1	45.1	29.4	40.3	57.4
Chittoor	43.1	62.6	77.6	20.2	36.4	55.8	31.9	49.8	66.8
Kadapa	43.9	63.1	75.8	17.8	32.4	49.5	31.2	48.1	62.8
Anantpur	40.8	55.9	68.4	16.2	27.6	43.3	29.0	42.2	56.1
Kurnool	40.0	53.2	66.0	17.1	26.0	40.0	28.7	40.0	53.2
Mahabubnagar	28.1	40.8	56.6	10.6	18.0	31.9	19.4	29.6	44.4
Ranga reddy	39.1	60.4	75.3	19.3	36.9	56.5	29.4	49.1	66.2
Medak	32.0	45.2	64.3	10.9	19.3	38.7	21.5	32.4	51.6
Khammam	33.2	50.0	66.1	17.7	30.5	47.4	25.6	40.5	56.9
Nalgonda	31.6	50.5	69.2	13.0	24.9	44.7	22.4	38.0	57.2
Andhra Pradesh	39.3	55.1	70.3	20.4	32.7	50.4	29.9	44.0	60.5

Note: Literacy rate is for 7+ age population.

Source: Census of India, Andhra Pradesh.

Table 10.3

Dropouts in Class I-V in Andhra Pradesh

Year	*All*			*SCs*			*STs*		
	Boys	*Girls*	*All*	*Boys*	*Girls*	*All*	*Boys*	*Girls*	*All*
1990–91	49.51	56.41	52.55	55.65	62.60	58.69	64.02	70.38	66.49
1991–92	52.50	57.37	54.62	60.56	65.03	62.50	63.20	69.60	65.59
1992–93	51.56	53.95	52.36	57.09	61.26	58.89	61.68	67.49	63.94
1993–94	55.50	55.91	55.68	59.27	63.94	61.32	72.48	78.08	74.63
1994–95	52.86	52.15	52.55	58.52	61.48	59.80	69.45	75.86	71.94
1995–96	51.28	49.35	50.44	56.20	57.27	56.66	67.93	75.25	90.82
1996–97	51.01	50.93	50.97	52.75	58.62	55.45	71.16	78.71	74.26
1997–98	44.36	46.77	45.48	51.45	57.15	54.10	71.11	78.14	74.05
1998–99	42.69	44.70	43.63	48.67	54.66	51.48	68.91	75.59	7174
1999–2000	39.42	41.23	40.28	45.73	50.45	47.96	66.69	73.75	69.75

Source: Commissioner and Director of School Education, Government of Andhra Pradesh.

These findings suggest that ST female adults could not avail of the desired benefit from literacy campaigns and/or from formal schooling facilities as compared to SC female adults in rural areas. We find that SC male adults could benefit from literacy campaigns and/or formal schooling facilities to improve their literacy position between 1991 and 2001. Even though the literacy level among adults is much better in urban areas than in rural areas, about 64.7 per cent of the ST female adults and about 47.6 per cent of the SC female adults in urban areas are illiterate (Table 10.3).

Educational Deprivation of Children

As is the case of literacy, there is also a significant disparity across social groups in children at school. The percentage of children in the 5–14 age group attending school was relatively low among SC/ST than the other communities. Many children belonging to these marginalised communities especially ST, are out of school and some are even engaged in economic activities. As per NSSO estimates the percentage of children in the age group 5–14 years attending schools during 2004–05 in ST, SC, OBC and other communities were 80.4, 86.6, 86.3 and 89.9 per cent respectively in rural areas and 94.3, 90.0, 89.5 and 92.7 per cent respectively in the urban areas. Gender disparities in school attendance across these communities are 22.6, 11.1 and 7.5 per cent respectively (Table 10.4).

The incidence of educational deprivation (i.e., percentage of children who remained out of school) is higher among children belonging ST and SC when compared to others. Between the SC and ST, the ST children are the most deprived. This is corroborated even by enrolment figures. Poor enrolment and high drop out rates were highest among ST children followed by SC and others.

Table 10.4

Out-of-School Children across Social Groups

(in per cent)

	Year	*SC*	*ST*	*Others*
Total	1981	63.8	80.6	57.3
	1991	59.8	73.9	46.9
	2001	35.9	23.1	20.4
Rural	1981	68.1	82.2	63.8
	1991	64.4	76.0	53.0
	2001	36.8	24.2	21.9
Urban	1981	41.1	56.3	38.2
	1991	39.0	51.7	32.5
	2001	25.3	17.8	16.9

Note: Figures presented in percentage.
Children of 5–14 years of age.

Source: Census 1981, 1991 and 2001.

Inter-district variations in attendance are much higher for girls than for boys among ST and SC communities. In the case of ST, the low attendance districts are Mahabubnagar, Medak, Guntur, and Rangareddy. The gender disparity in attendance is also relatively higher in these districts except for Guntur. For SC and others, the low attendance districts are Mahabubnagar and Kurnool, where gender disparity in attendance is also higher.

Female literacy and infant mortality can be used to represent education and health respectively. Before going to the trends in these two indicators, we compare the ranks of the districts (arranged by regions) for income poverty and education and health indicators. Significant regional disparities in relative deprivation and under development can be identified.

The rural poverty ratio varies from 16.2 in Kadapa to 39.7 per cent in Mahabubnagar. Female literacy varies from nearly 70 per cent in West Godavari to 33 per cent in Mahabubnagar, while infant mortality varies from 30 in Krishna district to 77 in Mahabubnagar. The ranks for rural poverty and the other two indicators show that there is no perfect correlation among these three variables. The bottom 10 districts for these three indicators show that four districts are common. These are: Mahabubnagar, Nalgonda, Kurnool, and Warangal. Apart from these Anantpur also figure in the bottom at least in two indicators.

Literacy and education levels are important human development indicators. One of the failures of development policy in India since independence is lack of focus on primary education. The percentage point changes between 1991 and 2001 for females and males are also given. The female literacy rates show that all the districts (except Hyderabad and Mahabubnagar), has more than 15 percentage points change between 1991 and 2001. In Mahabubnagar, the change is closer to 15 percentage points. The inter-district disparities declined significantly in the last decade. The co-efficient of variation for males declined from 15 per cent to 8 per cent while for females it declined from 35 per cent to 21 per cent between 1991 and 2001.

Health

Health status is measured by indicators such as mortality, morbidity, immunisation of children and pregnant women and their nutrition levels. The estimates for all these indicators indicate that STs and the SCs lag behind other communities. Mortality as measured by the crude death rate is marginally higher among the SC and ST. Infant mortality rate (IMR), which is an important indicator in the human development perspective, is highest among the STs (104) followed by SCs (97). The great difference between STs/SCs and the others in terms of IMR indicates the difference in development across these communities (Table 10.5).

Table 10.5

Health Parameters across Social Groups

Indicators	*2005–06*				
	ST	*SC*	*OBC*	*Others*	*Total*
TFR	2.75	2.51	2.26	2.00	2.25
IMR	104	95	70	47	71
Family Planning	48.5	52.2	61.3	63.6	59.6
Vitamin A	9.6	23.6	24.0	29.6	24.8
No ANC Checkup	25.9	8.1	7.2	2.9	7.3
Delivery at home	62.4	32.7	24.5	13.1	25.4
HW Visit	26.4	22.8	17.8	12.1	17.4
Nutritional Status of Women					
Mean Height (cm)	151.3	149.9	150.915	2.3	151.2
% < 145 cm	9.4	16.7	14.0	9.1	12.7
Mean BMI	19.1	19.4	19.9	21.7	20.3
% BMI < 18.5	44.2	44.8	40.6	26.9	37.4
% with Anaemia	48.6	56.0	48.5	47.9	49.8
Nutritional Status of Children					
Weight for Age					
% below –3SD	7.5	14.2	12.5	4.8	10.3
% below –2SD	45.9	43.4	39.1	29.7	37.7
Height for Age					
% below –3SD	18.5	20.7	15.1	10.1	14.2
% below –2SD	49.4	44.6	39.8	32.3	38.6
% with Anaemia	68.2	79.6	71.4	69.7	72.3

TFR (Total Fertility Rate), IMR (Infant Mortality Rate), ANC (Antenatal Care), HW (Health Worker), SD (Standard Deviation).

The nutritional status of women is crucial for their own health as well as the health of children. There are different indicators to measure the nutritional status of women. For instance the height of an adult woman also reflects the level of nutrition during childhood and adolescence. The height of a woman often indicates the level of risk of difficulty in childbirth and delivering a baby with low birth weight. Current diet also influences their nutritional status. Women from scheduled tribes/castes have a relatively poor diet that is deficient in fruits and green, leafy vegetables. Although there is no significant difference in terms of the mean height of the women, the percentage of women below 145 cm is highest among women belonging to scheduled caste.

The body mass index (BMI) which is a measure of weight to height is used to assess thinness or obesity. A BMI less than 18.5 indicates chronic energy deficiency in a woman. The mean BMI for SC/ST women is the lowest and the percentage of women whose BMI is below 18.5 is the highest among SCs and STs.

Anaemia is another indicator of nutritional status and it usually results from a deficiency of iron, vitamin B or other nutrients. Iron deficiency is the most widespread form of malnutrition in the world and in India and in Andhra Pradesh it affects about 50 per cent of the population. Across social groups, anaemia was highest among SC women (56%).

Nutritional status of children is an important aspect of their health and well-being. Nutrition status is expressed in standard deviation units (z-scores) from the median. Children who are under three years of age and below 2SD are considered to be undernourished and those below 3SD are considered to be severely undernourished. While weight for age is a composite measure of both chronic and acute under-nutrition, height for age measures linear growth retardation. Across social groups, the percentage children characterised as undernourished was higher among the ST community followed by SC when compared with the other children. Severity of under-nutrition was higher among SC children.

Chronic under-nutrition generally results from a failure to receive adequate nutrition over a long period of time or from chronic or recurrent diarrhea. Moreover, under-nutrition among children is strongly associated with their mothers' nutritional status and is more common in children whose mothers' height is less than 145 cm and BMI is below 18.5. Ultimately, it is strongly related to the living standards at the household level and children of households with a low standard of living are more likely to be undernourished than children of households with a high standard of living.

The other indicator of the health status of the population is access/utilisation of health care services. For this the indicators used are: immunisation of children and pregnant women and attention received at the time of delivery. For nearly 62 per cent of ST women and 33 per cent of SC women, child delivery took place at home.

The National Health Policy (1983) gives top priority to provide health services to people residing in tribal, hilly and backward areas as well as to the population affected by endemic diseases and vulnerable sections of society. Therefore, in order to provide better health care to SCs and STs, the norms for population coverage were relaxed. This is further supported by implementation of programmes like the control of communicable and other diseases and especially undertaking research on diseases to which SCs/STs are generally prone. Mobile dispensaries and camps organised wherever feasible, are catering to their needs at their doorsteps.

Infant Mortality Rates

Infant mortality is an important component of mortality in general and a crucial indicator of the health status of a society. The Infant Mortality Rate (IMR) unlike the crude death rate, remained lower than the rate in the country till the early 1990s. However, the difference was not striking in subsequent years, and it was high when compared to the other southern states. There has been a steady decline of IMR, particularly since 1971. Though IMR in the state declined from 106 in 1971 to 54 in 2007, it is still at an unacceptably high level (Table 10.6). This further suggests that in Andhra Pradesh, despite the early decline in IMR, the decline has become stagnant.

Table 10.6

Infant Mortality Rates and Period Variation

Year	*Andhra Pradesh*	*Karnataka*	*Kerala*	*Tamil Nadu*	*All India*
1971	106	95	58	113	129
1981	86	69	37	91	110
1991	73	77	16	57	80
2002	62	55	10	44	63
2007	54	47	13	35	55
		Variation (in percentage)			
1971–81	-23.3	-37.7	-56.8	-24.2	-17.3
1981–91	17.8	10.4	-131.3	-59.6	-37.5
1991–2002	-17.7	-40	-60	-29.5	-27
2002–07	-14.8	-17	23.1	-25.7	-14.5

Source: Sample Registration System (Various Issues).

Trends in Life Expectancy at Birth

The overall decline in death rate has resulted in a substantial improvement in the life span of people. It is estimated that the life expectancy for the country as a whole was 49.7 years in 1971–75 which had risen to 65.4 years in 2001–06. Similarly, in Andhra Pradesh also, life expectancy has improved over the years, i.e., from 48.8 years in 1970–75 to 63.9 years in 2001–06 (Table 10.7). The most notable fact is the improvement in both rural and urban areas and also among males and females. This, in turn, has resulted in women outliving men by 0.9 to 2.2 years in the state. There was a significant improvement of 10 years in life expectancy in the state from 1970–75 to 1981–85, which matched the pace of decline in the death rate.

Table 10.7

Life expectancy at Birth by Place and Sex

Period	*Rural*	*Urban*	*Total*	*Male*	*Female*
1970–75	47.3	57.2	48.8	48.4	49.3
1976–80	51.7	60.6	53.1	52.2	54.2
1981–85	57.1	63.8	58.4	57.2	59.8
1986–90	58.3	62.1	59.1	59.1	62.2
1991–95	60.7	65.1	61.8	60.3	62.8
1992–96	61.0	65.5	62.0	61.4	64.5
2001–06	NA	NA	63.9	62.8	65.0

Source: Sample Registration System (Various Issues).

Trends in Total Fertility Rate

The Total Fertility Rate (TFR) for Andhra Pradesh remained more or less stable at around 5.5 per woman during 1961–71. Within the state, the pace of decline was slow during the 1970s and mid-1980s. It took almost three decades to reach three children per woman but once this threshold was reached, the further decline to two children took just about 10 years. The rapidity of decline was faster in the decade from 1987–96 as compared to the other southern states.

The analysis of NFHS-2 data (James, 1999; James and Subramanian, 2005) showed that the literacy of mothers had no association with contraceptive use in the coastal region. Contraceptive use has increased in all the regions, which raises questions about the role of education as a prime mover in fertility transition. A further analysis reveals that exposure to cinema alone was found to be positively associated with the practice of family planning in Andhra Pradesh. A

Table 10.8

District-wise Trends in Total Fertility Rates

Districts	*1981*	*1991*	*2001*
West Godavari	3.9	3.0	2.0
Krishna	4.3	3.3	1.9
Guntur	4.1	3.2	1.9
Prakasam	4.6	3.5	2.3
Nellore	3.9	3.1	2.0
Chittoor	4.0	3.1	2.2
Kadapa	4.5	3.4	2.3
Anantpur	4.9	3.9	2.4
Kurnool	5.0	4.3	3.0
Mahabubnagar	4.9	4.5	3.1
Rangareddy	4.8	3.9	2.6
Hyderabad	4.2	4.1	1.9
Medak	4.6	4.2	2.9
Warangal	4.6	4.1	2.5
Khammam	4.7	3.7	2.3
Nalgonda	4.5	4.3	2.6
Andhra Pradesh	4.3	3.4	2.3

Source: Data for 1981 and 1991, RGI, Occasional Paper No.1 of 1997, Table 2.0, p. 88; Data for 2001, Christophe Z Guilmoto, S. Irudaya Rajan: 'District Levels Estimates of Fertility from India's 2001 Census,' *EPW*, February 16, 2002.

regional analysis indicated that exposure to mass media and asset holdings of the household were important in explaining acceptance of family planning in the coastal region of Andhra Pradesh. In the other two relatively backward regions of Telangana and Rayalaseema, the work participation rate of women was found to be positively related with the use of contraception.

District-wise comparison of fertility estimates during the last decade (1991–2001) reveals that the decline was faster in the districts located in the coastal region (for instance, Srikakulam, West Godavari, Krishna, and Guntur) than in the other regions. Some had reached the replacement level of fertility as early as 1996. The lowest fertility rate is observed in coastal region (2.1), followed by Rayalaseema (2.8) and Telangana (2.9). According to the reverse survival estimates from the 2001 Census data, the highest level of TFR was observed in Mahabubnagar district (3.1), and the lowest value of 1.9 in Guntur, Hyderabad, and Krishna (Table 10.8).

More recent data indicate that once the fertility decline gathered momentum, it fell at a faster rate in rural areas compared to urban areas so that rural-urban differences have virtually disappeared. According to NFHS-3 data for 2005–06, TFR in urban areas was estimated to be 1.7 and the rural TFR was higher by only 0.2 points in the state. Fertility differences by education of mothers or among social groups have also narrowed considerably leading to homogenisation in reproductive behaviour.

Table 10.9

Distribution of Ever-married Women with Low BMI and Anemia Levels

(in per cent)

Region	*Percentage of Anemic Women*				
	BMI<18.5	*Severe*	*Moderate*	*Mild*	*Total*
Godavari–Krishna	26.7	3.3	18.8	39.3	926
Southern	36.9	1.5	16.4	38.7	530
Low rainfall Rayalaseema	46.4	2.0	11.4	28.3	446
Hyderabad and Rangareddy	17.9	0.7	8.7	30.0	414
South Telangana	41.5	0.7	11.2	31.3	454
North Telangana	44.7	2.0	10.5	27.5	610

Source: Computed from NFHS-2 data.

Health and Empowerment of Women

National Family Health Survey-2 (1998–99) conducted in Andhra Pradesh collected information from 4032 ever-married women on socio-economic conditions in the age group 15–49. In this section, some indicators relating to women's levels of living and health status have been examined. The data are arranged by agro-climatic regions. Based on asset holdings, a type of living standard index is constructed for these women. It shows that the percentage of women with low living standards is nearly uniform across different regions of Andhra Pradesh. The exceptions are Hyderabad and Rangareddy region. The region is relatively backward while the latter one is more developed region. Even in Godavari–Krishna belt, the percentage of women with low living standards is quite high (Table 10.9).

NFHS-2 also provides nutrition of ever-married women. The percentage distribution of women with anemia and at different levels of haemoglobin shows that the highest percentage of women with BMI<18.5 is found in low rainfall Rayalaseema region. The percentage of anemia is relatively high even in other coastal regions. On the other hand, the under nutrition levels are lower for Godavari-Krishna belt.

Some indicators relating to health care availability shows that health facilities are relatively poor in Telangana region. Surprisingly, North Coastal region has better infrastructure facilities in Godavari–Krishna **belt** (Table 10.10).

Table 10.10

Region-wise Government Medical Facilities per One Lakh Population

Region	*Hospitals and Dispensaries*	*PHC*	*Bed*	*Doctor*
Godavari–Krishna	1.0	1.6	40.6	10.9
Southern	0.9	2.4	44.1	10.7
Low rainfall Rayalaseema	0.9	2.2	45.0	11.0
Hyderabad and Rangareddy	1.5	0.5	111.8	24.0
South Telangana	0.6	2.3	27.6	7.2
North Telangana	0.8	2.1	36.8	8.9
Andhra Pradesh	0.9	1.9	46.7	11.4

Source: Computed from NFHS-2 data.

The components of HDI show that there is no correlation between income and health/education for some of the districts. The rank in terms of per capita income is much higher than those of education and health for Medak and Khammam districts. On the other hand, the ranks for education are higher than those for per capita income in West Godavari, Krishna, Nellore, Chittoor, Kadapa, and Nalgonda. Similarly, health ranks are higher than those for income in the case of Krishna, Guntur and Kadapa. In other words, apart from looking at aggregate HDI, one has to examine the components of the index in order to have better policies.

In most districts of South Coastal Andhra, the index of human development was higher than the state average. In Telangana, districts like Rangareddy, Khammam and Medak had higher levels of human development than the state average.

The rate of change in HDI values during 1991–2001 was higher in those districts which had lower HDI levels in 1991. This indicates that the backward districts improved more than the relatively better developed districts. Therefore, there is some convergence of districts in terms of HDI.

Table 10.11

Ranks of Districts for the Components of HDI

Districts	*Income 2003–04*	*Education 2001*	*Health 2001*	*Overall*
West Godavari	4	1	3	1
Krishna	5	2	1	2
Guntur	6	7	2	4
Prakasam	8	10	9	10
Nellore	7	5	6	5
Chittoor	9	3	7	6
Kadapa	11	6	5	7
Anantpur	13	12	14	14
Kurnool	10	13	12	12
Mahabubnagar	15	15	15	15
Ranga reddy	1	4	4	3
Medak	2	14	10	9
Warangal	12	8	11	11
Khammam	3	11	8	8
Nalgonda	14	9	13	13

The analysis shows that there is significant regional disparities human development in Andhra Pradesh. However, the regional disparities seem to be declining in the 1990s particularly in the field of literacy and education. This is a good development. The backward regions seem to be catching up with the pace of developed regions. In the case of health, particularly women's health, it is clear whether the progress in backward regions is as fast as that of developed regions (Table 10.11).

Sustaining the social mobilisation and empowerment programmes should be a primary focus of the human development strategy. Again, the immediate focus could be in the districts and Mandals where poverty is prevalent. More attention has to be paid to capacity building of groups. The government should adopt a much more flexible approach depending, among other things, on the strengths of the village-based groups to handle their own affairs and take development in their own hands.

Policy Initiatives for Balanced Regional Growth

The level of literacy is perhaps the most important index of development of a society. Invariably, male literacy is higher than female literacy in any society. Often there may be significant gender gap in literacy. The true index of development of a society is the level of female literacy, which can be considered as the bottom line as far as literacy is concerned.

An important indicator of the quality of health care in a society is the infant mortality rate. As in the case of literacy, here also the bottom line is the female IMR. The national average is 64 which imply that out of every 1000 female infants born in the country, 64 will not survive till the first birthday. The lower the IMR the better health care a state enjoys. Andhra Pradesh has IMR below the national average.

In the case of literacy and education, the regional disparities have come down substantially because of the special programme launched by the Government during the 1980s and 1990s. The regional differences in the incidence of rural poverty have also been reduced significantly.

There are also important changes in human development indicators - especially education and health - which indicate a shrinking of disparities across the regions of the state. Interestingly, the greatest improvements appear to have been in the regions which have performed more poorly in terms of standard income growth measures.

Even after 50 years, the percentage of literate population in Telangana continues to be the lowest in the state, i.e., 37.00 as compared to 46.22 in coastal Andhra Pradesh, 44.96 in Rayalaseema and 71.52 in the capital city. This has happened because of uneven distribution of educational facilities in different regions of the state. For clarity, a region-wise analysis is made, selectively, comprising-school education and health sector.

To conclude, if the existing trends in differential rate of socio-economic development continue, regional disparities are bound to accentuate. Therefore, it is imperative that the present trends are arrested and preferably reversed.

References

Dev, S. Mahendra (2002) 'Human Development in Andhra Pradesh', in Krishna Rao Y.V. and Subrahmanyam S (eds), *Development of Andhra Pradesh, 1956–2001: A Study of Regional Disparities*, Hyderabad: NRR Research Center.

—— (2007). *Inclusive Growth in Andhra Pradesh: Challenges in Agriculture, Poverty, Social Sector and Regional Disparities, Working Paper No. 71*, Hyderabad: Centre for Economic and Social Studies.

James, K.S. and S. Subramanian (2005). 'Decline in fertility in Andhra Pradesh: A reexamination of conflicting arguments', in: Gulmoto, C.Z. and S. Irudaya Rajan (eds) Fertility Transition in South India, New Delhi: Sage Publications, pp. 357–84.

11

Opportunities and Challenges in Indian Higher Education

GANESH KAWADIA AND RADHIKA DIXIT

Today, the world economy is experiencing an unprecedented change. New developments in science and technology, media revolution, internationalisation of education and the ever expanding competitive environment are revolutionising the education scene. A paradigm shift has been noticed in higher education now-a-days, from 'national education' to 'global education', from 'one-time education for a few' to 'life-long education for all', from 'teacher-centric education' to 'learner-centric education'. Knowledge is the driving force in the rapidly changing globalised economy and society. Quantity and quality of highly specialised human resources determine their competence in the global market. Emergence of knowledge as driving factor results in both challenges and opportunities. The benefits of globalisation accrue to the countries with highly skilled human capital and it is a curse for the countries without such specialised human capital. Developing countries are further challenged in a highly competitive world economy because their higher education systems are not adequately developed for the creation and use of knowledge, India is one of such developing nations. India has recently witnessed a big boom in the BPO/KPO sector, which absorbs and requires a large proportion of skilled and trained population of the country. This trend is certain to continue and India faces the challenge of generating an appropriate supply response to retain its existing advantage. It should be noted that Indians spend nearly $4 billion annually to send their children abroad for higher studies and technical training. The real challenge therefore is to expand capacities in higher education to keep ahead of the curve of rising domestic and global demand. Because of interdependence and integration of world economy in recent years, the Indian higher education system has a new role and a challenge to provide to the nation and the world at large, skilled human power at all levels, having breadth of knowledge and confidence to effectively confront the social and economic realities. This paper is an effort to examine the current status of higher education system in India.

The specific objectives of the study are to study the trend of allocation of public funds in higher education in the country; to study the growth and composition of institutions of higher education; to study the extent of access to higher education; to study the degree of diversification in the field of higher education; to examine the issues of quality and governance in higher education; and to suggest appropriate measures to enhance accessibility and quality of higher education in the country.

Scenario of Higher Education in India

In the recent years, Indian higher education system has undergone massive expansion with the establishment of several universities, technical institutes, research institutions and professional/non-professional colleges all over the country to generate and disseminate knowledge coupled with the noble intention of providing easy access to higher education to the common Indian. In the initial phase of the development higher education, public/state initiatives played a dominant and controlling role. Most of the universities were public institutions with powers to regulate academic activities in their campuses as well as in their areas of jurisdiction through the affiliating system. Even the private institutions which were quite handful at that time enjoyed large scale financial support in the form of grants from public exchequer. Now, over the last one decade with the increasing demand for higher education in the country and the world, the framework of the higher education has undergone certain changes and there has been a considerable increase in private resource allocation in the field of higher education in the country.

Public Expenditure on Higher Education

Owing to continuous increase in the demand for higher education, there is a need for expansion and increasing the accessibility of higher education in the country. But if we look at the data of resource allocation for higher education, we find that the share of higher education in the government budget is on constant decline. It can be measured in terms of the share of higher education in Gross National Product (GNP). Starting from a very low figure of 0.19 per cent of GNP invested in higher education in 1950s, the share of higher education increased five fold by 1980s around one per cent of the GNP. But ever since, the allocation of resources is steadily coming down. It was around 0.56 per cent of GNP during 1990–91 and it further declined to around 0.4 per cent of GNP by mid of the 1990s and still continues with the same kind of trend. There has also been a constant decline in the percentage of planned expenditure of government on the university and higher education. This has emerged not only as a result of government's promise to provide compulsory and free primary education but also due to reform packages introduced in the late 1980s and early 1990s by the country. This imposed a heavy compression on the public budgets on education sector, more specifically so on higher education. Following the introduction of structural adjustment policies that include macro-economic stabilisation and adjustment, a fiscal squeeze is experienced in all social sector investments in many developing countries, including India. This has further trickled down to public expenditure on education in general, and higher education in particular. The figure below shows how the plan allocation for higher education, which went up to 28 per cent in the Fifth Plan period, has gone down to only 6 per cent in the Tenth Plan period:

Figure 11.1

% Plan Expenditure on Higher Education (%)

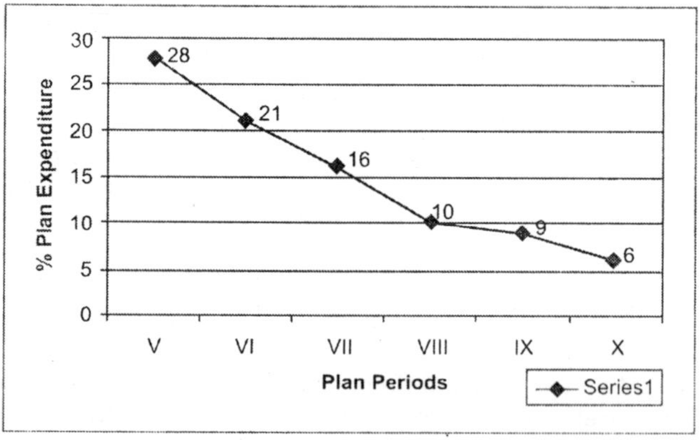

These clearly point towards the inability of the state to provide adequately for expansion and diversification of higher education, which ultimately paved the path for massive privatisation. The public funding thus is not in a position to take-up the challenging task of expansion and diversification of the higher education system in the country to meet the continuously growing demands. There is thus little option other than bringing in private initiatives in a massive way to meet the various challenges. The deregulating mechanism of controls started with the granting of 'autonomous status' to identified colleges in the 1970s. Some of these colleges have graduated further to receive the 'Deemed to be University' status in later years. Now, the country is on the threshold of the establishment of private universities in different states.

Private Initiatives in Higher Education

The extent and scale of privatisation could be realised by the fact that in 2000–01 out of the 13,072 higher educational institutions, 42 per cent were privately owned and run, catering to 37 per cent of students enrolled into higher education, i.e., approximately 3.1 million out of total 8.4 million. It is also evident that most of the expanding higher education sector took place in private unaided colleges or in self-financing institutions. Many government universities have granted affiliation to unaided colleges and many universities have authorised new self-financing courses even in government and aided colleges. It is felt that as of now more than 50 per cent of the higher education in India is imparted mainly through unaided private institutions. The growth of private institutes of higher education and the enrolments therein has been very rapid. The total number of higher education institutes further rose to 17,973 in the year 2005–06 in which the increase in the number of the private institutes has been more than double compared to the year 2000–01. The students enrolment also increased over this period from 8,399 to 10,481. Out of the total increase in the enrolments the private sector's share in the total has increased by 77 per cent during this period, which in itself shows the massification in the private higher education in the country. Table 11.1 shows the details of higher education institutions in India.

Table 11.1

Higher Education Institutions and Enrolment (by type of management)

Type (by Management/ Funding)		*Universities*		*Colleges*		*Higher Education Institutions*		*Enrolment (in thousand)*	
		2000–01	*2005–06*	*2000–01*	*2005–06*	*2000–01*	*2005–06*	*2000–01*	*2005–06*
Public	Government	24526	8	4097	4225	4342	4493	3443	3752
	Private aided	—	10	5507	5750	5507	5760	3134	3510
Private	Private unaided	21	70	3202	7650	3223	7720	1822	3219
Total		26634	8	12806	17625	13072	17973	8399	10481

Source: University Grants Commission (India) and Agarwal (2006).

Enrolment in Higher Education

Enrolment in higher education has been rising steadily since 1950–51. The enrolment rate was 0.7 per cent in 1950–51 which increased to 1.4 per cent in 1960–61 and further to 8 per cent for 2000–01. For 2003–04 the Gross Enrolment Ratio (GER) worked out to 9 per cent. The enrolment rate has continued to remain low compared even to some of the developing countries of Asia and Latin America. The GER in relative terms compares quite poorly with 60 per cent in USA and Canada; over 40 per cent in several European countries and more than 20 per cent in many developed and developing countries. International experience shows that no country has been able to become an economically advanced country if its enrolment ratio in higher education has been less than 20 per cent. The foremost priority therefore must be on enhancing access to higher education such that the GER is raised to a minimum threshold level of about 20 per cent for sustained economic development. In immediate terms, the Eleventh Plan has set the target GER of 15 per cent. Table 11.2 below shows the growth of enrolment in tertiary education (at doctorate, post-graduate, degree and diploma levels) during the period 1980–81 to 2003–04.

Table 11.2

Enrolment by Levels and Major Disciplines

Year	*PhD*	*PG*	*General Graduate (Art, Science and Commerce)*	*Technical Graduate (Engg., Medical, BEd)*	*Diploma*	*Total Higher Education (Degree, Diploma)*
1980–81	25417 (0.88)	291341 (10.12)	1886428 (65.67)	239267 (8.32)	430126 (14.97)	2872579
1990–91	32468 (0.66)	354216 (7.24)	3285776 (67.24)	416828 (8.53)	796686 (16.30)	4885974
2000–01	45004 (0.46)	647338 (6.73)	7244915 (75.36)	688625 (7.16)	987279 (10.27)	9613161
2001–02	53119 (0.54)	647016 (6.64)	7139497 (73.34)	790050 (8.11)	1104594 (11.34)	9734276
2002–03	65357 (0.60)	782590 (7.30)	7633125 (71.22)	1035701 (9.67)	1199785 (11.19)	10716558
2003–04	65525 (0.58)	806636 (7.20)	8026147 (71.65)	1110840 (9.91)	1191447 (10.63)	11200595

Note: The percentage share of each degree and diploma in the total higher education is indicated in the brackets.

Source: Selected educational statistics, different years.

It is clear from the above table that more than two third of the enrolment is still for general graduate education. The enrolment in this category of education is continuously increasing under the study period. The enrolments in post-graduate and diploma courses are less than 10 per cent of the total enrolments in higher education in each category. The share of these programmes is showing decreasing trend over this period.

The share of technical education is expanding but at a very slow rate. Its share is still less than 10 per cent. The biggest challenge of higher education is very low enrolments, less than 1 per cent in Ph.D. programme. Most of the institutes of higher education in the country are not able to promote such programmes because of lack of funds from the government or industries. University Grants Commission (UGC) has recently introduced the scheme of fellowship for all the students registered for Ph.D. in the Central Universities. But because of their poor coverage in the country, nothing much has changed in this sector. The other important issue is the lack of diversification in courses of higher education in the country. Although there is a constant rise in the percentage share of technological education in the total higher education but the change is very insignificant as compared to the share of general graduation. Most of the enrolments are still confined to general graduation degrees. Therefore in order to improve the enrolments at the undergraduate and post-graduate level, there is a strong need to develop more opportunities and choice based curriculums with more diversified and specialised courses which can fulfil the requirements of the growing economy.

Quality of Higher Education in India

The other important question which arises here is that whether this increase is only in the quantitative terms or also in the qualitative terms. The biggest challenge faced by the Indian higher education system today is to generate world class skilled and efficient manpower which could be absorbed by the global economy and not the mass contributing to the educated unemployed. The quality of the product of Indian higher education system matters equally along with its quantity. The massive quantification of higher education in our country has given birth to many questions related to its quality, equity and governance. Overall the years there has been tremendous increase in the size of higher education but the same cannot be

Table 11.3

Global Ranking of Universities

Countries	*Top 20*	*21–50*	*51–100*	*101–200*	*201–300*	*301–400*	*401–500*
UK	2	3	6	12	10	4	5
US	17	20	17	34	29	23	26
UK – US	19	23	23	46	39	27	31
World total	20	30	51	101	102	98	108
UK – US % in total	95	76.7	45.1	45.5	38.2	27.6	28.7
12 developing countries	—	—	1	9	12	11	17
% share of the 12	—	—	2	8.9	11.8	11.2	15.7

Note: The 12 developing countries are Argentina, Brazil, China, Chile, Taiwan, Egypt, India, Israel, Mexico, Singapore, and South Africa.

Source: Academic Ranking of World Universities (www.arwu.org)

said about the quality of higher education in the country. According to a study, out of 4,95,000 engineering graduates produced annually, only 8–10 per cent are of employable quality. Not only this, it is only on account of lack of quality and research in our higher education institutions that out of total 370 universities and comparable institutes of the country not even single qualifies to be in top 20 Universities of the World. Of all the Indian Universities only IISc and IIT Kharagpur appear in the 301–400 ranking in the Academic Ranking of World Universities (ARWU) 2007 (The ranking is based on the academic or research performance of the universities) (Table 11.3).

The sample study of National Assessment and Accreditation Council (NAAC) reveals that 66 per cent of colleges have been rated as 'B' while another 25 per cent are rated as 'C' grade and only the remaining 9 per cent are of 'A' grade quality. These grades are based on Universities' performance with respect to number of indicators, which include faculty strength in number per department and quality (qualifications/PhD degree), and both physical and academic facilities. Recently a well-known economist, Palapre Balakrishnan (2007) in his paper affirms that 'it is widely accepted by now that the quality of higher education provided by government in India has not kept pace with the quantitative expansion. This may be inferred from the fact that young Indians who are able to finance the move have now begun to leave the country soon after they finish school'. It is a very disheartening fact that even after such massive expansion of domestic higher education market, a large number of the young students are increasingly involved in the import of higher education from rest of the world. A survey that took place recently shows that there has been 20 per cent increase in the number of students flying abroad from the country for availing higher education from other countries. In an environment of global competitiveness it is important that Indian outcome of the higher education institutions must be as competent as graduates of any other country, not only in their scholastic attainments, but also in terms of the value system and richness of their personality. Unless the quality and standard of Indian higher education institutions is enhanced keenly and sustained at a high level through innovation, creativity and regular monitoring, it seems difficult for the Indian academia/professionals to compete in the world scene. Following steps can help in enhancing the quality of higher education in the country:

- The major contributors in the improvement of quality of higher education in the country could be; improvement in the staffing, i.e., improvement in the quality of trainers and teachers at the university level. In this direction there is strong need of introducing some new mechanism to induce talented, qualified, skilled and young effective people to join the distribution stream of higher education and lead Indian higher education to the new innovative and required destinations. This is definitely possible by providing adequate monetary returns for it as corporate and private sector. Providing better research facilities, more teaching fellowships, better service conditions, and probably faster promotional avenues linked with the research work and teaching performances and giving more autonomy in framing of curriculum are some of the measures, which could be adopted for faculty development and recharge.

- The second most important contributor in the quality enhancement is logical and scientific development of the curriculum. The curriculum should be developed in an integrated manner by involving experts from different fields with major focus on sharing of experiences in a holistic framework. A multidisciplinary curriculum must be developed with a view to cater to the needs and fulfillment of expectations of learners, teachers, parents, employers, and society in general. The curriculum should also be revised from time to time and should be flexible enough to accommodate new and desired changes from time to time to respond to the needs of industry, profession and community so that it does not become obsolete and outdated at any point of time.
- Imparting quality education will require better infrastructure, greater use of latest technology and equipments, proper teacher student ratio, better chances and facilities for holistic development of the learners, greater autonomy to the teachers along with increase in their accountability towards the students. There is also a need for proper governance of higher education system for ensuring its quality production and distribution.

Governance of Higher Education in India

It has been observed that policy framework of higher education is carefully planned at the level of the Planning Commission, Ministry of Human Resource Development and University Grants Commission. However, the policies are not fully implemented mostly because of faulty management of the institutions of higher education. The administrative structure of the universities, which was devised in the pre-independence period, seems to be still continuing. To meet the new challenges facing the system of higher education in the country there is a need of total overhauling of the structure of management of higher education institutions. This has become all the more necessary because of globalisation, which requires talent, competence, drive, initiative, and innovation at several levels. The biggest drawback of Indian higher education governance is its failure to generate sense of accountability in its overall system. Its working and problems are nowhere different from that of any other government department of the country, which suffers from several operational deficiencies such as duplication of procedures, long funding cycles, long approval process, delay in exams and admissions, fraudulent practices, etc.

For improving the governance of higher education, there is a need of limiting the interference of the government in the universities, so as to strengthen the university autonomy and accountability and to promote decision-making in its matters on the basis of merit. Compared to other countries, the decision-making power of Indian higher education institutions remains limited. Currently, only 204 colleges out of 17,000 are autonomous with freedom in admission policies and curriculum designing. Similarly, system governance based on strict rules for input into the learning process – a fixed teacher-student ratio, number of books and square feet of facilities per student – inhibits innovations at the institutional level and does not foster strong institutional capacity. There is an increasing acknowledgement that dynamic societies and economies require institutions that operate with a degree of independence, and can supply to the market graduates who have the necessary skills needed by the market. Market mechanisms are often more effective than university administrators and government officials in signalling the demand for diverse forms of learning and skills delivered to diverse groups of students.

The current system of higher education is examination centric and degree producers. Almost all universities (except Central Universities) are overloaded with examination work. They are not able to manage their academic calendar and there is extraordinary delay in the declaration of results. This over pressure of examination is not allowing them to go for innovative and creative development of courses. It is therefore important to divert some of the examination tasks to the autonomous and big institutes of higher educations. This will provide them with some energy and time to think for innovation and research for the betterment of society.

The role of teaching faculty in the process of governance should be increased by promoting their participation in the management bodies of the institutes whether private or government. To make the transformation of information easy and ensure its speedy implementation, the coordination between the colleges and the universities should also be improved. The use of new technologies of information and communication should be done for attaining administrative efficiency. The working of executive/academic bodies and other governing councils of the universities should be made transparent and free from any sort of political and bureaucratic interferences and pressure. The participation of the students in the governance should also be systematically increased on democratic grounds so as to add to the transparency of the framework and its working. Efforts should be made to simplify the process of governance and inculcate a sense of accountability at every level, i.e., at the level of university, colleges, educators and learners.

Conclusion

India is facing a great challenge in higher education, which is being masked by the success of very few professional schools. The success of the few institutions of excellence cannot deny the fact that the median higher education institutions in India have become incapable of producing students who have skills and knowledge. The process neither serves a screening or signalling function nor prepares students to be productive and responsible citizens. Consequently, students are forced to spend more years (and increasingly, large resources) in acquiring some sort of post-graduate professional qualification as they desperately seek ways to signal their qualities to potential employers. It would not be an exaggeration to say that India's current system of higher education is centralised, politicised and militates against producing general intellectual virtues. The fact that the system nonetheless produces a noticeable number of high quality students, has to do with the sheer number of students and the struggle at the high school to get admission into the few good institutions. The most acute weakness plaguing India's higher education is a crisis of governance. Its most visible manifestation is a crisis of faculty. The generation that was inspired by a broad commitment to the public good has retired or will do so soon. There is little likelihood of sufficient replenishment, given entrenched mediocrity in institutions with life-time appointments, few competitive pressures and abysmal governance. The result has been the academic equivalent of Gresham's law – the bad drives out the good. The prevailing political ideological climate in which elite institutions are seen as being anti-democratic, finds its natural response in political control to influence admissions policies, internal organisation, the structure of courses and funding. As quality deteriorates, students are less and less willing to pay the very resources without which quality cannot be improved. In India's case, the growth of private sector higher education institutions has been the answer and increasingly, the consumption of education abroad. However, as this analysis suggests, private sector investment has been confined to professional streams, bypassing the majority of students. Furthermore, it is plagued by severe governance weaknesses, raising doubts as to its ability to addresses the huge latent demand for quality higher education in the country.

References

Agarwal, Pawan (2006). 'Higher Education in India: The Need for Change', *ICRIER Working Paper No. 180*. New Delhi.

Palapre, Balkrishanan (2007). 'Higher Education in India: Will 6 per cent do it?' *Economic and Political Weekly*, September 29.

12

Disparities in Levels of Educational Attainment in India

A National Analysis

SANJAY KUMAR

At the time of independence, India inherited a system of education, which was not only quantitatively small but also characterised by structural imbalances. Only 18 per cent of the population was literate and only one child out of three had been enrolled in primary school. The low levels of participation and literacy were aggravated by acute regional and gender disparities. As education is vitally linked with the totality of the development process – education being 'the basic tool for the development of consciousness and reconstitution of society', in the words of Mahatma Gandhi – the reform and restructuring of the educational system was recognised as an important area of state intervention.

The need for a literate population and universal education for all children in the age group of 6–14 were recognised as crucial inputs for nation building and were given due consideration in the Constitution of India[1] as well as in successive Five-Year Plans. This has resulted in a manifold increase of spatial spread, infrastructure facilities and increased coverage of various social groups.

There has been a spectacular increase in elementary education during the post-independence period. The elementary education system of India has expanded into one of the largest systems in the world. The number of primary schools increased from 2,09,671 in 1950–51 to 5,72,541 in 1992–93; the corresponding increase in upper primary schools was from 13,596 to 1,53,921. These 7,26,462 schools together with 2.7 lakh non-formal education centres enrolled 150 million children as compared to 22.3 million in 1951. Universal provision of education has been substantially achieved at the primary stage. According to the Fifth All India Education Survey (1986), 94.5 per cent of the rural population had schools within a walking distance of 1 km and 83.98 per cent of the rural population had an upper primary school within a walking distance of 3 km.

Table 12.1

Literacy Level of India, 1951 to 2001

Year	*% of Literate*	*Decadal Change*
1951	18	—
1961	28	+10
1971	34	+6
1981	44	+10
1991	52	+8
2001	65	+13

Source: Census of India.

Since independence there had been several positive changes in India, increasing literacy being one of them. The efforts of the governments had been successful to a great extent. Over last 50 years there had been a tremendous increase in the level of literacy in India. At the time of independence, only 18 per cent of Indians could read and write, but now more than two-third of Indians have become literate. As per the 2001 Census, the literacy rate in India was 65 per cent. There had been a steady increase in the literacy levels, almost 10 per cent every decade. The decade 1991 and 2001 witnessed, 13 per cent increase in the literacy level, the highest increase in literacy compared to all previous decades (Table 12.1). It seems various schemes of the government for providing basic education to all the people (Sarva Siksha Abhiyaan, Adult Education Scheme, etc.) have been instrumental in making more and more Indians literate.

While it is true that there had been enormous increase in literacy levels, but at the same time it is also true that the increase has not been uniform across states, across localities and across social communities. While the Constitution of India guaranteed policies of protective discrimination for the deprived and the marginalised sections of society, namely, the *Dalits* and the *Adivasis* for providing level playing field for educational attainment, but even after so many years there is a gap in levels of educational attainment amongst various sections of society. There had been expansion in educational attainment, but what is bothering is the uneven expansion of educational attainment. The inequality in educational attainment is based on various factors, i.e., gender, class, locality, and caste. While theoretically all the citizens have equal access to the educational opportunities, but there is a situation of unequal access to the educational opportunity. Several factors affect the chances of equal access to opportunity of educational attainment.

While there are various kinds of disparities, the paper aims to explore the disparities in educational attainment in amongst people belonging to various caste groups. The paper also aims at comparing the degree of disparity amongst various sections of the four broad caste groups. The argument in the paper has been largely built upon the empirical evidences from the data collected from the National Election Study (NES), 2009.[2] Besides evidences from the NES 2009, the paper also uses data from the 2001 Census relating to literacy. The information collected about the educational attainment of each respondent in the Census has been used for analysing the level of educational attainment amongst different sections of society.

State-wise Pattern

While it is true that there had been enormous increase in the literacy rate in India over last few decades, but the pattern of increase in literacy had been very uneven. While literacy had increased manifold in many states, few states are still lagging behind. As per the 2001 Census, Kerala is the most literate state of India with 91 per cent literacy while Bihar remains the least literate with less than 50 per cent literacy. If on one hand Kerala is the only state to have crossed 90 per cent literacy, Bihar remains the only state to have below 50 per cent literacy. As per the 2001 Census report, only 47 per cent people in Bihar can read and write. Though there have been improvement in levels of literacy in Bihar between 1991 and 2001, but Bihar still remains the least literate state of the Indian Union. The states of Jharkhand, Arunachal Pradesh, Uttar Pradesh, and Jammu and Kashmir are marginally ahead of Bihar in terms of literacy. Odisha, which used to be the least literate state till few decades back, has made considerable improvement and attained 63 per cent literacy. There are large numbers of states, which have managed to attain nearly 70 per cent or slightly a higher level of literacy (Table 12.2).

Table 12.2

State-wise Pattern of Literacy Rate 1991–2001

State	*% Literacy rate 1991*	*% Literacy rate 2001*	*Decadal change*
Kerala	90	91	+1
Mizoram	82	89	+7
Lakshwadeep	82	87	+5
Chandigarh	78	82	+4
Delhi	75	82	+7
Goa	76	82	+6
Pondicherry	75	81	+6
Andaman & Nicobar Islands	73	81	+8
Daman & Diu	71	78	+7
Maharashtra	65	77	+12

Cont'd...

...Cont'd

Himachal Pradesh	64	76	+12
Tripura	60	73	+13
Tamil Nadu	63	73	+10
Uttaranchal	58	72	+14
Manipur	60	71	+11
Punjab	59	70	+11
Sikkim	57	69	+12
West Bengal	58	69	+11
Gujarat	61	69	+8
Haryana	56	68	+12
Nagaland	62	67	+5
Karnataka	56	67	+11
Chhattisgarh	43	65	+22
Madhya Pradesh	45	64	+19
Meghalaya	49	63	+14
Assam	53	63	+10
Odisha	49	63	+14
Rajasthan	39	60	+21
Andhra Pradesh	44	60	+16
Dadar & Nagar Haveli	41	58	+17
Jammu & Kashmir	NA	56	
Uttar Pradesh	41	56	+15
Arunachal Pradesh	42	54	+12
Jharkhand	41	54	+13
Bihar	37	47	+10

Notes: 1. Literacy rates for 1951, 1961 and 1971 censuses relate to population aged five years and above. The rates for the 1981, 1991 and 2001 censuses relate to the population aged seven years and above. The literacy rate for 1951 in case of West Bengal relates to total population including 0–4 age group. Literacy rate for 1951 in respect of Chhattisgarh, Madhya Pradesh and Manipur are based on sample population.

2. India and Manipur figures exclude those of the three sub-divisions, viz., Mao Maram, Paomata and Purul of Senapati district of Manipur as Census results of 2001 in these three sub-divisions were cancelled due to technical and administrative reasons.

3. NA: Not available as no census was carried out in Assam during 1981 and in Jammu & Kashmir during 1991.

4. Created in 2001. Uttaranchal Pradesh, Jharkhand and Chhattisgarh for 1981 and 1991 are included under Uttar Pradesh, Bihar and Madhya Pradesh respectively.

Source: Census of India, Office of the Registrar General, India.

Differences in Levels of Educational Attainment across Caste Groups

The hierarchy in the Indian caste system is largely based on the notions of purity and pollution. This hierarchy also seemed to have its impact on other aspects as well, levels of educational attainment being one of them. A comparison of the levels of educational attainment amongst the four broad caste groups indicate that there is a clear hierarchy on the level of educational attainment, quite similar to what we experience in the caste-based hierarchy. Amongst the four caste groups, the upper castes are the most educated with 78 per cent being literate. Compared to this, only 53 per cent amongst the Adivasis are literate, 58 per cent amongst the Dalits are literate and among the OBCs, 68 per cent are literate. The difference in levels of educational attainment is not restricted to the attainment of primary or the basic education, this difference in levels of educational attainment is much wider if we look at the proportion of people within each caste group who managed to achieve higher education. Amongst the upper castes, 5.1 per cent managed to complete their post-graduate education and another 18 per cent managed to complete their college education. The proportion of graduates amongst the OBCs is half the proportion of graduates amongst the upper castes. The situation is much worse if we look at the proportion of graduates amongst the Dalits and the Adivasis, the proportion of graduates amongst the Dalits and Adivasis are much less compared to the upper castes. Like the upper castes, even amongst the Dalits and Adivasis, large number of children begin their school education, many of them manage to complete their high school education as well, but very few of them manage to complete their college education. At every stage of educational attainment, the dropout amongst the Dalits and the Adivasis seems to be higher compared to the upper castes and the OBCs (Table 12.3).

Table 12.3

Caste Groups and Levels of Educational Attainment

(in%)

Caste Group	*Literate*	*Completed High School*	*Graduates*	*Post-graduates*
Upper castes	78	46	18	5.1
OBCs	68	33	9	2.4
SCs	58	24	6	2.0
STs	53	19	5	1.4

Source: National Election Study, 2009.

Differences amongst the Upper Castes

While it is true that the upper castes are more educated compared to others, but upper castes are not a homogeneous category and we find differences in levels of educational attainment even amongst various castes within the upper castes. In terms of attaining basic education, there is not much difference between various castes within the upper castes. The proportion of high school educated is more or less the same amongst all the upper castes, but the difference begins to surface once we try and look at the achievement in higher education. The differences are noticeable if we look at the proportion of graduates amongst various upper castes, but it becomes much sharper as soon as we compare the proportion of post-graduates within each caste of the upper caste section. Within the upper castes, the proportion of graduates is the highest amongst the Vaishyas, closely followed by the Brahmins and Kayasthas respectively. But the situation changes if we look at the proportion of post-graduates amongst various upper castes. In respect of attaining higher education, the Brahmins lead the race with 10 per cent of them being graduates, closely followed by the Vaishyas amongst whom 9.8 per cent have completed post-graduate education. Though we tend to believe that amongst the upper castes the Kayasthas are the most educated, but in reality they are lagging behind the Brahmins and the Vaishyas (Table 12.4).

Table 12.4

Detailed Castes and Levels of Educational Attainment

(in%)

Castes	*Literate*	*Completed High School*	*Graduates*	*Post-graduates*
Brahmins	88	62	28	10.0
Kayasthas	87	54	22	6.5
Rajputs	76	46	15	3.5
Bania/Jains	92	63	32	9.8
Other dwijas	87	57	23	5.2
Peasant proprietors (non-Diwajas non-OBCs)	76	45	18	5.7

Source: National Election Study, 2009.

Differences within the OBCs

If the year of 1990 was marked by a controversy regarding implementation of the Mandal Commission report, which recommended policy of reservation in central government jobs for those belonging to the OBC category, recently there had been a controversy regarding the policy of reservation for the OBCs in institutions of higher education. There are large number of castes within this broad category called OBC, which could be divided broadly into three groups, the 'peasant OBC', the 'artisan OBC' and the 'service OBC'. As the nomenclature suggests, the peasant OBCs are generally agrarian and depend upon agriculture for their livelihood. The castes classified as the peasant OBCs category are generally considered as socially and economically better compared to other OBCs. The peasant OBCs category includes castes like *Yadav, Kurmi, Koeri, Lingayat, Vokkaliga, Kamma*, and *Reddy*, etc. Similarly, the artisan OBCs category includes those OBC castes, which are engaged in artisan and craftsman work and they are considered lower in social and economic hierarchy compared to the peasant OBC. The artisan OBCs category includes castes like Kumhar, Sonar, Lohar, Barahi, Bunkar and various others generally engaged in craftsman work. The third category referred to as the service OBCs includes castes like *Nai, Dhobi, Teli, Kewat, Mudaliar, Beldar*, etc. Most of these castes are engaged in providing services to other people (Table 12.5).

Table 12.5

Levels of Literacy Amongst OBCs in Different Regions

(in%)

Region	*Literate*	*Completed High School*	*Graduates*	*Post-graduates*
		Peasant OBC		
All	66	33	9	2.5
South-West	71	38	11	3.2
Rest of India	64	30	8	1.9
		Artisan OBC		
All	71	35	10	2.5
South-West	78	34	10	2.6
Rest of India	70	34	9	2.1
		Service OBC		
All	67	32	8	2.1
South-West	72	36	8	2.2
Rest of India	71	35	10	1.8

Note: South-West region includes, Kerala, Tamil Nadu, Karnataka, Andhra Pradesh, Gujarat and Maharashtra.

Source: National Election Study, 2009.

Patterns of Educational Attainment Amongst OBCs

There is a shared belief that socially, economically and educationally, the peasant OBCs are the most well off, followed by the artisan and service OBCs. There may be differences in social and economic conditions of the people belonging to three different OBC categories, but the findings of the data indicate at the national level that there is hardly any difference in the levels of educational attainment amongst the OBCs belonging to the three different categories. Not only the proportion of literates are more or less the same amongst these three OBC groups, even similar proportion amongst the three OBC categories have managed to attain a post-graduate degree and similar numbers among them managed to complete their high school education and college education. While at the national level, there are hardly any differences in the levels of educational attainment amongst the peasant OBCs, the artisan OBCs and the service OBCs, but the differences began to surface once we divided the OBC castes into different regions of the country.

If we divide the OBC castes into two different regions, the OBCs in the south-west region and the rest of India, it seems the OBCs from the states in the South West region are better off in terms of educational attainment compared to the OBCs of the rest of India, which largely include the OBCs of the Hindi heartland. Though there is not much difference in the level of educational attainment amongst the artisan and the service OBCs in difference regions, but in respect of educational attainment, the peasant OBCs of the south-west region are certainly ahead of the peasant OBC in the rest of India. Amongst the peasant OBCs from south-west region, 3.2 per cent managed to complete their post-graduate degree, and another 11 per cent of them completed their college education, but amongst the peasant OBCs of the rest of India, less than 2 per cent could complete their post-graduate education and 8 per cent of them managed to complete their college education.

Disparities in Levels of Educational Attainment Among Dalits

Findings presented in previous sections clearly indicate, there are disparities in levels of educational attainment amongst the Dalits compared to other castes groups. The disparity is much sharper if we compare the level of educational attainment amongst the Dalits with the upper castes, while this disparity is less compared to other caste groups. The data from the NES helps in mapping the disparity in different localities, the disparity in the rural areas and disparity in the urban areas. It is important to figure out the disparity in levels of educational attainment in urban and rural locations since Dalits are more rural compared to other sections of population. Compared to India being 72 per cent rural, amongst the Dalits, 83 per cent of Dalit population lives in the villages and only 17 per cent live in urban locations compared to 28 per cent of India's population being urban. If we compare the disparity in educational attainment among the upper castes and the Dalits, the disparity is more or less equal both in the rural and the urban setting, but the disparity becomes glaring once we try and look at the pattern of attainment of higher education among the Dalits and the upper castes in rural and urban areas. The rural Dalits seems to be at an extremely disadvantageous position when it comes to attaining higher education. The deficit in the level of educational attainment between the upper caste and the Dalits is more or less equal if seen only in terms of attaining basic education, both in rural and urban areas, but this deficit is much higher when it comes to attaining higher education. The proportion of upper castes graduates in urban location is three times more compared to the proportion of Dalit graduates in urban locations. We find similar deficit amongst the urban upper castes and urban Dalits if we look at the proportion of post-graduates amongst these two groups. It seems that the dropout amongst the urban Dalits after high school education is much higher compared to the dropout amongst the urban upper castes, while the difference in this dropout amongst the two groups is smaller in the rural areas (Table 12.6).

Table 12.6

Locality and Levels of Educational Attainment amongst Dalits

(in%)

Locality and Caste Group	*Literate*	*Completed High School*	*Graduates*	*Post-graduates*
Rural Dalits	53	18	4	1.2
Rural upper castes	72	37	10	2.5
The deficit	–19	–19	–6	–1.3
Urban Dalits	75	41	13	4.8
Urban upper castes	88	63	31	9.6
The deficit	–13	–22	–18	–4.8

Note: The deficit – the difference between the level of educational attainment between the Dalits and upper castes.

Source: National Election Study, 2009.

Table 12.7

Levels of Literacy Amongst Dalits in Different Locations

(in%)

Region	*Literate*	*Completed High School*	*Graduates*	*Post-graduates*
Rural Dalits in Hindi heartland states	48	19	4	1.0
Rural Dalits in rest of India	63	23	5	1.3
Urban Dalits in Hindi heartland states	70	40	16	7.0
Urban Dalits in rest of India	81	46	13	3.8

Note: Hindi heartland includes states of Bihar, UP, MP, Chhattisgarh, Uttaranchal, Jharkhand, Delhi, HP, Rajasthan and Haryana.

Source: National Election Study 2009.

There are also differences in levels of educational attainment amongst the Dalits living in different parts of the country. Dalits constitute 16.2 per cent of India's population, while the Dalits could be found in almost all the states, but they are concentrated in the Hindi speaking states. Of the total Dalit population, 49 per cent of Dalits live in the Hindi heartland states, which include states of Bihar, Uttar Pradesh, Madhya Pradesh, Chhattisgarh, Uttaranchal, Jharkhand, Delhi, Himachal Pradesh, Rajasthan, Haryana, while 51 per cent of all the Dalits are spread in all other states. The Dalits of the Hindi heartland both in the rural and urban area as are less educated compared to the Dalits in other parts of the country. This is clearly indicated in the figures for the deficit presented in the Table 12.6, but when it comes to attaining higher education, the urban Dalits in the Hindi heartland have performed better compared to the rural Dalits of the rest of India. Compared to 7 per cent post-graduate amongst Dalits living in urban location in Hindi heartland states, there are only 3.8 per cent post-graduates amongst urban Dalits from rest of the country. Similarly, amongst the urban Dalits in the Hindi heartland, 16 per cent completed their college education, but amongst the urban Dalits, living in other parts of the country, only 13 per cent Dalits managed to complete their college education (Table 12.7).

Level of Educational Disparity Among Adivasis

Compared to the other caste groups, the Adivasis are the most disadvantageous group if seen in terms of level of educational attainment. Only a little more than 50 per cent of the Adivasis are literate even after decades of independence. The situation is worse if we try to look at the attainment of higher education amongst the Adivasis, only 1.4 per cent have managed to get a post-graduate degree, and only 5 per cent are graduates. Less than one-fifth of them have managed to complete their high schooling. These findings are not surprising, but what is important to note is the disparity between the adivasis living in the north-eastern states compared to the adivasis living in southern, western and Hindi heartland states. It is important to look at this pattern since 12 per cent of the Adivasis live in these north-eastern states even though these are thinly populated states. The level of educational attainment amongst Adivasis of the seven north eastern states[3] is better compared to the adivasis living in other parts of the country. The Adivasis of the north-eastern states are the most literate, 82 per cent of them have managed to get educated. This is one of the highest proportions of educated among people from any caste community. But it seems the dropout amongst them is very high since only one-third of the Adivasis in the north-east managed to complete their high school education. But amongst those who managed to complete their high school, large numbers also completed their college education which is clear from the fact that 10 per cent of them are graduates while 2 per cent of them managed to complete their post-graduate education. If compared the level of educational attainment of the Adivasis of the other regions/states, the situation is very bad (Table 12.8).

Table 12.8

Levels of Literacy among Tribal of North East and from Rest of India

(in%)

Region	*Literate*	*Completed High School*	*Graduates*	*Post-graduates*
Adivasis of North-East	82	33	10	2.0
Adivasis of rest of India	51	19	5	1.4
The Gap	**-31**	**-14**	**-5**	**-0.6**
Dalits in states other than North-East	59	26	7	2.1
Gap between Adivasis and Dalits in States other than North-East	**-8**	**-7**	**-2**	**-0.7**
Upper caste in states other than North-East	79	49	19	5.3
Gap between Advasis and Upper Castes in States other than North-East	-28	-30	-14	-3.9

Notes: North East includes states of Arunachal Pradesh, Tripura, Meghalaya, Manipur, Nagaland, Mizoram, Sikkim and Assam.
Rest of India includes all other state.

Source: National Election Study 2009.

If compared the level of educational attainment of the Adivasis and the Dalits in the states other than the north-eastern states, the situation of the Adivasis in these states is very bad compared to the Dalits. If we compare the level of educational attainment of the Adivasis with the upper castes in the states other than the north-eastern states, the situation is appalling. There is a gap of 28 per cent amongst the literates, 30 per cent gap with regard to the high school educated, 14 per cent gap in respect of college educated and 3.9 per cent gap between the Adivasis and the upper castes, if seen in terms of those who managed to get a post-graduate degree.

Difference in Levels of Educational Attainment across Religious Groups

Findings from the Census of India clearly indicate, there are differences in levels of educational attainment amongst people belonging to different religions. Though numerically small, Christians seem to be the most literate, not only in respect of the basic education but also in respect of higher education. Amongst the Christians, not only 78 per cent are literate, 4 per cent have managed to complete their post-graduate education, and 13 per cent have completed their college education. Hindus do not lag far behind the Christians as 3.5 per cent amongst them managed to attain a post-graduate degree while 12 per cent completed their college education. More than two-thirds of Hindus are literate. The Muslims do not lag far behind the Hindus if seen in terms of proportion of literates, but the disparity in educational attainment begin to surface if we compare the proportion of Muslims who managed to complete their high school education, or those who managed to complete their college education and also those who have a post-graduate degree. Compared to 3.5 per cent post-graduates amongst the Hindus, there are only 1.8 per cent post-graduates amongst the Muslims; there are even 4 per cent less graduates amongst the Muslims compared to the Hindus. There are also sizeable differences in the proportion of high school educated amongst the Hindus and the Muslims. In respect of high school education, the Sikhs and the Buddhists are not lagging behind the Hindus, but lesser proportion amongst the Buddhist and the Sikh manage to complete their college education (Table 12.9).

Table 12.9

Differences in Level of Educational Attainment Amongst Various Religious Groups

(in%)

Religion	*Literate*	*Completed High School*	*Graduates*	*Post-graduates*
Hindu	70	37	12	3.5
Muslim	68	29	8	1.8
Christian	78	43	13	4.0
Sikh	70	39	8	2.3
Buddhist	76	33	8	3.4

Source: National Election Study, 2009.

Disparities in Levels of Educational Attainment amongst Muslims

Muslims lag behind the Hindus with respect of levels of educational attainment. The aggregate picture indicates that though Muslims lag behind the Hindus in respect of educational attainment, the situation does not seem to be too bad for the Muslims with regard to educational attainment. The picture becomes clear only when we compare the Hindus and the Muslims at disaggregate level.

Table 12.10

Levels of Literacy Among Muslims

(in%)

Region	*Literate*	*Completed High School*	*Graduates*	*Post-graduates*
Urban Muslims	78	41	12	2.8
Urban Hindus	83	55	24	7.7
The gap	-5	-14	-12	-4.9
Rural Muslims	62	22	5	1.2
Rural Hindus	62	27	7	1.7
The gap	—	-5	-2	-0.5

Source: National Election Study 2009.

Table 12.11

Levels of Literacy Among Muslims in Hindi Heartland and Rest of India

(in%)

Region	*Literate*	*Completed High School*	*Graduates*	*Post-graduates*
Muslims in developed states	80	39	9	2.3
Hindus in developed states	70	39	13	3.8
The gap	+10	—	-4	-1.5
Muslims in rest of India	64	27	7	1.6
Hindus in rest of India	70	36	12	3.2
The gap	-6	-9	-5	-1.6

Note: Developed states include Andhra Pradesh, Kerala, Tamil Nadu, Karnataka, Maharashtra, Gujarat, Punjab, and Haryana.

Source: National Election Study, 2009.

Let us first compare the level of educational attainment amongst rural Muslims and rural Hindus and vice versa. There is not much gap in level of educational attainment between the rural Muslims and rural Hindus. Amongst both the rural Hindus and the rural Muslims, there are 62 per cent literate, and more or less equal proportions amongst the rural Hindus and rural Muslims managed to complete their school education as well as college education. Similar proportions amongst the rural Hindus and rural Muslims managed to complete their post-graduate education. But the difference in level of educational attainment is much higher between the urban Hindus and the urban Muslims. The Muslims living in urban localities lag behind the urban Hindus at all levels of educational attainment. The gap in level of educational attainment between the urban Hindus and urban Muslims begins at the level of attainment of primary education and the gap becomes much wider as one goes up higher in educational hierarchy. Amongst the urban Hindus there are 7.7 per cent post-graduates, compared to only 2.8 per cent post-graduates amongst the urban Muslims. The proportion of graduates amongst urban Hindus is twice the number of graduates amongst the urban Muslims. There is also a 14 per cent gap in the proportion of high school educated amongst the urban Hindus and the urban Muslims (Table 12.10).

Relative backwardness of the Muslims with regard to educational attainment is also evident if we compare the educational attainment amongst Hindus and Muslims in developed and underdeveloped states.[4] Muslims constitute 13.7 per cent of India's population and are spread in all the states in different proportions. These eight developed states account for 30 per cent of country's Muslim population while the rest 70 per cent is spread in various other states. Apart from these developed states there are large number of Muslims in states of Assam, Bihar, Uttar Pradesh, Jammu and Kashmir and West Bengal. The Muslims seem to be fairly educated in the developed states. In the developed states in respect of attaining basic education, Muslims are more educated compared to Hindus. In developed states, amongst Muslims 80 per cent are educated compared to only 70 per cent literate amongst the Hindus. In these states equal proportions amongst Hindus and Muslims managed to complete their school education, but the Hindus take a lead over the Muslims in respect of attaining higher education, i.e., completing college or much higher education. In developed states, amongst the Muslims, 2.3 per cent are post-graduates while amongst the Hindus 3.8 per cent are post-graduates (Table 12.11).

The disparity with regard to educational attainment among the Hindus and Muslims is more visible if we compare the level of educational attainment amongst Hindus and Muslims in underdeveloped states. The Muslims lag behind the Hindus in the underdeveloped states at all levels of educational attainment. While in developed states there are more literates amongst the Muslims compared to the Hindus, but in the underdeveloped states, the Hindus outnumber the Muslims with regard to the proportion of literates. This gap between the Hindus and the Muslims is much large if we look at the number of school educated in the underdeveloped states. The gap at no stage narrows down but one can notice that the Muslims consistently lag behind the Hindus in respect of educational attainment in underdeveloped states.

Caste/Class Dimension in Educational Inequalities

Caste is still an important factor, which influences the educational attainment of the people. The educational attainment is much higher among the upper caste compared to the OBCs, Dalits or the Adivasis even if they belong to the same economic class. Amongst the upper class upper castes, 11.6 per cent are post-graduates, 33 per cent are graduates and 68 per cent managed to complete their high schooling. Compared to this, amongst the upper class Dalits, only 7.9 per cent are post-graduates, 20 per cent managed to complete their college education and only 48 per cent managed to complete their high school education. The situation among the upper class Adivasis is quite similar to that of the Dalits, except that, the dropout amongst the Adivasis is much higher after completing their school education compared to what is experienced amongst the Dalits. Amongst the Adivasis, only 5.9 per cent managed to complete their post-graduate education while, 24 per cent of them managed to complete their college education. Amongst the upper class Muslims, there are only 4.7 per cent post-graduates and only 20 per cent managed to complete their college education (Table 12.12).

Table 12.12

Economic Class and Levels of Educational Attainment among Different Caste/Community

(in%)

Class/Caste	*Completed High School*	*Graduate*	*Post-graduate*
Upper Class			
Upper Caste	68	33	11.6
OBC	55	22	7.9
SC	48	20	7.9
ST	57	24	5.9
Muslim	51	20	4.7
Middle Class			
Upper Caste	61	24	5.4
OBC	51	17	4.0
SC	46	13	3.8
ST	46	13	2.5
Muslim	45	14	3.2
Lower Class			
Upper Caste	33	6	1.3
OBC	28	4	0.8
SC	23	4	1.0
ST	20	3	0.6
Muslim	21	3	0.5
Poor Class			
Upper Caste	17	3	0.7
OBC	13	2	0.5
SC	11	2	0.2
ST	10	2	0.5
Muslim	9	1	0.4

Source: National Election Study, 2009.

There are also differences in levels of educational attainment amongst the upper castes, OBCs, Dalits and the Adivasis even if all belong to the same economic background. The level of educational attainment is higher amongst the poor upper castes compared to the poor OBCs, poor Dalits and the Adivasis belonging to the same economic class. Amongst the poor upper caste, 17 per cent managed to complete their high schooling, compared to only 13 per cent amongst the poor OBC, 11 per cent amongst the poor Dalits and only 10 per cent amongst the Adivasis of the same economic class. But, the proportion of graduates and the post-graduates amongst people belonging to various caste groups from same economic class does not vary much. The level of educational attainment amongst the poor Muslims is the lowest, only 9 per cent amongst the poor Muslims are literate, and only 1 per cent of the poor Muslims managed to complete their college education.

The pattern of levels of educational attainment does not change amongst the middle class belonging to various castes. The influence of caste in levels of educational attainment can be clearly seen since the middle class upper caste is more educated compared to the middle class Dalits or the middle class Adivasis.

Conclusion

Modern education, i.e., education based on the advancement of knowledge and science in England and teaching in English at the secondary and higher levels in India was introduced by the British upon their arrival in India,[5] with the aim of creating a class of Indian elite that could help the British in ruling and administering the country. The British were not interested in the spread of mass education and were interested in creating a class of Indians which was 'British' in its thinking and approach. Thus, the prevailing backwardness in the field of education can to an extent be explained through the system put in place by the British, where even today higher education despite various efforts by the government is accessible to a select few. These 'privileged' sections of society who managed to attain education earlier compared to the masses, try to maintain their monopoly over higher education as it helps them to continue their dominance in the society.

The findings of the survey data presented in the paper clearly indicate, even after six decades of India's independence, there are disparities in levels of educational attainment. The disparity is perpetuated by various factors like caste, community, class, religion, locality, region and similar such groups and subgroups, but caste is still one of the most determining factors that influences educational mobility. The disparity in levels of educational attainment correspond to the system of caste hierarchy in India, higher is the social status of the caste, greater is their access to education and vice versa. The government with its commitment to provide basic elementary education to all, initiated various literacy programmes. It seems, some of the initiatives of the government did bring some results since though the gap in educational attainment is clear amongst various caste communities, i.e., the upper castes being more educated compared to the Dalits or the Adivasis, but generally the gap at the bottom of the pyramid of various levels of educational attainment is not large. Also the gap in the level of educational attainment at the starting level between various castes has narrowed down over the last few decades. The gap in the level of educational attainment is bigger if we look at the patterns of attainment of high school education or higher education.

These findings draw attention toward the issues of access to basic education. Though there would be hindrances to even the access of education, but largely at the level of basic education there does not seem to be the critical problem. The disparities in educational attainment begin to surface at the level of high school education or even higher education. There is a problem of higher number of dropout of children from the lower caste groups compared to those who belong to the upper castes. A higher rate of dropout may be more due to problem of access due to their poor economic condition or the need for engaging the children in various economic activities to support the family income. This could be one possible reason for the larger proportion of dropouts amongst children/students from the lower class also families. Possibly because of the poor economic condition of the people belonging to the lower castes, they are unable to continue the education of their children. Since the government is committed to giving free basic education, many of them do send their children to the government school where they do not have to pay any fee, but when it comes to higher education which is largely self financed the parents withdraw their children and engage them in other productive activities. The problem is more visible amongst the lower castes compared to the upper castes since the proportion of the rich would be much larger amongst the upper castes who can afford the expenses of higher education for their children, compared to the proportion of the rich amongst the lower castes people and vice versa.

But does that mean that the disparity in educational attainment only has an economic dimension and the differences in the levels of educational attainments is not influenced by the caste of the individual. Findings of the NES 2009 have clearly indicated that along with class, caste also influences the levels of educational attainment. There are differences in levels of educational attainment amongst people from same economic class, but belonging to different caste.

Clearly, caste and class both influence the levels of educational attainment. Neither being rich nor belonging to the upper caste solely ensures maximum access to the higher education. Class does influence the level of economic attainment, but caste identity of the person also affects his/her access to education. To solve this problem, there is a need for a two-way approach, which is a mix of both the caste and the class. Caste-based discrimination suggests, there is still a need for caste-based reservation, but there is also need for a policy of protective discrimination for people from economically weaker sections across different castes. The economic status of the people does influence the level of educational attainment, but caste background of the people also influences access to education.

Notes

1. The provision in the Indian Constitution regarding Right to Education for children below age 6–14 was placed under the Directive Principles of the State Policy. But, more recently, the Central Government has passed the Right of Children to Free and Compulsory Education Bill, 2008, which, makes the right to free education for children between age group 6 and 14, a fundamental right. The Bill also aims to reserve 25 per cent seats to weaker sections in private schools. The Union Minister for Human Resource Development, Kapil Sibal described the passing of this bill as 'harbinger of a new era for children to meet the challenge of the 21st century'. This is a historic opportunity for providing better future to children of the country, as there was never such landmark legislation in the last 62 years since independence.
2. National Election Study is a nation-wide study of people's opinion; attitudes and perception related to various issues relating to politics, society, and security and similar such issues. A total of 36,169 respondents were successfully interviewed from a list of over 59,000 respondents randomly selected using the most updated electoral rolls. The interviews were conducted at 2,808 locations spread across all the states barring the smaller ones like the Lakshwadeep, Dadar and Nagar Haveli, Andaman and Nicobar, etc. For more details about the methodology see National Election Study 2009: A Methodological Note, *Economic and Political Weekly*, September 26, 2009, pp. 196–202.
3. North-eastern states include states of Arunachal Pradesh, Tripura, Meghalaya, Manipur, Mizoram, Sikkim and Assam.
4. Developed states include states of Andhra Pradesh, Kerala, Tamil Nadu, Karnataka, Maharashtra, Gujarat, Punjab and Haryana.
5. A.R. Kamat, 'The Educational Situation', *Economic and Political Weekly*, Vol. 7, No. 26 (June 24, 1972), http://www.jstor.org/stable/4361515, accessed on April 7, 2010.

13

Quality Education under Sarva Siksha Abhiyaan

A Performance Appraisal

S.K. PANT

Education has always been perceived as one of the most important social inputs that has the capability for bringing about substantial transformation in the socio-economic and cultural life of the people, the region and the nation (Eleventh Plan, 2008). Ever since the launching of First Five-Year Plan in the early 1950s, efforts have been targeted not only towards enhancing its coverage but also providing the masses with quality education. The launching of a plethora of educational programmes in the ensuing various subsequent plan periods bears testimony to the fact about how serious our planners, social activists and nation builders were (Pant, 2009).

The impact of all these endeavours, however, has rather been a mixed one. On the one hand it has not only succeeded is increasing the state of physical infrastructure manifold times, enhanced the students enrolment rate and number of teachers in the schools but has also pushed the overall level of literacy from a mere 18 per cent in 1951 to over 65 per cent in 2001 (ibid.). But the flip-side of development has also been equally appalling, which has been manifested in the form of heightening of educational disparities that cut across gender, caste and regional domains, high level of dropouts at the primary and secondary levels, increasing marginalisation of the deprived sections of society and dilution in the quality of education (Kaul, 2002; NSSO 52nd Round; Visaria, et al., 1993).

Showing concern over these developments, the government appointed various committees to look into the overall functioning of education sector which suggested appropriate and relevant interventions.

Based on the recommendations of these committees, the government finally launched a very ambitious programme identified as Sarva Siksha Abhiyaan (SSA) in the whole country in 2001.

This programme not only aimed to universalise the elementary education through community ownership of school system, but also to address the issues of quality of education. All this was to be achieved through a series of social interventions in which the community had to play a key role (Sarva Siksha Abhiyaan, Framework for Implementation, MHRD, 2008).

What has been unique in this programme is its compatibility with other educational programmes that were earlier being executed independently. Now with SSA, the entire gamut of educational activities, which starts with early childhood care to elementary and secondary education, has been perceived holistically (ibid.). It is, perhaps, for the first time also that the programme solicits support of community to run with a missionary zeal.

Performance of SSA

The ensuing exercise attempts to analyse the performance of SSA in the 18 districts of eastern Uttar Pradesh. These districts are Mirzapur, Sonebhadra, Chandauli, Varanasi, Bhadohi, Mau, Ghazipur, Fatehpur, Ballia, Pratapgarh, Gorakhpur, Allahabad, Kaushambi, Maharajganj, Jaunpur, and Azamgarh.

However, due to time constraints, the performance of SSA in five contiguous districts, viz., Mirzapur, Sonebhadra, Chandauli, Varanasi, Bhadohi, and Allahabad has been deliberately selected to study the performance of educational achievements of the programme and study the trend of performance. For studying the achievement levels, the performance of students in all the sample districts has been taken up. The study finally identifies the factors that are militating against the scope of the programme. The study is confined to the period of 2007–08.

Further, for ensuing quality education under SSA, various social interventions have been envisaged, viz., provision of Teachers Learning Materials (TLM) grant, TLM being used by them, provision of training to the teachers, ensuring teachers school optimal ratio, provision of supervision of Block Resource Centre (BRC) and Nyan Panchayat Resource Centres (NPRCs), etc. An attempt has therefore been made to see how and to what extent these provisions have really helped the teachers engaged in SSA, to impart quality education.

The selection of sample has been made as per the SSA guidelines and 5 per cent of the schools in the whole district were randomly selected. However, care was taken to select every kind of school, even if its proportion was quite insignificant. For analysis purpose, we have taken up only the primary and upper primary schools. A brief methodology adopted for the study has been summarised below (Table 13.1).

Table 13.1

Profile of the Primary and Upper Primary Schools

Districts	*Primary School*		*Upper Primary School*		*Total (PS+ UPS)*	
	Total	*Sample*	*Total*	*Sample*	*Total*	*Sample*
Mirzapur*	1350	70	367	20	1718	90
Sonebhadra	1150	65	375	20	1525	85
Chandauli	915	49	339	19	1254	68
Varanasi	1015	51	325	16	1340	67
Bhadoi	564	30	273	14	837	44
Allahabad	2280	116	888	45	3168	160
Total of 18 districts	23295	1363	7748	474	31043	1837

*Initially 72 were selected but as it also has two new primary school which have been sanctioned during the academic years. They were, hence, not included for analysis purpose. Thus, the total number of primary school surveyed was 70.

Source: BSA Offices of the respective districts.

Thus, the total 514 sample schools selected for analysis, over 74 per cent belonged to primary level and remaining about 26 per cent to upper primary level, while the total number of schools selected from 18 districts was 1,837.

Teacher Learning Material (TLM) Grant Received and Utilisation Pattern

Under the SSA, the school teachers are provided grant under the head TLM grant whereby they can procure or even buy material to make course contents interesting sample to understand for the students. The study shows that none of the schools in all the six districts had received cent per cent grant, both at the primary as well as upper primary levels. The level of grant received by the teachers at the primary level varied between 75 per cent in Mirzapur to as high as 93 per cent in Allahabad while for upper primary level, the lowest proportion of schools getting grants was once again Mirzapur where about 73 per cent of the schools had received it, while its proportion for the Allahabad was 96 per cent. Further, the study also shows that while 68 per cent of the overall schools at the primary level in the whole sample had received the grants, its proportion for upper primary level was about 63 per cent (Table 13.2).

What has really been the cause for anxiety and disappointment was that lesser proportion of teachers who had already received this grant had utilised it for furthering the quality of teaching in the class. In other words, the teachers have not been able to appreciate the basic purpose of providing grant and they need to be motivated and sensitised for using it. Table 13.2 shows that in the case of Mirzapur, about 80 per cent of the teachers had utilised it for either buying the TLM from the market or for making it through inputs sought from the market. In the case of Sonebhadra it was much lesser at 64 per cent. The highest proportion of teachers utilising the TLM grants came from Allahabad where about 96 per cent of the total grant had been utilised at the primary school level.

Table 13.2

TLM Grants Received by Teachers

Districts	*Primary School*			*Upper Primary School*		
	Yes	*No*	*Total*	*Yes*	*No*	*Total*
Mirzapur	154 (75.0)	52 (25.0)	206	24 (73.0)	9 (27.0)	33
Sonebhadra	176 (84.0)	34 (16.0)	210	27 (77.0)	8 (23.0)	35
Chandauli	157 (83.0)	32 (17.0)	189	58 (83.0)	12 (17.0)	70
Varanasi	276 (88.0)	37 (12.0)	313	79 (95.0)	4 (5.0)	83
Bhadoi	91 (88.0)	12 (12.0)	103	40 (85.0)	7 (15.0)	47
Allahabad	398 (93.0)	32 (7.0)	430	148 (96.0)	6 (4.0)	154
Total of 18 districts	3428 (68.0)	1594 (32.0)	5022	1054 (63.0)	616 (37.0)	1670

Source: Field data, 2006–07; 2007–08.

The study further shows that the TLM grant utilisation pattern at the upper primary level was relatively much better and in Chandauli and Allahabad district the proportion of teachers utilising the grant was worked out to be cent per cent and 93 per cent respectively. However, for Mirzapur and Bhadoi district this proportion dropped to 67 and 63 per cent respectively. The overall level of grant utilisation for all the 18 district at the primary as well as upper primary levels was reported to be 76 per cent and 80 per cent respectively (Table 13.3).

Table 13.3

TLM Amount being Utilised by Teachers

Districts	*Primary School*		*Upper Primary School*	
	Yes	*No*	*Yes*	*No*
Mirzapur	123 (80.0)	31 (20.0)	16 (67.0)	8 (33.3)
Sonebhadra	112 (64.0)	64 (36.0)	21 (78.0)	6 (22.0)
Chandauli	137 (87.0)	20 (13.0)	58 (100.0)	- (0.0)
Varanasi	197 (71.0)	79 (29.0)	59 (75.0)	20 (25.0)
Bhadoi	67 (74.0)	24 (26.0)	25 (63.0)	15 (37.0)
Allahabad	381 (96.0)	127 (4.0)	137 (93.0)	11 (7.0)
Total of 18 districts	2603 (76.0)	825 (24.0)	842 (80.0)	212 (20.0)

Source: Field data, 2007.

Frequency of Utilisation of TLM by Teachers

Mere distribution and utilisation of TLM does not ensure improvement in the quality of teaching unless it is being regularly used by the concerned teachers. Thus, the regular and sustained utilisation of TLM goes a long way to enhance the quality of teaching. An attempt has also been made to study the pattern and frequency of utilisation of TLM by the teachers both at the primary as well as upper primary levels in the sample schools of the six districts, as well as for the whole sample schools of 18 districts.

The study of the frequency of utilisation of TLM provides a very disappointing picture as hardly 21 per cent of the total teachers in all the 18 districts at the primary levels as well as upper primary level respectively make use of TLM on regular basis. The study further shows that about 54 per cent of the teachers at the primary level and 52 per cent at the upper primary levels were utilising it occasionally, while the remaining 25 per cent and 27 per cent of the teachers at primary and upper primary level have, so far, not utilised it for the teaching purpose.

The scenario in the six districts also depicts a very disappointing picture as the proportion of teachers utilising the TLM material regularly was reported to be hardly 4 per cent in Bhadoi and was reported to be as high as 50 per cent in Chandauli district at primary level while hardly 22 per cent of the teachers of Allahabad and 50 per cent in Mirzapur were utilising it regularly at the upper primary level. What has been a major cause of concern is that quite a substantial proportion of teachers varying from 44 per cent to 21 per cent in Mirzapur and Allahabad were not utilising TLM at the primary level and equally substantial number of them were not utilising at the upper primary level (Table 13.4).

Table 13.4

Pattern of Utilisation of TLM by Teachers

Districts	*Regular*		*Some times*		*Never*	
	PS	*UPS*	*PS*	*UPS*	*PS*	*UPS*
Mirzapur	21 (17.0)	8 (50.0)	76 (62.0)	5 (31.0)	26 (21.0)	3 (19.0)
Sonebhadra	36 (32.0)	9 (43.0)	68 (61.0)	7 (33.0)	8 (7.0)	5 (24.0)
Chandauli	69 (50.0)	28 (48.0)	52 (38.0)	24 (41.0)	16 (12.0)	6 (11.0)
Varanasi	38 (19.0)	—	89 (45.0)	39 (66.0)	70 (36.0)	20 (34.0)
Bhadoi	3 (4.0)	—	35 (52.0)	18 (72.0)	29 (44.0)	7 (28.0)
Allahabad	131 (34.0)	30 (22.0)	173 (45.0)	82 (60.0)	77 (21.0)	25 (18.0)
Total of 18 districts	550 (21.0)	173 (21.0)	1395 (54.0)	442 (52.0)	658 (25.0)	227 (27.0)

Note: PS – Primary School; UPS – Upper Primary School.

Source: Field data 2006–07; 2007–08.

Frequency of TLM Utilisation by Students

There are two purposes of providing TLM in SSA. Besides providing necessary guidance and help to the teachers, it also supports and supplements the learning process of the students as well. The various models, charts and other items provided in the classroom help them (teacher and the taught) to comprehend the subject more objectively and prepare well. Thus, regular use of TLM enables the students to grasp and comprehend the subject matter in a much better way. Hence, an attempt has also been made to see to what extent the students make use of these TLM articles.

The study shows that in the majority of districts, the use of TLM by the students has been disappointingly low. In Mirzapur, in about 19 per cent of the schools, the students were making use of the TLM, in Sonebhadra, students in about 11 per cent schools were utilising TLM in their day to day learning. Except for Allahabad where in about 45 per cent schools, the students were using TLM articles, the overall usage in other sample districts was adjectively low. The analysis shows that the average level, for the whole of the 18 districts, was about 24 per cent at the primary level. Likewise, the study shows that the trend of TLM usage at the upper primary level was also quite disappointing. In Mirzapur, for instance, no student in any of the 20 sample schools was found to be utilising TLM in the studies; similarly in Sonebhadra hardly in 10 per cent of the schools, the students were found to be utilising TLM for furthering their studies. The two districts where the use of TLM was relatively higher were Bhadoi and Allahabad where about 43 per cent and 55 per cent of the schools encouraged the students to utilise TLM. The overall level of usage was reported to be 24 per cent and about 26 per cent at primary and upper primary levels respectively (Table 13.5).

Table 13.5

TLM Utilisation by Students in Sample Schools

Districts	*Primary School*		*Upper Primary School*	
	Yes	*No*	*Yes*	*No*
Mirzapur	13 (18.6)	57 (81.4)	—	20 (100.0)
Sonebhadra	7 (10.8)	58 (89.2)	2 (10.0)	18 (90.0)
Chandauli	5 (10.9)	41 (89.1)	3 (18.8)	13 (81.2)
Varanasi	14 (28.6)	35 (71.4)	3 (21.4)	11 (78.6)
Bhadoi	6 (20.0)	24 (80.0)	6 (42.9)	8 (57.1)
Allahabad	52 (45.2)	63 (54.8)	23 (54.8)	19 (45.2)
Total of 18 districts	321 (24.4)	999 (75.6)	112 (26.4)	313 (73.6)

Source: Field data, 2007.

School-Teacher Ratio

The SSA guidelines have clearly set up norms defining what should be the optimum ratio between the teacher and the school. Accordingly, there should be one teacher for every 40 children at primary and upper primary levels. Further, there should be at least two teachers in a primary school and one teacher for every class in upper primary school. One of the three teachers sanctioned under SSA for every new upper primary school will need to be a teacher with mathematics and science specific educational background. The guideline further reinforces that wherever there is a need for additional teacher at upper primary level, to maintain the pupil-teacher ratio of 40:1, the additional teachers sanctioned under SSA, if need to be provided, be recruited from Science/Mathematics background.

Thus, the school ratio holds a very crucial place for maintaining and imparting quality education. Accordingly, an attempt has also been made to study the school ratio pattern in the sample districts. The perusal of the table shows that the distribution pattern is highly skewed. In districts like Mirzapur, Sonebhadra over 68 per cent and 80 per cent of the schools, at the primary level, were having one teacher less. The situation, however, improved for districts like Chandauli, Varanasi, Bhadoi and Allahabad, where the schools having no teacher or only teacher were 15 per cent, 16 per cent, about 17 per cent and about 2 per cent respectively, which by no means could be discounted while considering the SSAs objective of universal coverage and imparting quality education respectively. The study further shows that there were about 10 per cent of the schools for all the 18 districts, which were either without teacher or having only one teacher.

Similarly, in the case of upper primary schools, the scenario is equally depressing. It could be seen that over 18 per cent of the schools for the entire 18 districts were either without teacher or were having only one teacher. The situation in the following two districts, viz., Mirzapur and Sonebhadra was quite precarious as the proportion of schools violating the SSA guidelines was 55 per cent, 15 per cent, 68 per cent, and 80 per cent of the total respectively. The study also highlights that some of the schools had more than adequate number of teachers, however their proportion at the primary as well upper primary level was quite marginal (Table 13.6).

Training Status of the Teacher

Training of the teachers form a very crucial and integral part of development that finally affects the overall quality of teaching and performance of the teachers. Under the SSA, the teachers are supposed to undertake training at multi-levels that includes induction training for newly recruited teachers to 10 days in service training for all teachers each years. Besides this they are also exposed to myriad amount of activities and

Table 13.6

Profile of the School-Teachers Working Ratio in Sample Schools

Districts	*No. of Teachers in Primary School*							
	0	*1*	*2*	*3*	*4*	*5*	*6*	*7 and above*
1	*2*	*3*	*4*	*5*	*6*	*7*	*8*	*9*
Mirzapur	1 (1.4)	47 (67.1)	16 (22.9)	5 (7.1)	1 (1.4)	—	—	—
Sonebhadra	9 (13.8)	43 (66.2)	13 (20.0)	—	—	—	—	—
Chandauli	—	7 (15.2)	23 (50.0)	8 (17.4)	7 (15.2)	1 (2.2)	—	—
Varanasi	7 (14.3)	—	1 (2.0)	—	7 (14.3)	7 (14.3)	3 (6.1)	24 (48.9)
Bhadoi	—	—	5 (16.7)	10 (33.3)	13 (43.3)	1 (3.3)	1 (3.3)	—
Allahabad	—	2 (1.7)	9 (7.8)	41 (35.7)	29 (25.2)	8 (5.9)	2 (1.7)	5 (4.3)
Total of 18 districts	19 (0.7)	122 (9.3)	149 (11.3)	420 (31.9)	352 (26.7)	128 (7.7)	63 (4.8)	65 (4.9)
Districts	*No. of Teachers in Upper Primary School*							
	0	*1*	*2*	*3*	*4*	*5*	*6*	*7 and above*
	10	*11*	*12*	*13*	*14*	*15*	*16*	*17*
Mirzapur	3 (15.0)	8 (40.0)	3 (15.0)	4 (20.0)	2 (10.0)	—	—	—
Sonebhadra	1 (5.0)	8 (40.0)	7 (35.0)	2 (10.0)	2 (10.0)	—	—	—
Chandauli	—	6 (37.5)	—	5 (31.3)	—	3 (18.8)	1 (6.3)	1 (6.3)
Varanasi	—	2 (14.3)	—	2 (14.3)	2 (14.3)	2 (14.3)	1 (7.1)	5 (35.7)
Bhadoi	—	1 (6.3)	2 (12.5)	7 (43.8)	2 (12.5)	1 (6.3)	1 (6.3)	—
Allahabad	—	6 (14.3)	8 (19.0)	10 (23.8)	3 (7.1)	5 (11.9)	5 (11.9)	5 (11.9)
Total of 18 districts	4 (0.9)	74 (17.4)	72 (16.9)	95 (22.4)	63 (14.8)	40 (9.4)	41 (9.6)	36 (8.5)

Source: Field data, 2007.

training sessions at various stages of their teaching career that helps them to broaden their understanding and perception. This exercise also equips them with the latest happening in the field of pedagogy.

The study of training status of the teachers both at the primary as well as upper primary level points out to a very depressing picture. It shows that the overall training level of teachers from all the 18 districts, at the primary level, was just about 53 per cent, while hardly about 32 per cent of the teachers were found to be trained at the upper primary level.

Further, the training profile of the teachers in the six selected districts also projects a very dismal picture. In Mirzapur hardly 21 per cent of the total teachers at the primary level and about 61 per cent at the upper primary level had received training while in Chandauli district about 23 per cent and 17 per cent of the teachers were found to be trained at primary and upper primary level. The situation in other remaining districts was equally appalling. Another disappointing aspect of the whole episode was that the training models did not uniformly cover all the teachers. It was found that quite a few of the teachers had received training in more than one subject. Hence when this aspect is also taken into account, the overall level of training drastically falls, which spells good signals neither for the teachers nor for the programme (Table 13.7).

Table 13.7

Details of the Training taken by Teachers

Districts	*Primary School*	*Upper Primary School*
	Total	*Total*
Mirzapur	44 (21.4)	20 (60.6)
Sonebhadra	165 (87.3)	57* (190)
Chandauli	43 (22.8)	12 (17.1)
Varanasi	203 (64.9)	38 (45.8)
Bhadoi	36 (35.0)	11 (23.4)
Allahabad	293 (68.1)	59 (38.3)
Total of 18 districts	2629 (52.6)	534 (31.9)

Note: Quiet a few of the teachers have received training in more than one subject which further lowers the overall level of training.

Source: Field data, 2007.

Absenteeism Pattern among Teachers

Quality of education also has a strong bearing on how consistent or regular the teachers are in the class. Thus, higher the level of consistency in the presence of teachers, the better will be the performance of students and vice-versa. An attempt has also been made to study the pattern of absenteeism of teachers in the school. The criterion adopted was to observe how many teachers were present in the school on the validation day.

The study of incidence of absenteeism among teachers both at the primary as well as upper primary level, by and large, was at par at about 18 per cent for primary and upper primary classes for all the 18 districts. It further shows that at both the levels, the incidence of absenteeism was more pronounced among the assistant teachers' category and least among the head teachers, which is truly a cause of concern because the onus of teaching is definitely more on the assistant teachers of the school and their subsequent absence is more likely to affect the quality of teaching. The analysis also shows the incidence of absenteeism was more visible in districts like Mirzapur, Sonebhadra, in particular and to some extent in Chandauli and Varanasi district respectively (Table 13.8).

Table 13.8

Incidence of Absenteeism among Teachers

Districts	*Primary School*				*Upper Primary School*		
	HT	*AT*	*SM*	*Total*	*HT*	*AT*	*Total*
Mirzapur	72 (20.8)	65 (38.5)	69 (26.1)	206 (28.2)	18 (16.7)	15 (46.7)	33 (30.3)
Sonebhadra	46 (6.5)	27 (33.3)	137 (13.1)	210 (14.3)	15 (26.7)	20 (30.0)	35 (28.6)
Chandauli	40 (7.5)	83 (44.6)	66 (30.3)	189 (31.7)	18 (22.2)	52 (17.3)	70 (18.6)
Varanasi	44 (18.2)	189 (31.2)	80 (13.7)	313 (24.9)	13 (23.1)	70 (11.4)	83 (13.3)
Bhadoi	23 (4.3)	29 (6.9)	51 (5.9)	103 (5.8)	11 (9.1)	36 (8.3)	47 (8.5)
Allahabad	107 (15.0)	131 (28.2)	192 (9.3)	430 (16.5)	33 (21.2)	121 (19.1)	154 (19.5)
Total of 18 districts	1151 (14.5)	1639 (24.5)	2211 (14.8)	5001 (17.9)	359 (15.6)	1314 (16.7)	1673 (16.5)

Note: Figures in parentheses denote percentage.
HT – Head Teacher.
AT – Assistant Teacher.
SM – Shiksha Mitra.

Source: Field data.

Teacher-Pupil Ratio

According to SSA guidelines, the quality of education and teaching can only be ensured when there is an optimum ratio between the teacher and the taught. It accepts the fact that if the number of students exceeds that stipulated limit, not only it adversely affects the quality of teaching but also the education. Accordingly, it accepts the optimum ratio as 1:40 or there should be one teacher for every 40 students.

The study of teachers and students ratio shows that this criterion is largely being followed both at the primary as well as upper primary levels which augers well for the programme. In fact in all the sample districts this ratio was well within the stipulated mark at the primary level, which substantiates the fact that this variable cannot be taken to be a militating factor so far as the performance of SSA is considered. However, at the upper primary level, except for Allahabad where ratio between teacher and student was worked out to be 1:25, in all the remaining districts it was well above the optimum mark and for district like Bhadoi, it was highly skewed at 1:47! All this implies that there was an urgent need for teacher recruitment at the upper primary level if the quality of teaching is to be ensured. Subsequently it also spells the need to sensitise and motivate the parent to send their wards to schools at the elementary levels, which will help in improving the teacher-pupil ratio also (Table 13.9).

Table 13.9

Teachers-Students Ratio in Sample Schools

Districts	*Primary School*			*Upper Primary School*		
	No. of Teachers	*No. of Students*	*TS Ratio*	*No. of Teachers*	*No. of Students*	*TS Ratio*
Mirzapur	206	—	—	33	—	—
Sonebhadra	210	6881	1:33	35	1908	1:55
Chandauli	189	6129	1:32	70	1558	
Varanasi	313	7540	1:24	83	3355	1:40
Bhadoi	103	930	1:09	47	6895	1:147
Allahabad	430	16277	1:37	154	3922	1:25
Total of 18 districts	5001	162797	1:33	1673	52318	1:32

Source: Field data, 2007.

Pattern of Supervision by Block Resource Centre (BRC)

Supervision and monitoring has been one of the essential and integral aspects of SSA guideline. It envisages that the states would accord priority to developing and regularly implementing monitoring systems to measure the quality related outcomes, *inter alia*, for students learning outcomes, teacher's performance, students and teachers attendance rates and a host of other school curriculum related issues.

These interventions basically are targeted to improve and enhance the overall functioning of the programme as well as enhancing the level of quality of teaching in the class by addressing the bottlenecks experienced by both the students and the school administration alike. An attempt has also been made to study the pattern of supervision by the block resource centres (BRCs) for primary as well as upper primary schools. The study of the supervision pattern of the sample schools does not provide an encouraging trend, while the overall level of supervision of all the 18 districts at primary level was reported to be about 58 per cent only which implies that the remaining about 42 per cent of the schools have remained unvisited by them. Likewise, the supervision level observed for the six selected districts also depicts a similar trend; while in the districts like Mirzapur and Chandauli the overall supervision level was reported to be about 73 per cent and 83 per cent respectively, in others it was not very high.

Similarly, in case of upper primary schools, while the overall level of supervision for 18 schools was estimated to be about 57 per cent, in four of the six districts, viz., Mirzapur, Varanasi, Bhadoi and Allahabad it was disappointingly low. Moreover, the in-depth account of supervision pattern revealed that the level of frequency of visit to schools further dropped with the locations of schools. In other words, the schools located at the far off distances from block headquarters were seldom visited, which does not augur well for the performance of the programme (Table 13.10).

Table 13.10

Pattern of Supervision by BRC

Districts	*Primary School*	*Upper Primary School*
Mirzapur	51 (72.8)	11 (55.0)
Sonebhadra	45 (69.2)	16 (80.0)
Chandauli	38 (82.6)	15 (93.8)
Varanasi	27 (55.10)	9 (64.3)
Bhadoi	21 (70.0)	9 (64.3)
Allahabad	52 (45.2)	23 (54.8)
Total of 18 districts	760 (57.7)	244 (57.4)

Note: Over 42 per cent of the total schools have never been visited by BRC. Hardly about 4 per cent of schools have been regularly visited.

Source: Field data, 2007.

Pattern of Supervision by NPRCs

The supervision pattern by the Nyaya Panchayat Resource Centres (NPRCs) of the sample schools, however, projects a relatively better account. It shows that, at the primary level for the whole of 18 districts, about 90 per cent of the school had been visited by them while the overall level of supervision in the selected sample district was also reasonably high except for Allahabad where about 84 per cent of the schools had been supervised. Likewise, in case of upper primary schools, the overall level of supervision for all the 18 districts was reported to be about 86 per cent. However, in the six sample districts it varied between as low as 75 per cent in Mirzapur to cent per cent in Varanasi and Bhadoi districts respectively.

Though the aggregate or macro picture appears to be quite satisfactory however, the micro-realities are very disappointing. The study also shows that there were around 17 per cent of the total schools which have never been visited by the NPRCs. The proportion of school that were being regularly visited was hardly 12 per cent. Thus, it could be said that without providing uniform and adequate coverage, the whole purpose of supervision gets defeated as it encourages complacency to seep deep into the system and demotivates the teachers from performing the duties as well (Table 13.11).

Table 13.11

Pattern of Supervision by NPRC

Districts	*Primary School*	*Upper Primary School*
Mirzapur	65 (92.9)	15 (75.0)
Sonebhadra	63 (96.9)	17 (85.0)
Chandauli	42 (91.3)	14 (87.5)
Varanasi	48 (97.9)	14 (100.0)
Bhadoi	30 (100.0)	14 (100.0)
Allahabad	97 (84.3)	37 (88.1)
Total of 18 districts	1179 (89.5)	367 (86.4)

Note: Frequency of visit – 17 per cent schools (total) which have never been visited by NPRC. Hardly about 12 per cent of the schools have been regularly visited.

Source: Field data, 2007.

Learning Achievements of Students

In addition, to document the learning achievements of students in the sample schools, around 35 to 40 students (both girls and boys) from each of the 18 districts were randomly selected from class five and class eight. Thus, the total sample consisted of 767 students from primary class and 792 students from class eight. Further, the competence level of the primary class student was tested for the two subjects, viz., Hindi and Mathematics whereas the students of class eight were tested for Hindi, Mathematics and English.

For the analysis purpose, the achievement scores were classified into the following broad categories:

(i) below 32 per cent: extremely poor or very weak;
(ii) 34 per cent to 44 per cent: below the minimum levels of learning (MLL);
(iii) 45 per cent to 59 per cent: minimum levels of learning (MLL); and
(iv) 60 per cent and above: near mastery or mastery.

Analysis of Achievements of Primary Students

The analysis of the performance of students of class five for the two subjects, viz., Hindi and Mathematics provides a very disappointing account. It can be seen that out of a total of 767 students, the performance of about 54 per cent was below 33 percentage points and another 15 per cent between 33 per cent and 44 percentage points. Together these two groups accounted, for about 69 per cent of the total students whose performance could be termed as below minimum level of learning. There were hardly about 13 per cent of the students whose achievement was of minimum learning levels while about 19 per cent of the students had either mastered or were near the mastery level.

Further, the gender-wise performance shows that the performance of girls was more disappointing as more than 73 per cent had failed to achieve the minimum learning level against 71 per cent of boys. Similarly, the subject-wise analysis shows that the boys performed marginally better than their counter part girls in both the subjects. The study also brings to the fore that the students were much better off in Hindi than Mathematics, as higher percentage was recorded as per obtained master or near mastery norm in Hindi (Table 13.12).

Table 13.12

Subject and Gender-wise Performance of Students

(Class V)

Marks Obtained (in percentage)	*Hindi*			*Mathematics*			*Total*		
	Boys	*Girls*	*Total*	*Boys*	*Girls*	*Total*	*Boys*	*Girls*	*Total*
Below 33	172 (44.8)	191 (49.9)	363 (47.3)	211 (54.9)	230 (60.0)	441 (57.5)	190 (49.5)	220 (57.4)	410 (53.5)
33 to 44	56 (14.6)	44 (11.5)	100 (13.0)	60 (15.6)	51 (13.3)	111 (14.5)	64 (8.3)	51 (13.3)	115 (15.0)
45 to 59	57 (14.8)	57 (14.9)	114 (14.9)	38 (9.9)	33 (8.6)	71 (9.3)	57 (7.4)	40 (10.4)	97 (12.6)
60 and above	99 (25.8)	91 (23.8)	190 (24.8)	75 (19.5)	69 (18.0)	114 (14.9)	73 (9.5)	72 (18.8)	145 (18.9)

Note: Figures in parentheses denote percentage.

Source: Field data, 2007.

Analysis of Achievement Levels of Upper Primary

The achievement levels of the students of class eight have been tested for three subjects namely Hindi, Mathematics and English. For this, a total of 792 students were randomly selected, of which about 51 per cent were girls and remaining about 49 per cent were boys. The students were given simple questions from their books of the relevant subject, which they had been taught in the ensuing academic year in the class.

The performance shows that about 49 per cent of the total had failed to obtain even 33 per cent marks while another about 20 per cent could score between 33 per cent and 44 per cent only. Together these two segments accounted for nearly 69 per cent of the total students whose performance was below the minimum learning levels. There were hardly about 16 per cent of the students whose performance was equivalent to minimum learning levels while remaining about 15 per cent of the students had achieved the mastery or near mastery norm.

The subject wise analysis reveals the performance students in Hindi was best followed by Mathematics and finally English. The proportion of students qualifying under minimum learning levels and mastery or near master norms together was 16 and 15 per cent respectively. The gender-wise study of the achievement shows that boys, marginally outstripped the girls (Table 13.13).

Table 13.13

Subject and Gender-wise Performance of Students

(Class VIII)

Marks Obtained (in percentage)	*Hindi*			*Mathematics*		
	Boys	*Girls*	*Total*	*Boys*	*Girls*	*Total*
Below 33	123 (31.8)	117 (28.9)	240 (30.3)	190 (49.1)	209 (51.6)	399 (50.4)
33 to 44	81 (20.9)	99 (24.4)	180 (22.7)	56 (14.5)	75 (18.5)	131 (16.5)
45 to 59	109 (28.2)	111 (27.4)	220 (27.8)	68 (17.6)	50 (12.3)	118 (14.9)
60 and above	74 (19.1)	78 (19.3)	152 (19.2)	73 (18.9)	71 (17.5)	144 (18.2)
Marks Obtained	*English*			*Total*		
	Boys	*Girls*	*Total*	*Boys*	*Girls*	*Total*
Below 33	213 (55.0)	238 (58.8)	451 (56.9)	190 (49.1)	199 (49.1)	389 (49.1)
33 to 44	69 (17.8)	61 (15.1)	130 (16.4)	75 (19.4)	81 (20.0)	156 (19.7)
45 to 59	40 (10.3)	39 (9.6)	79 (10.0)	61 (15.8)	67 (16.5)	128 (16.2)
60 and above	65 (16.8)	67 (16.5)	132 (16.7)	61 (15.8)	58 (14.3)	119 (15.0)

Note: Figures in parentheses denote percentage.

Source: Field data, 2007.

Major Outcomes

The study of the performance of Sarva Siksha Abhiyaan in the 18 districts of Uttar Pradesh provides an interesting account in itself. Though, the analysis of achievement levels of the students of primary as well as upper primary class provides a disappointing account of itself, however the analysis clearly highlights the anomalies and inconsistencies that have inflicted upon the implementation aspects of the programme. Some of them have been briefly summarised:

Iniquitous Distribution of TLM Grant

Teachers Learning Material (TLM) has been perceived as a significant break-through from the conventional method of textbook learning. It enables both the teachers as well as the students to grasp the subject in a much better way by using innovative and imaginative tools. It also brings in a fresh approach to break the monotony generated by conventional mode of teaching. Accordingly, the guidelines encourage the use of TLMs and accordingly sanction a token amount of grants, to be utilised by the teachers. However, the study clearly shows that quite a sizeable section of teachers have yet to receive the grants which severely curtails their innovative skills. Therefore, efforts are required to be made to provide grants to all the teachers in time. For this the monitory and supervision system needs to be strengthened, and the subsequent bottlenecks conflicting the process needs to be streamlined.

Limited and Sporadic Use of TLM

The analysis also reveals another disappointing aspect of TLM, which is their limited and sporadic use of the teachers and students alike. This only reflects that both communities (teacher and taught) have failed to appreciate its relevance and the use. All this was also contributing to the poor performance of SSA. Hence there is a need to motivate, sensitise and encourage them, through appropriate social intervention strategies, to use the TLM material to further the classroom teaching.

Disproportionate Pattern of Training

Under SSA, the training component of teachers has been accepted as an important and crucial part meant to import quality education. The guideline has proposed multiple types of on job training. The basic premise, perhaps, being that training prepares, sensitises and helps to broaden the perception of teachers besides equipping them with the latest information and techniques prevalent in the field of pedagogy.

The study of training pattern of teachers clearly shows that it has failed to provide them uniform coverage. The analysis also shows that not only the overall training status of teachers was disappointingly low, the practice of some teachers acquiring training in more than one discipline severely hampers the process of providing equitable opportunity to all teachers which not only results, in disproportionate skewed distribution pattern but also brings down the overall training level of teachers, that does not spell good either to the programme or its performance. Hence there is a need to correct/rectify this in balancing approach through better monitoring and supervision techniques.

Pattern of Absenteeism among Teachers

Incidence of absenteeism not only affects the sequence of teaching but also puts pressure on teachers to finish up the course in time which, many a times, hampers the quality of teaching. The study of teachers' absenteeism in the sample schools shows that the schools also suffer from incidence of absenteeism, and that has been a matter of concern. The study also shows that incidence of absenteeism was more pronounced among the assistant teachers on whom bulk of teaching rests, because the headmasters have to share the administrative work and other miscellaneous assignments of the school.

Therefore, efforts need to be made to encourage and motivate the teachers to be more regular in schools. Here the role of other local and grass root organisations like parents teachers associations (PTA), mother teachers association (MTA) or village education committees (VECs) needs to be redefined. They have to play a more positive, constructive and assertive role. SSA is a unique programme that encourages private-government partnership. Thus by invoking an element of social accountability into the school functioning, the problem of teachers' absenteeism can be effectively tackled.

Supervision Pattern

The SSA guidelines clearly recommended that the states would need to give priority to developing and regularly implementing, monitoring system to measure quality related outcomes, inter-alia, for students learning outcomes, teacher's performance, student and teacher attendance rates, etc., besides this it is also capable of measuring changes in classroom practices, impact of teacher training.

Accordingly an attempt has also been to study the pattern of supervision in the sample schools of the districts. The two bodies that have assigned the task of looking after the monitoring and supervision of sample schools were the block resource centres (BRCs) and the nyaya panchayat resource centres (NPRCs). The analysis clearly shows that the level of supervision of both agencies is far from satisfactory. The proportion of schools regularly being visited was hardly 4 per cent in case of BRCs and 12 per cent for NRRCs. There were about 42 per cent of the schools that have never been visited by BRCs and about 17 per cent by NPRCs.

It should be remembered that supervision exercise should not be taken as a fault finding exercise, it is rather an effective feedback mechanism that intends to facilitate two way information system enabling the authorities to act swiftly to counter any form of inconsistencies or anomalies cropping up in the course or functioning of programme. Hence, there is a greater need for toning up of this aspect.

Suggestions

The analysis of SSA clearly shows that the performance of programme has not been impressive. In fact it has, so far, not been able to provide quality teaching as was being envisaged of it. The analysis clearly shows that it suffers from many angles, which needs to be addressed on priority basis.

What has been a matter of concern that all the safeguard measures that have been envisaged in the guidelines have not been implemented in the true spirit of the programme. What should be done under these circumstances? What additional interventions needs to be done to put back the derailed programme, back on its track? Should government step in?

The study also shows that all through the implementation and execution stage, the people participation has been bare minimum. It should be remembered that no programme, how so beautifully designed, can work in isolation or vacuum. Moreover, SSA is supposed to be an example of public-private partnership. What we have seen so far that many of the organisations or bodies whose co-operation and support was solicited like the VECs, MTA, PTA, etc., were not playing their role effectively and unless these bodies are not fully activated or operationalised, the programme may not be able to perform effectively. Thus, an element of public accountability has to be resorted. In a democracy, the role of these institutions also needs to be redefined even if it may require relevant and appropriate amendments in the constitutions or by laws governing them.

References

Eleventh Five Year Plan 2007–2012, Vol. II Social Sector, Planning Commission, Oxford University Press, 2008.

Kaul, V. (2002). Early Childhood Care and Education in India Education Report, (ed.) by R. Govinda, New Delhi: Oxford University Press.

Pant, S.K. (2009). Universalisation of Education through Adult Literacy Programme. Some Empirical Evidences in India's Development Scenario Challenges and Prospects (ed.) by Yatindra Singh Sisodia, Jaipur: Rawat Publications.

Sarva Siksha Abhiyaan A Programme for Universal Elementary Education Framework for Implementation, Ministry of Human Resource Development, Department of Elementary Education, New Delhi, 2008.

Visaria, P. A. Gumbar, and L. Visaria (1993). Literacy and Primary Education in India 1980–81 to 1991 Differentials and Determinants, Journal of Educational Planning and Administration, Vol. III, No. 1, January, New Delhi.

14

Medium of Instruction in Schooling among Tribes in India

SUJIT KUMAR CHOUDHARY

Medium of instruction in schooling has been one of the debatable issues in contemporary India, especially after independence. However, the Government of India has made many attempts to consider the problems of language on the basis of region and community at the levels of policies and programmes. But the deprived sections of Indian society have been still facing this problem despite all the government policies and programmes. While going into details of this discussion, it is essential to look upon the historicity of language in general and as a medium of instruction in particular. On the international front, a new direction was suggested by a UNESCO Committee of Experts in 1951 which ruled out the saying that 'it is axiomatic that the best medium for teaching a child is the child's mother tongue' (UNESCO, 1953: 11). Furthermore, in 1990, the various policies for bilingual and bicultural education developed in different countries, received international support in the ILO convention for indigenous peoples. Articles 27 and 28 of ILO convention reconvened the right to independent forms of education and general language rights: 'Governments shall recognise the right of these people to establish their own educational institutions and facilities ... children belonging to the people concerned shall, wherever, practicable, be taught to read and write in their own indigenous language or the language most commonly used by the groups to which they belong' (ILO convention, 1990: 16). This convention gave strong encouragement to the governments of all countries to act more rigorously and justly in their language policies for indigenous people. In connection to this, a report on the conference 'Which Languages for Europe' organised by the European Cultural Foundation (1998) says, 'Do not restrict the number of languages to be used. Certain concepts, beliefs, sensations can only be expressed in the languages in which they are coined, shaped, experienced.' Here the point of consideration is that language is not only an issue restricted to India but is debated in the world over.

In India, the whole debate of language was started at the time of Mounstuart Eliphistone's 'minute' of 1823, in which he emphasised the establishment of schools for teaching English and the European Sciences. Subsequently, Macaulay, in his 'minute' of 1835 stated that the objective of the British government ought to be 'the promotion of European literature and science amongst the natives of India' (Choudhary, 2008). In addition, Macaulay in his 'minute' recorded as follows:

> To sum up what I have said, I think we are not fettered by the Act of Parliament of 1813; then we are not fettered by any pledge, express or implied; that we are free to employ our funds as we choose; that we ought to employ them in teaching what is best, worth knowing; that English is better worth knowing than Sanskrit or Arabic; that neither as the language of law, nor as the language of religion has the Sanskrit or Arabic any peculiar claim to our engagement that it is possible to make natives of this country good English scholars and that to this end our efforts ought to be directed. (cites in Dongerkery, 1967: 2)

In response to British education and language policy, organisations like the Brahma Samaj (1828), Arya Samaj (1875), Satyashodhak Samaj (1873) and others realised that education and language would play an important role in social reform and masses could be approached only in their languages and not in English. Agnihotri rightly points out, 'The British wanted to use the native languages of the people either to convert them to Christianity or to keep them in their stations; for people like Gandhi, Gokhale and Zakir Hussain, active use of the languages of the common people was a necessary requirement for freedom' (Agnihotri, 2001: 194). Scholars like Ramchandra, Munshi Zakaullah and Syed Ahmed Khan were convinced that a foreign medium makes the basic conceptual machinery incomprehensible to learners and also destroys their creative potential (ibid.: 195). Basu, on the other hand, points out that in India, 'the idea of national education emerged not to promote loyalty to the state, as in Europe, but in opposition to the system of education introduced by the colonial masters' (Basu, 1998: 55). Gokhale warned the use of English as a medium of instruction in a country of India's magnitude and complexity. The role of the mother tongue in education and socialisation was most emphatically recognised by the Zakir Hussain Committee (1938) working largely under the influence of Gandhi as is stated as:

> The proper teaching of the mother tongue is the foundation of all education ... Moreover, it is a means of introducing the child to the rich heritage of his people's ideas, emotions and aspirations, and can therefore be made a valuable means of social education while also instilling right ethical and moral values. Also, it is a natural outlet for the expression of the child's aesthetic sense and appreciation. (cites in Aggarwal, 1983: 54–55)

Moreover, the Kothari Commission (1966) drew attention to the importance of keeping the way of life and 'cultural and social needs of the people in mind' while planning the education of tribal communities. However, this appears to have been largely done to enable their integration with the 'mainstream' of education and society rather than with any principles of pedagogy in mind. In subsequent policy documents, mandatory references to tribal languages as mediums of instruction as well as developing of books in tribal languages for the early primary years are mentioned. However, little has been accomplished to make school meaningful for the tribal children (cited in Nambissan 2006: 33). According to information available, few of the tribal languages are used as medium of instruction up to class three but nowhere a strategy is spelled out for a transition from one medium to another. In 1976, 33 tribal languages were used as medium of instruction in the schools. Position of language in the school curriculum in India lists Angami, Ao, Karen, Kharia, Bodo, Chakhasang, Chang Naga, Garo, Hmar, Ho, Karen, Kharia, Khasi, Khiemnungar, Konkyak, Kuki, Lotha, Lushai, Manipuri, Mizo, Mundari, Nicobarese, Oreon, Phom, Rengma, Sangtam, Santhali, Sema, Yeimchungere, Seliang as tribal languages in school education. Since then Gondi, Kokbarok, Missing, Rabha, and Saora have been added as educational languages. While new languages are added, some of the old languages are discontinued as medium of instruction. They pass through stages of subordinate medium languages studied up to class two or three, after which they become subject languages and move towards oblivion (Pattanayak, 2001: 57). As the 1976 publication says, 'for instance in Meghalaya, Nagaland and Mizoram all the tribal languages are discontinued as medium but some of them like Mizo, Khasi, etc., are allowed to be studied as subjects up to the higher secondary classes' (ibid.).

In case of tribals from Munda and Oraon community, the language used as the medium of instruction has been an important factor in their response to the schools. Hindi is no doubt rudimentarily understood by some tribals. Still, for an overwhelming majority, both Hindi and English are equally considered in the category of foreign languages (Report On Public Instruction in Lower Bengal, 1865–66: 247). The introduction of Hindi would, therefore, hardly equip the tribals for smooth reception of Western education. The linguistic handicap, however, is only part of the total culture ensemble that has discouraged the tribals from making use of the new education (Bara, 2002: 130). Moreover, Varghese argues about the problem of linguistic identity in Chhotanagpur. In his words, 'Hindi terminology and even Hindi as first language is making big inroads in the tribal cultures of Chhotanagpur, even Christian missionaries, though always accused of fomenting tribal separatism, are opening Hindi medium schools, a development which may lead to the loss of the tribals' linguistic identity' (Varghese, 1993: 102). In the past, it has impelled the government as well as the German missionaries to adopt Hindi as a medium of instruction for the education of the tribals. It has also compelled the two agencies to incorporate in the curriculum some specific elements for the tribals, such as explaining the laws and government procedures and imparting basic literacy in the Kaithi script. According to the missionaries, 'what is called the court language, the mixture of Hindi, Urdu and Pharsi words, is a perfect crux for them (the tribals)' (letter dated 17 May 1876 from H. Onasch and 15 others to the Lt. Governor, Bengal, people relating to Chhotanagpur Agrarian Disputes, Vol. 1, p. 68). But to mould them in the best way, Dalton wanted that tribals would be educated through the medium of English and acquainted with English literature and science, even if the dose was going to be small (letter dated 11 June 1859 from Dalton to Young, Director, Public Instruction, Bengal, appended to Report on Public Instruction in Lower Bengal, 1869–70, p. 48). Hindi medium based education of the tribals, according to him, meant 'throwing them at the feet of the Brahmins through the instrumentality of Hindu teachers' (letter dated 31 July 1871 from Dalton to Thomson, officiating Secretary to the Government of Bengal, Singhbhum Old Records, Patna, 1958: 222). Dalton expressed these views in the context of Ho and Munda tribals, to whom the missionaries were having little success. So long as Hindi education was being conducted under the supervision of Christian missionaries, as in the tribal heartland of Ranchi district, he had no objection. Here, the Hindi medium based primary schools run by the missionaries at remote villages were feeders to the Central (English) schools (Bara, 2002: 143).

But the fact is that lack of communication network in tribal areas has miserably failed to produce desirable results. Even if students want to attend the school, infrastructural facilities are not accessible for them. Besides the major portion of welfare fund is diverted to concessional provisions with almost nothing left for the development of tribal language and cultures (Study by Agragamee, 1994; an NGO in Kashipur, Odisha). Hardly there is any effort to standardise and consolidate tribal languages, not to speak of callous negligence of their cultures and traditions in the curricula. In the introduction of the Linguistic Survey and Mapping for District Primary Education Programme (DPEP) districts of Odisha

(Academy of Tribal Dialects and Cultures, SC/ST Development Department, Odisha, October 1999) says, 'India has failed to meet the commitment of universalising primary education and ensuring a basic human right because of this language problem'. Hence, the situation of the tribal language as a medium of instruction has not been taken seriously so far as definite policy has been implemented. In this context, Pattanayak rightly points out as follows:

> In the present context of education in India, no policy is enunciated for the use of tribal languages in education. Being victims of development, many of them have become itinerants. No efforts are being made to bring the school to their door steps. Their languages are neither compulsory as first, second, third language, nor as optional languages. They are not perceived and are totally ignored. Their cultures are impoverished. (Pattanayak, 2001: 57)

In fact, the tribal schools in different parts of India are run by the Education Department as well as by the Welfare Department. Since the Education Department has better facilities, there inspection is more systematic. There are tribal schools which have not been inspected for years. Unlike rural and urban schools, the tribal schools may be classified as roadside schools and interior schools. The interior schools are seldom inspected and suffer from teacher absenteeism. Free books supplied by the Welfare Department are seldom in adequate number. As a result, the well to do among the tribal are also forced to buy books from the market and the major fact remains that no book is written in tribal languages. There is no strategy to link the home languages with their school language. The double alienation of the tribal children takes on toll (D.P. Pattanayak, Report of a Case Study on Educational Materials in the Learning Environment, 1999, sponsored by the UNESCO).

The education system bypasses the tribal languages. In some states, because of the acute protests, tribal languages are used as medium of instruction up to the class three. Bodo and Missing in Assam were two such languages. With inexperienced teachers and insufficient reading material these programmes are apologised for education. In any case, no strategy is adopted to link the home language with the school language. The Central Institute of Indian Language (CIIL) developed a programme of bilingual primary education. It started with reading and writing in the home language and speaking and understanding in the state language. Allotting 80 per cent of the available time for the home language and 20 per cent for the school language in the first year, by the end of the primary stage the time of allocation was reversed. By that time the learner had assumed sufficient competence in the school language to study in that language (Pattnayak, 2001: 54). This was tried out in some locations in the country. The result was exciting.

Khasi in Meghalaya was one language which offered a post-graduate course in that language. Yet another example is Santhali which is offered as a subject of examination at the end of the secondary stage in West Bengal. Koli in Maharashtra is one of the languages which are used at the primary stage. Same is the case of Jenu Kurubas in Karnataka (ibid.). Here the point of Govinda seems to be relevant as he says:

> Micro level evidence shows that interventions and initiatives like the mid-day meal scheme, creation of self-help women's groups, environment-building programmes under different projects, appointment of local tribal teachers, and developing partnership between school and village communities in the school management have helped tribals realise the importance of education and adopt a positive attitude towards the education of their children. (Govinda, 2002: 8)

If we look at the theoretical arguments made by Bernstein, Bourdieu and others that children coming from poor families lack an appropriate cultural capital, which is a culture of the upper class and hence becomes the justification behind their failure in school performance. The less privileged social groups are the obvious ones who are at the receiving end since the children experience school processes without any tangible continuity with their sociocultural life. In the whole context, school's concept of what is to be educated is socially constructed knowledge whereas knowledge is not a static entity, something out there and independent of the knower but a social invention heavily biased in favour of few powerful social groups that is articulated in school curricular and other pedagogical forms. Thus, the forms of knowledge that make up the school curriculum are related to the interest of particular class or professional groups that school curriculum is a product of pressure of certain vested interest groups (Kumar, 1991). In this context, Choudhary rightly points out:

> Generally, the medium of education is determined by the economic and social benefits that are likely to accrue to the learner. Be it basic education or higher education, the medium of education is determined on the basis of a complex mix of factors. What is significant is that in the contexts where specialised education is restricted to a small section of the society, the question of medium is sorted out more easily. However, once education is universalised the problem of medium takes on several unpredictable implications. (Choudhary, 2006: 50)

When tribal children are denied access to their own language in school, its immediate implication is to produce ungraspable distance between home and school for tribal children. This is also related to overall educational outcomes including achievements in school performance. Bernstein (1973), here, argues that children from different backgrounds use different linguistic codes, the elaborated code perform relatively better than the restricted code, since there is no fundamental difference from the language used in schools while children using restricted code experience difficulty in learning at schools and thereby, results in the failure of the latter in school performance. The argument is that the acceptance and the appreciation of the language and culture of tribal children by the school seem to lead to a positive identity of self worth and thereby, to effective educational achievement while the denial of their mother tongue in formal systems of schooling is to disconnect them from any tangible continuity from school and processes of schooling. This is seen to be very significant particularly for tribes since language remains distinguishing trait for many tribal groups and their self-identification (Salam, 2004: 30).

Quality Improvement through the Tribal Language as a Medium of Instruction

Most of the states have taken up activities for quality improvement of the tribal area schools. One of the issues identified by the states has been the problem faced by the tribal children whose home language is very different from the regional languages, which is the medium of instruction at the primary level, in addition to teachers' attitudes, textbooks and materials, curriculum and pedagogy, and teaching-learning process in tribal areas. However, an increasing number of researches strongly advocate the use of the mother tongue or home language as medium of instruction in early stages of education. This assumes great significance in the context of education of tribal children because their mother tongue is often quite distinct from the prominent languages in the state or regional languages. The tribal children face problems wherever teachers do not speak their dialect at all. From the perspective of language, it is felt desirable to have a local teacher from the same tribal community. Though research evidence also favour bilingual or multi lingual schooling in view of its positive consequences for cognitive development and social interaction processes, it would need special treatment for tribal children to be able to cope with.

In this connection, Assam has been the first state to prepare teacher training modules and separate teaching learning materials for the Bodo tribal language in 1995. Bodo is also a medium of instruction in some districts of Assam. The work on tribal language materials was undertaken through District Institute of Education and Training (DIET) staff and Block Resource Centre/Clusters Resource Centre (BRC/CRC) coordinators who belonged to the tribal community. Resource material in Bodo language has been prepared and all workbooks at primary stage have been translated and adopted in Bodo language. In addition, Garo medium workbook has been translated, adopted and distributed in the schools of Golpara district. In Madhya Pradesh and Chhattisgarh teachers' handbooks called Bridge

Language Inventory (BLIs) have been prepared in three tribal languages, viz., Gondi (Shahdol and Betul district), Kuduk (Raigarh) and Bhili (Dhar). Identified teachers were imparted training for use of BLIs in classroom set up. The teaching-learning package called Dham Dhama Dham was translated into Gondi and supplementary reading material Kopal was developed for tribal children. The class one textbook Bharati has been translated into tribal languages. Supplementary Total Literacy Mission (TLM) for tribal children has been developed in Jhabua district using local cultural form, i.e., folk tales, songs, proverbs, riddles to make the learning process interesting. In all, 450 teachers of 311 schools have been trained to use the supplementary materials.

In Karnataka, a textbook for class one and two has been developed and introduced in Soliga language. A handbook has been developed for sensitisation of teachers towards social and cultural specificities of the tribal societies. In Maharashtra, tribal language dictionaries have been developed. Language resource groups have been set up for Bhili, Pawara, Madia, Gondi, etc. Bridge material has been developed in Dhule district. Kerala has developed bilingual language materials at district level in Kasarkode, Waynad, Malappuram, and Palakkad.

Odisha took initiative to develop a comprehensive strategy for education of tribal children as early as 1997. It has initiated a number of activities for addressing the quality improvement of the tribal education. In addition, a large number of teachers have undergone attitudinal training which has had a significant impact on the attitudes of non-tribal teachers towards tribal children. Continuing efforts are being made to sustain the impact of the attitudinal training through block and cluster level meetings of teachers by including items for discussion on these issues in the monthly meetings. A linguistic survey and mapping has been completed by the Academy of Tribal Dialects and Culture in four districts - Kalahandi, Gajapati, Raygoda, and Keonjher. The state has also explored the use of folklore in primary education, which would help to tap the rich tradition of arts, crafts, music, songs, etc., in tribal societies. Stories and riddles have been collected for use by the teachers and classrooms.

Andhra Pradesh has developed bilingual dictionaries and teacher training has been organised in Warangal and Vizianagaram districts. For use of the bilingual material, research studies have also been undertaken on the issue of language and mathematics learning of tribal children. It has been decided to use the multi-level kits developed for tribal areas in Vishakhapatnam district in other tribal areas also. Gujarat has developed dictionaries in Dangi and Bhili dialects. A local work glossary in Dangi has been prepared and distributed in schools for class 1–4 in Dang district. Similarly, a local word glossary in *Adivasi* dialect has been prepared for class 1–4 in Banaskantha district and distributed in schools. The

Vidyasahayaks were given training on the use of these dictionaries. Gujarat has also initiated extensive work for preparation of Total Literacy Mission (TLM) in tribal languages. The TLM developed include flash cards for different languages and also cards for mathematics. These have been supplied to all schools in tribal areas. Bridge Language Inventory has also been introduced in Ho and Mundari languages in Ranchi district of Jharkhand. The acceptance of teachers by the community as one among them is critical for increasing the schooling participation in tribal areas. An understanding of and respect for tribal cultures and practices are important for teachers to gain this acceptance.

> The presence of tribal teachers, especially from the same community, has shown and improved school participation of ST children. Coming from the same community, it is believed that the teachers would understand and respect the culture and the ethos with much greater sensitivity. Studies suggest that teacher motivation contributes more to teaching – learning process than teacher competence. (Vaidyanathan and Nair, 2000)

Realising the importance of having teachers from the local community many states have appointed community teachers. In addition, para teachers in large numbers from the local community have also been appointed to give emphasis on the local language and culture. In this regard, the deployment of community teachers was first experimented in the late 1970s in Non Formal Education (NFE) and later in the formal school with the Volunteer Teacher Scheme of Himachal Pradesh (1984). Nineties saw spurt in the appointment of community teachers, who were from the local community and appointed by the gram panchayat for Village Education Committees. Different states have different schemes for appointing community teachers – Shiksha Karmi Scheme (Madhya Pradesh/Chhattisgarh and Rajasthan), Shiksha Mitra Yojana (Uttar Pradesh/Uttarakhand), Lok Shikshak (Bihar/Jharkhand), Andariki–Vidya Volunteer Scheme (Andhra Pradesh), Vidya Upasak Yojana (Himachal Pradesh), Shikshan Sevak (Maharashtra), Guruji (under EGS in Madhya Pradesh/Chhattisgarh), Shikshak (under Basti Shala Scheme in Maharashtra), etc.

In spite of different efforts made by the government and the local agencies in tribal areas, the tribal children have still been facing problems in classroom due to the huge difference between home and school language as it has not been implemented at the macro level. For instance, during my own fieldwork visits for my doctoral research in the State of Jharkhand, I have found that almost 55 per cent tribal children wanted to have their elementary education in their own dialect Santhali. In addition, we did not find the teachers from the same community, i.e., the Santhal, in adequate numbers, however most of the teachers belonged to local population.

In the concluding remarks, it may be said that the government in some tribal areas has made attempt to follow the principles advocated by the educationists and social reformers in general and Zakir Hussain Committee and thereafter Kothari Commission in particular so far as their local languages, more precisely tribal dialects, are concerned in providing education to the tribal children. It has been activated at the micro level and is restricted to some tribal areas only. However, in the recent times, it has been seen that government has been trying to help the deprived peoples as much as possible through making practical level programmes, such as implementation of Sarva Shiksha Abhiyaan (SSA) and the recruitment of Para teachers from the local people. However, the issue of language in the tribal education has not been taken seriously. At this point, it can be considered that there may be a problem of acceptance of the tribal language as a medium of instruction among the tribal communities; therefore, adequate and frequent dialogues with the tribal communities and with their leaders are required to prepare them on this issue. It is also suggested that there is need to address this issue through collaborative approach among the various sections of society and also to take help from the civil society organisations at the macro level.

References

Academy of Tribal Dialects and Cultures, SC/ST Development Department, Odisha, October, 1999.

Aggarwal, J.C. (1983). *Landmarks in the History of Modern Indian Education.* New Delhi: Vikas Publishing House.

Agnihotri, R.K. (2001). English in Indian Education. In C.J. Daswani (ed.), *Language Education in Multilingual India.* New Delhi: UNESCO.

Bara, Joseph (2002). Tribal Education, the Colonial State and Christian Missionaries: Chhotanagpur, 1829–1870. In Sabyasachi Bhattacharya (ed.), *education and the disprivileged.* New Delhi: Orient Longman.

Basu, A. (1998). National Education in Bengal 1905–1912. In Sabyasachi Bhattacharya (ed.), *education and the disprivileged.* New Delhi: Orient Longman, pp. 54–67.

Bernstein, B. (1973). *Class, Codes and Control.* London: Routledge and Kegan Paul.

Choudhary, Sujit Kumar (2006). Role of Language in Education and Formation of Social Status. *Journal of Indian Education*, Vol. XXXI, No. 3. November 2005. New Delhi: NCERT, pp. 42–51.

——. (2007). Women, Higher Education and Occupational Discrimination: An Indian Experience, *International Journal for Women & Gender Research.* Vol. 1, No. 1, January–June, 2007, pp: 72–74.

——. (2008). Higher Education in India: A Socio-historical Journey from Ancient Period to 2006–07. In Journal of Educational Enquiry, Issue 8, No. 1, July 2008. Australia: University of South Australia, pp. 50–72.

Dongerkery, S.R. (1997). *University Education in India*, Manaktalas, Mumbai.

European Cultural Foundation (1998). 'Which Languages for Europe', Amsterdam.

Govinda, R. (2002). *India Education Report.* New Delhi: Oxford University Press.

Govinda, R. and N.V. Varghese (1993). Quality of Primary Schooling in India: A Case *Study of Madhya Pradesh.* Paris: International Institute for Educational Planning; New Delhi: National University (Institute) of Educational Planning and Administration (NUEPA).

International Labour Organisation (1990). *Convention on Indigenous Peoples.* The Hague: International Labour Organization.

Kumar, Krishna (1991). *Political Agenda of Education, A Study of Colonialist and Nationalist Ideas,* New Delhi: Sage Publications.

Letter dated 17 May 1876 from H. Onasch and 15 others to the Lt. Governor, Bengal, people relating to Chhotanagpur Agrarian Disputes, Vol. 1.

Letter dated 31 July 1871 from Dalton to Thomson, officiating Secretary to the Government of Bengal, Singhbhum Old Records, Patna, 1958.

Nambissan, Geetha B. (2006). Between policy and pedagogy: Issues in the education of tribal children. *Biblio: September–October 2006*, pp. 32–33.

Pattanayak, D.P. (1999). Report of a Case Study on Educational Materials in the Learning Environment, 1999, UNESCO.

—— (2001). Tribal Language in Education. In C.J. Daswani, (ed.), *Language Education in Multilingual India.* New Delhi: UNESCO, pp. 48–57.

Report on Public Instruction in Lower Bengal 1865–66.

Salam, Jeebanlata (2004). *Social Exclusion and Education.* New Delhi: Indian Social Institute.

UNESCO (1953). *The Use of Vernacular Language in Education*, Monograph on Fundamental Education, Vol. 8. Paris: UNESCO.

Vaidyanathan, A. and P.R. Gopinath Nair (eds) (2000). *Elementary Education in Rural India: A Grassroots View*, New Delhi: Sage Publications.

Part IV

Governance Issues at the Grassroots Level

15

Human Development Scenario in Rural Areas

An Analysis of Human Dignity Index

G. PALANITHURAI

India is known for several paradoxes and of which the new paradox of achieving economic growth side by side with poor performance in human development (UNDP, 2009) draws the attention of academia who are interested in growth, equity and development and above all inclusive governance and inclusive development. Sixty years of democratic governance and development administration have brought unprecented transformation in the social, economic and political life of the people in India (Francine, 2005). On the whole, looking at the macro achievements in terms of economic growth, infrastructure development, institutional, industrial and market expansion, the performance of the stakeholders involved in building and developing the institutions are laudable and impressive. The development growth, the adaptability of the stakeholders, the capacity and capability of development participants have been excellent and consistent and put up an unprecented show in the respective domains in terms of performance by the stakeholders. By doing so the creative face of India has been projected (Bhagawati, 2004).

But, looking at the living conditions of the people in India one finds that the majority cannot lead a decent human life. The numerical strength of the people affected by poverty, inequality, illiteracy, malnutrition, anaemia, sanitation, poor water supply, poor hygienic living conditions, poor food security points to the dismal picture of the performance of the government and administration (Social Watch India, 2009). The present scenario of economic growth and human development in India has raised a fundamental question on the proposition that economic growth and development will achieve social development in a society. While seeing the existing conditions in human development a new proposition is emerging in the third world countries that the higher the economic growth, lower will be the social development. Equity will be the casualty in the process of economic growth. The role and responsibility, skill and capability of governing institutions in tackling the critical issues of development have been seriously questioned (Jalan, 2005).

Realistically one has to analyse why and how the development initiatives of the government and the market are being used effectively by the stakeholders to achieve tremendous results in economy. Why the same initiatives have not enthused the stakeholders and prompted them to participate in the process and make use of all the development initiatives of the government and other development institutions to achieve human development in the question now.

It is the minority or a class or the elites who are capable and skill-wise developed to make use of the development initiatives of the government and market institutions and achieve development. Indeed the very development initiatives are the result of the promptings of these elites or this class of people. The capability level is on par with the development opportunities and thereby all opportunities are being used and the governments are also enabling them to perform well. Hence the initiatives of the government are fully used for their development. Governments are rather made to act in such a way that the development elites are empowered in India, whereas, in the case of the masses their capacity, capability, skill, perception and ability to make choices are highly limited and hence they are unable to make use of the opportunities. As a result India cannot perform well in the social development sector.

Conditions of the People

One has to understand the present conditions of the people in India: 71 per cent of the people are in the rural areas; 58 per cent rely on agriculture for their livelihood; 60 per cent of the cultivable land relies on rainfed irrigation; 20 per cent of the people hold 80 per cent of the cultivable lands in India; 80 per cent of the farm and milch animals are with 80 per cent of the people. Our economy relies on industry and service sector for its growth and only 18 per cent comes from agriculture to the economy. The infrastructure and other institutional structures for development in the rural areas are weak, be it health, or education, or credit or market. Further, the development process is weakened by the poor understanding of the people about the process of development, governance and administration (Palanithurai, 1995).

Development Activities Still with Bureaucracy

It is to be noted here that, in the perception and understanding of the people, especially the people from the rural areas and more particularly the poor, the whole development process and activities are in the hands of officials and development brokers. Till date the nexus of the development brokers and the development bureaucracy has not been broken despite the demystification process of governance and administration being initiated through decentralisation of powers (Palanithurai, 2008). Till date not even 2 per cent of the whole development fund is channelled through the people's institution, namely 'panchayati raj'. The quantum has increased for development activities at the grassroots, but where it goes and how it goes, where it is being spent and how it is being spent is not known to the stakeholders, despite the presence of the Gram Sabha, which is supposed to know and which is equivalent to the Lok Sabha well within the powers conferred on it. It is so because our governance and administrative processes are still complicated, complex and mystified (Ragunanthan, 2009). The whole process of accountability is not built towards the stakeholders or people. The accountability built in the system is upward and not downwards as it was designed by the colonial administration. While in the case of federal government, under globalisation, reforms have been initiated and implemented and for every economic activity single window clearance has been established for the poor at the bottom, at the grassroots, even for a community certificate multi-window clearance is in practice. Till date people are not clear about the systems that are in operation in the development management at the grassroots. In this way our governance, development and administration are simplified for the elites and complicated and mystified for the poor (Palanithurai, 2008). For the elites governance and administration are shaped and reformed according to their own preferences as they are key players in the economy. For the people the same governance and administration are still in a complex form and they are in the hands of the bureaucracy and the bureaucracy is in the hands of the ruling elites. Hence the rich are participating in the process of development and achieving their targets and enjoying the fruits at the cost, the people and more particularly the poor. As a result of the above paradox we find one phenomenon constant. When Rajiv Gandhi was the Prime Minister, he made a statement that if one rupee is allotted for rural development, only 15 paise reach the needy at the grassroots. But now, as per the Planning Commission's study, 17 paise reach the needy. So the condition remains the same. When Rajiv Gandhi made such a statement civil society argued that 85 paise go for brokerage, which is almost a corrupt practice. But now a new label has been introduced: 83 paise go as transaction cost or administrative cost (Aiyar, 2010).

Nobody knows where it goes, how it goes, whether it goes legally or illegally, because the whole process of fund follows a circuitous route and managing the fund is complicated. Multiple institutions and organisations are funding development through their own field agencies bypassing the people's institutions – 'the Panchayat' – created legitimately by the Constitution.

Further, it is to be understood perspectively. Indian communities in the rural areas are living in diverse socio, economic, cultural and environmental settings. The diversities are unmanageable through the prototype models of development evolved by the federalists at the headquarters. Over a period of time, in our democratic governance and administration, we find much variation among the state governments and district administrations in handling development issues. In the past 60 years, our governance mechanism worked for industrialisation, marketisation and development of service industries. But the same governance and administrative machinery involved in development perform their task by doling out benefits to the people with the perception that the poor have to get the benefits as beneficiaries and, if they do not get the benefits, let them act as petitioners to submit petitions submissively to the bureaucracy. Such kind of administrative activities pushes people to the periphery and not towards the mainstream. People are outside the purview of development, governance and administration, but they are in a democracy and inside as voters. The citizens are not allowed to act as full citizens (Cohen, 2009).

Having realised the weaknesses in the system, Rajiv Gandhi wanted to bring the poor into the process of governance and development. By doing so, inclusive growth and inclusive development could be achieved. To achieve the above goal he designed decentralised democratic governance with the participation of people and he initiated action for incorporating the democratic decentralisation through constitutionalisation. This process ended with the enacting of the 73rd and the 74th amendments to the Constitution of India. This constitutionalisation should have altered the paradigm of governance and the process of development by including the hitherto excluded and by transforming the beneficiaries into stakeholders and development participants (Shivramkrishnan, 2000).

Dignity Index

People are reduced from the level of citizens to that of beneficiaries by increasing the delivery of benefits. Normally citizens have to manage their affairs on their own for which the government has to enable the citizens. As long as citizens are in a position to meet their needs on their own without depending on the government, the self-dignity of the people will be intact. The moment people are made to depend on the government for many of their needs; their self-dignity is be at stake and reduced. Thereby, the citizens take the position of beneficiaries and develop a perception that their life depends on the benefits from the government. The beneficiary syndrome gradually disempowers the people. Secondly, there is no assurance that benefits will reach the beneficiaries. The beneficiaries have to approach the office or officer to get the benefits. In the absence of the vision that beneficiaries have right to claim their benefits as entitlements, the beneficiaries are at the mercy of the officer. The feudal mindset in the society and the colonial mindset inherited by the administration have afflicted the officials and hence they behave as masters. As a result, there is no assurance to the people that they will get all their benefits as entitlements. Further, in our administrative and governance system, there is no assurance that benefits are given according to the needs of the people. In the absence of a match between the needs and the supply, competition will be intensive to get the benefits by any means. In the same way, the distributor of benefits will retain the power of discretion. This predicament deprives the beneficiaries of the benefits and implants another perception as 'petitioners'. As a person or a group is deprived of entitled benefits, the individual and groups become petitioners and submit petitions. Even the petitions are submitted very submissively. Here also they are deprived of their dignity as they do not claim their benefits as entitlements.

The benefits reach to the beneficiaries after a process of negotiations done submissively as beneficiaries and petitioners. This process further reduces the self-esteem of the citizens. Further, when they are unable to get their benefits even after submitting petitions as petitioners, they approach the elected representatives as voters. With the intervention of the elected representatives, benefits are obtained. The whole process makes the people further lose their pride as citizens. The above process empowers the elected representatives or officials and disempowers the people. It is a process by which citizens are reduced and are conditioned to lose self-dignity and self-esteem. Further, the rights of the poor, women and the marginalised are violated. While Human Development Index (HDI) is fixed for evaluation, self-dignity, social justice, justice indicators have to be integrated into HDI as bases for evaluation and monitoring (Sakiko, 2005). The poor and the marginalised live in subhuman living conditions. Indicators have to be developed for decent human living conditions. The condition of the people has to be evaluated on the basis of the above indicators.

Demystification

Human development issues are still mystified as a subject for experts. In human development, health and education have to be tackled effectively by both the departments and the communities. In our setting however, the above two subjects are meant for experts. Departments will create facilities by making use of the funds allotted but the created facilities have to be utilised only by the communities. In our society, governments create facilities but they do not see whether the created facilities are used or not. Toilets are being constructed by the departments but the toilets have to be utilised by the community for which a toilet culture has to be created. It is unfortunate that in India the subjects of human development are not made subjects of the people but made specialised subjects for the experts. All the indicators of health and education have to be converted into actionable points for the community. Now the panchayat institutions are in position of governance and administration. They should be given responsibility to attend to these issues for which the departments of health and education have to work with the panchayats. By doing so, participation of the people will be ensured (Sakiko, 2005).

From trimming the nails of the school going children, maintaining the mid-day meal centre, providing safe drinking water to the communities, screening the poor women medically to identify the anaemia level, ensuring 100 per cent enrolment of eligible children in educational institutions communities can take responsibility through the newly created panchayat institutions. But, unfortunately, panchayats have not been oriented to take up human development issues but they are oriented in construction and providing certain services. They are not professionals even in providing these services. It is unfortunate that both communities and the panchayat representatives are not oriented in human development activities. To orient the communities and panchayat leaders, the subjects have to be simplified and demystified. As I have been involved in preparing human development reports for two districts, I have done small exercises to involve the communities and youth in human development activities through panchayats. They are produced hereunder for understanding and action at the panchayat level (The Hunger Project, 2001).

- Enrolling all the children who have completed five years of age in school.
- Ensuring that the enrolled children continue their studies without dropping out.
- Conducting school annual day celebrations to enable the students to display their creative potential.
- Providing basic amenities like drinking water, toilet, playing ground and vegetable garden in the school.
- Creating a sanitation and toilet culture among the students.
- Establishing reading rooms to encourage the desire to learn among the villagers and putting to use the Ayyan Thiruvalluvar Library.

- Providing toilet facility and play things for children in the anganwadi and trimming their nails to ensure hygiene.
- Enrolling all the children who have completed two and a half years of age in the anganwadi and helping them to learn the habit of attending to their personal cleanliness.
- Ensuring the age-specific weight and the general health of children by providing them with appropriate balanced nutritious meal and ensuring the proper conduct of activities such as providing nutritious flour and mid-day meal under the Integrated Child Development Scheme.
- Preventing female infanticide by creating awareness among the villagers.
- Ensuring that all the children receive fully and properly the benefits of the immunisation programme.
- Creating an environment free of child labour.
- Adopting measures to prevent child mortality.
- Creating awareness among the people about gender equality.
- Ensuring that all deliveries take place only in hospitals.
- Creating awareness among women about prenatal and postnatal care.
- Helping women to fully receive the benefits of the activities under the postnatal child welfare schemes.
- Helping pregnant women to properly receive benefits such as prenatal care, medical examination, immunisation vaccines, nutritious flour and pregnancy assistance money.
- Providing the required minimum basic facilities in the sub-health centre.
- Helping the village health nurse to discharge her welfare functions well.
- Taking steps to ensure optimum utilisation of the women's sanitary complexes.
- Ensuring that all the people get safe drinking water.
- Completely eradicating open air defecation.
- Arranging for common public toilets and their proper use.
- Removing waste in order to create a sanitary village.
- Creating awareness among the people about the dangers to the village from non-degradable substances like plastics and polythene and taking steps for their prohibition.
- Augmenting finances by converting public wastes into fertiliser.
- Planting, rearing and protecting saplings in public places to transform the village into a green village.
- Ensuring minimum basic amenities to all the habitations in the village.

- Installing solar street lights.
- Ensuring that all eligible families get ration cards.
- Arranging issuing of *pattas* to those who own no house sites.
- Ensuring that essential commodities are properly available under the public distribution system.
- Building houses for houseless people.
- Eradicating untouchability and creating social harmony.
- Ensuring that the Adi Dravidar community gets all the due benefits.
- Organising poor women into self-help groups and helping them to achieve social and economic upliftment.
- Making all the arrangements required to enable the self-help groups to produce articles and to market them.
- Bringing together the village artisans into a federation, enhancing their manual skills and arranging for employment opportunities for them.
- Creating awareness to ensure that girls are married only after they complete 21 years of age.
- Identifying the families with weak, destitute, elderly people, poor widows, poverty-stricken artisans and guaranteeing their livelihood.
- Identifying the disabled and delivering to them due benefits.
- Showing the way to male as well as female self-help groups to function robustly.
- Motivating and guiding self-help groups to participate fully in public welfare activities and in Gram Sabha meetings.
- Repairing and maintaining water sources such as ponds, tanks, *ooranis* and *kanmois*, collecting rainwater in them and using them properly.
- Creating the right perspective among the people regarding the importance of water, water management and utilisation of water.
- Developing natural resources and protecting them from damage and degradation.
- Creating awareness among the people to cultivate medicinal plants in public places in the village and in habitations and to use them.
- Creating awareness among the people to effect changes in agriculture suitable to circumstances.
- Reclaiming common property resources from encroachment.
- Regulating common property resources and taking steps to augment the panchayat income through them.
- Reorienting the panchayat activities to a people-centred mode and carrying them out with people's participation.
- Transforming the panchayat into an arena for people's action.

- Transforming the people into social citizens and making them participate in all panchayat activities.
- Transforming the Gram Sabha into a forum for social upliftment instead of a forum for collecting grievances.
- Involving women and Dalits in a big way in all the activities of the village.
- Synergising the different organisations functioning in the village for development activities.

Tackling Human Development Issues

Observing the status of human development in the whole of India, one finds that the conditions are alarming and deplorable. We have three levels of government. They are federal, state and local. All these governments are working towards the welfare of the people. When all the three levels of governments are working for the well-being of the people through policies, schemes and resource allocation and implementation of the same in the field, why is India poor in human development? Primarily the issues of human development have not been focused on as major issues which can be tackled effectively by all the governments. It requires a new approach which is decentralised in nature and character (Swaminathan, 2009). The totality of the data about the conditions has to be desegregated to the level of the state.

Since we have state and district human development reports, it is easy to identify the status of human development of each state and each district. Targets can be fixed and accordingly the issues can be tackled by the state governments. Further the status and position of human development of the districts have to be further desegregated to the level of each block. Inter-block variations have to be analysed. The problem is that there is no consistent segregation of data below the district level. All officials working at the district level are coordinated by the District Collector through the district administration. We have representatives for governance at the block but the departments of the government are not made accountable to the Block Panchayat. In fact all the departments do not have an office at the block level and hence there is no coordinating agency to coordinate the activities of the departments at the intermediate level. Not only that, the government departments down below the district do not have uniform data breakup to the level of the Block Panchayat. The database varies from department to department depending on the administrative arrangement.

Human development issues can be tackled even down below the level of the block. Every gram panchayat has its own governance and administrative unit. But this unit does not have the data pertinent to the indicators of human development. Even the United Nations Development

Programme (UNDP) has embarked upon preparing Human Development Report at the district level only recently. Due to non-availability of data with breakup details for blocks and villages, the team which prepared the District Human Development Report in select districts had to not only prepare the report but also had to prepare the officials for this task. Thus, the data generation system down the district does not suit the governance arrangement at the block and village levels. The understanding and awareness level of the officials and the representatives of the people in the panchayati raj system about human development are poor. Hence to tackle the human development issues, micro actions are needed as the local bodies are activated through the new amendments.

Output to Outcome Analysis

We have policies, programmes, schemes, resource allocation, personnel in the departments of governments, both central and state, working for human development. Yet significant improvement could not be achieved. While analysing the reasons we find that for education we have schools, teachers and facilities yet enrolment is poor despite the presence of village panchayat representatives, school teachers and the education department. The reason behind all these failures is the absence of outcome analysis. In all departments, targets are fixed, resources are allocated, yet no responsibility and accountabilities are fixed for the outcome of all the above exercises. The departments of education and health are to be evaluated from the perspective of outcome not output. In many of the government departments achievements are seen in terms of the activities carried out and progress shown in terms of the activities performed not in terms of the impact the activities have created. Hence, outcome oriented evaluations are needed. Incentives and disincentives can be thought of in the department for personnel, based on the outcome achieved by them and not the activities carried out by them.

Action to be initiated at Grassroots

First the subject 'Human Development' has to be demystified and simplified to make the citizens understand what for and what is human development. It should be made a subject of the citizens rather than a subject for the experts. It should be just like a cell phone. It is a sophisticated technology which can be used by even an ordinary uneducated person. In this way this subject has to be simplified. Further it should be put in a campaign mode to create awareness among the people about human development and to mobilise the people for achieving the target in human development. It could be done through the Gram Sabha. A special Gram Sabha meeting can be convened every year for discussing all the issues of human development to which all the concerned officials have to be invited.

Panchayat leaders and the officials have to be trained in the issues of human development. They should not only be trained but they are to be intensively sensitised on this subject. Creating sensitivity is more important than creating awareness and providing training. On many occasions we find people knowledgeable but not sensitive. Unless sensitivity is created, the individuals cannot be driven or motivated to action.

Initiatives have to be taken to prepare a human development report for every gram panchayat for every year. In the same way development plan for every gram panchayat has to be developed. For both a development seminar has to be conducted. By doing so, people can be mobilsed for development action. In India, one can authoritatively say from the Tamil Nadu experience that people are mobilised, that too the poor, for politics but not for development. Poor people can be mobilised for development through micro-planning and preparing human development report.

While preparing plan document and human development report for every gram panchayat, data have to be generated on human development indicators from the respective department for each gram panchayat area. Data generation, data upgradation, data validation and maintenance mechanism have to be evolved. By doing so human development issues become core subjects of panchayat management. The mindset of the stakeholders, whether they are the officials, representatives of the people or the members of Gram Sabha, has to be changed in such a way that all their activities take place only for achieving human development.

To perform the above task, co-operation, involvement and role of the concerned officials of the department are imperative. Hence, the state governments have to place the service of the officials at the disposal of the panchayats.

For all the vital aspects of human development monitorable indicators have to be fixed and they are to be given to the different committees of panchayats for monitoring. For example health indicators are to be monitored through the actions of the health department officials by the public health committee of the panchayats. In the same way all the indicators are to be monitored through the activities of the respective departments by the other committees of the panchayats.

Every panchayat has to be provided with untied funds to fill up the gap while matching the needs of the people and the schemes of the government. While preparing the plan for every gram panchayat, a matching exercise must be carried for matching the needs of the people with the schemes and programmes of the governments. For many of the minor needs of the people there will not be any scheme with the government. To meet all those small needs untied funds are essential. This untied fund for filling up the gap in attending to the human development issues at the gram panchayat level is an imperative need. For example, to bring a sanitation and hygiene culture among the school going children, a nail clipper has to be purchased, toilet soap has to be purchased for hand washing, some other toiletries have to be purchased for keeping the school toilets clean and tidy. For all the above there is no provision in the existing schemes.

Panchayats have to be evaluated and based on the performance by rating, and incentives and awards have to be given to the panchayats based on the achievements. Instead of giving sectoral awards for sanitation, water supply and so on, human development awards have to be given to the panchayats every year based on evaluation. It could be done at district level, state level and national level.

For the presentation of micro plan for development and human development report, the services of the civil society organisations, school teachers, both in service and retired, and retired government officials can be utilised effectively. Mass media, especially electronic, are very powerful and hence they are to be utilised for awareness creation and knowledge dissemination.

To make this subject integral in the life of the people, it should be incorporated in the school syllabus under civics, which should be mandatory. Further, at the higher level, it should be an audit course for all the undergraduate and post-graduate programmes in the colleges and universities. For social science programmes it should be an elective subject for specialisation. To perform all the above, training modules of the officials and the panchayat leaders have to be thoroughly altered and a section on human development has to be incorporated. By doing so human development issues become citizen's issues and with the involvement of the people the above issues will be tackled.

Conclusion

To improve the living conditions of the people a series of steps have to taken. So far human development initiatives have been taken through increased allocation of resources, new policy initiatives, new schemes and programmes with the active involvement of the bureaucracy and the people. Instead of treating the people as active participants and citizens they are treated as beneficiaries of the schemes. If the problems are looked at nationally they seem to be deplorable and massive. To tackle the problems, they are to be looked at in a decentralised and desegregated manner at micro level. Having created the local bodies at the grassroots for governance and administration mandatorily, the responsibility of handling human development issues should be given to the local bodies. Planning at micro level for improved human living conditions with the active participation of the people will really solve the problems. To involve the people in the process of human development, the subject itself has to be demystified and simplified. Action has to be initiated for evolving micro plan, and to prepare human development report for each and every gram panchayat. A data management system has to be evolved at the gram panchayat level. People have to be conscientised on the issues of human development through Gram Sabha meetings. Panchayat representatives and panchayat officials have to be trained in human development issues. Panchayats have to be provided with needed resources to fill the gap in the plan activities. The officials and the elected representatives have to be trained and sensitised. Human development is the fundamental issue and hence it should be made a mandatory subject to be taught in the schools and higher educational institutions. Panchayats have to be incentivised through awards and prizes for their good performance in human development at the district, state and the national levels. Civil society organisations, retired officials, teachers and media can be used effectively, efficiently and professionally for the purpose of preparation of human development report and micro plan and for their dissemination. Panchayat committees can be involved in monitoring the progress of human development. All stakeholders can be involved in this process by conducting these activities at the grassroots level.

References

Aiyar, Mani Shankar (2010). Valedictory Address delivered in the Workshop on *Secularism and Inclusive Democracy* in Gandhigram Rural Institute, Gandhigram, January 8.

Bhagwati, Jagdish (2004). *In Defense of Globalisation,* New Delhi: Oxford University Press.

Cohen, Elizabeth F. (2009). *Semi-Citizenship in Democratic Politics,* Cambridge: Cambridge University Press.

Francine, R. Frankel (2005). 'India's Political Economy 1947–2004', *The General Revolution New Delhi,* New Delhi: Oxford University Press.

Jalan, Bimal (2005). *The Future of India: Politics, Economics and Governance,* New Delhi: Penguin.

Palanithurai, G. (1995). *Peoples Perception of Politics: An Indian Perspective,* New Delhi: Kanishka Publishers and Distributors.

——. (2008). 'Governance and Administration: Reforms at Grassroots', *The ICFAI University Journal of Public Administration,* Vol. 4: No. 4 (October).

——. (2008). *Rajiv Gandhi's Vision on Local Governance,* New Delhi: Concept Publishing Company.

Ragunanthan, T.R. (2009). 'Using RTI for Fiscal Transparency: The tail end of the canal – the Panchayats', National Workshop on *Globalisation and*

Decentralisation, Dr M.S. Swaminathan Research Foundation, Chennai, November 7.

Sakiko Fukuda-Parr (2005). 'Rescuing the Human Development Concept from the HDI: Reflections on a New Agenda' in a Sakiko Fukuda-Parr, A.K. Shiva Kumar (eds) *Readings in Human Development: Concepts, Measures and Policies for a Development Paradigm*, New Delhi: Oxford University Press.

Sivaramakrishnan, K.C. (2000). *Power to the People? The Politics and Progress of Decentralisation*, New Delhi: Konark Publishing Company.

Social Watch India (2009). *Citizens Report on Governance and Development 2008–2009*, Delhi: Daanish Books.

Swaminathan, M.S. (2009). 'Globalisation and Decentralisation', Dr M.S. Swaminathan Research Foundation, Chennai, November 7.

The Hunger Project (2001). *Village Development Plan: Meenaveli Village Panchayat*, Pudukottai District, Gandhigram.

UNDP (2009). *Human Development Report 2009*, New York: Palgrave Macmillan.

16

The Elusive Holy Grail of Tribal Self-Rule

An Analysis of the History behind PESA

RAHUL BANERJEE

Constitutional Riddles

A searingly hot summer afternoon in the month of April 2001 saw Motiabhai the Bhilala adivasi Patel of Katukia village in Bagli tehsil of Dewas district in Madhya Pradesh sitting among the ruins of his house and plaintively asking the then Chairman of the National Scheduled Castes and Scheduled Tribes Commission Shri Dilip Singh Bhuria whether as a citizen of India he did not have the right to live with dignity under his own roof. Prior to this in a secretly planned 'Operation Clean' the Government of Madhya Pradesh had carried out a sudden campaign of mass destruction and loot of the houses of adivasis who belonged to the Adivasi Morcha Sangathan without giving them any notice whatsoever and had killed four of its members when they protested enmasse against this blatantly illegal operation (IPT, 2001).

Shri Bhuria was too dumbstruck by the scale of destruction to say anything other than some words in consolation. Why is it that adivasis like Motia Patel have again and again been forced to ask this question in independent India without receiving any satisfactory answer? Why is it that despite constitutional safeguards and other ameliorative legislation adivasis continue to face the iron hand of state repression whenever they demand their rights in any significant manner? Why has the Panchayat Extension to Scheduled Areas Act, 1996 (PESA), which had initially been hailed as the long awaited panacea for all the ills of tribal mal-development, also been unable to deliver the goods to the tribals in the past decade in which it has been in force? Why indeed does tribal self-rule remain an elusive Holy Grail even after six decades of independence? To find the answers to all these burning questions it will be necessary to trace the history of various legal provisions leading up to the enactment of PESA and its later non-implementation over the past decade of its existence.

However, before beginning this historical analysis, it has to be mentioned that PESA like most other laws is gender-blind. Possibly because tribal society too, especially in the areas governed by the Fifth Schedule of the Constitution is highly patriarchal. There is a clear gender division of labour among the Bhils with the women having to do the domestic work and also take on the responsibilities of child bearing and rearing in addition to agricultural work. Socially too the women have an inferior status with little say in community affairs and are considered as commodities to be sold off for a bride-price at the time of marriage. Married women have to submit to polygamy and witchhunting and also have to veil their faces in front of elder male relatives on their husband's side. Women have no right of inheritance or to property. As with poor rural women elsewhere in India, the major burden of the modernising thrust introduced by the British and continued by the independent Indian state that has adversely affected the Bhils' traditional lifestyles has had to be borne by the women. This patriarchy and the lack of education and proper reproductive health services had resulted in the birth rate remaining uncontrolled further adding to the miseries of the women in particular and the Bhils as a whole through a population explosion (Rahul and Subhadra, 2001).

Mass participatory democracy in India was sabotaged at the very outset by the framing and adoption of a Constitution that retained a distinct centralised colonial character that considerably curbed the freedom of the people. The Constituent Assembly was not elected by universal adult suffrage but was the same as was formed by the British in 1946 with members from among the elite feudal, capitalist and professional classes mostly owing allegiance to the former. Moreover, the actual drafting of the Constitution had very little to do with the debates that did take place in this unrepresentative Constituent Assembly. The drafting was done by a set of Indian Civil Service bureaucrats led by the Constitutional Adviser Sir Benegal Rau. These bureaucrats who had been part of the British administration and were well versed in the techniques of repressive colonial rule authored a Constitution that retained the colonial and anti-people character of the Government of India Act, 1935 greatly discounting the new liberal democratic features such as the provision of Fundamental Rights and the affirmative sections for the scheduled castes and tribes. Thus, Jawaharlal Nehru's biographer Michael Brecher wrote,

> One of the striking features of India's new Constitution is the continuity with British-Indian practice. Approximately 250 articles out of 395 were taken either verbatim or with minor changes in phraseology from the Government of India Act 1935 and the basic principles remained unchanged. (Brecher, 1959)

Consequently, the British in reality transferred power in India at the time of independence in 1947 to a ruling coalition consisting of the nascent capitalists, the feudal classes and the bureaucracy (Bardhan, 1985). The capitalists looking ahead to the situation that would prevail after independence had come up with a national plan in 1944, popularly known as the Bombay Plan, which spoke of both strengthening their ties with imperialist capital and at the same time of protecting the Indian market from predatory penetration by the latter (Thakurdas et al., 1944). The Bombay Plan also envisaged the rapid development of basic infrastructure through heavy state spending garnered from exploitation of the labour of the masses and the vast natural resources. It specifically mentioned that the state must intervene to maintain law and order and restrict individual freedoms given the possibility of dissent from the masses against such a policy. No wonder then that G.D. Birla the doyen of the Indian capitalists gloated at the time, ' We have embodied large portions of the 1935 Act, as finally passed, in the Constitution which we have framed ourselves and which shows that in the 1935 Act was cast the pattern of our future plans' (Birla, 1968).

As can well be imagined this could only bode ill for the adivasis. The presence of articulate adivasi leaders like Khan Abdul Ghaffar Khan and Jaipal Singh resulted in the debates in the Constituent Assembly reverberating with eulogies for the inherently democratic and non-exploitative nature of adivasi communities and the expression of concern about enabling them to negotiate the process of integration into the modern economy to their advantage (GoI, 1954). Consequently, extensive provisions were made in the Constitution and many laws were passed for the protection and betterment of the adivasis. Nevertheless, the imperatives of modern industrial development as enunciated in the Bombay Plan and later embodied in the centralised planning process initiated from the early 1950s and the powerlessness of the adivasis in the face of the ruling coalition resulted in a policy of even greater intrusion into adivasi areas than in colonial times being adopted after independence to exploit the vast natural resources that these held.

The independent Indian government in fact continued the policy of the British of promising liberal natural justice on paper and suppressing it in practice to pursue a policy of extraction of resources to fuel modern industrial development in Britain. The British when introducing the first Government of India Act in 1858 had guaranteed to the people of India *inter alia* that due regard would be paid to the ancient rights, usages and customs of India while framing new laws and that these laws would be administered equally and impartially for the benefit of the people. Almost immediately, however, these principles were breached. The Indian Penal Code (IPC) was enacted in 1860 and the Code of Criminal Procedure (CrPC) in 1861. These laws, with some minor amendments only, are still in force today and have been codified in such a manner as to provide the administration with a handy means of suppressing organised public dissent. A more harmful law from the point of view of the adivasis was the Indian Forest Act 1864. Applying the principle of *res nullius*, which means that in case a particular property has no owner the British refused to recognise the customary community rights of the adivasis over the forests in which they resided and turned them over to the Forest Department created for this purpose. This law too in its newer 1927 version, which effectively converts the adivasis into trespassers in their own backyard, continues to be in force at present. Yet another law that disinherited the adivasis from their main resource of land was the Land Acquisition Act, 1894 which using the principle of eminent domain empowered the government to dispossess the private owner of a piece of land for some public purpose in exchange for a paltry compensation. Once again this law also has been retained and widely used to displace people, particularly adivasis, in independent India in pursuit of modern industrial development (Fernandes and Paranjpye, 1997).

The biggest lacuna of all was that Gandhi's conception of 'Gram Swaraj' or the promotion of grassroots democracy through the establishment of autonomous village republics was given a go by. Panchayati Raj was included in the Directive Principles of State Policy which were non-justiciable, that is, unlike the fundamental rights, these could not be enforced through the courts. Basic rights like that to free education, health and nutrition services and the means to a dignified livelihood too were included in this section. Thus provisions that could have created an aware, healthy and articulate population and provided them with an institutional structure for implementing their development according to their own genius and so curtail the power of the ruling classes were ignored totally by the governments both at the centre and the state after independence thus paving the way for the persistence of a form of internal colonialism and feudalism. Matters were compounded by the fact that fundamental rights too were not easily assured given the tremendous expenses involved in approaching the High Courts and the Supreme Court for redress. While the erstwhile princes, landlords and the capitalists often went to court to obstruct the path of justice for the poor, the latter could hardly afford to do so and so had to bear with the illegal actions of the ruling classes directly or through the organs of the state.

This in effect meant that the checks and balances that form a basic part of a liberal democratic set up, were disturbed in favour of the executive consisting of the council of ministers and the bureaucracy. The party system ensured that the council of ministers and its leader the prime minister would always be much more powerful than their fellow legislators. In the initial years after independence, the overwhelming majority of the Congress party and the charisma of its leader Nehru also meant that the opposition was not very vocal or effective in monitoring the actions of the government and parliament was reduced to being as ineffectual as a debating society. Moreover, preventive detention laws were enacted to silence the protests of people's organisations and their leaders outside parliament and thousands of such people were jailed. Finally the press too was not as combative and investigative as it is today and given the high level of illiteracy it did not have much of a reach. Thus the government and the bureaucracy rode roughshod over democratic niceties to push through a process of modernisation at the cost of the ordinary people by using colonial repressive laws and by flouting the progressive aspects of the constitution. The bureaucracy, which continued in its colonial mindset, was a power unto itself as it not only framed all the laws but also interpreted and administered them to the detriment of an illiterate and unaware populace.

The Tribal Dilemma

The tribals, as mentioned earlier, had special provisions included for their benefit in the Constitution. Those in the states of Assam, Meghalaya, Tripura and Mizoram were to be covered by the provisions of the Sixth Schedule while those in the states of Andhra Pradesh, Odisha, Jharkhand, Himachal Pradesh, Madhya Pradesh, Chhattisgarh, Maharashtra, Gujarat, and Rajasthan were to be covered by the provisions of the Fifth Schedule. The basic philosophy behind these provisions was that the tribals had a unique communitarian culture based on a subsistence non-accumulative lifestyle that was totally at odds with the consumerist culture spawned by modern industrial development. Thus, it was necessary to conserve this culture by secluding it from the aggressive thrust of modern development. The British administrator, anthropologist and social activist Verrier Elwin was the foremost proponent of this view and it was he who influenced Nehru in this matter and was the brain behind his *Panchsheel* for tribal areas which spoke of their development keeping in mind their uniqueness. However, given the tremendous imbalance of powers away from the grassroots level these noble ideas remained a pipe dream in reality.

The provisions under the Sixth Schedule purport to provide for a self contained code for the governance of the tribes living in those areas through the institution of autonomous district councils. Despite the fact that autonomous district councils gave some powers to the tribes in respect of determining many aspects of their life. These were limited by the greater powers of the states of which they were a part. In the case of Assam and Tripura, non-tribals who were in no mood to cede any substantial concessions to the tribals dominated the state legislatures and curbed the powers of the district councils. In the case of Meghalaya and Mizoram the tribal leaders at the state level usurped all the powers emasculating the district councils. Problems have been created by not giving sanction to the laws and rules passed by the councils and also by restricting the funds available to them to carry out developmental activities. Centralised development and immiserisation of the tribals has been the rule and the district councils have fallen well short of the aspirations of the people in the north-eastern states (Roy Burman, 1997).

The situation in the Fifth Schedule areas has been even worse. Section 5 of the Fifth Schedule reads thus:

(i) Notwithstanding anything in this Constitution, the Governor may by public notification direct that any particular Act of Parliament of the Legislature of the State shall not apply to a Scheduled Areas or any part thereof in the State or shall apply to a Scheduled Area or any part thereof in the State subject to such exceptions and modifications as he may specify in the notification and any direction given under this sub-paragraph may be given so as to have retrospective effect.

(ii) The Governor may make regulations for the peace and good government of any area in a State which is for the time being a Scheduled Area. In particular and without prejudice to the generality of the foregoing power, such regulations may:
   (a) Prohibit or restrict the transfer of land by or among members of the Scheduled Tribes in such area;
   (b) Regulate the allotment of land to members of the Scheduled Tribes in such area;
   (c) Regulate the carrying on of business as moneylender by persons who lend money to members of the Scheduled Tribes in such area.

(iii) In making any such regulation as is referred to in sub-paragraph (2) of this paragraph, the Governor may repeal or amend any Act of Parliament or of the Legislature of the State or any existing law which for the time being is applicable to the area in question.

Thus, theoretically it is possible for the Governor of a state, on the advice of the Tribes Advisory Council consisting of the tribal MLAs of the state, to prevent the application of or repeal the Indian Forest Act and the Land Acquisition Act. The most important aspect of these provisions is that the Governor may implement them so as to ensure 'peace and good government' in adivasi areas as the framers of the Constitution felt that this could be possible only if the adivasis were allowed to develop according to their own laws and customs. However, this has never happened because it is not a binding provision and only a suggestion like the Directive Principles of State Policy, which finally has to depend on the executive for its implementation.

Consequently, there has been neither peace nor good government in adivasi areas. The history of the past 60 years after independence is replete with innumerable struggles of the central Indian adivasis against the injustice meted out to them by the Indian state through the ruthless implementation of the Indian Forest Act and the Land Acquisition Act and the cynical non-implementation of the Fifth Schedule. There have been widespread protests by adivasi mass organisations. The most path breaking of these struggles has been that of the *Narmada Bachao Andolan* (NBA). Even though the NBA has not been able to prevent the construction of the big dams on the river Narmada it has through its mass struggles and legal activism effectively questioned the legitimacy of the Land Acquisition Act and the industrial development model that it serves. It has today created an atmosphere in the country wherein the fraudulent concept of 'eminent domain' of the State and its monopoly on deciding what is 'public purpose' has come to be questioned.

A non-government organisation (NGO) Samatha fought the Government of Andhra Pradesh's decision of giving of a lease to a private company to extract minerals in scheduled adivasi areas all the way to the Supreme Court which in a landmark judgement rendered in the light of the debates in the Constituent Assembly upheld that the intention of the founders of the Constitution when drafting the Fifth Schedule was that the adivasis should be protected from dispossession of their land and so even though the actual word in the constitution is that the Governor 'may' act for their benefit it should be read as 'shall' and has thus effectively prevented the transfer of adivasi land to non-adivasis (Samatha vs State of Andhra Pradesh, 1997 8 SCC 191). Theoretically, as mentioned earlier, the Governor of a state in which there are scheduled areas, as mentioned earlier, can on the advice of the Tribal Advisory Council (TAC) of that state have special laws enacted for these areas and also direct that laws enacted by the parliament or state legislatures should not apply to them. Indeed these provisions could easily have been used to prevent the application of such inimical laws as the Indian Forest Act, Indian Penal Code, Criminal Procedure Code and Land Acquisition Act. Thus, these provisions could have been used to seclude the tribals from the onslaught of modern development and allow them to gradually pick up the skills of negotiating a modern economy and polity. However, in practice, for a long time the TACs were not constituted or were there only on paper and the Governors never used their special powers to intervene on behalf of the tribals leading to massive land alienation due to development projects and deforestation and through debt bondage and other problems for the later. This is because these provisions are not binding on the Governor and suggest that he 'may' utilise them. So if the government does not implement these provisions he cannot be held responsible and taken to court for redressal.

The simmering discontent arising from this gross mis-governance led to the adoption of a new strategy for tribal development from the Fifth Five Year Plan onwards in 1974. Tribal areas were identified throughout the country and a special sub-plan was formulated for transferring funds to these areas for their development. It was found that many of these areas were not included in either the Fifth or the Sixth Schedule. This led to the amendment of the Constitution in 1976 so that newer areas in Andhra Pradesh and Himachal Pradesh could be included in the Fifth Schedule. However, this process was left unfinished in 1978 and even today many tribal areas in Karnataka, Kerala, Tamil Nadu and West Bengal are still outside the purview of the Fifth Schedule. This has meant that there has been gross misappropriation of the Tribal sub-plan funds and adequate benefits have not accrued to the people for whom they were intended. Indeed these funds have only served to co-opt the tribal elite into the ruling nexus.

The Promised Land

Obviously the lack of grassroots governance institutions was becoming more and more of a problem as the level of political awareness and literacy was increasing and the centralised trickle down type of development was coming apart at the seams. There was a need to provide a third tier of democratic institutions to take some of the pressure of accountability off the shoulders of the state and central governments. Consequently, the pressure building up within the mainstream parties and from various mass organisations and NGOs finally led to the passing of the 73rd Constitutional Amendment in 1992 making Panchayati Raj mandatory. As a result of a concerted campaign conducted by the National Front for Tribal Self-Rule, the Scheduled Tribal Areas were excluded from the purview of these amendments. Article 243M (4) (2) of Part IX of the Constitution envisages that 'Parliament may by law extend the provisions of this part to the Scheduled Areas ... subject to such exceptions and modifications as may be specified in such a law'. Thus, this was the first time that a central law had not been automatically extended to the Scheduled Areas. It was also stated that such a law enacted by Parliament would not amount to an amendment of the Constitution and could thus be passed by a simple majority. Provision for this special law was made keeping in mind the failure of the Governors to implement the enabling provisions of the Fifth Schedule.

There was, however, no enthusiasm shown by the central government to pass this special act and extend the provisions of the 73rd Amendment to the Scheduled Areas. Finally the Government of India constituted a Committee of Members of Parliament and Experts in 1994 to suggest the framework of the special law to be enacted for this purpose and the changes necessary in other Acts to accord with the spirit of the new Act. This committee, which has since come to be known as the Bhuria Committee after its chairman ex-MP Dilip Singh Bhuria submitted its Report on January 17, 1995. Some of the important recommendations of the Committee are as follows (Sharma, 1995):

(i) The community habitation like a hamlet rather than an administrative unit like a village should be the basic unit of the system of self-rule in tribal areas and this should be designated as the Gram Sabha.

(ii) The Gram Sabha would function on the basis of consensus.

(iii) The Gram Sabha would concern itself with all matters of day to day life including command over natural resources, resolutions of disputes, investigation and adjudication of all matters including debts and management of institutions such as schools, cooperatives, health centres, etc. It would also be responsible for execution of all developmental programmes including the selection of beneficiaries. The administrative personnel at the village level would function under its control.

(iv) The higher level institutions from the Gram Panchayat to the District Councils would all have appellate jurisdiction and would be able to undertake development works at their level and be constituted by people directly elected from the Gram Sabhas.

(v) The demographic structure of some tribal areas has undergone significant change because of heavy influx of population of non-tribals and so a majority of members in all elected bodies as also their chairman and deputy chairman should be tribals.

(vi) The tribal areas are mostly situated on the boundaries of administrative units, be they blocks, districts or states and so a reorganisation of tribal areas should be undertaken so as to constitute tribal administrative units with homogeneous social, economic, geographical and ethnic parameters. This reorganisation should be completed within two years.

(vii) Many tribal areas have not been included in any of the Scheduled Areas. The process of extension of scheduled areas that was started in 1976 came to a halt in 1978. This process should be restarted and all the remaining tribal areas should be included in scheduled areas within one year.

(viii) The Constitution should be amended to make the provisions of the Fifth Schedule mandatory and justiciable so as to rectify the indifferent functioning of the Tribal Advisory Councils and the total neglect of their responsibility with regard to Scheduled Areas by the Governors of the States. A Central Tribal Advisory Council should also be constituted.

These were radical recommendations except that they did not have anything in them for the women. Consequently once again the government did not show any intention of enacting the special act for extension of Panchayati Raj on these lines. Meanwhile Panchayat elections were announced in February 1995 in Andhra Pradesh. The Andhra Pradesh Government enacted a Panchayati Raj Act providing that only in blocks that had 100 per cent tribal population, the top posts for the various levels of panchayat bodies would be reserved for tribals and in Scheduled Areas where the tribal population was in a minority there would be no reservation whatsoever. Thus, the tribals who had already lost on the demographic front due to non-tribal influx and on the economic front due to land alienation were now also to lose on the political front due to the lack of a special law for the extension of Panchayati Raj to scheduled areas. This was challenged by Arka Vasanth Rao and others in the Andhra Pradesh High Court which held in its judgement of March 23, 1995 that the Andhra Pradesh Panchayat Raj Act 1994 was unconstitutional and so could not apply to the Scheduled Areas (Sharma, op. cit.).

This brought to the fore the serious problems that could arise in the absence of a special central act extending the provisions of Panchayati Raj to the scheduled areas. The National Front for Tribal Self-Rule stepped up its campaign to get this new law enacted. Meetings and mass rallies were held all over the country and intense lobbying was resorted to with the central government. Finally in desperation some of its members sat on an indefinite hunger strike at Rajghat in 1996. This combined with some more lobbying finally resulted in the preparation of a watered down version of the Bhuria Committee Recommendations, which was passed through parliament without debate and became the now famous PESA. PESA as it stands is a far cry from what is ideal for the tribals in the Fifth Scheduled Areas but something is better than nothing and it has already proved to be a headache for the central and state governments and a boon to *adivasi* mass organisations. The paramount nature of the Gram Sabha in tribal areas has been established even though it has not been vested with the wide-ranging powers that it should have. Most importantly for the first time in the history of the country, a law that has been drafted by the people and not by a bureaucrat, had been enacted. Thus, it provided an opportunity to small *adivasi* mass organisations to try and assert the power of the people at the grassroots level.

Illusion and Reality

The Madhya Pradesh Panchayati Raj Act was amended in 1997 in accordance with PESA and rules framed for its implementation in 1998. The Gram Sabha or village council had been made the paramount decision making body and so a special local government system to accord with *adivasi* lifestyle and culture had become a legal possibility. Mobilisation proceeded all over the Bhil *adivasi* dominated western Madhya Pradesh region to exert pressure on the administration towards implementing these provisions.

Since 1999 there had been deficient rainfall in this region. Whereas some tehsils of Barwani and Jhabua districts had been officially declared drought hit, others had not been so fortunate as the harvest there had not been less than the statutory level of 37 per cent of the normal harvest required for declaring a district or tehsil as being drought hit. Even after being declared drought hit paltry amount between rupees three and four crores each had been sanctioned for these two districts for relief works over and above the minimal amounts that are normally available through various Central Government schemes. The rest of the region had not even got these crumbs. The *adivasi* mass organisations launched a massive campaign for putting pressure on the government to carry out sufficient relief works. Plans for soil and water conservation works were prepared by the people and sanctioned by the Gram Sabhas and forwarded to the administration for action. Subsequently rallies, dharnas and even blocking of roads was undertaken. The *Adivasi Mukti Sangathan* organised a month long dharna in January 2000 in Barwani and later in Bhopal pressing for relief works to be started but could get extra sanction of only rupees one crore for the district. Even the allocations of cheap foodgrains for distribution to the Below Poverty Line (BPL) families through the public distribution system were not increased.

This failure on the part of the government to provide adequate relief work resulted in more number of *adivasis* having to migrate for work than is normally the case. The problem was that the whole western Indian region had been groaning under drought conditions. So even the places that normally offered work to the *adivasis* like the towns and cities of Gujarat and Indore and the intensive agricultural areas of the Malwa plateau and Gujarat had less work to offer. This combination of less available work and a higher number of migrant workers had depressed wages to well below subsistence levels all over the region.

The net result was that the *sahukars* were having a field day. The *adivasis* were forced to go to these *sahukars* in the absence of any other support system and bear the burden of usurious interest rates that had shot up to levels of 10 per cent per month and more. In Alirajpur tehsil of Jhabua district when the *adivasis* did not have even the money for the bus fare to migrate, they borrowed the money from the *sahukar*. When they returned after a fortnight or a month they paid back double the money borrowed. Reviewing the situation the *adivasi* mass organisations found that the only way in which things could be improved was for the government to take action under the various laws at its disposal against the *sahukars*. Since this was unlikely given the political power of the *sahukars*, plans were finalised for launching a mass action programme pressing for punitive action against them.

This campaign was to piggyback on the other ongoing campaigns for access to and control over the main natural resources of forests and water that were already underway. Given the persistent drought conditions the pressure on these resources had increased and so had the confrontation with the agencies of the state regarding their proper utilisation. The situation had become very tense in the areas of influence of the mass organisations by December 2000. A delegation of *adivasi* members of these organisations went to meet the deputy Chief Minister Jamuna Devi on December 2 to settle the matters. However, the latter categorically told them that they should give up their agitational methods and distance themselves from the non-*adivasi* activists who she alleged were foreign agents out to destabilise the state. She advised them to disband their separate organisations and join the Congress party instead!

The Madhya Pradesh government carries out a mass contact programme each year in the month of January called the Jan Sampark Abhiyaan ostensibly to take note of the problems being faced by the people. Led by the chief minister, all the ministers, secretaries and other government staff go to the villages in a weeklong programme to record the grievances of the people. Apart from a few symbolic actions this charade does not result in any widespread improvement in the quality of governance in the state and in the end becomes just a publicity stunt.

In the cabinet meeting held in January 2001 to review the Jan Sampark Abhiyaan, the spreading influence of the *adivasi* mass organisations was commented on and it was decided to crackdown on them. Subsequently a high-level meeting chaired by the Chief Secretary was held on February 17, 2001 in Bhopal to work out the modalities of this crackdown. It was admitted in this meeting that the lack of development and the corruption in government services had led to rising disaffection among the *adivasis*, which was snowballing into organised protests. However, it was categorically stated that the might of the state apparatus could not be allowed to weaken in the face of such protests even if they were spurred by valid grievances and so force would have to be applied to crush these organisations and recourse should be taken of such laws as the National Security Act and externment proceedings instituted if required to put a stop to the activities of these organisations (IPT, op. cit.).

The MLAs of the region held public meetings in various places along with the collectors, superintendents of police and other officers. Open threats were given in these meetings that unless the tribal organisations disbanded themselves, punitive action would be taken against their members. Following this repressive action began from the month of March against the *Narmada Bachao Andolan*, the *Adivasi Morcha Sangathan*, the *Adivasi Mukti Sangathan* and the *Adivasi Shakti Sangathan* involving raids by police and forest forces. In the severest of such crackdowns a huge force of some 400 armed personnel led by the collector descended on the villages of Udainagar sub-tehsil in Dewas district in the last week of March 2001 without any prior notice, destroying and looting the houses of the *adivasi* members of the sangathans and firing on them when they protested leaving four people dead in police firing and many others injured. The *adivasis* like Motia Patel who had begun to hold their heads high on the strength of the self-respect earned through organised action were forced into being cowering sub-humans once again. As is usual in such cases many activists were jailed by the administration on trumped up charges (IPT, op. cit.).

This is the chilling reality of PESA. The organs of the state, even in a tribal state like Jharkhand, will not normally countenance any challenge to their hegemony over power and resources and will always come down hard to crush people's movements using the various colonial repressive laws that they have at their disposal. Apart from these repressive powers they have considerable powers of co-option. The disbursal of funds for development through the panchayats has meant that the elections for these bodies are keenly fought for the privilege of having the power to use or misuse them. Thus, the unity of the traditional tribal Gram Sabha has been broken by the election system, which invariably pits *adivasis* against each other (Rahul, 1992). Moreover, the increasing penetration of modern media and entertainment into remote *adivasi* areas has meant that their traditional culture is disintegrating. Consumerism has made serious inroads into the earlier subsistence economy. Thus, the ideal tribal setting envisioned in the Bhuria Committee Report no longer exists in most Scheduled Areas. All this makes it even more difficult to implement the PESA in its true spirit.

Another contributing factor is that most *adivasis* have to migrate to non-tribal areas as the lands that they have are not sufficient to provide them with a sustainable livelihood. Thus, they come into contact with the mainstream consumerist culture and imbibe its values, especially the younger generation. Migration in fact further victimises Bhil women as they lose privacy and security in the destination labour places. Children lose the opportunity to pursue studies in schools and this is also a big blow for girls who can break with patriarchy only by studying and avoiding early child marriage at puberty which is the general custom among the Bhils.

The Way Ahead

Despite this reality check, the PESA does provide a greater space for legal and mass action to press for increased tribal autonomy. The repressive and co-optive powers of the state can be stretched to the limit by such actions if they are carried out in a concerted manner spread over the whole of the scheduled areas of the country. With the help of the judiciary and the media it may be possible to give weight to the contention that modern development cannot be carried out at the cost of the *adivasis*. Thus, there is a chance to ensure that basic principles of liberal democratic governance are not flouted with impunity by the state in tribal areas as they are being at present. The traditional *adivasi* lifestyle and culture is an anarchist one which negates the centralising thrust of the modern state system and the market economy. The latter are increasingly proving to be detrimental to both nature and human survival. Thus, the anarchism of the tribals has a lot to offer to human beings. The PESA is a first step in the direction of preserving and promoting tribal culture and thus ensuring a saner world involving more sustainable resource use and equitable inter-personal relations than the one we are living in (Rahul, 1997). Proof of this can be found in the fact that the leaders of the Chiapas indigenous people's movement in Mexico have used it as one of the reference points for the formulation of their own draft constitution.

The passage of the National Rural Employment Guarantee Act (NREGA) and the Right to Information Act, 2006 has considerably enhanced the effectiveness of PESA. There are now many instances throughout the country of small mass organisations in Fifth Schedule Areas taking advantage of the provisions of these later acts and using them to fulfil the promise of self rule mentioned in PESA. Similarly many *adivasi* mass organisations have conducted long drawn campaigns which have resulted in the enactment of the Scheduled Tribes and Other Forest Dwellers (Recognition of Rights) Act, 2006 which tries to give teeth to the provisions of the Fifth Schedule and nullify the historical injustice done to the *adivasis* through the implementation of the Indian Forest Act.

One such mass organisation in the western Madhya Pradesh region in Alirajpur district is the Khedut Mazdoor Chetna Sangathan (KMCS) which has been mobilising the local Bhil tribal population on rights issues for over two and a half decades (Banerjee, 2008). Apart from rights based mobilisation the KMCS has taken up soil, forest and water conservation work on a large scale through voluntary participation in defiance of the negative attitude of the government and the bureaucracy, and are showing positive results. The streams running through the villages where the organisation is active have water flowing perennially even though there are many motor pumps on them drawing water from it for irrigation. Now with the MNREGS the organisation has considerably increased its mobilisation work.

The foregoing discussion makes it abundantly clear that ultimately tribal self-rule will be possible only if there is conscious community mobilisation at the grassroots level in support of this. As we have seen macro level policies have also led to the decay of the traditional communitarian practices of the Bhils and so a revival will have to be attempted at a decentralised level by the Bhil communities themselves. Especially as such communitarian culture will also save the natural resources and have a mitigating effect on climate change (Cruz, 2009). One of the foremost votaries of such communitarian approaches to the management of common pool natural resources, Elinor Ostrom, has recently been awarded the Nobel Memorial Prize for the Economic Sciences in 2009 thus putting the imprimatur on the validity of this approach (Ostrom, 2001). So, the way ahead lies in persisting with the synergistic implementation and further refinement of people oriented tribal laws so as to ensure peace and good government in tribal areas as envisaged in the Fifth Schedule of the Constitution.

References

Banerjee, R. (2008). *Recovering The Lost Tongue: The Saga of Environmental Struggles in Central India*, Hyderabad: Prachee Publications.

Bardhan, P. (1985). *Political Economy of Development in India*, New Delhi: Oxford University Press.

Birla, G.D. (1968). *In The Shadow of The Mahatma*, Mumbai, quoted in S.K. Ghosh (2001), *The Indian Constitution and Its Review*, Mumbai: Research Unit for Political Economy, p. 131.

Brecher, M. (1959). *Nehru: A Political Biography*, London, quoted in S.K. Ghosh (2001), *The Indian Constitution and Its Review*, Mumbai: Research Unit for Political Economy, p. 421.

Cruz, RVO. (2009). Climate Change and Watersheds: Issues and Concerns, http://pemsea.org/pdf-documents/ccef_ruz.pdf accessed on September, 24, 2009

Fernandes, W. and V. Paranjpye (eds) (1997). *Rehabilitation Policy and Law in India: A Right to Livelihood*, Delhi and Pune: Indian Social Institute & Econet.

Government of India (1954). *Constituent Assembly Debates (CAD)*, Lok Sabha Secretariat, Delhi.

—— (1996). Panchayat Provisions (Extension to Scheduled Areas) Act.

Indian People's Tribunal (2001). *Terrorism sans Terrorists: An Enquiry into the Firing on Bhil Adivasis in Dewas M.P.*, Mumbai.

Ostrom, E. (2001). An Institutional Approach to the Study of Self-Organisation and Self-Governance in CPR situations, in U. Sankar (ed.) *Environmental Economics*, New Delhi: Oxford University Press.

Rahul (1992). Rhetoric Versus Reality: The State, Jawahar Rozgar Yojana and People's Participation, *EPW*, December 19–26, 1992.

—— (1997). Reasserting Ecological Ethics: Bhils' Struggles in Alirajpur, *EPW*, Vol. 30, No. 3.

Rahul and Subhadra (2001). Schooling of Tribals in Madhya Pradesh: Problems and Prospects, *Journal of Educational Planning and Administration*, Vol. X, No. 1.

Roy-Burman, B.K. (1997). Sixth Schedule and Seventy-third and Seventy-fourth Amendments of the Constitution (mimeo), DCRC, University of Delhi.

Sharma, B.D. (1995). *Whither Tribal Areas: Constitutional Amendments and After*, New Delhi: Sahayog Pustak Kutir.

Thakurdas, P. et al. (1944). *A Brief Memorandum Outlining a Plan of Economic Development for India*, Mumbai.

17

Democracy in an Indian Village

Interaction of Gender, Caste and Poverty

SANJAY SINGH AND SHAILJA SINGH

India became more democratic with reference to participation of men, women and other disadvantageous groups but it became less democratic in terms of democratic principles and ideologies after independence. The caste and faction ridden politics at local level in the village to the national level signifies the decline in democratic principles. The parochial attitude with reference to women and other disadvantageous groups lead to hardships in terms of economy and development. The distribution of political power, education and economic opportunity to the disadvantageous group, mainly dalit and women community, is the important indicator of development and decentralised governance. The change of grassroots democratic system from developmental to political unit shows a shift in the orientation and participation. The inclusion of dalit and women in the political process has initiated a new dimension to the grassroot democratic system. In the hierarchical traditional structure social distances were clearly defined and were more or less rigidly maintained. There was hardly any scope in this structure for people at the two ends of the hierarchy to sit together and discuss their private affairs on equal terms. As long as the traditional structure persists, the cognitive map or archetype of elite class is likely to continue. But, the new leadership that controls the affairs of panchayat differs from the traditional elite of the village. This difference exists not only in terms of caste, class but in terms of gender also. Earlier, the power structure was complete without including the factor of women in it. But, the policy change and promotion of women in politics led to the change in power structure. The present paper is based on the micro field study of one of the smallest units of democratic governance, the village panchayat of Lucknow district from period 2003–07. This time period has provided the researcher to perceive the challenges with respect to governance in the village and the observations shall be helpful for making future strategies for the village development. The emphasis in the present study is on economy, gender and caste. These variables are observed in the context of the politics and governance of village panchayat. The change in the power structure of the panchayat under study led to the change in the socio-political configuration. This process of change leads to creation of not only new relations but also of new values, attitudes and aspirations. This process of change provides scope to the researcher to enter into new network of interpersonal relations where village, caste and other traditional bonds are observed in interaction with one another.

Economic Structure

Before understanding the ethos of democracy, it is imperative to understand the economic context of the panchayat. The panchayat constitutes of mainly four villages. Each village is dominated by different caste group people; the economic structure of all four villages is different. Therefore, any interaction in terms of politics suggests an interaction in terms of inter-village, inter-caste and inter-economic sphere.

Village Suvansipur

The economy of the village is based mainly on agriculture. Therefore, there exist different categories of people associated with different processes of agricultural production. These categories include owner of the land, tenants and labourers. These together complete the economic structure of the village. The economic structure of the village Suvansipur is not autonomous in nature. The village is related to the external economy. What is produced in the village is not all consumed there. The process of agricultural production is dependent on relationship beyond the boundaries of the village. In other words, one can say that the village is not self-sufficient.

The organisation of agriculture is such that most of the villagers are dependent upon one another for their livelihood. Since the village mainly consists of *Yadavas* therefore any understanding of the process of socio-economic relationship may be understood in terms of class division only.

There are certain stages in the agriculture cycle at which there is a heavy demand for labour. The demand of the extra labour force is basically met by the landless labourers of other castes of the panchayat, namely, the *Jatavs, Nats* and *Pasis*. The peppermint crop is grown just between two major seasons of wheat and paddy. Preparation for the paddy crop begins nearly two months before they sow the peppermint crop. The peppermint crop not only gives them good economic returns, it also demands extra labour and investment. But it makes the land fertile for the next paddy crop.

The production process is socially organised as it involves relations between different categories of individuals. The basic division within the class structure is between owners and non-owners of the means of production, i.e., ownership and non-ownership of the land. Before understanding the class structure of the village one thing which is important to highlight is that the village is mono-caste village as the hamlets associated with this village inhabited by different caste groups is given the status of a separate village. Since these hamlets are away from the main village, they do not affect the physical setting of the village.

If the division of the village on the basis of landownership is done, it suggests that all the families do possess some area of land. The small land holder though depends upon others but this dependency is not absolute because all the families in the village have cattle and these cattles not only provide them with milk and ghee, they provide them with some cash after selling the milk to the milkmen (*dudhiya*). The ownership of land is vested in people with same social background (in terms of caste) and different economic background. Therefore in terms of caste they create a homogenous community but in terms of economy or class they create a heterogeneous community. The distinction can be made on the basis of two categories: landowners and tenants with small landholdings.

The majority of people are engaged in agricultural work. Majority works on their own land but some others besides working on their own land prefer to work on the lands of others as tenants. This constitutes the basis of economic and social ties between the different classes of people in the village. The landholder and tenants do not constitute a separate category concretely as the tenants also possess some small landholdings with them.

The classes that one perceives in this village are not separated into watertight compartments. Some individuals belong to one or more of them.

Village Rajapur

This is the only village of the panchayat which is inhabited by the people of different caste group. Therefore the economy and the interaction of social and political forces have different connotation and meaning.

The village is inhabited by *Pasis, Yadavas, Muria* (vegetable producer), and *Thakurs* but there is no brahmin caste group. The land basically belongs to *Yadavas* and *Thakurs*. The other caste group possesses small landholding or no land, that is they are landless workers. The *Yadavas* hold the maximum landholdings. The economy of this village is also based mainly upon agriculture. In this village there exist different categories of people associated with different occupations. These categories in this village are different than those existing in the village Suvansipur. The categories include owners of the land, tenants, labourers, landless labourers and some shopkeepers. These together constitute the economic structure of the village. The village consists of many castes therefore the process of socio-economic relations may be understood in terms of class as well as caste division.

The important point to be noted here is that the higher the caste of an individual, the higher is the class ranking. The *Yadavas* and *Thakurs* are the higher caste group, they possess maximum land holdings and therefore they constitute the higher class group of the village.

The crops as usual are paddy and wheat with peppermint as the supporting crop. The village supplies workforce to other villages. In contrast to Suvansipur, the cattle economy is normally absent. Only few families practice and depend upon cattle economy. The landholding with the people is also very small and that is why it is not sustainable. The majority of the people are engaged in agricultural work. Therefore, the ownership of land is an important factor for the determination of the class.

Most of them work as a labourer at the brick-kilns. They get a handsome amount there in comparison to those working on the farmlands. In the agricultural cycle when there is a heavy demand of labour the demand is actually met by *Nat, Pasi* and the *Chamar* landless labourers.

Village Puhuppur

This is the village inhabited mainly by *Nat* people. Basically, *Nats* are the nomadic tribe. During 1960s they came to this village. The local zamindar has given nearly 200 bighas of land to them. As a result of this, a large number of *Nat* people inhabited this village.

The village has three *Thakur* families and four *Yadav* families, others are *Nat* families. The *Yadavas* and *Thakurs* possess the maximum land holdings. *Nats* have very small landholdings and majority of *Nat* families do not possess the land.

The traditional occupation of the *Nats* is 'beggary', and they still profess this occupation. Most of them work as landless labourer. They also engage themselves in the cattle caring for others, for which they are paid. The consumption pattern of *Nat* is very lavish. They drink liquor in the evening from whatever they have earned during the day. In a truly democratic sense, males as well as females enjoy the drink.

The pattern of interaction in terms of socio-economic framework shows that they work on the lands of *Yadavas* and *Thakurs*. The basic division within the class structure is no doubt between owners and non-owners of the means of production. But, in terms of interaction, the majority population group of *Nat* is considered to be outsider to the major cultural system of the village. Therefore, in terms of the economic interaction, the *Nats* work for the upper caste group and depend upon them. This dependency as a small landholder or no landholder of the *Nats* upon upper caste or class is not absolute because, they have the option of beggary as well as they are the major suppliers of the workforce to the kilns and other small industries.

Village Shivrajpur

This village is a collection of four hamlets. Earlier, this village was the part of village Suvansipur. This village has also got the status of Ambedkar village during the regime of Mayawati government. But this status provided all the facilities to the village Suvansipur and these four hamlets were neglected. After the separation from the village Suvansipur the condition of these four hamlets is not very good. Only one hamlet is properly connected to the main road by *kharanja*, while the other three have *kaccha* approach road.

The *Jatavs* are the dominant population group in this village. They are basically small landholders while majority of them are landless labourer. They work on the lands of the upper caste for their livelihood. They also supply a major workforce to the agriculture during the peak season. Cattle economy is nearly absent.

Table 17.1

Primary Occupation in the Four Villages (Number of Households)

Category	*Suvansipur*	*Puhuppur*	*Rajapur*	*Shivrajpur*
Agricultural	40	48	32	30
Service	01	—	01	—
Shop/Seller	02	04	03	02
Labour	03	47	06	23
Any other	—	05	—	—

Table 17.2

Beneficiary of Indira Awas Yojana

Village	*SC*	*General*	*Total*
Suvansipur	0	3	3
Shivrajpur	24	5	29
Rajapur	0	0	0
Puhuppur	58	14	72
Total	82	22	104

The economic system of the above four villages suggests that agriculture plays a very dominant role in the process of production. Though other activities and occupations are important, they mainly depend upon agriculture, which does not provide a kind of economic independence to them. The overall scenario with respect to economy suggests a poor status (Table 17.1). The beneficiaries of Indira Awas Yojana are drawn in majority from SC category in two villages which clarifies that the SC community is receiving this benefit but at the same time in other villages there is not a single beneficiary from the SC category (Table 17.2).

The organisation of production is based upon relationship between different classes (the pattern shows that high caste group exhibits the characteristics of high class group). These classes are created by the ownership and non-ownership of land. Though the class relationship that emerged as a result of land relationship is important but it is not absolute. Because a major section gets its livelihood from other allied activities significantly as working in kiln and other small industries.

Role of Women

The links between gender subordination and property need to be sought in not only the distribution of property between households but also in its distribution between men and women and in not only who owns the property but also who controls it. Gender equality in legal rights to own property does not guarantee gender equality in actual ownership, nor does ownership guarantee control. The distinction between law and practice and between ownership and control are especially critical in the context of gender, for most South Asian women there are significant barriers to realising their legal claims in landed property, as well as to exercising control over any land they do get (Agarwal, 1994).

In most societies today it is men who largely control wealth generating property. Even property that is under state, community, or clan ownership remains effectively under the managerial control of selected men through their dominance in both traditional and modern institutions. Men as a gender, exercise dominance over the instruments through which their existing advantages of property ownership and control get perpetuated much as the institutions that enact and implement laws.

Case 1

Rama Devi aged about 36 years works on the peppermint plant. She was the only female member working over there. On my question of what share are you going to get? She replied that everything belongs to her, as it is a family affair. The fact was that she was only working; others were sitting around the plant chatting and enjoying the whole process.

The main constituent of the economic organisation is agriculture. The participation of women in the agricultural activities is very important. Though in the traditional set up the ownership of the land is confined to the men, the women irrespective of this fact participate and contribute to the economy of the village.

Out of the four villages, only village Rajapur and Puhuppur have *Thakur* caste group. In the traditional caste hierarchy other than *Brahmin*, *Thakur* and *Vaishya* are at the top. The womenfolk of these caste groups do not participate in the outside chores. But, the womenfolk of the other caste groups participate not only in the household chores but also outside the household. The population of the four villages may be divided into *Nats*, *Yadavas*, *Pasis*, *Jatavs* and *Thakurs*. Of these caste groups, only *Thakurs* restrict the women from working. The womenfolk of the *Nat* community are basically involved in agricultural as well as non-agricultural activities, within the confinement of household as well as outside. Not only this, they sometimes involve themselves in the begging activities as they are outside the caste hierarchy of the Hindu system. Therefore there are no restrictions on them regarding status degradation.

The womenfolk of the *Pasi*, *Jatav* and *Yadava* caste groups are participating in the activities of the agriculture. They work outside the confinement of the household. Though in some *Yadava* families there is restriction but in other caste groups there is no restriction on the participation and activities related to the productive processes, i.e., agriculture and allied activities.

Case 2

Woman pradhan Amarkali's step son Prakash (originally he is the nephew of the pradhan), during the election campaign promised a widow of *Chamar* caste that her name shall be included in the list of beneficiaries of the Indira Awas Yojana. But for that she has to vote in favour of the pradhan. He made such type of promises to many individuals during the whole election campaign.

Women provide the major workforce to the agriculture and other allied activities outside the household. They are overburdened with work as they have to manage the affairs of the household as well as work outside. This provides them with little time to think of the other activities. Not only this, their share in the income coming from the agriculture activities is controlled by their male counterparts.

Daniel Thorner (1992) emphasises that the primary aim of all the classes in the agrarian structure is not to increase their income by adopting more efficient methods, but to experience in higher level of social prestige by abstaining from physical labour as much as possible. They prefer not to think in terms of undertaking the degrading fieldwork themselves. In order to increase their social prestige, the first to abstain from the fieldwork is the womenfolk of a particular caste group. It is in fact the will of their male counterparts to withdraw women from work to increase their social prestige. This is clearly visible in terms of certain *Yadava* caste group women in the village.

Socio-cultural Structure

The division of panchayat may be done with reference to different caste groups dominating different villages. In village society, caste division plays a role both in actual social interaction and also in ideal scheme of values. Members of different castes are expected to behave differently. These differences are sanctioned by Hindu religion. The present village panchayat shows a very different kind of religious model with one of the social group – *Nat* community. The *Nats* are neither Hindus nor Muslims. They follow the cultural values of both Hindus and Muslims.

If one goes by the population of a particular caste, it suggests that village Puhuppur is dominated by *Nats*, village Suvansipur by *Yadavas*, Rajapur by *Pasis* and Shivrajpur by *Jatavs*. This domination in terms of population is not absolute in the sense that other caste groups are also present in these villages but their number is less in comparison to the dominant caste group.

It is important to point out here that the different caste groups live in different parts and in chunks, but they never consider themselves as separate identities. But as far as *Nat* community is concerned, they are isolated from the mainstream culture and are considered as a separate identity. The whole of the panchayat may be categorised on the basis of caste division into three strata. First, *Yadavas*, second *Nats* and third one constitutes of *Jatavs* and *Pasis*. These three groups form the different strata. They occupy different positions in the economic, political and ritual system. The *Nats* though have adopted many elements of the main culture are still considered to be outsiders.

In order to initiate a cultural interaction, the *Nats* had two groups at their disposal, one Muslim group and the other Hindu group. The *Nats* were willing to interact with these new groups and in the whole process they were ambivalent about whom to imitate. This situation of ambivalence created a crisis in the cultural system of *Nat*. This crisis is just a crisis of cultural dilemma a mix of the question acceptance by the other group. The attitude and reaction of the other group towards *Nats* was of awe and distance. They consider *Nat* community an adivasi community possessing a very strange culture that is entirely different from their own. The claimants of land increased due to fragmentation. The land unit that any household possessed thus was not sustainable for agriculture as they could not use any technology to produce any cash crop. Due to this they also adopted cattle caring for others.

Case 3

Urmila, wife of Ayodhya aged about 35 years, of *Pasi* caste told me that *Nats* are adivasi. They can eat everything including non-vegetarian. She said that they do not follow any ritual but on each and every occasion they drink. She said that they seem to be an altogether different cultural group. As the *Nats* were always ready to accept the cultural items from these two groups, they accepted the cultural traits from these groups. They chose the name from the Muslim as well as from Hindu cultural system. They adopted both the Muslim and Hindu customs in their marriage ceremonies. Not only this, they tried to maintain their own culture while adopting the cultural traits of other groups.

Case 4

Madan Lal, a candidate from *Nat* community, was a contestant for the post of pradhan. When I interacted with him he told me that his name is Majan. Though his name is Madan Lal in the voter list and other documents but his friends and relatives call him by the name of Majan. Madan Lal is a Hindu name while Majan is a Muslim name. When I enquired about this, he told me that they are not the original inhabitants of this place. They started a settled life in early 1960s. In this process, they came in contact with both Hindus as well as Muslims. As a result of which, they adopted and assimilated the cultural traits of both the communities.

Nats are economically not well-off and they spend their major resources on eating and mainly drinking. Each and every member of the community, except children is habitant of drinking in routine life. The whole process of a nomadic tribe becoming settled, capturing seat of power, loosing that power and once again resorting to begging, completes a circle.

The traditional caste hierarchy does not conform to the politico-economic relations. The *Nats* who have no place in the social structure attained formal political power. The other caste groups do create a stratification system, but the system is imperfect in the sense that the hierarchy does not conform to the traditional structure. The *Thakurs* though enjoy a higher status in comparison to *Yadavas* and other caste groups of the panchayat but due to socio-economic and population size the *Yadavas* act as a dominant group. Not only this, the *Nats* who remained in power for nearly a decade, do take dictates from the *Yadavas* instead of *Thakurs*. So in the local hierarchy the *Yadavas* dominate. The *Chamars* and the *Pasis* are at the bottom of the caste hierarchy and are not in a position to influence the socio-cultural and political configuration. Though a *Pasi* is the pradhan of the panchayat, the whole process of political assertion is manipulated by the *yadava* caste group. The present study conforms to the concept of dominant caste given by Srinivas (1995).

Political Structure and Distribution of Power

The objective of this part is to arrive at an understanding of the manner in which power is distributed in the village and the role of the women in the power sharing process. The political processes have been examined in relation to the panchayats, local elites and the emergence of new women group owing to reservation policy.

The manner in which power is distributed leads to a division of village community into different categories. One category consists of those who have power and another of those who are deprived of their rights. There is a third category which formally has power due to reservation but due to socio-cultural and economic circumstances cannot assert that power, this includes womenfolk in the village. The groups derive their power from different sources. For example one group derives its power from the ownership and control of the land and other group derives that power from the support of the numerical strength of their caste group members.

The power blocs are dependent upon number of factors. Caste, class and gender play an important role. A leader can command power even though his caste and class position is low. The population sise and the reservation to women in panchayat act as an important factor for the dynamic role of women in power structure of the panchayat.

Earlier, the panchayat was composed of individuals enjoying varying degrees of power and influence. But now due to reservation, the schedule caste and particularly women, who were always confined to household chores, now take part in the affairs of the village. The entire panchayat is subdivided into different wards and election to the panchayat is on the basis of wards. Therefore each and every segment gets some representation. Due to reservation, the disadvantaged section, particularly schedule castes and women also get representation. The present panchayat though lost the status of 'panchayat headed by a woman, still consists of nine female members out of eleven members excluding pradhan. Out of the eleven members each and every caste group is represented except *Thakur* caste group' (post-election 2005 scenario).

The panchayat pradhan enjoys power in the village. The power is conferred to him by his official position. A distinction can be made between power and authority. Authority is power which is legitimised; it operates within an institutional framework. The pradhan has a certain measure of authority. He can impose his will even despite resistance from others.

Case 5

Jagdish, age about 60 years, *Nau* (barber) by traditional caste system, inhabitant of village Puhuppur had a shop on the panchayat land. Earlier he had worked with a business caste *Rastogi* (worked as an agent to extract money from those who borrow money from moneylender). He said that earlier pradhan had no problem over the location of his shop. But the present pradhan has given him a notice and he has to shift his shop. The interesting fact is that Jagdish belongs to the same village as the present pradhan. This suggests how arbitrarily a pradhan can assert his power. According to Jagdish, the previous pradhan was nice to them as she never confronted with them.

Case 6

Rajaram, aged 32, *Jatav* by caste is inhabitant of village Shivrajpur. He is not the original inhabitant of the panchayat but is residing in this place with his maternal grandparent. The panchayat earlier allotted some land to his family. But, after the death of his grandparents, the present pradhan has given him a notice to vacate the land. He said that some land belongs to him but has no documentary proof. He told that there is great problem of drinking water but there are no hand pumps for us, whereas the *Yadavas* who are affluent have the governmental hand pumps in their vicinity. When I pointed out that it is they who were responsible for the defeat of the female pradhan, he regretted his decision and said the earlier one was good as she and her family never interfered in their affairs.

Case 7

Urmila, aged about 52 years inhabitant of village Suvansipur talked about the affairs of the village. According to her the earlier pradhan was the puppet in the hands of affluent *Yadavas*. The female pradhan and her family used to respect only a particular group of *Yadava* family. The present pradhan is doing good work. He initiated the construction of road (kharanja) and drainage system. It was the partiality done by earlier pradhan in favour of chosen *Yadavas*, which led her to loose her seat.

The above case studies reveal that the lower caste group for example *Chamar* and *Nau* (barber), etc., opposed female pradhan in the election in order to have a change. There was no apparent reason for them to oppose and oust the female *Nat* pradhan. The situation with reference to the *Yadavas* is different in the sense that *Yadavas* as such do not constitute a single category. There is a clear cut division in the *Yadavas* and the caste group is clearly stratified in terms of the resources. The *Nats* are supported by the upper class *Yadavas* who are numerically less in comparison to lower and average class *Yadavas* who opposed female *Nat* candidate in the election.

The meetings of the panchayat are held in accordance with procedure. Meetings of the panchayat are often postponed and sometimes meetings are held without all the members being notified in advance. Not only this, the decisions are taken by pradhan in advance and it is only the formality for the members to sign the papers.

The very concept of panchayat, which suggests that 'panch parmeshwar' (god speaking through five) decision was respected by the people. There was consensus and respect among the people towards this panchayat. But in the present panchayat the structural conditions for this consensus do not exist. The panchayat is representing the interests of a particular community. There is a sharp division between different caste and class group. These differences lead to opposition which could not be resolved by harmonious adjustment. The panchayat is characterised by unequal participation and domination of different groups. Though there is representation in the panchayat from all the sections but they are not treated equally. During the female pradhan regime, the *Nat* caste got the privilege and the upper class *Yadavas* were the decision-makers. But now it is *Pasi* caste group which enjoys the privileged.

Though the *Thakur* caste group is at the top of the traditional caste hierarchy but in the present power structure due to the policy of the government and the changes in the demographic structure of the village, they are marginalised in the power dynamics. Till 1960, they were in power in the village political structure. The supremacy of *Thakurs* was challenged by a common *Yadava* man. The story told by Shyam Lal of village Suvansipur is as follows: 'Fatte, a poor *Yadav* challenged the supremacy of the zamindars by fighting panchayat election against them. He won the election. The zamindars filed a petition against the election result. Fatte was illiterate and therefore was unaware of the result. The Hakim at the tehsil told him that he won the election and the petition of the zamindar was rejected'.

After this incidence the *Yadavas* remained in power for a long time except for sometime period when *Thakurs* gained power during early 1980s for a small time period. After this once again *Yadavas* captured power at the panchayat. The reservation in panchayat for the 'schedule caste woman' category brought *Nat* caste group in the power dynamics of the panchayat. They dominated the panchayat for 10 years and lost their supremacy in the election of 2005 when seat was reserved only for 'scheduled caste' category. In the elections of 2005 only Amarkali, fought as a woman candidate, others were male candidates. The seat of power was captured by Ayodhya Prashad from *Pasi* caste group of village Rajapur.

This power shifting suggests the circulation of power with respect to the village. The seat of power circulated from Puhuppur to Suvansipur to Rajapur. This circulation of power may also be viewed with respect to caste. The seat of power was first captured by *Thakurs* then it went to *Yadava*, *Nat* and *Pasi* caste group respectively. The whole process of circulation included all the major villages and caste groups except village Shivrajpur and the caste group *Chamar*. One important aspect of the whole power distribution suggests one more important variable in the whole process. This is the rise of a woman to the formal seat of power in the panchayat. This rise and assertion of the woman is not the result of any movement neither it was the efforts of the women. It was in fact imposed upon them. But their experiences in the panchayat for a long period of time boosted their confidence and they fought for the election when the seat was de-reserved from 'scheduled caste woman' category to 'scheduled caste' category.

The *Thakur* caste group, deprived of their superior position, was unprepared to participate in the governance of the village under the new reservation policy. They were first challenged by *Yadavas* and then new reservation policy made them to stand at the margin. The idea of sitting in a panchayat where their voice may be weaker than that of others did not appeal strongly to them. They tried to remain aloof from the affairs of the panchayat. Economically and demographically (population size being very small), they were not in a position to even influence the dynamics of power structure. This dynamics is very well managed by *Yadava* caste group, who due to their population size and economic power, do have considerable influence upon the power dynamics of the village panchayat.

Case 8

Bachan Yadav, aged about 55 years, is a school master in the nearby primary school. He is economically very strong due to his landholdings and the resulting income. His son owns the public distribution shop (Kotedar). He said that during land consolidation (chakbandi) campaign the *Nat* pradhan worked arbitrarily and due to this the configuration of land went against the villagers. He said that *Nats* are illiterate and they do not possess much land so it did not affect them. He said that in every affair they took my opinion but in this they worked according to their own will. Therefore, we (*Yadava*) decided to favour another candidate for the post of pradhan in the election of 2005. He said Ayodhya Prasad, a *Pasi* candidate and above all, his student, was supported by them, and he won. He said that Ayodhya is literate man and he will work better than the *Nats*.

Therefore the *Yadava* leader is dictating the terms as to who the pradhan of the panchayat would be. The *Yadavas* earlier supported *Nats* in order to avoid the power assertion by others, particularly by *Chamars* and *Pasi*. Now they are supporting a *Pasi* candidate in order to provide a lesson to the *Nats*. *Yadavas* are acting as the dominant caste group of the panchayat.

But this dominant caste group is not at all absolute and consolidated. The *Yadavas* are divided into mainly three categories. First category consists of those families which possess land, are economically well off in terms of cattle, etc., and earlier enjoyed the seat of power. Second category consists of those families who have average landholdings and create for themselves self-sustaining life chances with some surplus through their hard work although they never enjoyed the power. Third are those families which possess a marginal landholding, may or may not have cattle and they manage their life with these meagre resources.

Nats are the favourite of all the categories for *Yadavas*, who had enjoyed power earlier and by supporting *Nats*, tried to maintain their influence. This patronage given to the *Nats* by this *Yadava* group led to certain benefits to this group. Due to this other *Yadava* group felt deprived. Therefore, in this election they (second and third category *Yadava*) showed their voting power and ousted the *Nat* woman from the seat of power by electing a man from *Pasi* caste group.

The influence of *Yadavas* in the local political structure is evident from the fact that a *Yadava* candidate is continuously winning the seat of member of Block Development Council (BDC). The constituency for the post of BDC is wider than the village panchayat, therefore other villages are also included in it. In order to ensure that the panchayat retain its representation, the *Yadava* candidate was supported by the panchayat unanimously and consequently he won. There was no challenge from the panchayat. This is suggestive of the fact that the dynamics of power structure is governed by the *Yadavas* and they are instrumental in bringing about any change in the local political structure.

Conclusion

The *Nats* are unable to participate fully in the affairs of the panchayat. The reason is mainly attributed to the fact that their social, economic and ritual position is low. They are excluded from the mainstream socio-cultural life of the village. Though the seat of power remained with them for nearly more than a decade, still they are taking dictates from the *Yadavas*, who are major dominant caste of the panchayat. *Thakurs*, due to low population size and economic factors, try to avoid the activities of the panchayat.

The main reason behind the passive status of the *Nats* in the affairs of the panchayat is their weak economic position. They are dependent upon other landowners particularly *Yadavas* for their source of livelihood. Though this reason is not absolute because they follow their traditional profession of begging, but still this can be one of the major factors hindering their participation.

The *Nats* have taken their social, economic and political inferiority for granted. This applies only to *Nats* but other caste groups of *Jatavs* and *Pasi* also feel such type of inferiority. This kind of inferiority has been conditioned from generation to generation.

But, now due to change that is brought about by the reservation in the panchayat, a different type of interaction pattern has emerged. Earlier the lower caste groups *Jatav, Nat* and *Pasi* felt embarrassed in discussing social and political matters on equal terms but now this situation no more exists. The lower caste groups now share and bargain the socio-political and economic spheres with upper castes.

The pradhan and other prominent opponents appear to form the centre of a lose clique of close friends and supporters who backed them in village conflicts. These supporters are not incorporated as formal parties in village politics. They are drawn mainly from the residential area where the leader himself lives. Frequently they appear to be linked through kinship ties with the leader.

The womenfolk do not form any faction or interest group. They are following the footsteps of their male counterparts. Though a woman remained in power for a long period of time, and during the election campaign the women participated enthusiastically but their group formation in terms of any common interest could not come to the surface.

The reason which is more suggestive is that *Nat* leader who remained in power for such a long period of time was considered to be an outsider with reference to the mainstream socio-cultural system. Therefore, any unity in terms of the interest of women could not get any recognition. There was no frequent interaction as the *Nat* considered to be ritually low and outside the socio-cultural system of the mainstream. Therefore the women could not be mobilised in the particular sense of group formation and participation.

Political change, social mobility and economic advancement lead to the creation of not only new relations but also of new values, new attitudes and new aspirations. This process of political mobilisation provides scope to the individual to enter new networks of interpersonal relations in which village, caste and other traditional bonds though are decisive but not absolute. With the system of reservation the disadvantaged section particularly women are coming to the forefront.

The class positions have acquired a relative autonomy but still they are not free from the caste position. The political and legislative changes, the numerical strength and rise of women as a category for political competition led to the loosening of caste but this is not absolute as all the variables have to interplay within the premises of caste.

In order to produce some natural mobilisation and change the artificial and superficial effort of only providing reservation will not work, the economic rights of these women representatives must be ensured. Women need a more favourable background to attain the same power positions men do (Vionello, 2004). Thus, in order to bring sustainability to the process of participation and empowerment, the women must get some privileges.

References

Agarwal, Bina (1994). *A Field of One's Own (Gender and land rights in south Asia)*, Cambridge University Press.

Srinivas, M.N. (1995). *Social Change in Modern India*, New Delhi: Orient Longman.

Thorner, Daniel in Dipankar Gupta (eds) (1992). *Social Stratification*, New Delhi: Oxford University Press.

Vionello, Mino (2004). 'Gender difference in access to and exercise of power', *Current Sociology*, Vol. 52, 3 May.

Part V

Efforts for Livelihood, Social Security and their Future Needs

18

Creating New Options for the Poor

A Case Study of Gujarat

JHARNA PATHAK

Agriculture is one of the most promising instruments for reducing poverty and securing local livelihoods. One of the critical conditions required for agricultural sector is to ensure that good governance structures and related policies are in place at all levels. Weak governance in agriculture led to major problems during the 1980s and 1990s when strong state interventions were undermined by structural adjustment programmes, emphasising the role of markets. Policy biases, underinvestment, mis-investment and lack of capacities underpin weak governance in agriculture. In spite of the recommendations of the World Development Report (1982) for improving governance[1] in order to improve agriculture, very little has been achieved in that regard to date. To address these issues, Tribal Development Department (TDD) has initiated the programme of involving private hybrid seed manufacturers, non-governmental organisations (NGOs) and public sector in diffusing hybrid maize seed in tribal belts of Gujarat along with other inputs and agricultural extension services. This paper focuses on the roles of the public sector, private sector and civil society in diffusing technology among farmers.

Recent Changes in Maize Crop in Gujarat

Gujarat is one of the five major maize growing states of our country. It is mainly grown by tribal farmers of Panchmahals, Dahod, Vadodara, Sabarkantha, Banaskantha districts of Gujarat. Maize is not only a staple food for tribals of North Gujarat, but also a major source of income and employment for rural households. Therefore, the development of maize sector was always a priority for the government and so it tries to improve productivity of the crop, thereby increasing the income earned from cultivation.

Since the initiation of the Green Revolution in the mid-1960s, Gujarat has done remarkably well in meeting the food needs of the growing population. From 1987–88 to 2005–06, Compound Growth Rate (CGR) of area under hybrid maize crop was higher (1.04) than that of total area under the maize crop (Table 18.1). In 2005, area under hybrid maize was nearly 70 per cent of the total area cultivated under maize crop. This has shown an increase over a period of 17 years. Table 18.1 shows that yield of maize has increased from 330 kg/ha in 1987–88 to 1581 kg per hectare in 2005, (at CGR of 1.03%). Increase in yield was a result of gradual replacement of traditional varieties by modern varieties (Hybrid). Two types of maize cultivation could roughly be distinguished: firstly, the commercial, high input production maize grains and the small-scale, semi-subsistence production exemplified by most of the maize producers in tribal belts of Gujarat. Though birth of the Green Revolution can be traced to hybrid maize,[2] many important maize producing areas of the state like Panchmahal and Dahod have remained largely untouched by these new technologies (Table 18.2).

For the whole of Gujarat, the percentage change in area where maize was grown in the year 2005 was nearly 10 per cent of that in the year 1995. During these years, Panchmahal showed a decline of 36 per cent in the area under Maize crop. However, production of maize crop in Gujarat during these years has increased by 69 per cent while yield has increased by 54 per cent. In Panchmahal, production increased to 76 per cent while yield declined to nearly 37 per cent. Year-wise analysis shows that the percentage change in growth rate of area under maize in Gujarat increased in the year 2001. Later, it declined (Table 18.2). Compound growth rate of area, yield and production under Maize crop in Gujarat shows very little variation. In central and northern regions of Gujarat where there is an increased diffusion of Maize seeds, there has not been a perceptible change in area, production and productivity over the years. From Table 18.3, it was clear that net irrigated area in both Dahod and Panchmahal was declining over the years. This might be one of the reasons that constrained the area under maize[3] cultivation in Panchmahal districts. The yield growth however has remained moderate in the rain-fed systems and diffusion of technology of improved seed variety has not taken place in tribal districts of Gujarat. Farmers still use traditional low-yielding varieties in a large proportion of area and use fertilisers in sub-optimal amounts when they adopt modern varieties due to the uncertainty of returns from investments and the limited capacity of risk taking at the subsistent level (Seigler and Puckridge, 1995).

Table 18.1

Area and Average Yield per Hectare of High Yielding Varieties of Crops

Year	Area under Maize ('00 hectares)		Percentage of Hybrid to total	Percentage of Maize			% of Cereals to total food crops	Yield (kg/ha.)
	Total	HYV		To total cropped area	To total cereals	To total food crops		
1987–88	3420	1223	35.76	—	—	—	—	330
1988–89	3550	1574	44.33	—	—	—	—	1363
1989–90	3563	1550	43.50	—	—	—	—	1536
1990–91	3662	2103	57.42	3.6	9.9	7.2	72.6	1406
1991–92	3834	2150	56.08	3.6	10.3	7.4	72.5	1199
1992–93	3829	2300	60.07	3.5	9.7	7.0	71.7	1537
1993–94	3883	2350	60.52	3.6	10.4	7.5	71.6	1077
1994–95	3960	2360	59.60	3.5	10.1	7.2	71.4	889
1995–96	4154	2000	48.15	3.8	11.4	8.0	70.3	1030
1996–97	4185	2108	50.37	3.8	11.5	8.0	69.8	1591
1997–98	4308	2300	53.39	4.0	12.5	8.8	71.0	1660
1998–99	4424	2865	64.76	4.0	12.8	8.7	67.9	1695
1999–2000	**4456**	**2770**	**70.84**	**4.0**	**13.9**	**9.4**	**67.6**	**1317**
2000–01	4620	2470	53.46	4.4	15.4	10.4	67.6	800
2001–02	4904	2818	57.46	4.5	15.2	10.2	67.2	1969
2002–03	4645	3086	66.44	5.0	16.8	11.3	67.5	1706
2003–04	4845	2666	55.03	4.4	15.0	9.8	65.7	1717
2004–05*	4595	2980	64.85	—	—	—	—	898
2005–06*	4600	3230	70.22	—	—	—	—	1581
Mean	4181	2363	—	—	—	—	—	1332
Standard deviation	464	542	—	—	—	—	—	408
Variance	215593	293556	—	—	—	—	—	166564
Minimum	3420	1223	—	—	—	—	—	330
Maximum	4904	3230	—	—	—	—	—	1969
Compound growth rate	1.02	1.04	—	—	—	—	—	1.03

* Figures are based on final forecast report.

Source: Directorate of Agriculture, Gujarat State, Gandhinagar.

Table 18.2

Percentage Change in Area, Production and Yield and Compound Growth Rate of Area, Production and Yield of Maize (Kharif) in Gujarat (Year 1995–96 to 2005–06)

Districts	*Dahod*	*Panchmahal*	*Gujarat*	*Dahod*	*Panchmahal*	*Gujarat*	*Dahod*	*Panchmahal*	*Gujarat*
	Area			*Production*			*Yield*		
1995–96	—	—	—	—	—	—	—	—	—
1996–97	—	53.5	0.7	—	55.5	55.7	—	4.1	54.5
1997–98	—	11.3	2.9	—	6.9	7.4	—	–6.5	4.3
1998–99	—	–2.2	–5.2	—	4.5	–2.7	—	5.0	2.7
1999–2000	—	–39.8	–4.2	—	35.2	–27.6	—	–47.5	–24.4
2000–01	—	0.3	–2.1	—	–49.4	–42.8	—	–49.6	-41.5
2001–02	—	10.9	15.8	—	267.1	206.6	—	231.4	164.6
2002–03	—	7.3	4.7	—	11.1	–10.4	—	3.6	–14.5
2003–04	—	–51.4	4.3	—	–66.0	5.0	–65.0	–30.0	0.6
2004–05	0.2	7.8	–5.2	–64.9	–46.5	–50.4	124.8	–50.4	–47.7
2005–06	–12.3	2.1	–0.6	97.3	99.7	75.1	–100.0	95.8	76.1
1995–05	**–12.0**	**–35.9**	**10.0**	**–30.6**	**76.3**	**68.9**	**–21.2**	**–36.8**	**53.5**
Yearly growth rate	–4.0	–3.3	0.9	–10.2	6.9	6.3	–7.1	–3.3	4.9
Compound growth rate	0.938**	0.913***	1.02***	0.833	1.03***	1.02***	0.888	0.936***	1.000***

Source: Directorate of Agriculture, Gujarat State, Gandhinagar.

Table 18.3

Growth Rates of Net Area Irrigated in Tribal Districts of Gujarat between the Years 1990–91 to 2003–04

Districts	*Intercept*	*Slope (b)*
Panchmahal	3843.74***	(–) 0.72*
Dahod	4215.16***	(–) 0.56
Southern region*	1986.58***	5.51**
Central Region**	1994.71***	2.63
Northern region***	2014.91***	0.01
Total Tribal districts****	**1980.20*****	**5.90****
All Gujarat	**1959.93*****	**1.28*****

Source: Computed from data collected from Directorate of Agriculture, Gujarat State, Gandhinagar.

The success of high-yielding varieties in the rainfed systems will depend on the investment in research on improved seed technology in public and private sectors and also on how the government addresses issues of diffusing these technologies among poor farmers. There was also the issue of the social acceptability of hybrid seed. So, it might take a long time before improved technologies reach farmers and make a substantial contribution towards increase in maize production. This calls for the importance of providing extension services to these farmers. However, extension services is a public good with high externalities and thus, complete privatisation is neither desirable nor feasible.

With an aim to doubling the income of tribal farmers of Dahod and Panchmahal districts of Gujarat state within five years, an initiative in public-private partnership was undertaken under a project named Sunshine. The goal was to provide modern farm inputs like hybrid seeds, fertilisers and extension services to farmers with a belief that it would result in an increased agricultural productivity. Public subsidisation of extension to small farmers was justified on two counts. First, small farmers were unaware of the benefits of improved technologies and second small subsistence farmers derived considerable non-monetary benefits (including better nutrition and health) from adopting hybrid seeds.

During this intervention, steps to develop infrastructure for facilitating linkages of inputs and outputs were considered. Monsanto India Limited (MIL), subsidiary of the parent company named Monsanto, which is the leading global provider of technology based solutions and agriculture products that improves farm productivity, was invited to play a key role in the project along with NGOs and the government. In the year 2007, TDD reviewed the pilot study on the performance of MIL in the project named Project Rainbow. Under this project, Dekalb corn seeds were given as free samples to farmers in 13 taluka covering 300 villages. Through this project, a safety net was created for the poorest and vulnerable households in the form of providing free inputs to farmers. Observations from this intervention led to the need for (i) initial investment support for seeds and fertilisers, (ii) education on the right cultivation practices, and (iii) marketing linkages form a critical input for the sustainability of the intervention. The generation of economic surplus for farmers and the commercial viability of the procurement of the grain purchasers were both critical elements. Therefore, high density was more important than the spread. These observations of the project encouraged the government to widen the scope of the work. They extended their partnership with MIL and provided hybrid maize seed and other inputs to nearly 27,290 farmer beneficiaries from two districts namely Dahod and Panchmahal. To meet these objectives, TDD of Gujarat acquired 612 million tonnes of corn seed from MIL, 12,000 million tonnes of fertiliser from Gujarat State Fertiliser Corporation (GSFC), 720 corn shelters with the aim of providing one to each village.

There is no empirical evidence from farm-level experiences of impact of hybrid maize in these areas. To address this issue, Gujarat Institute of Development Research (GIDR) initiated a study in the year 2008 to evaluate experiences of farmers regarding the adoption of hybrid maize varieties. The overall goal of this study was to understand the method adopted by the government to diffuse hybrid maize growing technology among poor farmers of Dahod and Panchmahal districts facing a decline in productivity of maize crop and thereby income from cultivation. It also aimed at studying increase in benefits, if any, accruing to farmers growing maize using hybrid seeds in comparison with benefits earned by farmers who grew maize using the conventional seed variety. As this project Sunshine was in the nascent stage, this study attempts to examine the full process of seed distribution by identifying strengths, weaknesses and opportunities for establishing effective seed delivery system with the aim of increasing the productivity of maize crop with dual purpose of food-feed varieties/hybrids, particularly with the rural poor. By analysing this intervention, attempt was made to understand how the private partner should be encouraged to play a leading role in diffusing technology? What were the appropriate roles for the public and private sectors? Can the private sector deliver services more efficiently? What were the implications for this intervention on small-scale farmers?

The remaining part of the paper was organised as follows: The next section outlines the background history of the seed industry and hybrid maize development in India. The paper goes on to describe about the Project Sunshine, which was a step to build public-private partnership in section third. Section fourth gives a detailed investigation of the study area, methods adopted to distribute hybrid seeds in the area, types and quantity of seeds, fertilisers and other inputs distributed, benefits accrued to farmers growing hybrid maize with respect to conventional maize variety, total costs incurred if they grow incurring costs on inputs and so on. Major conclusions and implications for research and policy are presented in section fifth. Here, we discuss ways in which public-private partnership would result in agricultural development of the area is discussed.

Experience of Hybrid Maize Development in India

In the past, though the Indian seed market was one of the largest, it was exclusively supplied by locally produced seeds (seeds retained by farmers of major food crops like wheat, rice, sorghum, millet, corn, and pulses) for many years, and the largest volume of seed trade involved exchange of established self-pollinating varieties. Public sector involvement in the seed industry on a national scale began at the beginning of the 'green revolution' with the establishment of the National Seed Corporation (NSC) in 1963, which was charged with the responsibility of promoting seed industry development from production through processing, storage and marketing, and establishing a system of quality control. It was soon found that the effective deployment of hybrid varieties in India was not possible without a strong commercial seed industry. Consequently, following the easing of government regulations by implementing a new seed policy in 1988, the private sector seed companies started playing a major role in seed development and marketing. The composition of the seed industry, by volume of turnover, had reportedly reached a ratio of 60:40 between the private and public sectors. While some of them (like Cargill) entered through joint venture partnerships with Indian seed companies, some others already had a presence in India through affiliate companies (like Hindustan Lever). They identified potential crops for hybridisation and started research and development activities. Typically, they concentrated on hybrids, mainly corn, cotton, sunflower, vegetables, and flowers (more recently on rice), and they now account for a major share of commercial production of these seeds in India (http://dacnet.nic.in).

A Case of Public-Private Partnership: About Project Sunshine

Seed delivery system in general and hybrid maize seed delivery system in particular were important for agricultural development in rainfed areas of Dahod and Panchmahal districts of Gujarat. Farmers of these areas used to save seeds from own harvest for sowing in subsequent period. Consequently, this leads to lowering crop yield from such seeds. The reasons for slow adoption of hybrid maize seeds were lack of private sector involvement in the seed industry, maize grown under varied agro ecological conditions, farmer's low expectations of gains in yields brought by HYVs, predominance of small farmers in growing maize seeds, higher cost of seed and additional inputs and so on. These constraints were at odds with the goal of bringing useful technology to the poorest (who are least likely to participate in commercial markets).

TDD realised the need for diffusing hybrid maize seeds among tribal farmers with an aim of increasing income of poor tribals. The major dilemma for most governments, however was, who should sit in the driver's seat in the extension system – the public sector, the private for-profit sector, the private non profit sector, or some combination of the three? With the aim of diffusing hybrid maize seed in tribal belts, TDD had signed Memorandum of Understanding (MoU) with MIL under this programme, to provide access to hybrid maize seed named Dekalb Corn to farmers of Dahod and Panchmahal district. Under this public-private partnership programme of diffusion of hybrid technology, the government procured seeds from MIL and fertilisers from the Gujarat State Fertiliser

Corporation (GSFC) and distributed the same to farmers. Dairy Cooperative and NGOs helped department in identifying beneficiaries and distributing agricultural inputs and so on. Inputs distributed under this programme were as follows:

(i) 612 million tonnes of seed acquired from MIL.
(ii) Fertiliser of 12,000 million tonnes acquired from GSFC.
(iii) 720 Corn Shellers were purchased with the aim of providing in these villages (One shelter per village).
(iv) MIL was invited to play a key role in the project along with NGOs and the Government.

Functions and scope of various partners are given below:

Organisations	*Functions*	*Scope*
MIL	Was required to provide seeds, manpower, extend crop-technical support and facilitate linkage for output purchase.	• Will supply the Dekalb corn hybrid seeds through D-SAG at distributor invoice price. • MIL's liability will be limited to providing quality seeds (genetic and physical purity) only. • Provide technical knowledge and managerial staff to work with ground level staff of NGO, Panchmahal Dairy, etc. Provide farmer education on cultivation practices. • MIL will conduct farmer meetings in villages. • On crop management/Agronomy, etc. • On post harvest care, etc. • MIL will coordinate with the output industry and facilitate procurement of output.
NGOs/ Panchmahal Dairy	Were required to recruit supervisors and coordinate with Gram Mitra, MIL and District Administration which would help facilitating in proper implementation of the project. They also distributed seeds to target farmers.	• Identify the villages and form village committees. Provide village wise seed and fertiliser requirement to DSAG. Receive the seeds on behalf DSAG and distribute to the villages. • Provide manpower and work with MIL for farmer support. • Report periodically to district authorities, apex body and TDD.
Gujarat State Fertiliser Corporation (GSFC)	To supply fertiliser at village level.	• Will supply directly to the village committees against the advice of the DSAG.

Cont'd...

...Cont'd

National Agricultural Bank of Rural Development (NABARD)	Will provide insurance coverage.	
Tribal Development Department	Was supposed to supply mechanical shellers in each village. Moreover, for the proper implementation of the programme, it was planned to set up the Village Level Committee.	• Select the taluka, provide funds for the project to DSAG. All project costs will be borne by TDD, including project insurance. • The apex body under the leadership of TDD will coordinate and periodically review the progress of the project.
D-SAG	Receive funds from TDD and make payments against inputs.	• Receive funds from TDD to purchase inputs. • Take village-wise demand from NGOs, Panchmahal Dairy and raise purchase order to MIL (with 50 per cent advance and delivery advise), GSFC, etc. After receipt of the stocks make balance payments against the inputs procured.

Others	
Role of Village Committee	• Consists of 4–5 members from the village • Facilitate input distribution with NGO/gram mitra • Facilitate farmer meeting, informing, gathering farmers • Facilitate end produce selling • Identify and finalise community hall for storage of seed (timeline to be decided). Ensure that the hall is in proper condition with no leakage/moisture • Seed and fertiliser should be properly stored covered with Tarpaulins • Prepare list of interested farmers (beneficiaries) and projected demand to NGO • Distribute fertiliser to farmers with all records • Collect original invoice from GSFC and distribute to farmers providing a copy of same to DSAG • Work with MIL/MDO for technical training for the village
Role of Gram Mitra	The guideline specifies that there should be one Gram Mitra responsible to carry out his duties in two villages. The project manager, on behalf of TDD at district level would review the work undertaken by him every fortnightly. His functions were: • Prepare village committee in targeted villages • Closely work with village committee for finalising beneficiaries and their purchase requirement

Cont'd...

...Cont'd

	• Coordinate with GSFC for soil testing by providing five soil samples from each village • Ensure availability of community hall in proper condition • Facilitate NGO, village community for seed distribution • Working closely with farmers at village level for proper agronomic management
Role of Project Manager	• Dedicated resource for project in DSAG payroll • In charge of the project on behalf of TDD at the district level • Coordinating with NGO, Panchmahal Dairy • Review progress of Gram Mitra and supervisors of the NGO • Review crop data of farmers from NGO and Gram Mitra with the team of MIL • Coordinating with MIL team for the implementation of the work • Collect purchase order from Supervisors and submit to Project In-charge
Role of Project In-charge	• Dedicated resource for the project in DSAG payroll • In-charge of the project on behalf of TDD at the state level • Would be a part of apex body and would be responsible for the follow up of meetings and decisions taken by the apex body at the district level • Review progress of Project Manager • Coordinating with MIL at state level for further scheme
Role of Supervisor	There is one supervisor for 10 Gram Mitra. His duties were the following: • Would be in NGO payroll • Supervise Gram Mitra • Coordinate with Gram Mitra for committee formation • Taluka-wise village identification • Coordinate with Gram Mitra for meetings with farmers and distribution of inputs • Support farmers in sowing crop and managing agronomic requirements • Facilitate gram mitra in collecting and reporting crop performance data • Facilitate MIL/MDO for conducting field shows • Support village committees in selling farm produce • Facilitate in collecting 50 per cent of the total credit requirement to purchase inputs on behalf of villagers • Responsible for the Maize Sheller • Identify depot for fertiliser storage and distribution • Compile village committee purchase orders and submit to NGO/Project Manager • Compile monthly crop update report and submit to NGO/Project
Manager/ MIL TM	15 days plan for reviewing the project needs to be prepared by NGO and the project manager, they have to review it every fortnightly
Role of Project Administrator	Would be in DSAG payroll Already existing

Source: Field survey.

Despite the conceptual attractiveness of partnerships in form of Project Sunshine, the question that we tried to ask in this study was whether such partnerships cater to the larger interest of the community or just to the interests of MIL? Has the public expenditure been justified? Has these partnerships in fact contributed to the primary goal of the TDD such as increasing the income of small landholders from agriculture or meeting broader social goals like creating value for commodities produced in the tribal areas? Answering these questions would help us highlight benefits and weaknesses of this programme. This paper aims to respond to these questions by providing empirical evidence from farmers of Dahod and Panchmahal districts of Gujarat.

Study Sites and Data Collection

The analysis draws from a database of 3,000 beneficiaries of Project Sunshine, which was implemented in rainfed areas of Dahod and Panchmahal districts of Gujarat. Under this project, free Dekalb corn seeds and fertilisers were given to 30,000 farmers residing in seven talukas and 497 villages of Dahod and Panchmahal districts. For the purpose of this study, we selected 10 per cent of total beneficiaries, i.e., 2,465 farmers from Dahod district and 535 farmer beneficiaries from Panchmahal districts, which totalled to 3,000. The list of beneficiaries was obtained from the TDD. As these beneficiaries were scattered across seven talukas and 497 villages, we arranged villages in ascending order of beneficiaries. Villages with median number of beneficiaries of the project were selected for an in-depth interview along with couple of villages above and below the median.

Summary of Major Findings

As the aim of Project Sunshine by the TDD was to increase the income of marginal and small farmers of Scheduled Tribe (ST) population living below the poverty line, programme made it mandatory for the implementing

Table 18.4

Percentage Distribution of Households Living below Poverty Line and Caste by Districts

Particulars	*Districts*		*Total*
	Dahod	*Panchmahal*	
BPL households	99.0 (2440)	98.5 (527)	98.9 (2967)
Caste			
Schedule Tribe	100.0 (2464)	99.6 (533)	99.9 (2997)
Other Backward Caste	0.04 (1)	0.4 (2)	0.1 (3)
Total (N)	2465	535	3000

Note: Figures in parentheses indicate number of observations.

Source: Field survey.

agency to distribute hybrid seed of maize crop along with inputs like fertilisers, pesticides and so on among these groups on the basis of the priority. Therefore, it was vital to explore caste composition and BPL status of beneficiary households in selected tribal districts. Table 18.4 shows that out of 3,000 beneficiaries of this project, 99 per cent families were living below the poverty line. Barring three households, the rest belonged to the ST. The reason for such a distribution could be due to the sampling procedure, where beneficiaries were selected for the detailed study from the project which was directed to benefit ST population.

Distribution and Actual Use of Hybrid Maize Seed

In order to understand diffusion of technology among farmers, series of questions were asked pertaining to type of maize seed sown in the year of the inception of the programme and the conventional seed sown in the past years. It was found that before the initiation of the programme, almost all farmers (99%) reported to have grown maize crop in kharif season (Table 18.5).

Out of the total beneficiaries, nearly 90 per cent of total households reported to have cultivated maize using hybrid seed given by the TDD during kharif season while 74 per cent of total households have reported to have grown conventional variety of maize seed in their plots of land. This shows that majority of farmers have grown both the varieties of maize in their small tract of land. Free distribution of hybrid seed encouraged farmers to cultivate it. However, this did not deter them from cultivating conventional variety of maize. This helped us in comparing yield between two types of seeds.

Table 18.5

Percentage Distribution of Respondents reporting Quantity of Seeds Used in Cultivating Maize using Conventional and MIL Seed Varieties

Types of Seeds	*Kharif*		
	Dahod	*Panchmahal*	*Total*
	Maize cultivated in the last year (2007–08)		
Hybrid	1.0 (24)	7.3 (39)	2.1 (63)
Local (Desi)	99.0 (2423)	92.7 (495)	97.9 (2918)
Total	82.1 (2447) [81.6]	17.9 (534) [17.8]	100.0 (2981) [99.4]
	Conventional Maize cultivated in the current year (2008–09)		
Local (Desi)	86.0 (1908) [63.6]	14.0 (311) [10.4]	100.0 (2219) [74.0]
	Maize using MIL seed (2008–09)		
Hybrid	81.5 (2195) [73.2]	18.5 (499) [16.6]	100.0 (2694) [89.8]

Note: Figures in parentheses indicate number of observations and figures in [ ] indicate percentage to total.

Source: Field survey.

For partnership to become successful, partners have to share responsibilities, jointly contribute resources and funding and mutually derive the benefit from goods and services. If these tasks were not carried out, cost of partnership would increase. In order to explore the extent of duties dispursed by the partners, we investigated amount of seeds, fertilisers, pesticides given by partnering agencies and amount of inputs used by beneficiaries. To our satisfaction, nearly 87 per cent reported to have been given 10 kgs of hybrid maize seed (Table 18.6). However, there were instances where 8 per cent farmers reported to have been left out in getting this benefit of hybrid seed of maize. There were 4 per cent of farmers who had reported to have obtained maize equal to 5 kgs or less. At one extreme, we could trace nine farmers who reported that they received less than one kg of seed, while on the other end; some farmers stated that they had received in excess of 20 kgs of hybrid maize seed. Table 18.6 shows that 79 per cent utilised seeds given to them while the balance 11 per cent of the farmers used less than or equal to 5 kgs of seed. Nearly 10 per cent beneficiaries reported to have not used the hybrid maize seed that was given to them. As seeds were given for free and farmers were growing on an experimental basis, they were not convinced about the returns accruing from the hybrid maize. Consequently, some farmers stored hybrid seed variety to be used in the Rabi season (31%) while the same per cent of farmers reported to have given it away to their relatives. This suggests that high returns earned from maize crops grown using hybrid seed would motivate farmers to cultivate hybrid seed.

Besides seeds, implementing agency was also required to distribute 150 kgs of chemical fertilisers. When we investigated whether the above claim was received by the beneficiaries, we noted that nearly 92 per cent of respondents agreed of having received chemical fertilisers (Table 18.6). Of them, 96 per cent of farmers have reported to have received 150 kgs of fertilisers while 4 per cent of beneficiary farmers have either received less than the required quantity of fertilisers (minimum was 0.5 kgs) or more than the required norm (maximum was 300 kgs) specified by the department. Nearly 86 per cent of beneficiaries reported to have used the given quantity of fertilisers. When we enquired about reasons for partial use of fertilisers, we realised that nearly 47 per cent farmers reported that as they were not convinced about the quantity of fertilisers to be used as advised by the staff of NGOs so they relied on their past experience (Table 18.6). At the outset, such an analysis would appear unimportant, yet, since this programme was one of its kinds of intervention boasting about zero leakages in inputs, an attempt at exploring the extent of such leakages would help the implementing agency in strengthening monitoring work of input distribution and reducing transaction cost which are crucial for public-private partnership (PPP) to function.

Table 18.6

Percentage Distribution of Households Reporting Quantity of Seeds Given, Quantity of Seeds Used and Reasons for the Change

Details	*Seeds*			*Chemical Fertilisers*		
	Districts			*Districts*		
	Dahod	*Panchmahal*	*Total*	*Dahod*	*Panchmahal*	*Total*
			Inputs received			
Yes	91.8 (2262)	93.8 (502)	98.0 (2764)	91.7 2261)	93.6 (501)	92.1 (2762)
No	8.2 (203)	6.2 (33)	2.0 (236)	8.3 (204)	6.4 (34)	7.9 (238)
		Quantity of inputs given (seed = 10 kgs and fertilisers = 150 kgs)				
Did not get	8.2 (203)	6.2 (33)	7.9 (236)	8.3 (204)	6.4 (34)	7.9 (238)
Less than the distributed quantity	5.1 (125)	1.5 (8)	4.4 (133)	1.7 (41)	0.6 (3)	1.6 (44)
Distributed quantity	86.4 (2130)	92.0 (492)	87.4 (2622)	87.5 (2158)	91.4 (489)	88.2 (2647)
More than the distributed quantity	0.3 (7)	0.4 (2)	0.3 (9)	2.5 (62)	1.7 (9)	2.4 (71)
			Quantity of inputs used			
Did not get	10.5 (259)	6.4 (34)	9.8 (293)	9.7 (240)	6.9 (37)	9.2 (277)
Less than the distributed quantity	12.5 (307)	4.3 (23)	11.0 (330)	5.0 (123)	5.2 (28)	5.0 (151)
Distributed quantity	76.8 (1894)	89.0 (476)	79.0 (2370)	85.1 (2098)	87.5 (468)	85.5 (2566)
More than the distributed quantity	0.2 (5)	0.4 (2)	0.2 (7)	0.2 (4)	0.4 (2)	0.2 (6)
Total	**82.2 (2465)**	**17.8 (535)**	**100.0 (3000)**	**90.3 (2465)**	**93.1 (535)**	**90.8 (3000)****
			Reasons for using inputs partially			
Given late	30.4 (69)	27.4 (69)		23.1 (27)	6.1 (6)	15.3 (33)
Stored for Rabi	27.3 (62)	30.6 (77)	60.0 (15)	16.2 (19)	82.7 (81)	46.5 (100)
Given to relatives	32.6 (74)	30.6 (77)	12.0 (3)	37.6 (44)	3.1 (3)	21.9 (47)
Others*	9.7 (22)	11.5 (29)	28.0 (7)	23.1 (27)	8.2 (8)	16.3 (35)
Total	90.1 (227)	100.0 (252)	9.9 (25)	54.4 (117)	45.6 (98)	100.0 (215)

Note: Figures in parentheses indicate number of observations.

* Others reasons for fertilisers include small landholding, unaware about the use of seeds/fertilisers, used fertilisers used in growing other crops, believed that excess use of fertilisers will adversely affect the productivity of crops.

** did not report.

Source: Field survey.

Total Cultivated Area under Conventional and Hybrid Maize

Out of the total 13,480 acres of land cultivated by farmers in Dahod and Panchmahal districts, nearly 65 per cent of area was cultivated under maize crop. Of this, nearly 31 per cent of the area was sown using hybrid seed distributed by TDD and in the rest; maize using conventional seed was grown. Nearly 48 per cent of the land in the study area was irrigated and the rest was unirrigated. Panchmahal accounts for greater area under irrigation (68%). This also gets reflected in irrigation intensity (Table 18.7). This implies that Panchmahal enjoys better availability of sources of irrigation compared to Dahod district. Table 18.7 shows that maize was

Table 18.7

Percentage Distribution of Cultivated and Irrigated Area by Seasons

Details (in %)	*Season*	*Dahod*	*Panch-mahal*	*Total*
Total maize cultivated (in acres)	**Total**	**7065**	**1632**	**8696**
Total maize cultivated to total cropped area	Total	65.0	62.7	64.5
Conventional maize cultivated to total cropped area		69.3	65.4	68.6
Hybrid maize cultivated to total cropped area		30.7	34.6	31.4
Maize cultivated	**Kharif**	**87.7**	**90.3**	**88.2**
	Rabi	**12.3**	**9.7**	**11.8**
Conventional maize to total maize cultivated	Kharif	83.1	85.2	83.5
	Rabi	16.9	14.8	16.5
Hybrid maize to total maize cultivated	Kharif	98.0	100.0	98.4
	Rabi	2.1	—	1.6
Total maize irrigated to total irrigated area		19.7	29.1	22.3
Total crop irrigated to total cultivated crops	Kharif	18.0	55.3	24.6
	Rabi	75.8	84.9	77.4
	Total	42.4	68.2	47.4
Total maize irrigated (in acres)	**Total**	**908**	**516**	**1425**
Conventional maize irrigated to total irrigated area	Kharif	0.7	25.5	5.2
	Rabi	98.9	99.7	99.1
	Total	17.3	36.5	20.7
Hybrid maize irrigated to total irrigated area	Kharif	0.9	22.4	5.4
	Rabi	95.6	—	95.6
	Total	2.9	22.4	6.9
Cropping Intensity		**180.2 (2460)**	**196.4 (534)**	**183.1 (2994)**
Irrigation intensity		**134.3 (1772)**	**201.2 (394)**	**149.3 (2166)**

Note: Figures in parentheses indicate number of observations.

Source: Field survey.

largely grown in kharif season. Majority of area under kharif maize was rainfed unlike that in the Rabi season. Table 18.7 clarifies that the dependence on sources of irrigation was relatively higher during Rabi season as compared to Kharif. Predominant source of irrigation is well followed by rivers, ponds, etc. (Table 18.8).

Table 18.8

Percentage Distribution of Respondents reporting Sources of Irrigation Used in Cultivating Maize using Conventional and MIL Seed Varieties

Sources of irrigation	*Kharif*		
	Dahod	*Panchmahal*	*Total*
Conventional maize cultivated in the last year (2007–08)			
Well	100.0 (15)	96.8 (122)	97.2 (137)
River/Kotar		0.8 (1)	0.7 (1)
Pond, tank		0.8 (1)	0.7 (1)
Canal		1.6 (2)	1.4 (2)
Total	10.6 (15)	89.4 (126)	100.0 (141)
Conventional maize cultivated in the current year (2008–09)			
Well	94.4 (17)	96.8 (60)	96.3 (77)
River/Kotar	5.6 (1)	3.2 (2)	3.8 (3)
Total	22.5 (18)	77.5 (62)	100.0 (80)
Maize using MIL seed (2008–09)			
Well	94.7 (18)	96.6 (112)	96.3 (130)
River/Kotar	5.3 (1)	3.4 (4)	3.7 (5)
Total	**14.1 (19)**	**85.9 (116)**	**100.0 (135)**

Note: Figures in parentheses indicate number of observations.

Source: Field survey.

Yield and Returns on Maize Crop

Yield and production of unirrigated kharif maize assumes importance as it is a staple crop in this tribal belt which is grown under rainfed conditions. Hence, any intervention resulting in an increased yield of the crop would go a long way towards increasing the food security and income of tribal population of the area.

Table 18.9 shows that yield of maize obtained from hybrid seed was nearly 37 per cent higher than that obtained from conventional maize seed. Better availability of irrigation has improved the yield in Panchmahal compared to that of Dahod district. When yield was converted to gross returns by multiplying yield with its farm gate price, we observed that gross returns obtained from hybrid seed was nearly 38 per cent higher than that of maize grown using traditional seed. Farmers growing maize using hybrid seed in Panchmahal taluka enjoyed higher gross returns from the crop.

Table 18.9

Average Yield of Maize Grown using Traditional and Hybrid Seed, Labour Day, Labour Cost, Total Costs and Gross and Net Returns Earned from Maize Cultivated using Traditional and Hybrid Seed

Taluka/ Districts	*Yield of Maize grown using Traditional Seed (per acre)*	*Yield of Maize grown using Hybrid Seed (per acre)*	*Yield difference grown using hybrid and traditional seed*	*Total Cost (₹/acre)*	*Gross returns of Maize using traditional seed (₹/acre)*	*Gross returns of Maize using hybrid seed (₹/acre)*	*Difference of Gross Returns earned in Maize grown using hybrid and traditional seed (%)*	*Net Returns from hybrid seed (₹/acre)*
	Kharif							
Dahod	476 (2361) [457]	692 (2170) [509]	**546** **{33.6}**	7792 (2447) [2565]	5236 (2346) [7047]	7691 (2143) [8977]	{34.2}	–1056 (2447) [8797]
Panchmahal	607 (523) [371]	934 (495) [477]	**155** **{45.6}**	7871 (534) [2113]	9737 (517) [14133]	14965 (490) [22000]	{55.1}	5861 (534) [21392]
Total	499 (2884) [445]	737 (2665) [512]	**712** **{36.5}**	7806 (2981) [2490]	6049 (2863) [8927]	9045 (2633) [12788]	{37.5}	183 (2981) [12346]

Note: Figures in parentheses indicate number of observations: figures in [ ] indicate standard deviation and figures in { } indicate difference between yield and gross returns earned from hybrid and traditional seed and percentage change in yield and gross returns earned from hybrid seed.

Source: Field survey.

In order to understand whether hybrid seed was profitable for farmers, we enquired about cost that farmer would incur on inputs like seeds, fertilisers, pesticides, labour, and so on. These are the costs which farmers will have to bear when government withdraws the programme. The total cost of production of maize was ₹ 7,806 per acre (Table 18.10). Cost of production of maize by farmers in Panchmahal district was higher than that of Dahod district. Major component of this cost component was labour (Table 18.10).

Table 18.10

Average Total Quantity of Inputs and Average Costs of Inputs by Talukas and Districts

Districts	*Quantity in Kg/acre*				*Labour days*	*No. of Watering*		*Cost in ₹ /acre*						
	Seed	*Urea*	*DAP*	*Potash*		*Required*	*Received*	*Seed*	*Urea*	*DAP*	*Potash*	*Total*	*Total Labour cost*	*Total cost*
Dahod	12	51	28	37	23	5	5	125	229	336	112	537	7163	7792
	(2447)	(2297)	(2110)	(9)	(2465)	(787)	(782)	(2430)	(2297)	(2110)	(9)	(2302)	(2447)	(2447)
	[8]	[64]	[34]	[27]	[4]	[1]	[1]	[106]	[289]	[408]	[81]	[660]	[2461]	[2565]
Panchmahal	11	47	32	18	24	5	5	156	213	386	53	582	7200	7871
	(534)	(471)	(456)	(2)	(534)	(149)	(148)	(528)	(471)	(456)	(2)	(475)	(534)	(534)
	[6]	[34]	[23]	[11]	[3]	[1]	[1]	[168]	[151]	[280]	[32]	[390]	[2081]	[2113]
Total	12	50	29	34	23	5	5	131	226	344	101	544	7169	7806
	(2981)	(2768)	(2566)	(11)	(2999)	(936)	(930)	(2958	(2768)	(2566)	(11)	(2777)	(2981)	(2981)
	[8]	[60]	[32]	[26]	[4]	[1]	[1]	[120]	[271]	[389]	[77]	[622]	[2397]	[2490]

Note: Figures in parentheses indicate number of observations and figures in [ ] indicate standard deviation.

Source: Field survey.

Weakness in the Distribution Process

Use of Seeds and Chemical Fertilisers

Out of the total households who reported to have benefited from hybrid seed distributed by MIL, all except 56 beneficiaries were found not to be using seeds that were given to them (Table 18.11). Delay in distribution of seeds and fertilisers after the onset of monsoon was the primary reason for not using seed (49 beneficiaries) and chemical fertilisers (10 beneficiaries). However, they believe that they will be using these inputs in the next year.

Table 18.11

Distribution of Respondents Reporting Reasons for Not Using Seeds and Chemical Fertilisers Given by MIL

Details	*District*		*Total*
	Dahod	*Panchmahal*	
Seed given late	87.3 (48)	100.0 (1)	87.5 (49)
Others	12.7 (7)		12.5 (7)
Total	98.2 (55)	1.8 (1)	100.0 (56)
Chemical fertilisers			
Fertiliser given late	10	0	10
Others	5	1	6
Total	15	1	16

Note: Figures in parentheses indicate number of observations.

Source: Field survey.

Project Sunshine not only calls for distribution of seeds and fertiliser but also agricultural extension services. The aims of agricultural extension were to provide farmers with information that would enable them to make good decision in farming, help in transferring appropriate technologies from research and other sources to the farmer's field with an aim of eliminating poverty and hunger by improving production of the staple food, i.e., maize and increase food security. With this background, we attempted to examine types of agricultural extension services provided, types of agencies rendering these services and so on. To our surprise, no attention or little attention was paid to such an important component of the programme. Nearly 3 per cent of farmers had reported to have received training in sowing maize mainly at the time of seed distribution. Majority of them had received it only for a day. Nearly 71 farmers out of 86 farmers who have received training implemented it while growing maize and majority of them had reported increased production (Table 18.12).

Table 18.12

Percentage Distribution of Households Reporting Training and Exposure Visits Undertaken, Types of Training Provided, Sources of Training, Activities Learnt, Duration of Training, Subject Matter of the Training and Level of Implementation of Learnt Information

Details	*District*		*Total*
	Dahod	*Panchmahal*	
a. Training Received			
Yes	2.3 (56)	5.6 (30)	2.9 (86)
No	97.7 (2409)	94.4 (505)	97.1 (2914)
Total	82.2 (2465)	17.8 (535)	100.0 (3000)
b. Exposure Visits			
No	100 (2465)	100 (535)	100 (3000)
Total	82.2 (2465)	17.8 (535)	100.0 (3000)
c. Activities Learnt During the Training			
Method of maize sowing	100.0 (56)	100.0 (30)	100.0 (86)
Total	65.1 (56)	34.9 (30)	100.0 (86)
d. Duration of the Training			
1 day	98.2 (55)	90.0 (27)	95.3 (82)
2–3 days of training	1.8 (1)	10.0 (3)	4.7 (4)
Total	65.1 (56)	34.9 (30)	100.0 (86)
e. Time When Such Training was Given			
At the time of distributing seed	100 (56)	100 (30)	100 (86)
Total	65.1 (56)	34.9 (30)	100.0 (86)
f. Sources that Provided Training			
Training by Panchmahal dairy	57.1 (32)	80.0 (24)	65.1 (56)
Others*	42.9 (24)	20.0 (6)	34.9 (30)
Total	65.1 (56)	34.9 (30)	100.0 (86)
g. Subject Matter of the Training			
To maintain proper distance of the maize seed while sowing	84.1 (37)	93.3 (28)	87.8 (65)
Others	15.9 (7)	6.7 (2)	12.2 (9)
Total	59.5 (44)	40.5 (30)	100.0 (74)
h. Implemented the advice given during the training session			
Sowing as per the information	60.6 (43)	39.4 (28)	100.0 (71)
i. Benefits received by following the advice			
Better growth of HYV maize	97.4 (38)	95.8 (23)	96.8 (61)
Save seed through proper distance	2.6 (1)	4.2 (1)	3.2 (2)
Total	61.9 (39)	38.1 (24)	100.0 (63)

Note: Figures in parentheses indicate number of observations.
* Others include 16 respondents reporting that they have received training from staff of MIL, 11 stated that NGO named
Sadguru trained them and the rest three did not know who trained them.

Source: Field survey.

Other Weaknesses of the Programme

(i) Some raised doubts about the certification of Dekalb hybrid seed.

(ii) MIL prescribed nearly doubled the quantity of nutrients (fertilisers) advised by agricultural universities.

(iii) Farmers stated in the discussion that release of varieties of maize were not superior over the popular varieties currently grown by farmers.

(iv) Lack of inter-institutional coordination/network for development and promotion of new varieties through better utilisation of available germplasm across R&D institutions.

(v) No special incentives for plant breeders to produce enough breeder seeds. Emphasis was only given to the hybrid seed by MIL.

(vi) Lack of regulation on pricing of seeds by the public sector.

Public-Private Partnerships as a Means for Agricultural Development

Partnerships by various agencies in distributing hybrid seeds to tribal farmers constitute a complex decision wherein each partner considers not only their own costs and benefits, but also those of other partners. Hartwich, Janssen and Tola (2003) suggest that there were five steps to consider: (i) identification of the common interest space; (ii) negotiation and design of the partnership contract, including legal, funding, and governance issues; (iii) implementation; (iv) evaluation of achievement; and (v) deciding whether the partnership will continue if objectives were not yet achieved, or if there were new and promising objectives to pursue in the partnership arrangement. Barring the last step, each of these steps was followed by TDD and MIL in the Project Sunshine. Proper monitoring and control of the programme by government and NGOs at different levels helped in proper selection of beneficiaries and plugging leakages. An attempt to plug leakages over time would improve the potential of such partnerships to earn profit from gradually improving work relationships and becoming strategic in absence of which such flexible arrangements may simply be phased out. It was believed that existence of the following conditions facilitated this partnership:

> *Existence of a common interest space.* Over generations, tribal farmers of the study area were growing conventional variety of maize. Lack of availability of sources of irrigation was also the prime reason for these farmers for becoming risk-averse in growing hybrid seed which requires increased use of fertilisers, pesticides and water. MIL had the interest of marketing hybrid maize seed. In absence of this partnership, diffusion of this technology for cereals like maize would have been a costly affair in these rainfed areas. However, such a diffusion of technology had the potential of

increasing income of small and marginal farmers, which was the objective of the government.

Expectation of positive private cost-benefit ratios by the private sector entities and public sector participating in the partnership. Such partnership was not without cost. The direct cost of implementation of this project by the department was ₹ 7,354 per beneficiary (Table 18.13). This cost was not inclusive of other transaction costs – i.e., costs of information search for partners, negotiation, screening, monitoring, coordination, and enforcement of contracts and institutions.

Table 18.13

Details of the Types of Costs Incurred and the Amount Spent

Details	*Volume (million tonnes)*	*Cost (₹ lakh)*	*Percentage to total*
Soil testing cost	1000	0.674	0.04
Seeds	612	612	35.2
Mechanical Sheller	720	144	8.3
Fertilisers*			
Urea	10800	512.2	29.5
DAP	36000	336.2	19.3
MOP	2880	134.1	7.7
Fertilisers total		**982.5**	56.5
Total input cost		1739.2	**100.0 (91.0)**
	Implementation Cost		
MIL	97.04	56.1	
NGO and Dairy Cooperative	48.4	28.0	
D-SAG	17.6	10.2	
Storage cost	10.0	5.8	
Total Implementation Costs		**173.0**	**100.0 (9.0)**
Total project cost		1912.2	**100.0**
Cost per beneficiary was ₹ 7,354			
Cost per acre was ₹ 2,655.8 acres			

* Standard per acre dose of fertiliser: Urea=150 kg; DAP=50 kg; MOP=40
* Standard cost per kg: Urea = ₹ 4.80; DAP = ₹ 9.34; MOP = ₹ 4.44
* Seed cost= ₹ 100/kg

Sheller cost@ ₹ 20,000

3 villages per cluster: ₹ 2,000 per cluster for input distribution Insurance cost was ₹ 47.84 lakhs.

Note: Figures in parentheses indicate percentage to total project cost.

Source: D-SAG, Gandhinagar.

It is against this that the benefit accrued from this partnership was analysed. It was clear that average change in yield of hybrid as compared to MIL was 712 kgs/acre (Table 18.7). As cost of production was borne by the government, increase in yield accounted for an increase in returns of ₹ 2,921 per acre to the farmers (Table 18.7). Comparing the cost of implementation of this project per beneficiary growing one acre of land, it was evident that farmers have gained from such a partnership. But still this figure needs to be viewed with precaution. As these were initial years of partnership, there was an every possibility of benefits outweighing the cost of intervention. In future, if the government withdraws from such partnerships and when the costs in inputs used for maize cultivation will be borne by farmers, these additional earnings would get reduced to ₹ 1,094 per acre (Table 18.7). This earning was not substantial to motivate farmers to adopt hybrid seed. This explains the reason as to why growing maize using hybrid seed had not diffused in this area. This was all the more a reason for the government to intervene. However, during the recent years when government was interested in diffusion of technology, greater benefits would accrue to farmers. This would happen only when there was a greater synergistic effect from mutual contribution resulting in greater benefits than those that could be achieved if the activities were carried out by each partner responsibly. Such an effect can be built over time. As the MIL has benefited in terms of its entry into the new market and have benefited from this partnership, it would be apt for the company to take up the role of providing agricultural extension services in these areas. This would help them in understanding agro climatic and socio-economic characteristics of the area which would in turn assist them in improvising upon hybrid seeds to suit the need of the area. However, there was a need for the MIL to travel an extra mile by providing extension services to farmers growing hybrid maize. Moreover, in the situation when government has been grappling with some of the constraints of providing agricultural extension services, such a move by the private partner would strengthen their partnership with the government. This would go a long way towards improving the efficiency of farmers in cultivation of maize. Such an effort would result in synergistic effects from active collaboration between public research organisations and private sector entities.

Conclusion

In view of the challenges facing farmers today, the structural transformation of agricultural extension systems around the world was unavoidable. Several countries are actively pursuing greater involvement by the private non-profit and for-profit sectors as a means of improving the effectiveness and sustainability of agricultural extension systems. Capitalising on the comparative advantage of each of the different sectors helps to ensure the success of this endeavour. However, the first major issue was who will pay for the extension service along with diffusion of inputs related knowledge – the government, farmers, or private non-profit organisations? The incentive driving public and private agents to enter partnerships was usually the interest in reaping the benefits, be they private or social benefits. Here there was a need to distinguish between benefits resulting from the innovation itself and from the partnership arrangement. Private benefits received by farmers from diffusion of hybrid seed consist of increased farm production and productivity. Private benefits from partnering include access to knowledge and technology. Social benefits from innovations include increased agricultural production and productivity of maize for marginal and small farmers as most of it was used for home consumption, sufficient food supply for the poor. Social benefits from partnering include joint learning; reduced time lags in the adoption of technology. While we emphasise on the benefits of partnering, it should not be construed that this method was the only or preferred option in diffusing the technology among poor farmers. However, when weighed against the only prevailing alternative, i.e., public agriculture extension services which have largely failed in the area, there was no exaggeration of the fact that such a step of increasing farmers' incomes through improved productivity was an important element in agricultural development and poverty reduction strategies. Any methods which improve adoption of improved technologies like use of improved variety of seeds and sustainable farm management practices open new opportunities to meet these challenges. Public-private partnership has been used as a vehicle for diffusion of technology among small and marginal farmers. However, vital element of agricultural extension system needs to be weaved into the programme of private-public partnership and should be given the same importance as input distribution policy. Further, for efficiency and effectiveness of the programme, steps need to be taken to initiate an inter-institutional coordination and networking research for the variety testing and release. There was a need to review the variety release process to shorten the breeding cycles. There was a need for strengthening infrastructure (modern processing and storage, better markets), introducing agricultural extension services immediately after the release of new hybrid seed as a parallel activity helping farmers to familiarise with new seed variety.

Notes

1. Good governance has a number of dimensions: political stability; the rule of law; voice and accountability; effective governments; regulatory quality and control of corruption, among others.

2. Henry Wallace, the initiator of the Rockefeller Foundation's agricultural research programme in Mexico in the 1940s founded one of the first and most successful hybrid maize seed companies in the USA. When the Rockefeller Foundation shifted its attention to India, the initial emphasis was also on hybrid maize. As we trace the history of hybridisation in India, Maize was the first cereal crop to undergo rapid and widespread technological transformation. The experience gained with maize deeply influenced other crops. The success of technological change in maize production on a global scale, reflected in continuing yield increases, was heavily based on the use of so called *high yielding varieties* (HYVs).
3. Though traditionally, it was a *kharif* crop from past few years. It was also being cultivated in *Rabi* season because of high yield levels and low cost of production.

References

Hartwich, F., W. Janssen, and J. Tola (2003). 'Partnerships for Agricultural Innovation: Lessons from Partnership Building between the Public and the Private Sector in Latin America', Paper presented at the Conference on Innovation and Learning in a Globalised World, Experiences of Developing Countries, Eindhoven: Eindhoven Centre for Innovation Studies.

Seigler, R.S. and D.W. Puckridge (1995). 'Improving Sustainable Productivity in Rice-Based Low-Land Systems of South and South-East Asia', *Geo Journal*, 35(3), pp. 307–24.

World Bank (1982). *World Development Report 1982 on Agriculture and Economic Development*, New York: Oxford University Press.

19

Implementation of MNREGS and Its Impact on Livelihood Structure in Rural Madhya Pradesh

TAPAS KUMAR DALAPATI

The Constitution of India emphasises 'decent work' under Directive Principles of State Policy (DPSP). Article 41 of the DPSP states that 'the state shall, within the limits of its economic capacity and development, make effective provision for securing right to work ...'. Similarly, there is emphasis on the conditions of work and level of wages under Articles 42 and 43, which state that 'the state shall make provision for just and humane conditions of work and for maternity relief. The state shall endeavour to secure work at a living wage, conditions of work ensuring a descent standard of living and full enjoyment of leisure and social and cultural opportunity by suitable legislation or economic organisation or in any other way, to all workers, agricultural, industrial or otherwise, and, in particular, the state shall endeavour to promote cottage industries on an individual or cooperative basis in rural areas'. The UN Covenant on Economic, Social and Cultural Rights, 1966 to which India is a signatory, makes similar declarations about right to work. Despite these declarations our country has not been successful in promoting right to work. Low level of productive employment generation in the aggregate, the persistence of poverty and low educational levels are the most significant failures of

Indian development strategy till now (Ghosh, 2006). The ensuring of rural employment is further facing acute crisis due to neo-liberal economic reforms of the past one and a half decade.

Against this background, the notification of National Rural Employment Guarantee Act (NREGA) of September 7, 2005 is a unique step towards realisation of economic right to work as envisioned in the DPSP which strives to ensure socio-economic justice in rural areas in the contemporary situation. The Act seeks to provide for the enhancement of livelihood security of the households in rural areas of the country by providing at least 100 days of guaranteed wage paid public employment in a financial year to every household whose adult members volunteer to do unskilled manual work. Specifically, the Act seeks the 'creation of durable assets and strengthening the livelihood resource base of the rural poor'. The Act envisages a collaborative partnership between the Centre and the state governments through a set of operational and the non-negotiable guidelines, while leaving considerable scope to the state governments to formulate the details of works and other aspects of the programme.

While the MNREGS itself builds upon a long history of wage employment programmes in India, it is different in the sense that it is a guarantee, not reversible with any changes of government; provides scope for implementation by local groups and agencies; devolves considerable powers to local panchayats; mandates a high quality of condition of work through provisions for medical aid, drinking water, shade, and crèche. On the worksite it encourages the use of the Right to Information and social audit to ensure transparent and effective implementation. Among the expected outcomes of implementation of MNREGS in India are an increase in employment and purchasing power of the people; augmenting participation of women workforce; strengthening of rural infrastructure through creation of durable assets; regeneration of natural resources that provide the livelihood resource base of local rural economy; increase in productivity in agriculture and reduction in distress migration from rural areas.

National and State Level Analysis of Rural Labour

Pattern of Employment

In India, the total number of agricultural workers has been estimated at 253 million as of 2004–05. They form 57 per cent of the workers in the total workforce. About 249 millions of them are in rural areas and that works out to 73 per cent of the total rural workforce of 343 millions. Nearly two-thirds of the agricultural labourers (64%) are self-employed or are farmers and the remaining 87 millions, a little over one-third (36%)

are agricultural labourer. Almost all these wage workers (98%) are casual labourers.

Studies indicate decline in growth rate of agricultural and rural employment during 1993–2000 compared to the preceding decade, by all measures of employment (Chadha and Sahu, 2003; Bhattacharya and Sakthivel, 2004). Agricultural labourers are mainly engaged for manual work in cultivation such as sowing, reaping, harvesting and total employment in manual cultivation also showed a dismal rate of growth of 0.7 per cent per annum during the period 1994–2000 (Srivastava, 2006). A number of factors contributed to this slow down in employment in agriculture sector. Prime among these was a lower investment in irrigation, drought proofing and agricultural research because of which, there was no intensification of farming in rainfed and dry-land areas. This also led to slowing down of land augmenting technical changes. Further, institutional factors led to acceleration in the adoption of labour saving changes particularly due to rising wages during the 1980s. There is a shift away from agriculture to more remunerative non-agricultural employment among the rural workers. There are, thus, both demand and supply constraints on employment generation in the agricultural sector. Employment days for agricultural wage labourers are characterised by great degree of uncertainty because of seasonality of manual operations such as sowing, weeding, harvesting, etc., in crop cultivation. There are ups and downs in employment days depending on the agricultural performance during the year. For years when agriculture has been good and monsoon has been appropriate employment days are higher and vice versa (NCEUS, 2008).

The male–female gap in wage employment days is also significant for agricultural labourers. The wage employment days available for female agricultural labourers were 196 in 1993–94, which declined to 184 in 2004–05. Wage rates, as observed earlier, were also much lower for females, while male wage was 1.4 times higher than that of the female agricultural labourers. These average days of employment for wage labourers conceal a great deal of regional variations. There are no fixed hours of work as there are no laws to act as guidelines for the working conditions of agricultural workers. Wage labourers are subject to long working hours at meagre wages well below the minimum wage limit. Further, due to lack of opportunities, there is high level of unemployment and underemployment leaving the labourers with little bargaining power. Further, seasonality in agricultural operations is a major reason why the labourers have to migrate to other regions to look for work during lean periods.

Unemployment and Underemployment

Unemployment rate, which is the number of persons unemployed per 100 persons in the labour force, is computed for usual status agricultural labourers by current daily status (CDS). According to the NSSO, EUS Survey 2004–05, the unemployment rate for agricultural labours by the CDS is quite high in rural areas by any standard; 16 per cent for men and 17 per cent for women. This is the visible measure of underemployment or underutilisation of labour time of agricultural labourers. The daily status rate also reflects the underemployment during the week and the intermittency of employment and uncertainty in availability of employment. The underemployment of usual status agricultural labourers by CDS rates increased during the decade 1993–94 to 2004–05. In fact, the CDS unemployment rate was exceptionally high at 16 per cent in 2004–05. In 2004–05, the female unemployment rates were higher in both the cases compared to the males.

The report on the employment and unemployment survey for the 61st Round gives a measure of the invisible unemployment rate by asking the usually employed if they were more or less regularly employed throughout the year. Among the various categories, proportion of those usual status workers who did not consider themselves more or less regularly employed was the highest for casual workers, particularly so in agriculture. It is more than double of the self-employed and four times of the regular workers. In a nutshell, agricultural labourers/casual workers in agriculture have high rates of unemployment and underemployment due to irregularity of and non-availability of employment. This makes the group even more vulnerable and creates insecurity in regular flow of income. Thus, to meet their subsistence levels and supplement their income during lean periods, they need to migrate to adjoining semi-urban and urban centres, which further worsens their situation and makes them subject to forced or bonded labour (NCEUS, 2008).

Against this background, the recent enactment of a national legislation of guaranteeing manual work to all those seeking rural workers is called Mahatma Gandhi National Rural Employment Guarantee Act (MGNREGA). It is essentially a form of social protection to cover the employment gap for the working poor and enable them to realise at least minimum wages relevant for the area. Proper implementation of the MNREGA goes a long way in not only assuring a minimum income for the rural working poor but also contributes to enhancing the reserve price of such labour which is currently so low that it is nothing but starvation wages (i.e., one that will not help cross the poverty threshold). At this juncture, when MNREGA is going to complete its four years of implementation, it is necessary that we study and examine the issues and challenges faced by it and its impact upon rural livelihood structure.

Rural Labour in Madhya Pradesh

Madhya Pradesh has predominantly been an agrarian economy which shows co-existence of poverty and prosperity in the state. The state's socio-economic profile describes an economy of rural mass, poverty and growth led by agriculture. Despite five decades of planned economic development, Madhya Pradesh continues as an underdeveloped BIMARU[1] state. If we analyse the percentage share of agricultural workers in total rural work force, it is 82.5 per cent out of which share of male and female workers is 79.1 and 88.1 per cent respectively in 2004–05 (NSSO, 2006). Out of the total rural workers, farmers constitute 61.4 per cent and 38.6 per cent belongs to agricultural labourer category (NSSO, EUS Survey 2004–05). In the same survey it is found that out of the total agricultural labourers, STs and SCs constitute 35.9 and 28.5 per cent respectively. If we look into the data of Rural Labour Enquiry Report 1999–2000, an SCs agricultural male and female labourer earned ₹ 30.1 and ₹ 24.44 for male and female respectively in Madhya Pradesh. Further, this amount is quite dismal for ST agricultural labourers households in the state. Against this background, introduction of MNREGS is like a silverlining where sizeable section of households depend upon agricultural labour for their livelihood.

The paper is based on the findings of a larger research project on Management of National Rural Employment Guarantee Scheme: Issue and Challenges in Madhya Pradesh undertaken during 2007–08. The study is based on survey of 16 MNREGS villages across the eleven agro-climatic zones from four districts (Dhar, East Nimar, Shivpuri and Sidhi) of Madhya Pradesh. In this study, 320 randomly selected MNREGS participants' households and 16 Gram Panchayats functionaries were interviewed to analyse implementation as well as impact of MNREGS in Madhya Pradesh during 2007–08. The paper is divided into seven parts, the first and second part introduce MNREGS and illustrate the structure of rural labour in India and Madhya Pradesh, the third part highlights features of implementation of the programme, fourth part analyses perception of the beneficiaries about impact of the MNREGS on participants households part highlights impact of MNREGS upon the rural labour structure in Madhya Pradesh and last part concludes the paper.

Implementation of MNREGS in Madhya Pradesh (2007–08)

In this study of management and implementation of MNREGS in Madhya Pradesh, analysis of land ownership among participants shows that 59 per cent are landless, 17.5 per cent are marginal farmers, 22.5 per cent are small farmers and only 0.93 per cent households are large farmers. In this study, it is found that majority (60.0%) of participating respondents in MNREGS are illiterate, 14.0 per cent are educated up to class four, 11.2 per cent are educated up to class eight, 8.12 per cent are educated up to class nine, 4.6

per cent are high school pass and only 2.5 per cent are educated above class ten. Occupation-wise it is found that majority (58.4%) of the participant households' main occupation is agricultural labour, 19.3 per cent households belong to the background of agricultural self employment, 15.6 per cent participants households are in the background of non-agricultural labourer and 5.0 per cent households' main occupation is non-agricultural self employment. When social background of the respondents are analysed it is found that majority of beneficiaries (42.1%) are from scheduled tribes and 21.5 per cent belong to scheduled castes category. The participation of other backward castes is reported as 32.1 per cent, whereas only 4 per cent of general caste participated in the wage employment programme.

Table 19.1

Availability of Job Card

Job Card	*Total*
Own job card	299 (93.4)
Joint with some other household	12 (3.8)
Several job cards	2 (0.6)

Note: Figures in parentheses are percentage.

Source: Field survey.

The first and foremost salient feature of MNREGS implementation is registration of the job seekers at the Gram Panchayat through an application and issue of job cards to the concerned individual household. The job card is an essential legal document. It has information about job seeking adults of the households and their photographs. Job card records date of application for work, date of work and remuneration paid to the workers. This legal document is non-transferable and helps to ensure transparency and protects labourers against corrupt practices. In this study of implementation of MNREGS in Madhya Pradesh, it is found that out of 320 beneficiaries, 93.4 per cent have their own job card issued in their name. Only 3.8 per cent of the beneficiaries have job cards with some other households. It has also been identified that there are few cases of ownership of more than one job card. The cases of having joint job cards with other households and of multiple job cards are an outcome of subdivision of joint family into various nuclear families (Table 19.1).

Table 19.2

Possession of Job Card

Possession of Job Card	*Total*
In possession	259 (80.9)
Lost	2 (0.6)
Someone else	58 (18.1)
Not clear	1 (0.3)

Note: Figures in parentheses are percentage.

Source: Field survey.

Under the provisions of the MNREGS, job card should be in the custody of the household to whom it is issued. It is not transferable to others in any case. During the study, it is found that 80.9 per cent of the beneficiary households have physically owned a job card at the time of survey. Remaining 18.1 per cent of the households reported that the job card is kept by someone else (Table 19.2). When questioned about whereabouts of the job cards, 29.2 per cent of the beneficiaries said that the job card was with the sarpanch and 70.7 per cent beneficiaries said that the card was with the panchayat secretary. When investigators grilled the sarpanch and secretary, they said that the job cards were withheld by them to open account in a bank or post office. When the information is analysed across social categories, it is found that sarpanch and secretary have kept the job cards of illiterate scheduled tribes beneficiaries, who are mostly unaware that how important is job card for their employment.

Table 19.3

Money Given for Obtaining Job Card

Money Given for Obtaining Job Card	*Total*
Paid	103 (35.3)
Not paid	217 (64.7)
Job card ₹ (mean)	5.56

Note: Figures in parentheses are percentage.

Source: Field survey.

It is the responsibility of the gram panchayat to timely issue job cards to the applicant household. Photograph of adult members who are applicants have to be attached to the job cards by the Gram Panchayat functionaries. Under the MNREGS, the cost of the job card and photograph is borne by the MNREGS programme itself. However, it is found that 35.3 per cent of the beneficiaries have given an average of ₹ 5.56 to get a job card in Madhya Pradesh (Table 19.3).

Under MNREGS, applications for work should be generally submitted to Gram Panchayat by the job seekers. The application in writing should include registration number of the job card, date from which employment is required, and number of days of employment required. A single application may be given for number of days in different periods during the year for which employment is required. A joint application may also be submitted by several applicants. A worker having job card may directly apply at the work site. However, lack of formal application form should not be a ground for denying work to any job seeker as this is against the spirit of the MNREGS.

In the study of implementation of MNREGS in Madhya Pradesh, it was found that only 5.6 per cent of the beneficiaries applied for job through a written application and 30 per cent beneficiaries asked for job

Table 19.4

Category of Request

Category of Request	*Total*
Not clear	36 (11.3)
Written application	18 (5.6)
Informal request	96 (30.0)
No (not approached)	170 (53.1)

Note: Figures in parentheses are percentage.

Source: Field survey.

Table 19.5

Availability of Job within Stipulated Time

Did you get work within 15 days	*Total*
Yes within 15 days	104 (32.5)
Yes within 30 days	131 (40.9)
Yes after 30 days	72 (22.5)
No response	13 (4.0)

Note: Figures in parentheses are percentage.

Source: Field survey.

through informal requests to the panchayat functionaries. Most interestingly, majority of the households (53.1%) never applied for job by any means and directly worked for MNREGS (Table 19.4). In this case, the demand-driven approach is negated during the implementation process of MNREGS and the scheme is implemented like erstwhile wage employment programme. However, it is a fact that people have been getting work without demanding for the same, but the important thing is that due to lack of awareness about MNREGS, a real job seeker is not liable to get an unemployment allowance only because he has not applied through the proper channel. When it was asked as why the participating households did not apply for job, 53.4 per cent households did not respond to the question. However, 18.8 per cent households reported that they were not aware that it was necessary to apply for the job and 20.6 per cent households said that they were unaware about the procedure to apply for the same.

It is mandatory under MNREGS that an applicant should be given work within 15 days of the submission of application, otherwise he or she is not eligible for getting unemployment allowance. In Madhya Pradesh, it is found that only 32.5 per cent of the beneficiaries have got work within 15 days of submission of their application, 40.9 per cent of the beneficiaries said that they were allocated work within a month of their application and 22 per cent beneficiaries accepted that they have got work only after 30 days (Table 19.5). However, the interesting fact is that not a single beneficiary has received any unemployment allowance despite being late in getting employment within the prescribed period of 15 days. This fact shows lack of awareness among the job seekers and apathy of the panchayat functionaries for giving unemployment allowances.

Under MNREGS, a household has the right to demand up to 100 days of unskilled work within a year. In this study, it is found that each participating household get an average employment of 48.6 days during 2007–08 in Madhya Pradesh. The average working days per respondent during the year 2007–08 was recorded as 23.14 during this period (Table 19.6).

When we look into the average earnings generated through MNREGS in Madhya Pradesh, it is computed as ₹ 3,395.61 per households during 2007–08 for all sample districts.

Under MNREGS, the Gram Panchayat is the most important agency for executing MNREGS works. The MNREGS envisages that at least 50 per cent of the works in terms of cost can be executed by Gram Panchayat. In this study, it is

Table 19.6

Availability of Employment under MNREGS

Particular	*Total*
No. of days worked by the respondent (mean)	23.14
No. of days worked by the all HH members (mean)	48.60
Total wage earnings (mean ₹)	3395.61

Source: Field survey.

found that 80.6 per cent beneficiaries reported that MNREGS works have been executed by Gram Panchayats, 9.1 per cent of the beneficiaries reported that MNREGS works have been implemented by beneficiary committee and only 1 per cent reported that works have been implemented by Block officials (Table 19.7).

Under MNREGS, various kinds of works can be undertaken by the workers but most of the works are of unskilled nature. In Madhya Pradesh, in its first phase of MNREGS implementation most of the (65.3%) beneficiaries reported that they have been assigned with earth digging and carrying of the same. Around 4.1 per cent beneficiaries reported that they are involved in breaking stones and only 5 per cent reported that they are involved in some sort of skilled work (Table 19.8).

The salient intention of MNREGS is to provide a basic employment guarantee in rural areas along with creation of durable assets for sustainable development of livelihoods for the people. According to the Schedule I of the MNREGS various works including water conservation, drought proofing, irrigation, land development, renovation of traditional water bodies, flood control and rural connectivity can be undertaken as MNREGS work. However, other works can be undertaken in consultation with central government from time to

Table 19.7

Agency for Implementing MNREGS work

Agency for execution of works at the village level	*Total*
Gram Panchayat	258 (80.6)
Voluntary organisation	6 (1.9)
Beneficiary committee	29 (9.1)
Block officials	1 (0.3)
Others	23 (7.3)

Note: Figures in parentheses are percentage.

Source: Field survey.

Table 19.8

Category of Work undertaken at Work site

Category of Work undertaken at Work site	*Total*
No response	65 (20.3)
Digging and or carrying earth	209 (65.3)
Breaking stones	13 (4.1)
Skilled work	16 (5.0)
More than one task	15 (4.7)
Other	2 (0.6)

Note: Figures in parentheses are percentage.

Source: Field survey.

Table 19.9

Type of Assets Created

Types of Assets Created	*Total*
Tank	54 (16.9)
Check dam	17 (5.3)
Well	35 (10.9)
Other water harvesting structure	1 (0.3)
Land improvement	2 (0.6)
Kuccha approach road	148 (46.3)
Pucca approach road	8 (2.5)
Other	2 (0.6)
Unclear	53 (16.6)

Note: Figures in parentheses are percentage.

Source: Field survey.

time. In Madhya Pradesh, 46.3 per cent beneficiaries reported that *kuccha* approach roads are the main assets created under MNREGS during 2007–08. Other important works undertaken under MNREGS are tanks (16.9%), wells (10.9%), check dams (5.3%), *pucca* approach roads and land development (0.6%) (Table 19.9). It is evident from the analysis that most of the assets are created under rural connectivity and water harvesting related works in Madhya Pradesh.

Perception about Impact of MNREGS on Beneficiaries' Households

National Rural Employment Guarantee Act was implemented in Madhya Pradesh from February 2006. In this study of management and implementation of MNREGS in Madhya Pradesh, it is found that total working days provided under MNREGS in Madhya Pradesh is only 6.7 per cent of the total days available for work among the beneficiaries' households. If we calculate the average income from MNREGS, it is calculated that average households wage income is ₹ 3,178 for the year 2007–08.

Table 19.10

Impact of MNREGS on Participating and Non-Participating Households

Impact of MNREGS on Households	*Participant Households (%)*
Proportion of households reported MNREGS is 'very important' for the family	175(54.7)
Proportion of households reported MNREGS brought 'significant change' in life	138(43.1)
Proportion of households reported MNREGS helped to 'avoid going hungry'	146(45.6)
Proportion of households reported MNREGS helped to 'avoid migration'	154(48.1)
Proportion of households reported MNREGS helped to 'send children to school'	129(40.3)
Proportion of households reported MNREGS helped to 'cope with someone's illness in the family'	124(38.8)
Proportion of households reported MNREGS 'repaid their debts'	123(38.4)
Proportion of households reported MNREGS helped to 'give up work they didn't want to do'	116(36.3)
Proportion of households reported MNREGS helped to 'create useful assets in the village'	143(44.7)
Proportion of households reported MNREGS helped to 'rise market wage'	137(42.8)
Proportion of households reported MNREGS resulted 'in scarcity of labour in peak season'	124(38.8)
Proportion of households reported MNREGS resulted in 'decrease of productivity of labour'	129(40.3)

Note: Figures in parentheses are percentage.

Source: Field survey.

In this study, it is found that 54.7 per cent participants reported MNREGS is very important for their family and 43.1 per cent households accepted that MNREGS has brought significant changes in their life. Among the beneficiaries, 45.6 per cent beneficiaries reported that due to MNREGS they were able to avoid hunger, 48.1 per cent beneficiaries stated that due to MNREGS they were able to avoid migrating out in search of job. About 40.3 per cent households reported that due to MNREGS their dropout children were able to join school, 38.8 per cent households accepted that they could treat family member's illness due to the MNREGS earnings. Among the beneficiaries 38.4 per cent reported that they were able to repay their debts due to MNREGS earnings. Among the beneficiaries 44.7 per cent reported that due to MNREGS useful assets have been created in the village. It is reported by 42.8 per cent beneficiaries that MNREGS has enhanced local wage rate, 38.8 per cent households reported that it has created scarcity of labour during peak agricultural season. It is also reported by 40.3 per cent households that MNREGS resulted in decrease of productivity of labour because MNREGS has higher wage rate than local wage rate and there is no adequate surveillance for works to be done (Table 19.10).

Share of MNREGS in Employment, Income and Household Expenditure

In the rural areas of Madhya Pradesh, people generally engage in agricultural self-employment, manual labouring in or outside village in agricultural and non-agricultural sector or remain unemployed. In this study of MNREGS, it is found that a household is available for an average of 741 man days (2007–08). Out of the total man days available for work, MNREGS provides job for only 6.7 per cent man days of work for a household. It is also found that in an average rural household people remain unemployed for 35.1 per cent of the total man days available for work despite implementation of MNREGS since 2006 (Table 19.11).

Table 19.11

Employment and Unemployment among Participant Households in MNREGS

Employment and Unemployment during 2007–08	*Percentage*
Proportion of working days under MNREGS	6.7
Proportion of working days under non-MNREGS wage work	29.5
Proportion of self-employment days	28.7
Proportion of unemployment days	35.1
Average household total days available for work	740.9

Source: Field survey.

It is calculated that among the sample, an average household generates a total annual income and total wage income of ₹ 22,999 and

₹ 14,151 respectively, during 2007–08, out of which MNREGS income is around 14.7 per cent of total income and 23.9 per cent of the total wage income of a household. Though, MNREGS involved only 6.7 per cent of the total working days available for work, it generated 14.7 per cent of the income for the beneficiaries family. This is because wage rate under the MNREGS is almost double in comparison to the local wage rate in the labour market. This shows that due to MNREGS wage income of beneficiary households has increased significantly (Table 19.12).

Table 19.12

Wage Income from MNREGS of the Total Wage Income of the Participant Households in MNREGS during the Year 2007–08

Wage Income during 2007–08	*(in ₹)*
Average MNREGS income per household	3,395
Average non-MNREGS wage income per household	10,756
Average total wage income	14,151
Average total household income	22,999

Source: Field survey.

It is found in this study that overwhelming (75.3%) beneficiaries used the MNREGS income for purchasing food items and those who have very significant income (16.6%) are able to invest the MNREGS wages on building durable assets for them (Table 19.13).

Table 19.13

Utilisation of Wage Income from MNREGS among the Participant Households

Description of Utilisation of MNREGS Income	*Participant Households*	*Average Wage Income From MNREGS*	*Percentage of MNREGS Income from Total Wage Income*
Education	4(1.3)	1380.00	4.8
Food	241(75.3)	3740.70	15.0
Accessibility of assets*	53(16.6)	5568.10	18.2
Debt repayment	1(0.3)	650.00	3.1
Working capital	2(0.6)	2477.00	14.7
Savings	1(0.3)	1785.00	3.4
Health care	4(1.3)	1380.00	4.8

*Purchasing of durable goods and house repair.

Note: Figures in parentheses are percentage.

Source: Field survey.

Share of MNREGS in Women Employment, Income and Expenditure

In this study, it is found that in 91 per cent beneficiary households, women worked under MNREGS. Among the sample, 35 per cent respondents were women workers. With respect to female participation in the MNREGS, it is found that MNREGS provided only 6.5 per cent of man days to the females of a household in the year 2007–08. Even after the implementation of MNREGS, female unemployment man days are accounted for 36.6 per cent of total female man days available for work in a household (Table 19.14).

Table 19.14

Employment and Unemployment during the Agriculture Year, 2007–08

Employment and Unemployment during the Agriculture Year 2007–08	*Percentage*
Proportion of female working days under MNREGS	6.5
Proportion of female working days under non-MNREGS wage employment	27.5
Proportion of female working days under self-employment	29.6
Proportion of female unemployed days	36.6
Average total female days available for work	296

Source: Field survey.

In this study, it is found that 34.8 per cent of MNREGS income is generated by the women workers. However, they accrued for generating 32.7 per cent and 32.4 per cent income in non-MNREGS wage income and total wage income of the household respectively during the year 2007–08 (Table 19.15).

Table 19.15

Wage Income of Females among the MNREGS Participants Households

Female Wage Income during 2007–08	*Percentage*
Proportion of female MNREGS income in total MNREGS household income	34.8
Proportion of female non-MNREGS income in total non-MNREGS household income	32.7
Proportion of female wage income in total household wage income	32.4

Source: Field survey.

In this study it is also found that in 62.5 per cent households of MNREGS, women workers keep their wages with them. In households, where women keep their wages with them, 5.9 per cent women use their wages for personal use. Among the women beneficiaries, 28.1 per cent use the wages for personal food consumption and 26.5 per cent of them use the wages for livelihood improvement, e.g., accessibility to assets, working capital, savings, and repayment of debts. Evidently it is found that MNREGS has generated a sense of empowerment among the MNREGS women workers to spend their wages for their own livelihood improvement (Table 19.16).

Table 19.16

Use of MNREGS Wages by Women

Description of the Parameters of Empowerment	*MNREGS Women Participant Households*		*MNREGS Women Non-Participant Households*		*Total House-holds*
	House-holds of women who keep the wages with them	*House-holds of women who do not keep the wages with them*	*House-holds of women who keep the wages with them*	*House-holds of women who do not keep the wages with them*	
Number of sample households	200(62.5)	97(30.7)	20(6.3)	3(0.9)	320 (100)
	Use of Wages				
Personal use	19 (5.9)	1 (0.3)	4(1.2)	0	24 (7.5)
Personal use for food	90 (28.1)	46 (14.3)	7(2.1)	2 (0.6)	145 (45.3)
Personal use for human development (education and health)	8 (2.5)	4(1.2)	0	0	12 (3.7)
Personal use for livelihood improvement (accessibility to assets, working capital, savings, and repayment of debts)	85 (26.5)	26(8.1)	9(2.8)	1 (0.3)	121 (37.8)

Note: Figures in parentheses are percentage.

Source: Field survey.

Impact on Labour Relations in the MNREGS Villages

This section deals with the impact of MNREGS upon the village (Gram Panchayat) as a whole where various sections of the society have different level of repercussions of MNREGS for their livelihood. This section describes the responses from the Gram Panchayat schedule responded by Gram Panchayat functionaries at Panchayat level. There are 16 Gram Panchayats from four districts, from where data have been collected. In this study, it is found that in four (25%) Gram Panchayats there is no change evidenced in the availability of casual labour. In rest of the 12 Panchayats (75.0%) where there is a decline witnessed in the availability of casual labour, in nine (56.3%) Gram Panchayats people opine that it is because of MNREGS and in three (18.8%) Gram Panchayats people say that MNREGS is not responsible for this decline. In rural areas different modes of wage payment are in vogue. The casual labourers are paid in daily, weekly, fortnightly, monthly, half yearly, or annual mode. In the case of the 16 panchayats studied, in three (18.8%) panchayats it is found that there is no change in the mode of wage payment for casual labourers. In rest of the 13 panchayats (81.2%)

where shortening of time period of payment is witnessed, seven (43.8%) Gram Panchayats reported that mode of wage payment has been shortened but MNREGS is not responsible for the same. However, in six (37.5%) panchayats people opined that MNREGS is responsible for shortening the time of wage payment because of shortage of casual labourer. Due to shortage of casual labour, the employer has to pay the wages regularly and within a very short period of a day or a week to retain the casual labourers with them. In the rural areas of Madhya Pradesh *hali* (attached labour) system has been prevalent, in which a wage labourer has to be attached to an employer for a year against a fixed amount of cash or kind. This kind of attached labour system provides the employer round the year supply of labour for a fixed amount. This kind of arrangement is not influenced by seasonal scarcity of labour in the peak season. In this study, it is found that in seven (43.8%) panchayats, the availability of attached labour has not been changed over the time. In rest of the nine panchayats (56.2%), where scarcity of attached labour was witnessed, three (18.8%) panchayats opined that the scarcity is not caused by MNREGS and six (37.5%) Gram Panchayats are of the opinion that it is caused by implementation of MNREGS in the respective panchayats.

MNREGS is being implemented in Madhya Pradesh since February 2006. Before the implementation of MNREGS, the average agricultural wage rate was ₹ 50.12 and ₹ 38.78 for male and female labour respectively, for normal agricultural operations. Due to implementation of MNREGS, it is assumed that wage rate has been increased in the villages in the peak agricultural seasons. This section examines whether there is any change witnessed in various seasons and percentage change in the wage rate in the study villages.

Table 19.17

Percentage Change in Agriculture Wage Rate Male Peak Season in Gram Panchayat, 2007–08

Response	*Panchayat (%)*
Low change (1 to 25%)	14 (87.5)
Medium change (26 to 50%)	2 (12.5)
Total	16 (100)

Note: Figures in parentheses are percentage.

Source: Field survey.

It is found, that in the entire 16 (100%) Gram Panchayats male wage labour in peak agricultural season has been increased. It is reported that only in two (12.5%) Gram Panchayats a medium level of change is witnessed. Whereas, a low level of wage rate change is found in 14 (87.5%) Gram Panchayats (Table 19.17).

Table 19.18

Percentage Change in Agricultural Wage Rate Child Peak Season in Gram Panchayat, 2007–08

Response	*Panchayat*
No change	2 (12.5)
Low change (1 to 25%)	6 (37.5)
Medium change (26 to 50%)	7 (43.8)
High change (51% and above)	1 (6.3)
Total	16 (100)

Note: Figures in parentheses are percentage.

Source: Field survey.

In this study, it is found that there is no change in child wage labour in two (12.5%) Gram Panchayats witnessed in peak agricultural season. A low change of wage rate is witnessed in six (37.5%) Gram Panchayats. A medium level of change is reported from seven (43.8%) Gram Panchayats. In one panchayat a high percentage of change in child wage labour was also reported in the peak agricultural season (Table 19.18).

If we analyse the wage pattern change among male, female and children, it is found that wage rate significantly increased among the child labourer and medium increase of wage labour is reported in case of male wage rate. The female wage rate has increased at a very low level in comparison to child and male wage labour. This may be due to the scarcity of male and female wage labour during peak agricultural season; child wage labourers are given more lucrative wages to retain them during the peak season to manage the agricultural work. This is because child labour is prohibited under the MNREGS. Analysis of average wage rate of harvesting season (wheat: February–March) during 2006–07 and 2007–08 shows that average wage rate has increased at the rate of ₹ 3.20 for male and ₹ 3.74 for female in all districts. It is important to note that the real increase in the wage rate is more in case of females than the male, though the actual wage rate is low among the females in the respective districts.

Conclusion

The study found that MNREGS has somehow succeeded in providing employment security to the downtrodden section of the society during scarcity of employment. Though, MNREGS has been giving employment security to the rural poor, its performance is not up to the mark in providing 100 days employment to each needy household. It is found that

MNREGS is able to cater to only one-third of the total unemployment days to the households of the beneficiaries who are available for work. MNREGS has been arresting hunger, dropout of children, indebtedness and out migration of labour from rural areas. Rural wage rate has been increasing and there is a change witnessed in the earlier labour relations prevalent in the villages due to MNREGS. Demand driven approach of the MNREGS is not fully utilised by the rural poor as very few number of beneficiaries are applying for job in a proper channel. Only providing employment to the poor is not enough, MNREGS should be converged with other development programmes to ensure sustainable livelihood of the poor. After four years of implementation, rural people are not fully aware of their rights under MNREGS, therefore adequate measures should be taken to 'conscientise' the people about right to work under MNREGS. MNREGS has ample potentialities to speed up the wheel of rural development and it can be achieved with the active coordination between state, institutions and civil society organisations.

Note

1. BIMARU refers to Bihar, Madhya Pradesh, Rajasthan, Uttar Pradesh, and Odisha.

References

Bhattacharya, B.B. and S. Sakthivel (2004). 'Economic Reforms and Jobless Growth in India', *Working Paper Series No. E/245/2004,* New Delhi: Institute of Economic Growth.

Chadha, G.K. and P.P. Sahu (2002). 'Post-Reform Setbacks in Rural Employment Issues that Need Further Scrutiny', *Economic and Political Weekly*, May 25, pp. 1998–2026.

NSSO (2006). *Employment-Unemployment Situation in India 2004–2005*, Round 61, Report No 515–I and II, Ministry of Statistics and Programme Implementation, Government of India, New Delhi.

NCEUS (2008). *Report on Conditions of Work and Promotion of Livelihoods in the Unorganised Sector (2008)*, National Commission for Enterprises in the Unorganised Sector, Government of India.

Srivastava, R. (2006). 'Trends in Rural Employment in India with Special Reference to Agricultural Employment Issues in India', *Paper presented at the Conference on Labour and Employment Issues in India*, July 27–29, 2006, New Delhi, Organised by Institute for Human Development (IHD) and World Bank.

20

Tribal Livelihood and Poverty Issues

A Study of South-Western Madhya Pradesh

NEERAJ K. JAIN

Madhya Pradesh ranks fourth in India in terms of rural poverty with 37.2 per cent head count ratio (HCR). It comes after Odisha, Bihar and Assam which have a higher rural poverty HCR. The south-western region[1] of this state has been unexpectedly the highest in terms of this HCR which is 68.2 per cent (Sah and Bhatt, 2008). The south-western region has the highest poverty HCR in comparison to other regions of Madhya Pradesh. On the other side, this region scores the second highest rank in terms of the HCR in India after southern Odisha. Barwani and Khargon of this region were the part of erstwhile West Nimar district, which was ranked next only to Jhabua (in Malwa region) in terms of overall development index and poverty incidence among the 45 districts of undivided Madhya Pradesh (Sah and Shah, 2003).

An overwhelmingly demonetised economy, very thinly commercialised and survival oriented subsistence farming are some of the basic characteristics of historically rooted deprived and alienated tribal society in this state. Earlier dynasties, the British rule, opportunistic and exploitative behaviour of the elite society and development induced displacement played important role in depriving and marginalising the tribal society. Moreover, population pressure-induced land fragmentation and resource depletion further intensified this deprivation. Given the above livelihood struggle, their inaccessibility to education, health and modern agriculture and markets have also created obstacles for the tribals in coming out from poverty trap. Poverty dynamics in rural India, especially across various socio-economic groups, is of varying nature. Tribal society, among these groups, has been identified as the most distinctive population segment, as this group is found to be the most vulnerable in terms of its percentage in poor with their high concentration in most economically deprived section, i.e., casual labour. The nature of poverty and its issues in tribal society are concerned with their special kind of livelihood struggles.[2] Casual agricultural labour and cultivators, possessing poor resource base and indulging in poor land and occupational rigidities are more likely to fall into poverty trap (Mehta and Shah, 2003; Radhakrishnan et al., 2003; Bhalla, 2003). Crop failure and shock like situations force them for seasonal migration. Though, this migration makes people capable to cope with current crises, it deprives them from social capital and basic civic amenities made available to them at native place. They also suffer from lack of voice in newly formed Panchayati Raj Institutions (PRIs) as active members of Gram Sabha. In this way, multiple deprivations cause them to remain as marginalised section of society.

Hulme, Moore and Shephered (2001) emphasised on five freedoms conceptualised by Amartya Sen in 1995 for making appropriate policy analytical approach, i.e., deepening the understanding of who is 'chronically poor' and why this happens. Sen (1999) in this connection further argued that development is about the pursuit of five freedoms – political freedom, economic freedom, social opportunity, transparency guarantee, and productive security. These freedoms make one's livelihood sustainable. Multiple deprivations of the poor or vulnerable groups make them incapable in optimising their livelihood. The most recent dimension in poverty debate is the transfer of poverty from generation to generation or the prolonged poverty of a household. More clearly, poverty now is viewed as multidimensional non-freedom that pushes the affected into a vicious circle of poverty (Sah, 2003; Sah and Bhatt, 2008; Hulme, Moore and Shephered, 2001). A complex relationship, however, exists among capabilities, assets, activities/entitlements and livelihood outcomes (Claynton, Dent and Dubois, 2002; Sen, 1995). Sah (2004) argues that the economy performs within the impersonal laws of markets. These economic institutions govern the production and distribution of goods and services. Although in theory, the markets are equal opportunity providers, in practice they also marginalise. Markets provide signals to producers to allocate resources in production processes. The state control on either price or technology or distribution, network results in distorting the price signals. Consequently, either the producer misjudges the size of the market or the market would not be cleared within the price-distorted environment.

The increasing role of public interventions has also started a new debate between issues of income poverty and human poverty.[3] The nutritional adequacy is implicitly captured into income poverty as it measured on the basis of per capita Monthly Consumption Expenditure (MCE) that includes food consumption to ensure minimum required calorie intake of 2,100 in urban area and 2,400 in rural area. But, it is evident by NSSO figures and through studies made by various researchers[4] that the decline in income poverty does not get reflected in nutritional adequacy and reduction in hunger. This paper is also investigating this controversy whether income poverty is sufficient to address human poverty or not?

Data and Methods

The analysis has used primary set of data collected from 149 households from six villages, of which, two belong to each of the three blocks – Barwani (administrative centre), Sendhwa (commercial centre) and Pati (remote block) of Barwani district. The households are categorised as severe poor, moderate poor and non-poor. On the basis of official norms[5] of monthly per capita expenditure (at market prices) of ₹ 245 for identifying households below poverty line, the equivalent Annual Per Capita Expenditure (APCE) of ₹ 2,950 is used. The households having less or equal to ₹ 2,000 (nearly two-third of threshold) are considered as severe poor households with APCE from ₹ 2,001 to ₹ 2,950 are taken as moderate poor; and households with APCE more than ₹ 2,950 are assumed to be non-poor. APCE has been estimated by aggregating food and non-food expenditure for one complete year. Food expenditure has been estimated for average or normal month of the year; however, non-food expenditure has been estimated for the whole year. APCE and its pattern at disaggregate levels have also been investigated to assess their livelihood pattern. For the investigation of variations within or between the distinguishing groups, F-ratio test through one way ANOVA has been used. Other socio-economic indicators, e.g., calorie intake, sickness, access to schools, etc., have been studied across both – various economic or poverty groups. Occupational pattern and rigidities in employment, and marketing and finance rigidities have also been identified in relation to poverty.

Profile of Sample Villages

The six villages exhibit significant differences in terms of demographic pattern, social composition, civic and agricultural amenities. Two villages – Balkuan and Balwari – have significantly greater proportion of non-tribal population, while other four villages possess negligible non-tribal population.

Non-tribal population segment in Balkun and Balwari is located in a well-organised place and around market place. Tribal population, irrespective of villages, is widely spread over distantly located hamlets called falias, many of which have very poor access to basic civic amenities

Table 20.1

Socio-economic Profile of the Sample Villages and Access to Market and Amenities

Particulars	*Village*					
	Balkuan	*Dhamnai*	*Osada*	*Palwat*	*Ramkola*	*Balbari*
Household	601	205	351	247	231	1260
Population	3712	1412	2787	1826	1673	6761
Sex ratio	998	929	919	947	1040	930
ST population	2106	1367	2317	1823	1652	1765
SC population	397	45	187	0	6	216
Literacy	56% 71.1%(M) 42.8%(F)	32.7% 46.7%(M) 16.9%(F)	11.4% 15.8%(M) 06.7%(F)	12.8% 15.9%(M) 9.5%(F)	16.2% 23.3%(M) 09.2%(F)	56.7% 67.5%(M) 45.2%(F)
Work participation rate	51.1% (main) 00.2% (marginal)	55.6% (main) 19.1% (marginal)	53.4% (main) 22.7% (marginal)	47.4% (main) 23.3% (marginal)	47.7% (main) 19.6% (marginal)	36.1% (main) 19.9% (marginal)
Cultivator	68.5%	62.2%	48.2%	81.6%	89.2%	27.3%
Agri. labour	27.1%	36.4%	48.2%	16.5%	9.1%	40.5%
Industries	0.5%	0.1%	0.3%	1.2%	0%	1.6%
Other	4.0%	1.3%	3.3%	0.7%	2.7%	30.6%
Health care	1.01–sub PHC 2. 4–5 Pvt doctor	Hospital at Balwari (10 km)	PHC at Pati (6 km)	PHC at Pat (5 km) PHC Gandhawal (3 km)	Sub PHC Charharia (8 km) Phanora (6 km)	01–PHC 09–Pvt. Doctors
PDS	FPS in village itself	Not in village	Not in village	Not in village	Not in village	FPS
Drinking water	Nal Jal yoyna, wells Well and Hand Pumps in Falias	Well Hand Pumps	Wells and major by Hand pumps	Wells and major by Hand pumps	Wells and major by Hand pumps	Tank-90,00 0 Lt. Nal No. – 653 Hand Pumps and Wells
Irrigation	Tubewell- 40–50, Well- 100–200	Tubewell- 4–5, Well- 40–50	Tubewell- 01, Well- 10–12	Tubewell- None, Well- 10–12	Gohi River, Well- 50–60 Tubewell- 15	Tubewell- 25–30, Well- 250
Roads	Pakki- Main village Kachchi-Fal ias	Kachchi	No	No	Kachchi	Pakki – Main village Kachchi- Falias
Near market	Village itself	Barwani (10 km)	Pati (6 km)	Pati (5km) Gandhawal (3 km)	Charharia (8 km) Phanora (6 km)	Village itself

Source: http://www.censusindia.net and field visit observations.

and market. Irrigation and technology diffusion in agricultural is also differing across the villages. Balwari and Ramkula of the Sendhwa block are found with strong agricultural base, on account of which, migration is relatively less in these villages even after greater economic opportunities in Sendhwa and its surrounding places in cotton ginning mills. In Ramkula, Gohi river is the main source of irrigation. While Balkuan and Balwari are mainly irrigated by tubewells. Although, most of these tubewells are owned by big farmers, it has created an opportunity for villagers for agricultural labour. In Dhamnai, Osada and Palwat, the irrigation is mainly done by traditional wells. However only in Dhamnai where digging the tubewells is prohibited, one can find water even in summer months. One of the striking features of the Palwat and Osada of the Pati block are their most sparsely inhabitant households across distantly located falias with hilly and undulating farming land. Moreover, this area is the most affected area with drought. Though the Gohi river is passing nearby these two villages, its benefits are limited to a few households. Balwari is found with urbanising trend, as the access to civic amenities is the best among all sample villages and it has relatively more developed market.

Discussion reveals the fact that Sendhwa can be considered as most developed block among the three. The people of the Sendhwa block have easy access to employment in agriculture and cotton ginning factories, running in or around the block. Subsequently, from employment and commercial points of view, Barwani is considered to be a less developed block. Pati is considered as backward block in the same sense.

About 38 per cent of total sample households have been identified as economically poor in terms of APCE. The estimate is not significantly different from state average. The poverty incidence in same region is however, much lower than that of the poverty estimated by Sah and Shah (2003).[6]

Poverty incidence is varying significantly across villages and blocks, categorised on the basis of degree of backwardness, as most backward block, is found with almost half of households falling under poor category. Osada village, which is relatively more backward in terms of socio-economic profile discussed in section one, is found to be the most vulnerable in terms of poverty incidence. About 62 per cent of households are found poor with most of them as very poor in Osada. Palwat in the same block ranks next to it. Barwani and Sendhwa blocks are found to have a relatively low poverty incidence. Only 35 and 25 per cent of sample households respectively are found to be poor in Barwani and Sendhwa blocks respectively. The variations in poverty across blocks are indicating direct relationship between poverty incidence and backwardness. Highly backward block is more likely to have more poor households.

Table 20.2

Poverty Profile of Sample Households across Development Blocks

Poverty group	*Block**			*Total*
	Pati	*Barwani*	*Sendhwa*	
Very poor	12 (24)	10 (20)	4 (9)	26 (17)
Moderate poor	15 (29)	8 (15)	8 (17)	31 (21)
Non-poor	24 (47)	33 (65)	35 (74)	92 (62)
Total	51	51	47	149

* associations with poverty are significant at 5 per cent level of significance.

Note: Figures in parentheses are percentage.

Source: Field survey.

Consumption Expenditure and Pattern

The sample average of APCE of sample households across blocks is ₹ 4,231.90. This seems to be relatively higher when compared with other estimates[7] for tribal people. The reference year witnessed relatively good rainfall in comparison to previous consecutive four years.[8] A relatively good agriculture of 2004–05 may have resulted in low incidence of economic poverty of 38 per cent. In order to investigate economic deprivation, and factors other then good rainfall or climate, a further introspection of APCE is needed.

Table 20.3

Annual per capita Consumption Expenditure (APCE) and Percentage Share of Food Consumption across Development Blocks

Poverty group	*Head*	*Development block*			
		Pati	*Barwani*	*Sendhwa*	*Total****
Severely poor	APCE	1895	1717	1864	1822
	Food item per cent*	(72)	(65)	(50)	(66)
Moderate poor	APCE	2548	2569	2568	2558
	Food item per cent	(59)	(60)	(55)	(58)
Non-poor	APCE	5729	5388	5401	5477
	Food item per cent	(49)	(43)	(46)	(46)
Total	APCE	3882	4226	4618	4232
	Food item per cent**	(58)	(50)	(47)	(52)

*variations are significant across blocks at 5 per cent level of significance.
**variations are significant across blocks at 1 per cent level of significance.
***share of food and non-food expenditure is significant for all poverty groups.

Note: Figures in parentheses are percentage.

Source: Field survey.

Although, APCE across blocks does not vary significantly, share of food expenditure in APCE is varying significantly across blocks particularly for severely poor category. Severely poor households of most backward block, Pati, are found with the highest share of food expenditure in APCE. They spend about 72 per cent of their APCE on food consumption, while this per cent is 65 and 50 for Barwani and Sendhwa respectively. It reveals that the propensity to consume is determined by the combination of poverty intensity and backwardness. The percentage share of food and non-food expenditure in APCE for sample households is 52 and 48 per cent respectively. But, the share of food expenditure in APCE is significantly low for non-poor irrespective blocks. Among non-poor 54 per cent of APCE is spent on non-food items. Among poor, specially severely poor, the share of APCE in non-food items is significantly less.

To understand, why the households having high share of food expenditure, have been called vulnerable, Table 20.4 discusses the non-food expenditure pattern of the households.

Table 20.4

ANOVA results for APCE distribution across Groups divided on the Basis of Poverty, GCA and Development Blocks

Non-food expenditure head	*Expenditure as Average of APCE*	*Poverty*		*Block*		*Remark*
		F-value	*P-value*	*F-value*	*P-value*	
Cloth	13	NS		NS		
Cosmetics	3	NS		4.27	0.01	Lowest in Pati
Travelling	5.5	2.63	0.07	NS		Lowest among severely poor
Education	1.5	NS	NS			
Social affairs	8.3	10.6	0	5.68	0.01	Lowest in Pati and highest in Sendhwa and non-poor
Alcoholic Consumption	4.7	9.16	0	NS		Very high among non-poor
Medical	**9.8**	4.03	0.02	NS		Lowest in severely poor and highest in non-poor
Fuel	2.4	NS		3.08	0.05	Lowest in Pati

NS = Not significant.

Source: Field survey.

The major heads on which larger share of APCE is spent are clothing, travelling, social affairs, alcohol consumption, and medical facilities, i.e., health. Almost 41.3 per cent of APCE is spent on these items. Excluding clothing heads from these major head of non-food items, the share of APCE spent on social affairs, consumption of alcohol, health and travelling is significantly varying across poverty groups. It is only social affair head, the share of which is varying significantly across blocks. The households of Sendhwa are found to be spending the largest share of APCE on social affairs. All kinds of major expenditures, varying across poverty profile, are significantly high among non-poor. The consumption of alcohol and expenditure on social affairs are the social compulsions in tribal community for their social status and belongingness on the one hand, while health and travelling expenditure are the basic civic needs on the other. However, it is only non-poor, who are able to spend substantive amount of money on these heads - social affairs, alcohol consumption and health.

The expenditure on basic civic amenities - health and travelling - is significantly low among severely poor. This indicates that severely poor can make only for their survival needs such as food, shelter and cloth. The severely poor are deprived not only from basic civic needs but also from social belongingness as they are not able to meet the needs of social affairs and alcohol consumption.

Social Vulnerability

Expenditure and its pattern alone cannot be considered a perfect measure of quality of life. Equally important is the calorie intake and access to health and education services. These accesses also determine the economic and social deprivation. The Planning Commission of India, in its Eleventh Five Year Plan document states that the country's economic status is directly dependent on the health of its population that contributes largely to its productivity. If malnutrition is not addressed, the country would suffer predominantly due to physical and mental disorders, learning impairment among children and loss in productivity among others.

Despite the emphasis given on the need of nutritional adequacy and inclusion of nutritional norms in estimating poverty, the poverty estimates of Planning Commission, itself do not incorporate nutrition. Further, the Tendulkar Committee (2009), formed for reviewing various poverty issues, suggested that 'given the poor correlation between calorie consumption levels and nutritional outcomes, the calorie norms for estimating the poverty should be abandoned'. It recommended new method[9] that involves the consideration of the present all-India urban poverty line as the basis for every other poverty line. However, it added that with the present all-India urban poverty line as the basis, the identification of its parity levels should be made separately at the state level for rural and urban areas. It postulated that new poverty line will meet not only food expenditure requirement but also those of important basic needs like education and health.

The increasing importance of poverty issues in state policy interventions need a very careful attention on current developments of poverty related issues. Our analysis shows not only the significant correlation between Daily per Capita Calorie Intake (DPCCI) and APCE, but also indicates that non-poor may also be nutritionally deficient. The correlation coefficient DPCCI and APCE is '0.6' at 1 per cent level of significance.

Table 20.5

DPCCI across Blocks and Poverty Groups

Block/GCA	*Calorie Consumption per Person per Day*			
	Poverty Profile			
	Very poor	*Moderate poor*	*Non-poor*	*Total*
Pati	1773.70	1640.23	2574.38	2118.00
Barwani	1371.53	1692.54	2373.86	2058.06
Sendhwa	1438.24	1686.66	2334.39	2109.03
Total	1559.16	1614.13	2412.85	2094.90

Source: Field survey.

The DPCCI is 2,094 among total sample households (Table 20.5). The average DPCCI is much below then the standard set for rural area, which is 2,400 DPCCI. The DPCCI is 1,559 among very poor and 2,413 among non-poor. Although, average DPCCI is much below than the sample average of 2097 for poor, for non-poor it is only a little more than 2,400, which is calorie-intake line to define nutritionally deficient people of rural India. The calorie-intake, however, is also varying significantly across poverty profile irrespective of development block.

Table 20.6

Nutritional Deficiency across Poverty Profile (No. of Households)

Poverty profile	*DPCCI category*		
	Less then 2400	*More or equal to2400*	*Total*
Severely poor	23 (92)	2 (8)	25(100)
Moderate poor	30 (97)	1 (3)	31 (100)
Non-poor	43 (48)	46 (52)	89 (100)
Total	96 (66)	49 (34)	145 (100)

Note: Figures in parentheses shows percentage of total households in respective category.

Source: Field survey.

The incidence of nutritional deficiency, as per prevailing norms, is the highest among very poor and moderate poor. About 95 per cent of the economically poor sample households are nutritionally deficient, while about half of non-poor are also nutritionally deficient. Only 34 per cent of total sample households are found having DPCCI more than 2,400. While, the poor share only 38 per cent in sample households on the basis of APCE,

66 per cent of sample households are falling under poor calorie intake or nutritional deficiency (Table 20.6). If we compare these findings with the calorie norms of 1,800 calories per capita per day for India as suggested[10] by the Food and Agriculture Organisation (FAO), then only 37 per cent of the sample households are found to be nutritionally deficient with only 18 per cent of poor and about two-third of poor (Table 20.7).

Table 20.7

Nutritional Deficiency (FAO norms) across Poverty Profile (No. of Households)

Poverty profile	*DPCCI category*		
	Less then 1800	*More or equal to1800*	*Total*
Severely poor	16 (64)	9 (36)	25 (100)
Moderate poor	22 (70)	9 (30)	31 (100)
Non-poor	16 (18)	73 (82)	89 (100)
Total	54 (37)	91 (63)	145 (100)

Note: Figures in parentheses shows percentage of total households in respective category.

Source: Field survey.

It is evident that although the APCE and DPCCI have positive and significant correlation, yet the nutritional norms is not a true indicator for poverty estimation. The reason lies in the fact that food consumption that meets calorie needs is not determined merely by food expenditure; rather, it depends also on individual's physical requirement and habits. Our analysis also shows that the DPCCI of about half of non-poor households is less than 2,400 calories. This is 18 per cent for less than 1800 calories. However, this analysis does not indicate that expenditure based poverty estimation should not incorporate the nutritional norms. The analysis intends to put further a serious concern towards meeting minimum energy needs as these are not met by not only poor but also by non-poor to some extent. The distribution of respondent households shows that both poor and non-poor are equally prone to fall sick and suffer from various diseases (Table 20.8).

Table 20.8

Percentage Households under Various Kinds of Sickness across Poverty Profile

Poverty profile	*Percentage Households*			*Total number of respondents*
	Normal	*Severe*	*Prolonged*	
Very poor	24	64	12	23
Moderate poor	16	58	26	30
Non-poor	22	62	16	43

Source: Field survey.

Despite the fact that the incidence of nutritional deficiency is significantly higher among non-poor, the spread of sickness – categorised as normal, severe, and prolonged – is not varying significantly across poverty profile. Incidence of severe sickness is the highest among the sample households irrespective of their poverty profile. Almost 62 per cent of households are found to be suffering from severe illness.

The most striking feature of tribal community is their inability to access the health care services. Most of them have never gone to Primary Health Care Centres (PHCs). Many of the poor, suffering from any type of health problem have never gone to any doctor or even to private health clinics. It is only Balkuan village of Barwani block where some people are receiving the private doctor services. Despite the better civic amenities in Balwari, the sample households do not avail services of any private doctor or PHC. It is observed in Balwari that non-scheduled tribes or elite class households residing in or around market or civilised street normally go to PHC. But local residents have reported about usual shutting down of PHC because of the irregularity and drinking habits of '*Swasthya Karmies*'. In Balwari, the most common diseases are Lucaria, popularly known as '*Yoni-Resab or Safed Pani*' and appendices that many time leads to premature death in absence of proper treatment. At private clinics, the treatment is very costly for these diseases.

Both literacy and education seeking behaviour are found least among poor than among non-poor. Across blocks, the literacy and education seeking behaviour is found least in Pati. It is observed that differentials in education seeking behaviour across poverty profile are rooted in the backwardness of area.

Table 20.9

Number of Households with Not-going School-age Children

Block	*Percentage households (of total valid cases)*				*Valid cases (No.)*
	Very poor	*Moderate poor*	*Non poor*	*Total*	
Pati	71	71	21	58	38
Barwani	88	17	54	62	34
Sendhwa	50	57	48	51	37
Total	67	56	54	57	109
Cases (No.)	21	27	61	109	

Source: Field survey.

This is evident from the fact that the percentage of households with children attending school does not vary across poverty profile in most developed block Sendhwa whereas it is the highest among very poor of Pati and Barwani blocks (Table 20.9).

Livelihood Struggle

Income deprivation causes inadequate consumption of food and other necessary consumables on the one hand and deprivation in terms of basic civic amenities – education, health, and transportation on the other. Both these failures cause further marginalisation of tribals in terms of low productivity, indebtness and low credit worthiness. In turn, the household is caught under vicious circle of poverty popularly known as chronic poverty (Sah and Shah, 2003).

It is observed that about 72 per cent of sample households selected mix strategies of occupations (Table 20.10). The most developed block, Sendhwa is found with highest per cent of households solely dependent on single occupation in comparison to other blocks. Cultivators are dominant among these occupants in Sendhwa with 24 per cent. About 60 per cent households of total sample are engaged in local labour (either among single or mix occupational groups).

Table 20.10

Per Capita Income (₹) of Households belonging to Various Occupations across Poverty Profile and Block

Occupational Category		*Expenditure based poor*			*Block*			*Total*
		Severely poor	*Moderate poor*	*Non poor*	*Pati*	*Barwani*	*Sendhwa*	
Single Occupation	Labour	1914 (23)	2917 (28)	4776 (9)	3874 (10)	2106 (17)	4377 (19)	3302 (15)
	Migration	—	863 (3)	2806 (2)	2158 (6)	—	—	2158 (2)
	Land	—	4162 (7)	9228 (13)	1825 (6)	—	10325 (24)	8504 (9)
	Other	—	—	3333 (2)	—	1667 (2)	5000 (2)	3333 (1)
	Total	1914 (23)	2953 (38)	6717 (26)	2745 (22)	2066 (19)	7522 (45)	4956 (28)
Mix Occupation[11]	LL	2407 (42)	3534 (26)	3669 (33)	2803 (18)	3416 (41)	3572 (40)	3364 (33)
	LdM	2935 (23)	1623 (10)	4159 (13)	3315 (33)	—	4008 (9)	3447 (14)
	LbM	5833 (4)	2495 (7)	3930 (7)	3087 (8)	4742 (10)	—	3823 (6)
	All	1394 (4)	—	6437 (7)	1620 (4)	8136 (8)	4233 (2)	5716 (5)
	Other mix	2129 (4)	2965 (19)	6586 (15)	3886 (16)	6535 (21)	4575 (4)	5339 (14)
	Total	2672 (77)	2943 (62)	4623 (74)	3204 (78)	4878 (81)	3742 (55)	3960 (72)
Grand Total		2497 (100)	2947 (100)	5170 (100)	3114 (100)	4272 (100)	5431 (100)	4241 (100)

LL: Local Lobour, LdM: Land Practice and Migration, LbM: Labour and Migration.

Note: Figures in parentheses show the percentage of total households of respective category and cccupation.

Source: Field survey.

Table 20.10 shows the average per capita income (PCI) of the households belonging to various occupations across poverty groups and blocks. PCI is significantly low among severely poor and households of Pati, which is the most backward block among the three. The average PCI for severely poor, moderate poor and non-poor is ₹ 2,497, ₹ 2,947 and ₹ 5,170 respectively. It is ₹ 3,114, ₹ 4,272 and ₹ 5,431 in Pati, Bawani and Sendhwa respectively. The above compiled facts reveal that single occupant non-poor are able to earn excessively high from all types of occupations. In total, their PCI is ₹ 6,717 which is more than three times as that of severely poor and two times as that of moderate poor. The earnings of single occupant poor and those belonging to Pati and Barwani are less than overall average PCI. For non-poor and households of Sendhwa, the PCI of single occupants is more than overall average. Most of the households of Pati and Barwani are characterised not only as mix occupants but also as those with PCI higher than that of their overall average.

Both self-employed and casual labour in agricultural activities are found to be least income generating occupational groups, especially among severely poor. 65 per cent of severely poor, who belong to either or both of these two occupational groups, earn the least. Migration, in such circumstances, becomes an inevitable livelihood option for these people.

The above discussion revealed that income capabilities of the sample households are the determinants of their occupational structure. Because of the low capabilities of earning, the poor and the households of the backward and less developed blocks have to opt for a mix strategy. Landlessness, rainfed agriculture, low access to the local labour are some of the reasons,[12] why these people are doing so; poverty drives people to diversify their livelihood strategies.

Poverty Correlates

On the basis of above discussion on poverty associations and to explore the nature and causes of poverty in tribal society, the correlates have been determined (Table 20.11). In order to determine the poverty correlates across poverty profile, we have categorised sample households in poor and non-poor only.[13] The table is grouped, for the various correlates, into four categories – first, assets and capabilities; second, outcomes in terms of income and agricultural output; third, coping mechanism; and fourth, social investments and government supports. Table 20.11 shows the significant association of poverty with only gross cropped area (GCA) and degree of backwardness of block among 'assets and capabilities' category.

Table 20.11

One-way ANOVA and χ^2 results for Different Socio-economic Indicators across Poverty Profile of the Households

Process	*Indicator*	*Average*	*Test*	*Minimum Significance level (P-value)*	*Remark*
Assets and Capabilities	Total present asset (₹)	10097	ANOVA	NS	
	Asset[14] change (increase/decrease)	——	χ^2	NS	
	Landholding (Acre)	2.5	χ^2	NS	
	GCA (Acre)	3.16	ANOVA	0.05	'NP' have 1.8 times of the poor
	Irrigation *(% for valid cases, i.e., only for cultivators)*	37.34	ANOVA	NS	
	Backwardness	——	χ^2	0.05	Households of backward block are more prone to be poor
Outcomes	Calorie intake (DPCCI)	2094	ANOVA	0.00	'NP' is 1.5 times of 'P'
	Total production (₹)	19232	ANOVA	NS	
	Yield (₹)	2883	ANOVA	0.02	'NP' is 1.7 times of 'P'
	Total income (₹)	29626	ANOVA	0.10	'NP' is 1.7 times of 'P'
	Per capita income (₹)	4240	ANOVA	0.00	'NP' is 1.9times of 'P'
	Marketable surplus (₹)	46.4	ANOVA	0.00	'NP' is 1.7 times of 'P'
Coping Mechanism	Migration (No. of households)	——	χ^2	NS	
	Migration share in income *(% for only for migrants)*	0.61	ANOVA	0.10	'P' is 1.3 times of 'NP'
	Migration days per households *(% for only for migrants)*	413	ANOVA	NS	
	Local labour (No. of households)	——	χ^2	NS	
	Local labour share in income *(% only for labourers)*	0.67	ANOVA	0.05	'P' is 1.2 times of 'NP'

Cont'd...

...Cont'd

	Local labour days per households *(% only for labourers)*	484	ANOVA	NS	
	Loan last year's total expenses (₹)	6417	ANOVA	0.02	'NP' is 1.8 times of 'P'
	Long-term debt (₹)	178848	ANOVA	0.02	'NP' is 1.9 times of 'P'
	Self-management of last year's expenses (%)	33.49	ANOVA	0.01	'NP' is 2 times of 'P'
	Credit management of last year's expenses (%)	60.25	ANOVA	0.08	'P' is 1.25 times of NP'
Social Investments and Supports	Expenditure in long sik (₹)	4364	ANOVA	0.00	'NP' is 3.5 times of 'P'
	Child birth expense (₹)	1813	ANOVA	0.00	'NP' is 2.5 times of 'P'
	Health expense (₹)	8995	ANOVA	0.01	'NP' is 2.7 times of 'P'
	Death expense (₹)	2066	ANOVA	NS	
	Literacy	35.5	ANOVA	NS	
	Panchayat wage benefits (₹)	180	ANOVA	0.07	'NP' is 3.3 times of 'P'
	PDS	—	χ^2	NS	

Note: 'P' stands for poor; and 'NP' stands for non-poor.

Source: Field survey.

Total present asset and landholding size is not found significantly associated with poverty on the one hand, the GCA is significantly high among non-poor. Among 'income' category, agricultural yield, per capita income, the marketable surplus and total income are significantly higher among non-poor than that of poor.

Among the indicators of 'coping mechanism', distress situations, e.g., the long-term debt, loan for routine expense, percentage of last year's expenses, managed through credit resources, are significantly higher among poor than that of non-poor. While the migration is not varying significantly, the share of migration in income is significantly higher among poor than that of non-poor. Expenditures in current year's prolonged sickness are significantly higher among non-poor than that of poor, the major expenses on death and health in last 10 years are also significantly higher among non-poor than that of poor. Under coping mechanism categories, the shares[15] of labour and migration in total income are significantly higher among poor than that of non-poor. As far as the social and state supports are concerned, only wage benefit through panchayats are found significantly varying across poverty groups. It is found that the non-poor are getting wages from panchayats more than three times as compared to poor.

Conclusion

Poverty issues in south-western tribal Madhya Pradesh can be discussed in two perspectives. Firstly, the people's deprivation in terms of low access to nutrition and basic civic amenities including education and health is very high among poor. Secondly, the lack of choice among poor for the livelihood options in terms of occupational opportunities, credit worthiness, compulsory migration, low productive employment, etc. Incidence of poverty is low among those tribal households who have higher agricultural productivity and high double cropped area. But, frequent crop failure and agricultural slack periods have resulted in aggravating poverty. Migration, though, is not varying significantly across poverty profile;[16] the households of Pati block (most backward) have shown significantly high dependency on migration income. Significant association of poverty with gross cropped area (GCA) and backwardness causes low access of poor to income generating strategies. Interestingly, Pati block is found with significantly low agricultural productivity and higher share of kharif cropped area in gross cropped area (GCA). Irrigation is significantly low in backward block, i.e., Pati. This shows that while irrigation is not significantly varying across poverty profile, it is major determinant of poor agricultural performance. While, the migrating households are significantly more in Pati and even non-poor migrate from the block, only non-poor are migrating in other blocks, Barwani and Sendhwa. Moreover, the share of migration income is about three-fourth of their total income in Pati, while it is only one-third and one-fourth in Barwani and Sendhwa respectively. The poor agricultural performance and high dependency on migration indicates that poor households located in backward region opt for seasonal migration as a compulsory livelihood strategy. In other words, it can be argued that migration is a common feature of those households who face economic poverty.

Beside their economic marginalisation, the tribal poor also pass through social deprivation. The nutritional deficiency is high and access to health care services is low among poor households. It would be important to note for the policy implications, that nutritional deficiency in sample is about 68 per cent against economic poverty incidence of 38 per cent. This means that poverty when measured on nutritional standard is twice of that measured on expenditure standard. The marginalisation process, which makes poor people socially deprived, can also be understood by the expenditure pattern; non-poor are spending significantly more of the share of APCE on non-food items, social affairs, travelling expenses, alcohol consumption and medical expenses. The non-food heads are social compulsion in a tribal society. Among social sector investment, access of poor to education and health is significantly less, as most of them are not sending their school age children to school.

Policy Implications

Despite the distinguishing poverty alleviation programmes, the state could not succeed in converting low paid rural livelihood options into productive employment. The situation is worst in case of poor and backward areas. Any effort, towards future strategy in view of making people's livelihood sustainable would be meaningless without looking into the multidimensional aspects of poverty. The policy implications in the light of above conclusions can be identified in the following two forms: first, for improving income and employment opportunities and second, providing nutritional security to poor.

Strategic Planning for Income and Employment Opportunities

Low productive employment and underemployment in remote rural areas is the main determinant of poverty. Livelihood in these areas is totally agriculture based. Agriculture is the only major activity in tribal area that not only creates employment for cultivators but also for non-cultivating households in terms of agricultural labour. Irrigation and lack of technology adoption is the main problem especially among poor and households located in remote tribal areas, categorised as backward area. Irrigation is crucial for agricultural productivity in the remote tribal areas. This would not only bring agricultural prosperity but also will check the seasonal migration. Therefore, all those activities that conserve water would be the first priority for removing poverty from the tribal areas. Agricultural credit through cooperatives for agricultural inputs and digging wells may be one of the important ways of making agriculture self-supporting. Guidance for the use of fertiliser, pesticides, harvesting techniques should also be focused upon. Migration is found to be major livelihood activity of backward area on account of indifferent agricultural production and frequent crop failures. The strategic plan for such complex livelihood problems in tribal society is a prime concern in order to sustain employment generation within the village. At the village level, the community, through participatory approach or panchayat, can maintain various reserves[17] – seed, water, food grain, etc. (Swaminathan, 2003). This will not only improve farm income and labouring opportunities in the villages but also reduce the out-migration and make rural livelihood sustainable.

It is also observed and understood in the field visits and through various discussions held with experts and voluntary organisations that the objective of bringing decision making nearer to people cannot be achieved without people's participation in newly formed PRIs. Capacity building programmes for making common rural people aware and vigilant must be initiated and encouraged through distinguishing state agencies and NGOs and voluntary organisations.

Nutritional Security

The decline in poverty HCR during 1990s, i.e., in neo-liberal period of the Indian economy had provided a further opportunity to many of the critiques of the income poverty measurement for using it in policy interventions. They highlight the increasing agrarian distress, depression and farmers' suicides in the same period that witnessed lower agricultural growth (particularly food grain production). Overemphasis on feed-grain[18] and export oriented production in comparison to direct food grain, post reform period had created acute shortage of food grains on the one hand; had also opened new areas of spending on non-food items – transport, cosmetics, health services, etc. – on the other. Utsa Patnaik, categorically, blamed on cut in state's rural development spending in the presence of fast economic growth, for increase food grain prices and increase in income disparities, which attributes to unemployment rise and cut in food consumption among low income groups. This in turn, affects calorie intake adversely that is mirrored in successive surveys of the National Nutrition Monitoring Bureau (NNMB). The NNMB has consistently confirmed in successive surveys that the main bottleneck in the dietaries of even the poorest Indians is energy and not protein as was hitherto believed ... the data also indicates that the measurement of consumption of cereals can be used as a proxy for total energy intake. This observation is of considerable significance as it helps to determine rapid, though approximate, estimates of energy intake at the household level (National Nutrition Monitoring Bureau, 1997).

In present study also, it is important to notice that incidence of nutritional deficiency in sample is about 68 per cent against economic poverty incidence of 38 per cent. This implies that a sizeable section of non-poor is also deficient nutritionally. It also means that conspicuous consumption on non-food items, such as social affairs, alcohol consumption, etc., places these non-poor above poverty line. But, their nutritional intake is low to such an extent that they suffer nutritional insufficiency. The calorie intake during 1990–98 has been decreased by 1.53 per cent, while an increase of 0.23 per cent had been observed during 1970–1990 (Ravi, 2000). The trend during 1970–98 is disturbing in the sense that emphasis on mere increasing the access of people to health and education facilities will not be sufficient in policy interventions based on income poverty. The strategic need is to see the nutritional deficiency either as a component of the poverty estimation or as an additional basis for policy interventions. The study strongly recommends that viewing poverty only on the basis of consumption norms is not sufficient for policy interventions. Equally important is to estimate and examine the nutritional poverty. Because the high incidence of nutritional deficiency in comparison to expenditure based poverty, misguides and underestimates the plights of marginalised sections. Without addressing human poverty that is linked with agricultural growth, income disparities and irrational reform oriented shift of land resources, the Millennium Development Goal of halving the poverty in real sense will not be met in the Indian context.

Notes

1. The south-western region of Madhya Pradesh consists of five districts, viz., Barwani, Khargon, Khandwa, Betul and Hoshangabad.
2. Poverty in remote rural areas is closely associated with size and quality of land but agriculture being only a part of the livelihood during a shock.
3. Human poverty captures the nutritional adequacy and hunger, as discussed by Jayati Ghosh (2010).
4. For example: G.M. Antony and A. Laximaiah (2008), Banerjee(2008) and U. Patnaik (2008) through data of 55th and 61st round of NSSO.
5. As used by Sah (2003).
6. The main reason for this difference was poor agriculture and bad monsoon in 2002, when this researcher has estimated the poverty incidence in tribal belt of Barwani district (see for detail, Sah and Shah 2003).
7. Estimates made by Sah and Shah (2003).
8. As per the discussion held with villagers during survey.
9. From comments by R. Ramakumar, http://www.macroscan.org/cur/dec09/print/prnt231209Tendulkar_ report.htm.
10. Quoted by R. Ramakumar in his comment on 'The Tendulkar Report: A Small Step Forward' (2009), http://www.pragoti.org/node/3727.
11. 'LL' stands for Local Labour; 'LdM' stands for Land and Migration; 'LbM' stands for Labour and Migration; and All for Land, Labour and Migration.
12. See variables GCA and backwardness under assets and capabilities category of the poverty correlates in Table 20.9. Also see Migration and Local labour share in income under coping mechanism category of the poverty correlates in Table 20.9.

13. However, to discuss poverty association in detail, the earlier sections analysed the nature and associates of poverty by categorising them into three groups -severe poor, moderate poor and non-poor.
14. The asset value is calculated on the basis of present market prices of various assets.
15. The share of labour and migration in total income among poor are respectively 1.2 and 1.3 times of non-poor.
16. Though half of poor in comparison to one-third of non-poor are migrating the other migration indicator like migration intensity, migration income, female share in migration are not varying significantly across poverty group.
17. Tribal families in Koraput district of Odisha have initiated a community food and water security system consisting of field Gene Bank, Village Water Bank, Village Seed Bank and Area Grain Bank.
18. For modern food-feed competition, see U. Patnaik, 'Origins of the food crisis in India and Developing countries', http://monthlyreview.org/090727patnaik.php, and Utsa Patnaik, Theorizing poverty and food security in the era of economic Reforms. En publication: Globalization and the Washington Consensus: its influence on democracy and development in the south, Gladys Lechini (ed). Buenos Aires: CLACSO, Consejo Latinoamericano de Ciencias Sociales, 2008.

References

Antony, G.M. and A. Laximaiah (2008). *Human Development, Poverty: Health and nutrition situation in India*, Indian J Med Res 128, August, 2008, pp. 198–205.

Bhalla, Shiela (2003). *Casual labourers in rural areas (draft),* Paper presented in IIPA-CPRC Seminar, New Delhi, November 4–5.

Claynton, Dent and Dubois (2003). *Rural Planning in Developing Countries,* Earthscan India, New Delhi.

Ghosh, Jayati (2010). *Poverty reduction in China and India: Policy implication of recent trends*, Desa working paper No. 92.

Hulme, David, Karen Moore and Andrew Shepherd (2001). *Chronic Poverty: Meaning and Analytical Frameworks,* Chronic Poverty Research Centre, IDPM, Manchester.

Mehta, Asha Kapoor and Amita Shah (2003). *Chronic Poverty in India: Incidences, Causes and Policy,* World Development, vol. 31, (no. 3), Great Britain.

Patnaik, Utsa (2006). *Poverty and Neo-liberalism in India*, Based on Rao Bahadur Kale Memorial Lecture delivered at Gokhale Institute of Politics and Economics, Pune, February 03, 2006.

——. (2008). *Theorizing poverty and food security in the era of Economic Reforms*, Enpublicación: Globalisation and the Washington Consensus: its influence on democracy and development in the south. Gladys Lechini (editor). Buenos Aires: CLACSO, Consejo Latinoamericano de Ciencias Sociales.

——. (2009). Origins of the food crisis in India and developing countries, Monthly Review (July–August 2009), http://monthlyreview.org/090727patnaik.php.

——. (2010). *A Critical Look at Some Propositions on Consumption and Poverty, Economic & Political Weekly* February 6, 2010, Vol. xlv, no. 6.

Radhakrishna, Hanumant Rao, Ravi and Sanbi Reddy (2003). *Chronic Poverty, Food Insecurity and Malnutrition in the Nineties*, Paper presented in IIPA-CPRC Seminar, New Delhi, November 4–5.

Ravi, C. (2000). *Complete Demand System, Welfare and Nutrition: An Analysis of Indian Consumption*, Data, unpublished Ph.D. Thesis.

Sah, D.C. and Amita Shah (2003). *Chronic Poverty in South Western Madhya Pradesh: Has Anything Changed*, Paper presented in IIPA-CPRC Seminar, New Delhi, November 4.

Sah, D.C. (2003). *Conceptual Preamble to in-depth Study: Chronic Poverty in Remote Rural Areas, CPRC Methodology Workshop*, CPRC, New Delhi, November 6.

——. (2004). 'Markets and Democratic Decentralisation', *Indian Social Science Review*, Vol. 6 (1), January–June.

Sah, D.C. and Bhatt A. (2008). *Trapped in Poverty: Chrono Poor in Remote Tribal Areas*, Jaipur: Rawat Publications.

Sen, Amartya and Jean Dreze (1995). *India: Economic Development and Social Opportunities*, New York: Oxford University Press.

——. (1999). *Poverty and Famines; Hunger and Public Action; and India: Economic Development and Social Opportunity*, New York: Oxford University Press.

Swaminathan, M.S. (2003). *Technological Change and Food Production: Implications for Vulnerable Groups, (draft)*, Paper presented in IIPA-CPRC Seminar, New Delhi, November 4–5.

Sundaram, K. and Suresh D. Tendulkar (2001). *NAS-NSS Estimates of Private Consumption for Poverty Estimation: A Aggregate Comparison for 1993–1994*, January 13.

——. (2003). *Poverty Among Social Economic Groups in India in 1990s* EPW, December 13.

Index